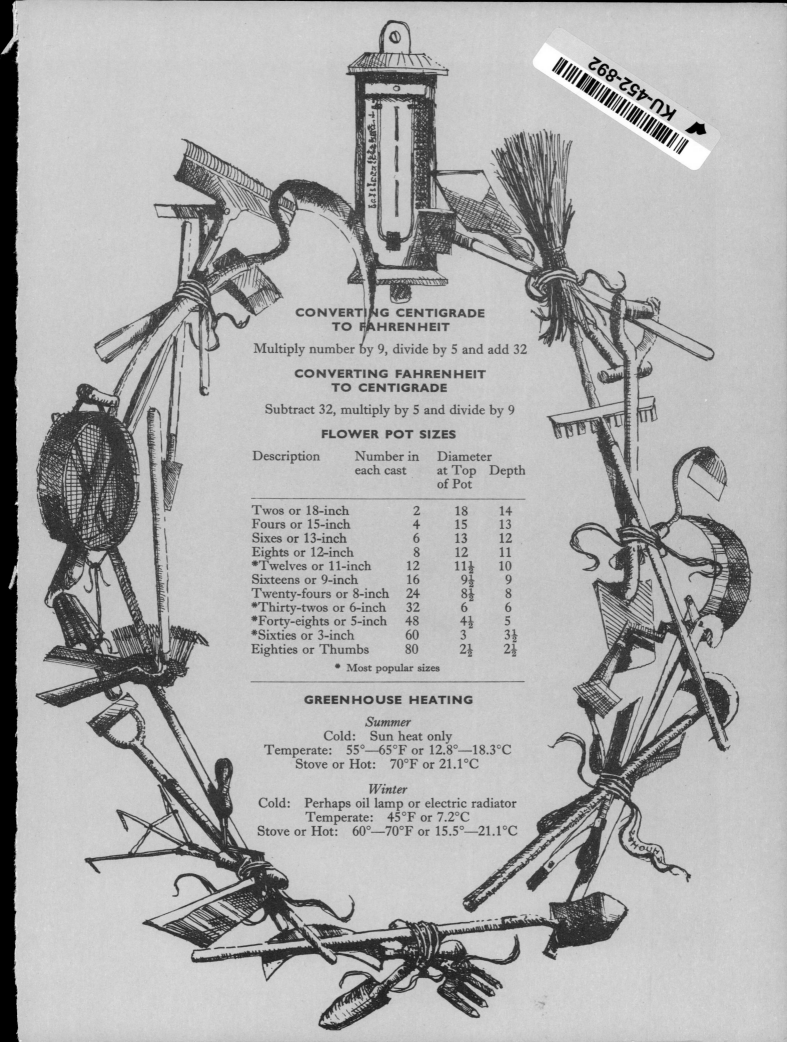

CONVERTING CENTIGRADE TO FAHRENHEIT

Multiply number by 9, divide by 5 and add 32

CONVERTING FAHRENHEIT TO CENTIGRADE

Subtract 32, multiply by 5 and divide by 9

FLOWER POT SIZES

Description	Number in each cast	Diameter at Top of Pot	Depth
Twos or 18-inch	2	18	14
Fours or 15-inch	4	15	13
Sixes or 13-inch	6	13	12
Eights or 12-inch	8	12	11
*Twelves or 11-inch	12	$11\frac{1}{2}$	10
Sixteens or 9-inch	16	$9\frac{1}{2}$	9
Twenty-fours or 8-inch	24	$8\frac{1}{2}$	8
*Thirty-twos or 6-inch	32	6	6
*Forty-eights or 5-inch	48	$4\frac{1}{2}$	5
*Sixties or 3-inch	60	3	$3\frac{1}{2}$
Eighties or Thumbs	80	$2\frac{1}{2}$	$2\frac{1}{2}$

* Most popular sizes

GREENHOUSE HEATING

Summer
Cold: Sun heat only
Temperate: 55°—65°F or 12.8°—18.3°C
Stove or Hot: 70°F or 21.1°C

Winter
Cold: Perhaps oil lamp or electric radiator
Temperate: 45°F or 7.2°C
Stove or Hot: 60°—70°F or 15.5°—21.1°C

GARDENING
in colour

**An all-the-year-round
Picture Encyclopedia**

by Frances Perry, M. B. E.

HAMLYN

LONDON · NEW YORK · SYDNEY · TORONTO

contents

Chapter decorations by
DAVID HUTTER
Front cover photograph by Valerie Finnis
Back cover photograph H. Smith

© Copyright 1963 by FRANCES PERRY
ISBN 0 600 01601 3

The Hamlyn Publishing Group Ltd
Astronaut House • Feltham • Middlesex • England

First impression 1963
Fourteenth impression 1980

Printed in Czechoslovakia by Severografia, Liberec
52011/14

introduction

A love of flowers is part of our heritage. In spite of a wealth of alternative interests and the constant encroachment by buildings — which reduce acreages year by year — gardening is still our greatest national hobby.

The longer I live and the more I learn about plants — the less I know, for gardening is one of those things which has constantly to be revised and brought up to date. This book does not set out to be an authoritative treatise on every aspect of gardening, although I have tried to mention most of the features which are found in our homes and gardens — including ideas for flat dwellers and the house-bound.

The compilation of an illustrated book of this scope calls for assistance and goodwill from many people, and I am particularly indebted to the horticultural trade, who have been more than generous with photographs and pictures. Amongst a host of grower friends

I should particularly like to thank Sir Clayton Russon and Mr Angus Barber of the House of Cuthbert, Mr Jack Carver from Messrs E. & J. Woodman, Messrs Walter Blom & Sons, Sir Oliver Leese and Fison's Horticulture Ltd, who have given me help beyond all expectations. I am also indebted to Anne Ashberry; Bakers of Codsall; The Cement and Concrete Association; The Farmer and Stockbreeder; Fidler's Seeds Ltd; Fisk's Clematis Nurseries; Geo. Bunyard Ltd; *The Grower;* Valerie Finnis; J. E. Downward; Jeremy McCabe; Keith Luxford Ltd; Laxton Bros; E. Lyall; Malby & Co.; Mullard Ltd; The National Trust; Robert Hall Ltd; R. & G. Cuthbert Ltd; Rolcut Ltd; Samuel Dobie & Son; Samuel McGredy; Samuel Ryder Ltd; *The Smallholder and Home Gardener;* Shell Horticulture Ltd; Sutton & Sons; H. Smith; Stella Coe; The Electricity Council; T. H. Everett of New York; Unwins Ltd; Vilmorin-Andrieux of Paris; Wilh. Schacht of Munich; Wilkinson Sword Co.; Wood & Ingram; W. & R. Perry, together with a number of other firms and manufacturers whose pictures are acknowledged individually.

On the manuscript side I should like to express my thanks to Mrs E. Lyall for assistance with the chapter on Flower Arrangement and my colleagues K. J. Spackman and D. L. Ibbotson for help with the Fruit and Vegetable sections.

My husband has helped in many ways — whilst Mr J. Gilbert and his colleagues at Paul Hamlyn have given me the kind of assistance than an author prays for.

I hope those who turn the pages of this book may derive some fraction of the pleasure I have felt in compiling it, and that they too will continue to enjoy the peace and pleasure which flowers and gardens so amply provide.

Frances Perry

Garden Design

Good gardens do not happen. They develop! One cannot expect to make a good job of them without some knowledge of the soil and the plants that it can grow; and to this knowledge must be brought artistry, good taste and a sense of fitness and proportion.

Many new gardens are taken over as a bare piece of ground, with nothing in them but soil, weeds and builder's rubbish. Others may be in better shape but dull and unimaginatively planned, both from the point of view of planting and design.

The making of a garden is a responsibility and a challenge, for every site is different and creates individual problems. Even a narrow strip, identical at first sight to hundreds of others, can be used in an individual way. Planting a group of trees or creating several levels relieves the flatness, whilst irregularly shaped borders, instead of the more usual oblong beds, take away the straight-lined effect. Even in the smallest plot is should not be possible to view the whole garden at a glance. It should be full of surprises, with each turn of the path revealing fresh vistas or disclosing new interests.

IF YOU ARE BUYING A HOUSE AND ARE FOND OF GARDENING AVOID:

1. An exposed site on a north or east hill slope. It is likely to be in shade most of the day.
2. Poor, stony or very sandy soil.
3. Ground subject to waterlogging.
4. Thin soil lying over hard rock.
5. Very windswept areas, unless there are possibilities of breaking the force of the elements.
6. Noted frost pockets (especially for fruit).
7. Too many tall trees — Elms, Poplars, etc. on neighbouring properties, as these will rob the soil of light and food.

THE PLAN

Do not attempt any constructive work or planting until you have made a plan of the site. This is most important for certain mistakes cannot be rectified. Felling a large tree, which is later found to have effectively masked a distant gasometer, is a case in point.

The type of soil may dictate certain plantings; Rhododendrons, for example, will not thrive on chalk and poor, sandy soils create problems for Roses and fruit trees. The essence of garden planning is a sense of proportion and fitness, with the trees chosen to fit the soil and site. The area must first be considered as a whole and then broken down into its component parts or features.

Plan of Campaign

Stand with your back to the house and make your first assessment from this angle. This is, after all, the view most frequently seen. Are there any features worth retaining? Which things should be hidden?

All gardens have certain natural assets. Exploit these, whether they consist of an interesting archi-

Foliage and water – Wakehurst Place
By courtesy of the National Trust and Fisons Horticulture

Old-fashioned garden – Barrington Court
By courtesy of the National Trust and Fisons Horticulture

tectural feature, a fine tree or even a distant view of a river or hill. Mark these for retention in your plan.

Inevitably, however, there are some things which are best hidden. Unattractive outbuildings, pipes running down the sides of the house, clothes lines, neighbours' sheds — or in extreme cases, their entire gardens. Climbing plants and shrubs can work wondrous transformation scenes. For quicker results erect trellis or rustic fencing (interwoven panels or wattle hurdling). See p. 247.

Privacy

If the garden is really to be used, privacy is essential. Some form of enclosure is therefore a prime necessity. Shrubs and hedges, though they take time to establish, are very permanent. Fences and screens give quick coverage but deteriorate in time and are usually more costly to erect. The ideal plan is to plant a hedge and protect it in its early years with hurdles or interwoven fencing. Details of hedging plants and screens can be found on pp. 246 and 282.

'Open Plan' gardens are obligatory on some housing estates, but even here much can be achieved by skilful group planting of shrubs and trees. These can eventually provide quiet nooks and corners, hidden from neighbouring plots.

Recreational Features

A garden should be designed for the whole household, not just the gardener. So recreational areas must be left, and provision made for cut flowers, herbs and decorative features.

Leave the greatest expanse of open ground close to the house. This may be designed for tea parties, lawn games or simply for relaxation. The area may be terraced, crazy-paved or put down to lawn; the

Lawn and flower beds – basic essentials of a well designed garden   Fisons Horticulture

great thing is to keep it near the house — not only for convenience but to create an air of spaciousness from nearby windows.

Other Features

Once the boundaries are enclosed and lawn area planned, the borders and special features can be decided. There are many aspects of gardening, but certain points should be remembered:

1. The utilitarian side of gardening needs to be away from the house and also screened from view. Potting sheds, compost heaps, vegetables and fruit should be kept to the back of the plot and masked from the ornamental garden. Flowering hedges, a pergola covered with climbers growing up posts or pillars or clumps of shrubs make useful barriers between the vegetable and flower garden.

2. Herbs should be grown near the kitchen door, for convenience in picking.

3. Flower borders with scalloped edges or small oval beds cut in the lawn take the formality away from a narrow, oblong plot.

4. Check on plants which will tolerate shade before ordering same.

5. Hard paths are essential in those places which take a great deal of wear: e. g. the vegetable plot, leading up to the potting shed or greenhouse, and around frames. Elsewhere, paths can be made of a variety of materials — grass, stepping stones (on a lawn), gravel, brick, cobbles or crazy-paving.

6. Site rock and water gardens in a sunny position.

7. Keep the garden neat whilst work is proceeding, grass over all but the path and vegetable areas and cut out beds as required.

8. Site the greenhouse within reasonable access of light and water.

9. Pastel or white flowers show up best in poor light. Use these for distant effects from the house in the evenings, or to brighten gloomy spots.

10. A choice of levels gives character to a garden and adds to its interest.

11. To cut down labour, utilise lawns, water, and permanent plants to the full.

12. Remember winter and extend the interest all through the year by planting some of the plants recommended (See p. 288).

A Berkshire garden, designed by Russell Page O.B.E., F.I.L.A. and made by William Wood & Son Ltd

Soils & Fertilizers

GETTING THE BEST OUT OF YOUR SOIL

Soil must be in healthy condition in order to raise good vegetables and flowers. It contains many organisms and ingredients, which, by good cultivation becomes fertile LOAM. Whether we garden on chalky, stony or heavy clay soil it can always be converted to loam by adding those substances lacking in its natural condition.

Most soils contain a mixture of the following materials:

1. *Mineral Particles*. Composed of various-sized rock fragments, broken down through the years from larger rocks. Fragments smaller than pebbles eventually become sand, silt or clay.

2. *Water*. Soil water contains both dissolved mineral and vegetable salts and may be present in quantity (in wet weather) or under drier conditions as a film surrounding both mineral and organic particles. It is taken up by the root hairs and passed to all parts of the plant. The salts are retained, with part of the water; surplus moisture is passed off through the leaves as water vapour. Thus food and moisture reach the plant via the soil water.

Clearing the site of weeds

Digging a trench

Applying manure

Forking over

3. *Air*. The upper soil layers contain the same gases as are found in the air. But there is more carbon dioxide and less oxygen. This is because plant roots breathe. They take in OXYGEN and give off CARBON DIOXIDE. Fresh manure also gives off carbon dioxide during decomposition, so there can easily be too much carbon dioxide in the soil if we use fresh animal dung or compost. This could adversely affect the plant roots.

4. *Humus*. When plant and animal remains fall on, or are dug into the ground they are gradually broken down by earthworms, bacteria and other organisms. Partially decayed vegetable or animal material is known as HUMUS. It provides food, enables light soils to retain moisture and improves aeration and drainage on heavy land.

The main practices of cultivation are digging and manuring, hoeing, raking and planting.

DIGGING

Single Digging

The spade is inserted in the soil, taken out when full and inverted ahead of the work. Usually a shal-low trench is removed at the start and the soil taken to the spot where digging will end. The operator then works along the row, taking out the soil, or SPIT, and turning it into the trench, making another trench in the process. It is usually done in spring or summer.

Double Digging

Also known as bastard trenching, each layer of soil remaining in its proper layer. Thus the top spit finishes on top and the second spit beneath it.

Start by taking out a trench 2 ft. wide, removing the soil to the end of the plot. Now get inside the trench and fork over the second or underneath spit, adding organic manure if required. Turn the next top spit on this and fork the subsoil as hitherto until all is finished. Finally, place the first spit removed in the last trench. This digging should be done in autumn. The surface should be left rough so that the frost may act on it.

True Trenching

The soil is taken out *three* spits deep, the first and second spits being reversed. Sometimes used for Sweet Peas.

Ridging

Useful for very heavy soils. Start as for double digging by taking out a 2 ft. trench. Mark out a strip 2 ft. wide running the length of the plot. This leaves three spade widths of soil (8 in. each) which are placed in the centre of the trench, one after the other, leaving a ridge. Continue in this way until the plot is finished. Should be practised in autumn.

Hoeing

Hoes are used to stir the surface of the soil. The Dutch Hoe is invaluable in summer for weed control and is pushed backwards and forwards. Draw hoes are used to draw drills (the operator working backwards) and for weed control when he walks forward.

Raking

Among a number of uses, rakes are invaluable for removing debris and stones from lawns, soil and smooth gravel surfaces.

Planting

The main tools used for planting are dibbers, trowels, and handforks.

LIME

Lime is the chief basis of soil fertility, providing a real plant food — as distinct from sand or pure clay, useless for plant nourishment. It counteracts sourness, and breaks up heavy clay soil, thus making for better drainage. It also makes other plant foods

Sowing Peas. Drawing a drill using flat part of hoe on well-prepared ground
Fisons Horticulture

Sowing the seed
Fisons Horticulture

available, acting on humus and setting free the elements necessary for plant growth.

Some plant diseases e.g. Club Root of Cabbage, occur more often on lime-deficient soils. Many pests, such as slugs and wireworms dislike lime.

DOES YOUR SOIL NEED LIME?

Lime deficiency is indicated by:
1. A mat of undecayed vegetable material on surface of grass land with poor, wiry foliage. Sorrel, Dock, Bracken and Ling much in evidence.
2. Repeated failure with leguminous crops e.g. Peas, Beans, Sweet Peas.
3. Grass dying in patches and no Clover.
4. Chemical soil tests.

N. B. Soils can be acid, neutral or alkaline, with a wide range of degrees of acidity. This is known as the pH value, the figure pH 7:2 standing for the neutral point. Lower figures than this indicate acidity (increasing as the figures become lower). Soil testing outfits can be bought from chemists and sufficiently accurate results obtained from them by means of colour tests. Briefly, most of these work by mixing a little top soil (2—3 in.) with water, leaving this to stand and testing the liquid with prepared litmus paper or special liquid. The resultant colour achieved will indicate the state of the soil — pink being very sour, orange sour, green neutral and blue-green alkaline.

Applying Lime

Gardens can be *overlimed*, so only apply when necessary. The best time is after digging in autumn, but should manuring have been carried out during that period, delay it until February. Spread material on the ground: do not dig it in.

Types of Lime

Hydrated Lime Acts quickly, safe to use close to plants. Use ¼ lb. per sq. yd. according to acidity.

Ground Lime and Gypsum Slow acting but safe. Use twice as much as quantities above.

Lime must not be given to Rhododendrons, Azaleas, Eucryphias, Heathers, Lithospermums and most bog plants.

Do not mix lime with animal manures, including guano and poultry manure, nor sulphate of ammonia or superphosphate of lime.

CLAY SOILS

Clay soils are often called heavy soils, being weighty to lift and difficult to work. Drainage is frequently bad and they are usually acid, clinging to the feet in wet weather.

Clay particles provide the smallest soil fragments, so they pack down very closely. Also, each separate

Filling in the drill   Fisons Horticulture

3. Work in plenty of organic materials — strawy manure, peat, leaves, rough compost or hop manure.
4. Apply lime or gypsum in spring if this seems necessary but avoid using it near lime-hating plants such as Rhododendrons and Camellias.

Clay soils are usually quite rich in plant foods, but tend to be cold. They are unsuitable for early crops, but often good later in the season, for they do not dry out as easily as chalk and sandy soils. Primroses, Foxgloves and Wild Carrot are common plants of clay soils.

SANDY OR STONY SOILS

Sandy soils drain quickly because the soil particles are large. They cannot hold moisture, the ground is poor, and without special cultivation suitable only for a restricted range of plants. Early crops may be successful, but drought is the enemy later on.

Build up the moisture-retentive powers by continually turning in organic material. Compost, peat, leafmould, chopped up turves and rotted dung are all suitable, especially pig and cow manure. Another idea is to sow the ground with Rape or Mustard (using approximately ½ lb. of seed for every 6 sq.yds.), digging the resultant plants into the soil just before they come to flower. Sandy soils are warm, dry and light in colour.

If You Have a Sandy Soil You Should:
1. Dig in bulky manures frequently to keep up the humus content.
2. When lime is required, ground chalk is better than hydrated lime as it is slower to dissolve. Cultivated soils will probably require a lime dressing every third year or so.
3. Sulphate of potash (1-2 oz. per sq.yd.) is beneficial to Sweet Peas, Tomatoes, Violets and other crops. Apply in spring.
4. If nitrogen is needed give it in the form of organic manures. Quick-acting fertilisers such as Sulphate of Ammonia and Nitrate of Soda are not recommended. They cause very rapid growth but wash out of the soil too quickly. Common plants of sandy soils are Brooms, Cornflower, Bracken and small Bindweed.

CHALK SOILS

Chalk soils are very variable, for their fertility depends largely on the depth of soil overlaying the chalk bed formation. If the top soil is thin the ground will be poor and hungry, but if fairly deep a good garden can be obtained. They are often sticky and soft in wet weather.

particle is surrounded by a sponge-like substance called a COLLOID. In wet weather these absorb moisture and become sticky, pressing the particles still more tightly together. In dry weather they lose moisture and shrink — forming characteristic clay soil cracks. This colloidal property can be destroyed by:
1. Burning clay and mixing it with the soil (almost impracticable because of the cost).
2. Adding lime, gypsum or certain proprietary soil materials.
3. Digging the soil in autumn.

If You Have a Clay Soil You Should:
1. Provide artificial drainage if exceptionally wet, either with pipes or by digging one or more deep holes at the lowest point, filling to within a foot of the top with stones, clinkers, crocks, old bricks etc., and covering to normal level with soil. Water drains down from the top soil layers. Another idea is a bog and water garden at the lowest point.
2. Dig the soil in ridges to expose the greatest possible area to influence of weather. Do this before the winter rains set in and fork the area over during a dry period around March.

If You Garden on Chalk, Remember:

1. Build up a good layer of topsoil by working in as much manure and compost as possible.
2. Do not dig too deeply into the chalk strata.
3. Green manures are beneficial.
4. Despite underlying chalk, lime is sometimes deficient in the top layers. Test if doubtful.
5. Potash is often deficient so use sulphate of potash ($\frac{1}{2}$-1 oz. per sq.yd.) or wood ashes (8 oz. per sq.yd.) as a spring top dressing.

Certain plants will not grow on chalky soils, notably Rhododendrons, Camellias, Azaleas, many Heathers, Gentians and *Iris kaempferi*. The lime locks up the iron in the soil and prevents them using it so that the plants are known as CALCIFUGES. The Iron Chelate 'MURPHY SEQUESTRENE' counteracts this so that the leaves become green and the plants grow normally. Apply in late winter or early spring, simply as a soil dressing. If dry weather follows application, the ground should be well watered.

Typical plants of chalk soils are Scabious, *Clematis vitalba*, Guelder Rose (*Viburnum lanata*) and Bird's Foot Trefoil (*Lotus corniculatus*).

PEAT SOILS

Peaty soils are uncommon, but do occur in fen or boggy areas. Peat is composed of excessive quantities of humus and is associated with waterlogging. The soil is usually very acid, dark brown in colour, fibrous and spongy in texture.

If You Have Peat Soil You Should:

1. Drain it.
2. Add lime occasionally to correct acidity.

Peat soils, thus treated, are particularly good for bulbs, potatoes and most market garden crops.

Typical weeds of peat soils are Heathers, Sphagnum Moss, Sedges and Rushes.

THE ORGANIC MANURES

We can never have too much organic matter dug into the garden. Whilst in the humus (or half decomposed state), it acts as a sponge in light soils to retain food and moisture; and in heavy clay it provides a drainage filter between the soil particles.

In the last stages of decomposition the dissolved salts are taken up by plant roots.

Animal Manure

All animal manures should be well rotted before use. The smell will disappear when this stage is reached, but meantime store under cover as rain washes out a lot of the goodness. Spread the manure

Phacelia, an annual for any soil except the waterlogged
Copyright Samuel Dobie & Son

Rudbeckia 'Dwarf Bambi' can be grown on sandy soils

W.J. Unwin Ltd

Heathers flourish on peaty soil

in autumn and dig it in, mixing it well with the top foot of soil; on very wet soils it can be applied in spring.

Poultry Manure

Very rich and must never be used fresh. Store under cover for 6 months, mixing it with one-third of its bulk of dry soil or broken up peat moss, turning heap occasionally. May also be mixed in the compost heap. Good for top dressing such plants as Strawberries, Sweet Peas, fruit trees, Tomatoes etc. Never mix with lime or wood ash.

Seaweed

Has local value only and is particularly useful on light soils. Apply directly and dig in during autumn or use as top dressing in spring.

Sewage

Good substitute for farmyard manure, especially on light soils, but varies considerably, so ask for an analysis before purchase. Use with lime.

Peat

Nutrient value low, but can hold as much as 90 to 95% water, so very useful on light or porous soils. Supplies an abundance of humus. Useful as a mulch in summer to keep top soil moist or can be dug in the top 3 in. during autumn. Moss peat is best for potting. Sedge peat is more acid, but excellent for Rhododendrons etc. If soil is dry, soak peat first.

Leafmould

Another good source of humus, Oak and Beech leaves being best. Turn heap occasionally and keep moist; dig in when rotted.

Spent Hops

Refuse from brewing industry. Use as a mulch in summer and dig in the following autumn.

Green Manure

Very useful if manure or compost are short. Sow Mustard or Rape on bare ground in July—August and dig in during October and November. Clover, Turnip, Vetches and brown Peas may also be dug in before they come to flower.

Dried Blood

Excellent but expensive. It is included with many proprietary fertilisers. Apply as top dressing ($\frac{1}{2}$-1 oz. per sq.yd.), or use in compost-heap.

Hoof and Horn

Slow acting, chiefly nitrogenous and phosphatic fertiliser, the constituent of several well known horticultural manures. Also included among the base fertilisers of the John Innes Potting and Seed Composts. Good for fruit and Rose trees.

Sundry

Fish Guano is made from the refuse from herring and cod fisheries, dried and powdered; Bonemeal is of animal origin; Guano is the manure from seabirds; and Bark-fibre is made from pulverised tree bark. Use of these organic materials depends to a great extent on cost and availability.

Soot

Weathered soot is a nitrogenous manure which helps to lighten heavy soils and may be used as a spring top dressing (5 oz. per sq.yd.).

THE INORGANIC FERTILISERS

Also known as artificial fertilisers, these are manufactured manures, normally used as top dressings during the growing season. They are quick acting and provide the plant with some special food requirement at short notice. However, they *cannot improve the physical condition of the soil* and must not be used continuously without humus of some kind.

Plant foods include carbon, hydrogen, oxygen, nitrogen, phosphorus, potassium and calcium — known as the 'major' elements; also iron, magnesium, sulphur, manganese, copper, boron, molybdenum, zinc and possibly chlorine — usually called intermediate or 'trace' elements.

17

The three principal requirements which plants need in large supplies are NITROGEN, PHOSPHORUS and POTASSIUM.

Nitrogen

This is essential to growth, both leaves and stems needing it in quantity. Grass, Lettuce and other 'leaf' crops show remarkable lushness after a dressing of nitrogen, although too much can cause soft growth and encourage disease.

Sulphate of Ammonia. Apply in spring 1 oz. per sq.yd. Not so good for acid soils.

Nitrate of Soda. Top dressing along the rows. Quick acting. 1 oz. per sq.yd.

Nitro-chalk. Safer than preceding, but unsuitable for lime-hating plants and chalky soil. 1–1½ oz. per sq.yd.

Dried Blood. Rake in at sowing time; 1–2 oz. per sq.yd.

Lack of nitrogen shown by stunted plants and small, very pale leaves.

Phosphates

These induce sturdy growth — especially of the roots and speed up flowering, fruiting and ripening.

Superphosphate of Lime. Quick acting. Rake in at any time with established plants, or before sowing and planting with crops and annuals. 1–2 oz. per sq.yd.

Basic Slag. Slow acting, can remain in the soil for several years. Apply in autumn. Good on acid soils. 5–8 oz. per sq.yd.

Bonemeal. An organic material. Used as a soil dressing like most inorganic fertilisers. Slow acting and safe. Apply in autumn, 2–4 oz. per sq.yd.

Lack of phosphate is often shown by stunted growth, also purpling leaves.

Potash

Increases disease resistance and improves colour and quality of fruit and flowers.

Sulphate of Potash. Apply any time, raking it in on the soil surface. 1–2 oz. per sq.yd.

Wood Ash. Organic origin. Quick acting, rake in any time of the year. 6–8 oz. per sq.yd.

Lack of potash is indicated by browning or scorching round leaf edges. Susceptible to disease.

POINTS TO REMEMBER

1. Never let artificial fertilisers touch the leaves of plants.
2. Do not use more than the amount recommended.
3. Do not apply these fertilisers too deeply.
4. Liquid fertilisers should not be put on dry soil; water soil first.

Venidium fastuosum, a plant for sandy soils
Copyright Samuel Dobie & Son

Compound Fertilisers

These are balanced fertilisers manufactured for specific needs: e.g. feeding Tomatoes, vegetables, Roses etc. They contain various percentages of nitrogen, phosphates and potash to suit particular crops and give excellent results.

Liquid Feeds

These must be diluted with water and applied to the plot with a watering can. The results are rapid. Particularly good for pot plants, but suitable for all crops. Apply during the actual growing season and follow maker's instruction.

The Compost Heap

There are various methods and schools of thought concerning the practice of compost making. But, provided the ultimate result yields a dark brown or blackish mass, with little trace of the organic ingredients, the compost can be used in exactly the same way as decayed animal manure.

Electric Hoe/Tiller   Tarpen

Pulsatilla vulgaris, thrives on chalky soil

This breakdown of organic material is brought about by soil bacteria. If the heap is waterlogged, they cannot breathe; if too dry they cannot work, and the material shrivels; whilst in winter it is too cold for their normal activities. The aim of the compost maker is to provide conditions suitable for rapid breakdown. Most materials of vegetable origin can be used, except woody twigs, diseased plants, grass clippings from the first cut (after using selective weedkiller) and persistent weeds like Bellbine.

Use soft vegetable and flower stems and thinnings, Pea and Bean stalks, tea-leaves, eggshells, ordinary weeds, peelings, grass cuttings, straw, leaves, peat, wood ash, Bracken, crushed Cabbage stalks and even small quantities of animal manure (e.g. rabbit, chicken, etc.).

To accelerate the decomposition use between the layers one of the proprietary accelerators such as 'Bio Compost Maker' or sulphate of ammonia alternated with hydrated lime. Some gardeners sprinkle with nitro chalk or nitrate of lime.

1. Select a sheltered, easily accessible spot, away from the house.
2. Dig out a shallow pit approximately 3 ft. wide.
3. Spread a layer of coarse vegetable material, crushed Cabbage stalks, Bracken etc. to a depth of 4–5 in. This asists drainage and lets in air.
4. Dust the heap with sulphate of ammonia or one of the proprietary accelerators.
5. Spread another layer of refuse (a little animal manure can be added if available) to a depth of 6–9 in. Tread firmly.
6. Dust with hydrated lime (or proprietary material).
7. Add another layer of garden refuse.
8. Apply sulphate of ammonia.

Continue in this way until the heap is 3 ft. or so in height. Water in dry weather. A movable wire mesh or light wood frame helps to keep the heap tidy.

As one heap is finished start another. After 3 or 4 months the heap is ready for use.

Straw Compost

Straw compost is an excellent source of humus and particularly useful when other organic matter is in short supply. To make it:

1. Buy a bale of straw, undo it and tease out the material. Soak thoroughly with a garden hose.
2. Make a flat-topped heap of wet straw, approximately 1 ft. deep.
3. Sprinkle with dried blood.
4. Make another layer of straw.

Continue in this way until the heap is high enough. Water occasionally in dry weather. The compost is ready in approximately 4 to 6 months.

Herbaceous Borders

The herbaceous border consists of plants of similar type and growth habit. The majority of these die to the ground annually; most of them are hardy enough to present no wintering problems and can remain for considerable periods in the same positions without replacement. As the plants grow in stature so they smother weeds and reduce maintenance problems. They also produce a greater number of flowers and consequently assume more colourful effects.

A collection of mixed perennials cannot be kept at the peak of perfection for months on end, so one either resorts to 'fill-ups' — using annuals, bulbs, or bedding plants like Dahlias and Pelargoniums — or else plants for particular periods of brightness when the garden is most used, as in June or September.

Few true herbaceous perennials come to flower before March, and even then their numbers are limited, but by including a few of the smaller shrubs in the planting scheme one provides a background of very permanent plants and ensures winter colour. Particularly useful shrubs in this respect are *Daphne mezereum*, *Viburnum fragrans*, Wintersweet (*Chimonanthus fragrans*), *Garrya elliptica* and the winter-blooming heathers.

PLANNING AND PREPARATION

The first essential for a successful border is a plan of campaign. Work should proceed as follows:
1. Site the border; 2. Prepare it for planting; 3. Make a planting plan on paper; 4. Undertake the planting.

Siting

A sunny situation is an advantage since a greater variety of plants can be chosen. For twin borders in the open or one running across the garden, the taller plants will go in the centre and the smaller ones to the sides. In a boundary position, however, as against a fence, hedge or wall, there will be more scope, as several graduating lines of plants can be

Herbaceous border at Wisley

fitted in, with the taller types at the back.

Make the border as wide as conveniently possible, even up to 12 or 15 ft. if space allows, with 5 ft. as a minimum. Anything narrower becomes just another flower bed. Bear backgrounds in mind, too. They protect the border and provide a setting for the flowers. Clipped Beech or Hornbeam hedges give effective protection and their green and gold foliage tints blend harmoniously with most flower colours. Yew provides a solid, deep green background although it takes time and labour to keep in trim.

Preparing the Soil

The main soil types, their characteristics and management are discussed in pages 12–19. In general the cultivation of the herbaceous border will follow along these lines. One special factor must, however, be borne in mind. Perennial plants stay in the ground for many years, so that annual digging and clearance is impossible. Deep preliminary cultivation and the use of organic and slow-acting fertilisers act as a long-

Polyanthus

term insurance policy, as the manurial benefits are felt for years. In subsequent seasons mulches of peat, compost, spent hops or rotted dung keep the soil healthy and in good heart.

So dig the border over (two spits deep if possible) and have plenty of organic material incorporated in the upper soil layers. If done in autumn, the ground has time to settle before spring planting. If there are many weeds, adopt the measures suggested on p. 295 beforehand.

Seedling weeds are normally destroyed by cultivation, but a very dirty piece of land should be left to lie fallow for a season before planting.

Platycodon grandiflorum   H. Smith

Kentranthus ruber

Making the Plan

Make a scale plan before planting the herbaceous border.

Having fixed the outline, pencil in the various planting sites, dovetailing one into another like the pieces of a jigsaw. In a 5 ft. border there may be only two or three depths of these but wider beds will obviously accommodate more. Finally, enter the names and numbers of plants required for every section, having due regard to their height, growth span and other features.

The chief points to consider are:

1. *Height and Growth Span*

In borders with a background keep the tallest plants to the rear and low-growing ones in front. Beds designed to be seen from two sides should have tall perennials in the centre and graduate downwards on either side.

Growth span indicates the area covered by a given plant in three years' time. Individual specimens rarely make an effective display and for a bold splash

Catananche coerulea major

21

Hemerocallis 'Pink Lady'

The position of the border can also influence colour planning. White and yellow flowers are excellent for a border viewed from a distance (as from a house), while blues and reds give a warmer touch and brightness to any dark background.

4. *Soil Suitability*

The texture of soil can be improved but its nature cannot be changed. Naturally wet land is not the best medium for any plants which must have good drainage, while lime haters (calcifuges) are seldom likely to flourish on chalk.

5. *Fragrance*

Not many border perennials are noted for fragrance, but for those who rate perfume in flowers as a desirable attribute Paeonies, Lilies, Monarda and Dianthus can be recommended.

6. *Individual Characteristics*

Other special traits may influence your final choice. The most important are:

UNTIDINESS AFTER FLOWERING—examples: Poppies, Aconitums. Plant in a mid-row position with later developers in front; new growths of the latter will mask the dying-down processes of the earlier plants.

MOISTURE LOVING PLANTS — examples: Astilbes, Trollius and Monarda. Incorporate plenty of organic material in the planting area and mulch with peat or compost in spring. This keeps up the moisture content of the soil.

PLANTS WHICH CANNOT TOLERATE STANDING MOISTURE — examples: Gaillardias, Catananches and Scabious. A common characteristic of southern European plants and the cause of much 'dying out'. Work sand or grit in around the planting area and drop a handful of sand at the bottom of the hole before planting. A mulch or collar of small pebbles or granite chippings round the crowns of particularly susceptible specimens prevents standing water in their vicinity.

LIME HATERS — Dress the soil in the vicinity with iron chelate. See p. 16.

INVASIVE PLANTS examples: some Michaelmas Daisies, Macleaya and Helianthus. Never site these next to particularly delicate species and be prepared to lift and divide the roots every three or four years. Slate slabs thrust endwise into the ground prevent plant roots from extending under the soil.

FLOPPY PLANTS Delphiniums, some of the newer Michaelmas Daisies and Poppies are examples of plants which often flop over their neighbours through sheer top-heaviness, or they may be beaten down after a storm. To prevent this they must be staked early in the year, using canes, or twiggy Pea-sticks. These should be thrust into the ground between the young shoots when they are only a few inches high.

of colour it may be necessary to plant anything up to a dozen roots of the same variety in one section.

2. *Season*

Borders designed to look their best at any given time should be composed of plants which normally come to bloom at that period. All-purpose borders can include a few very early and a few very late plants, but must be so arranged that the later varieties like Asters, Phlox and hardy Chrysanthemums mask the dying-down stems of earlier plants like Lupins, Paeonies, Poppies and Geums.

3. *Colour*

Clever colour groupings are the test of a good herbaceous border, although the pattern should not be too frequently repeated. The brighter shades need to be spread and very vivid colours like orange, scarlet and purple separated by paler flowered blooms or silver foliaged plants such as *Artemisia stelleriana* and *Stachys lanata*.

PLANTING The great majority of herbaceous plants can be moved in the autumn and spring: i.e. from end September until April. Early planting ensures sufficient warmth for new roots to be made. Herbaceous perennials should not be moved in frosty weather and stock received from nurserymen during cold spells should be kept in dryish soil in a shed or greenhouse until the weather breaks. Some species are best not disturbed during the autumn or winter, especially Pyrethrums, Scabious, *Aster amellus*, Catananche and — in heavy soils — Delphiniums and Lupins. Plant these in March or April.

Rake over the soil before planting and place labels (with appropriate names and numbers) in their corresponding sites with the border plan. This will prove a great help during planting and cut out the need for constant adjustments and measurements.

Set the roots firmly, up to the old planting mark — no deeper or shallower — and water the plants in if the ground seems dry. Next day loosen the earth and remove footmarks with a hoe or rake.

ROUTINE WORK IN THE HERBACEOUS BORDER

THE FIRST SEASON

Make sure that the border is never allowed to dry out, suppress weeds, stake plants and watch for pests and diseases. Newly planted perennials are in no fit state to withstand severe disease attacks.

Frost may lift newly planted subjects out of the ground, so tread or press the plants back into the earth as soon as possible *after* each thaw.

Campanula glomerata superba   Copyright Samuel Dobie & Son

Acanthus mollis

23

Wind also often damages freshly planted perennials, rocking the taller subjects precariously. Early staking can prevent this happening.

Soak the ground thoroughly during a drought and apply an even mulch of compost to the soil or cover it with black polythene. This will prevent evaporation and so conserve moisture.

Interplanting with annuals or bedding subjects may be necessary to provide interest and colour. Clumps of bulbs will also bring brightness early in the year. By the second season most perennials will probably be sufficiently established to fill their allotted space, and the annuals can be discontinued.

Established Borders

When frost begins to blacken stems, cut growths hard back and remove to the compost heap. Now fork between the plants (using a short tined fork which will not damage the roots), adjust or renew labels and put a mulch of leaves or weathered ashes over the crowns of the more delicate species, such as Eremuri in their first years and such winter intolerant subjects as *Dicentra spectabilis* and *Morina longifolia*.

Red Hot Pokers (Kniphofia) retain their leaves all winter, but these may be shortened and pulled together over the crowns and knotted, or else tied with raffia or string. Water seeping into the crowns and freezing may have fatal effects.

Around February lightly fork between the plants, turning in or removing any leaves or straw used for winter protection. Weed control is the rule from now on, so keep the hoe plying between the plants but remove large specimens by hand.

Plants which require staking should be attended to in early April; Pea-sticks will provide excellent support for all but the very robust, and should not show when the plants come to flower. Plants which produce straight, top-heavy stems, like Delphiniums, need individual stakes, preferably coloured green so that they are inconspicuous.

Later work consists mainly of weeding, hoeing and the removal of spent flowers. These should not be encouraged to go on to seed. Seed production weakens a plant and the resultant seedlings can play havoc with your planting scheme. The removal of the first batch of flowers often encourages secondary blooms later in the summer, particularly with Delphiniums, Lupins and some of the Campanulas.

A spring mulch is advisable, especially with such 'hungry' plants as Paeonies, Delphiniums and Lupins. This, together with an occasional autumn dressing of bonemeal (4 oz. per sq. yd.) or a mixed general fertiliser, takes care of all feeding problems.

Renovations

Every three years or so it will be necessary to overhaul most borders. Those plants which resent disturbance such as Paeonies, Eryngiums, Dictamnus and Hostas, should be left alone, but any which require splitting should be lifted, divided and replanted. Do this in early autumn, tackling one section of ground at a time.

Anthemis 'Grallagh Gold'

Helleborus orientalis

24

List of Plants

At the end of these descriptions, the first figures indicated give approximate heights, followed by time of flowering, rough growth span after three years, and method of propagation (D. division; S. seed; S.C. soft cuttings; R.C. root cuttings; L.C. Leaf cuttings). For details of these methods see p. 232) * denotes Good for cutting.

ACANTHUS Bear's Breeches

Decorative foliage plants, often with thorny leaves. Very im pressive in key positions, with large flower spikes packed with white, purple and green flowers, which can be dried. Flowers better in sun.

A. mollis is the most commonly planted. Leaves heart-shaped, deeply cut, 2 ft. × 1 ft.; *A. spinosus*, leaves shining dark green, deeply cut, flowers noble; *var. spinosissimus*, glistening white spines on dark foliage.

3—4 ft.   Summer   4 ft. sq.   R.C. or S.

ACHILLEA Milfoil; Yarrow

A large and variable family, majority easily grown in well drained soil and sunny situation. Group for major effect. Plant autumn or early spring.

MEDIUM HEIGHTS

A. clypeolata, masses of finely cut leaves and flat heads densely packed with small, bright yellow flowers.

1—2 ft.   July—Sept.   2 ft. sq.   D.

A. millefolium, the Wild White Yarrow, has produced a number of coloured garden forms, the best being 'Cerise Queen', rose-cerise; 'Crimson Beauty', crimson; 'Fire King', deep red; *rosea*, pink; *rubra*, deep pink. All have deeply-cut, ground-hugging leaves and leafy stems carrying terminal plate-like heads of flowers.

2 ft.   June—Aug.   2 ft. sq.   D.

A. ptarmica carries quantities of small white Daisy flowers on branching stems. All parts pungent smelling. Varieties include 'The Pearl', 'Perry's White' and 'Snowball' double.

1½ ft.   June—Aug.   2 ft. sq.   D.

A. taygetea. Garden variety with silvery, pinnate leaves and flat heads (2—4 in. across) of pale yellow flowers.

1½ ft.   June—Sept.   2 ft. sq.   D.

TALL KINDS

A. filipendulina. Handsome, back of the border plant, needing no staking. Loves sun and well drained soil. Large flat heads of bright yellow flowers and deeply cut, pinnate, strongly aromatic foliage. Cut blooms dry well. Varieties include 'Parker's Var.', 'Gold Plate' and 'Coronation Gold' which grows shorter (2½ ft.), 'Canary Bird', 'Flowers of Sulphur' (2½ ft.) and 'Sungold' (1½ ft.).

4—5 ft.   July—Aug.   3 ft. sq.   D.

*ACONITUM Monk's Hood

Handsome plants with glossy, palmately cut foliage, and spikes of helmet-shaped flowers. Roots poisonous. Favour deep, rich, moist soil which must not dry out, in sun or half shade. Leave plants alone when happily situated.

Among the best are *A. carmichaelii*, deep purple-blue, *var. wilsonii* flowers blue or violet, and the form of this known as 'Barker's Var.' (which may reach 6 ft. and flowers Sept.—Oct.), also *A. napellus* a very variable species with white, deep blue, violet and bicolour forms in blue and white.

3—5 ft.   June—July   2 ft. sq.   D. or S.

ADENOPHORA Gland Bellflower

Campanula-like plant, with nodding, short-stalked, funnel-shaped flowers, mostly blue, on slender stems. Leaves oval or heart-shaped at base but often toothed and oblong on the flower

Dianthus 'Bravo'   W. J. Unwin Ltd

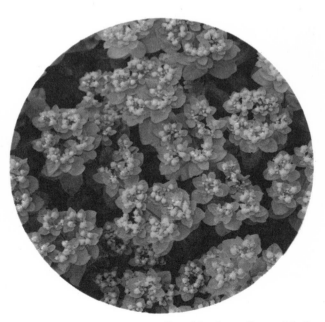

Euphorbia epithymoides   Copyright George Bunyard & Co

25

Althaea – Double Hollyhocks   Copyright Samuel Dobie & Son   **Achillea 'The Pearl'**   Copyright Ryder & Sons

stems. Plants resent disturbance so leave alone in a warm, sunny or partially shaded spot.

A. bulleyana, rich lavender-blue, and *A. potaninii*, light blue, are most commonly grown species.

2—3 ft. July—Aug. 2 ft. sq. S. sown directly after gathering.

ADONIS Pheasant's Eye

Early flowering plants for the rock garden or front of the border. Large, Buttercup-like flowers nearly 2 in. across and soft, finely cut, Fennel-like foliage. Arrange in groups in full sun or partial shade. Disappear after flowering so be careful not to fork them out or smother with neighbouring plants.

A. amurensis has single and *var. plena* double, golden flowers. Other forms have white, rose and red striped, also, rarely, yellow and green flowers. *A. vernalis* is single yellow and flowers April—May.

8—12 in. Feb.—April. 1 ft. sq. D.(spring) or S. sown immediately after gathering.

AJUGA Bugle

Hardy, carpeting plants for front of the border or as weed suppressors amongst perennials, best in damp or heavy soils. *A. genevensis* has oblong, coarsely toothed, deep green leaves and spikes of blue, white or rose flowers. *A. reptans*, with green leaves in the species has many fine foliaged varieties, e.g. *variegata*, leaves edged and splashed with cream; 'Rainbow', leaves mottled with dark red, purple and yellow; *atropurpurea*, purplish-blue. All have spikes of blue flowers.

6—9 in. June—July. 1 ft. sq. D.

*ALSTROEMERIA Peruvian Lily

A showy genus with tuberous rootstocks, but not hardy everywhere. Give plenty of sun and a well drained situation and protect from frost in first winter. Once established, will continue for years.

Remove soil 2 ft. deep, breaking subsoil with a fork. Return 6—8 in. of sandy soil and brick rubble; plant the rootstocks in spring, barely cover and leave. As growth starts add a little soil and continue until the trench is filled.

Flowers are funnel-shaped, many in a head on smooth stems; leaves soft green, smooth and narrow. Make good cut flowers but only if given about half an inch of water. **A. aurantiaca* is the best known and hardiest species with orange flowers, often spotted with chocolate. Varieties with larger or better coloured

blooms include 'Dover Orange' and 'Moerheim Orange'.
3 ft. June—Sept. 2 ft. sq. D.

A ligtu Hybrids from this Chilean species provide an exciting range of colours — flame, cerise, orange, pink, rose and yellow. All good for cutting but not as hardy as the previous species. Succeed in warmer areas or can be reared in frames.
1½—4 ft. June—July. 2 ft. sq. S.

ALTHAEA Hollyhock

An old-fashioned plant, recently out of favour because of leaf disease called Hollyhock Rust. Copper sulphate dusts and proper planting help to combat the trouble. Double varieties come fairly true from seed; single kinds are more doubtful.

Plant in deeply dug, well manured soil, with crowns 2 in. *below* soil level. Sand round the roots helps the drainage. Set in clumps of 3 for good effects. They need plenty of sun.

Varieties with white, yellow, rose and many shades of red can be obtained, with single or double flowers. Seed should be sown under glass in Feb. or March; out-doors in May or June.
6—8 ft. July—Sept. 3 ft. sq. S.

*ANAPHALIS Pearl Everlasting

Grey foliaged plants with crowded heads of white, 'everlasting' flowers. Useful for planting between brighter coloured plants. The flowers may be dried. Well drained, rather poor soil suits them best. Sun or partial shade. *A. margaritacea* and *A. triplinervis* are very similar.
1½ ft. August 1 ft. sq. D.

ANCHUSA Bugloss

Coarse perennials with rough, hairy stems and leaves but showy inflorescences covered with small, bright blue flowers. They need well drained soil and plenty of sun and for most spectacular effects should be raised annually. *A. azurea* has large blue or blue-purple flowers, but its varieties are more pleasing especially 'Morning Glory', 'Pride of Dover', 'Opal', 'Dropmore' and 'Royal Blue', in shades varying from pale to deep gentian blue.
3—5 ft. Summer 3 ft. sq. R.C.

A. caespitosa. Vivid front row perennial, forming dense mounds 15 in. high and as much across, covered with Gentian-blue florets. In dry soils is sometimes flowers itself to death, best prevented by cutting back some of the stems to allow a little basal growth above ground before winter. If done in August or Sept. cuttings can be taken in autumn and rooted in cold frames.
1¼ ft. May—Aug. 1 ft. sq. C.S. or D.

ANEMONE Windflower

Easily grown plants, the majority more suited to the rock garden, but the following useful in the border for spring or autumn flowers.

SPRING FLOWERING

A. canadensis, white starry blossoms and buttercup-like leaves in May; needs shade. 1—2 ft. S.; *A. caroliniana*, purple or whitish. 9 in. May. S.; *A. rivularis* and *A. sylvestris* both with white, somewhat drooping flowers, the latter fragrant. Moist soil and light shade. 1 ft. April.

AUTUMN FLOWERING

A. × hybrida, often known as *A. japonica*, or Japanese Anemones, are really hybrids of European origin. Do well in sun or shade and are free flowering, with single or double rose-like flowers and handsome, deeply cut leaves. Representative varieties are 'Charmeuse', double pink; 'Honorine Jobert', single white; 'Kriemhilde', pale pink, semi-double; 'Louise Uhink', semi-double, white; 'Prince Henry', single, purplish; 'Queen Charlotte', single, deep pink and 'Whirlwind', semi-double, white.
2—3½ ft. Sept.—Oct. 2 ft. sq. R.C.

Achillea 'Coronation Gold'

Anemone japonica 'Honorine Jobert'   Copyright R. & G. Cuthbert

Herbaceous border at Hampton Court   Michael Holford

ANTHEMIS Chamonile

Aromatic, deeply cut silvery foliage and large, usually yellow, single Daisies, are characteristic of this genus. All require full sun and a fertile soil with good drainage. *A. cupaniana* makes a useful edging subject, being short (1 ft.), with silvery Fern-like leaves. Flowers white. June—Sept. **A. sancti-johannis* has Pyrethrum-like flowers of bright orange with blooms 1½—2 in. across. **A. tinctoria* has produced some good garden forms, excellent for cutting, the best being 'Beauty of Grallagh', deep golden; 'E.C.Buxton', lemon-yellow; 'Golden Dawn', double gold; 'Grallagh Gold', bright gold, flowers sometimes 2½ in. across; 'Perry's Var.', gold and 'Roger Perry', deep gold.

2—2½ ft.   July—Aug.   2 ft. sq.   D. or S.

AQUILEGIA Columbine

Old garden favourites, suitable for any well drained soil provided this does not dry out in summer. Prefer light shade and for best effects should be allowed to colonise. Wide range of colours, either with long spurs at the backs of the flowers or short spurs (Granny's Bonnets)

1½—2½ ft.   July—Oct.   1½ ft. sq.   S. or D. for named sorts.

Alstroemeria ligtu

*ARMERIA Thrift

Hardy, evergreen plants with ground-hugging, grassy foliage and almost round heads of pink or white flowers. Almost any soil; full sun. *A. maritima* is the rock garden species (6—9 in.) with pink, white or deep rose flowers. *A. plantaginea* is a better border plant with large, globular heads of pink flowers. *Var.* 'Bee's Ruby', bright ruby red. *A. pseudoarmeria* is also known as *gigantea*; colours vary from pale pink to brick red.

1½ ft.   Summer   1 ft. sq.   D. or S. sown as soon as ripe.

ARTEMISIA Wormwood

Aromatic plants, including herbs, chiefly useful for their silvery foliage. All except *A. lactiflora* (which requires moist, almost boggy soil) need well drained conditions and sun. *A. gnaphalodes*, *A. ludoviciana*, *A. nutans* 'Silver Queen' and *A. stelleriana* are all useful. Flowers insignificant.

2—3 ft.   Late summer.   2 ft. sq.   D. or S.C.

A. lactiflora has flowers congregated together in large creamy-white plumes. Foliage, Chrysanthemum-like.

4—5 ft.   Late summer.   2½ ft. sq.   D.

*ARUNCUS   Goat's Beard

A. sylvester. A noble plant for a damp situation, with handsome pinnate foliage and impressive plumes of creamy flowers. Rich soil and half shade.

4 ft.   June.   3 ft. sq.   S. or D.

ASTER Michaelmas Daisy

A large and important family of easy cultivation, especially useful in autumn. Except for one yellow species *(A. linosyris)* the colours range through white and pink to deep red and from palest blue to deep mauves and purples. Earliest forms start to bloom in July, others go on until frosts; heights vary between a few inches and 6 ft.

The fibrous rootstocks made for easy division, although *A. amellus* must only be disturbed in spring or immediately after flowering. Softwood cuttings strike readily in spring.

Most Asters flower best in full sun and can be given a front, mid or back row position, according to height. Michaelmas Daisy varieties also make an attractive late summer border. There are three main groups:

A. amellus. These come into bloom about August, grow on average about 2 ft. high and have very large flowers (2 in. or so across). Varieties include 'Advance', deep violet; 'King George', violet-blue; 'Lady Hindlip', deep rose; 'Nocturne', rosy-lavender; 'Red Fire', almost red and 'Rudolf Goethe', large pale mauve.

2 ft.   Aug.—Oct.   2 ft. sq. D. in spring or S.C.

A. novae-angliae. Tall growing, with rough, hairy stems and leaves and many petals (florets) to each bloom, closing at night. Varieties: 'Barr's Pink', rosy-purple; *'Harrington's Pink'*, rose-pink; 'Snow Queen', white; 'Mrs. S.T. Wright', rosy purple.

3—4 ft.   Aug.—Oct.   3 ft. sq.   D. or S.C.

A. novi-belgii. Smooth leaves, branching stems with masses of flowers but very variable in height, from the cushion types a few inches high, to 6 ft. Colours white, pink to red and pale mauve to purple. Dozens of varieties including 'Mount Everest', 4 ft. and 'Alaska', 2½ ft. both white; 'Ada Ballard', 3 ft. mauvy-blue; 'Alderman Vokes', 3 ft., salmon-pink; 'Beechwood Beacon', 3 ft. deep rosy-crimson; 'Eventide', very large violet-blue, 3½ ft.; 'Peace', lilac pink, 3½ ft.; 'Sunset', glowing red, 3 ft.; 'Margaret Rose', bright rose, 9 in.; 'Countess of Dudley', shell pink, 1 ft.; and many others.

Variable.   Sept.—Oct.   1—3 ft. sq.   D. and S.C.

*ASTILBE False Goat's Beard

Beautiful plants with feathery plumes of white, pink, or red flowers and palmately-divided leaves. Moderate sunshine and deep, fertile damp soil essential. Particularly fine for water garden with Ferns, Primulas and moisture-loving Irises.

A. x arendsii. The best for garden purposes, especially varieties like 'Avalanche', white; 'Cattleya', orchid-pink; 'Burgkristal', coconut-ice pink; 'Fanal', garnet-red; 'Montgomery', deep red and 'Granat', crimson.

2—3 ft.   July—Aug.   2 ft. sq.   D. or S.

Aster 'The Cardinal'   Copyright Samuel Dobie & Son

*BERGENIA Megasea

Useful, early flowering perennials, with round, leathery leaves and fleshy spikes of usually pink flowers. Sun or shade, but flowers better in former; any garden soil. *B. cordifolia*, pink is species most commonly grown, but there are varieties with purplish, white and bright pink flowers.

1 ft.   March—April   1 ft. sq.   D.

BRUNNERA Siberian Bugloss

B. macrophylla, also known as *Anchusa myosotidiflora*, has large, rough, heart-shaped leaves and sprays of small, blue Forget-me-not-flowers. Spread rapidly if not watched. Likes damp soil and tolerates shade.

1—1½ ft.   April   1 ft. sq.   D. or R.C.

*CAMPANULA Bellflower

The perennial members of this large family like a moist soil with good drainage, in sun or light shade. Most smaller kinds seed freely so may be allowed to colonise wilder parts of the garden. Many make tap roots so do not transplant well, but seedlings or rooted cuttings move satisfactorily when young. *C. glomerata* has clustered heads of funnel-shaped, rich violet flowers at the ends of the stems. 1—2 ft.; *C. lactiflora* is a tall species (4—6 ft.) with loose panicles of white or blue-tinged flowers, which in 'Loddon Anna' are more pinkish. Magnificent plants, especially near Delphiniums. *C. persicifolia*, approx. 2 ft., makes a slender flower spike, festooned with wide open, bell-shaped flowers. Varieties snow white, lavender, deep and China blue forms; both single and double. Other good species are *C. latifolia*, 4—5 ft., *C. pyramidalis*, 5 ft.; and *C. trachelium*, 1—3 ft. All have blue and white flowered varieties.

May—July.   2 ft. sq.   D.S.   S.C.

*CATANANCHE Cupid's Love Dart

Forms a close rosette of rough, grey, narrow leaves from which spring many soft lavender-blue flowers, which may be dried. Plenty of sun and very well drained soil. *C. coerulea major* is the best; *var. alba* is white.

2 ft.   June—Aug.   2 ft. sq.   R.C.

CENTAUREA Knapweed

Thistle-like plants, but foliage without prickles. Most kinds like full sun, any soil. *C. dealbata* has globular flower heads of rosy-purple which in *var. steenbergii* become cyclamen-pink.

1½ ft. *C. macrocephala*, large yellow heads, and rough, oblong leaves. 3—4 ft. *C. montana* will grow in sun or shade and has white, yellow, blue or pink flowers — like large Cornflowers. 1½ ft. *C. glastifolia* is another good yellow species. 3—4 ft.

Various   Mid-summer   1—3 ft. sq.   D.

*CEPHALARIA Yellow Scabious

Back of the border subject, making a tall, branching plant covered in summer with large, soft yellow, Scabious flowers. *C. gigantea* is the best species and grows in any good garden soil, sun or semi-shade.

5 ft.   June—July.   3 ft. sq.   D. or S. (sown outside in April).

CIMICIFUGA Bugbane

Autumn flowering perennials for a damp place. Sun or half shade. Buttercup-like leaves and branching stems with drooping short spikes of creamy flowers. *C. americana*, *C. japonica*, *C. racemosa* and its *var. simplex* are all similar; the last named perhaps the best.

3 ft.   Late summer   2 ft. sq.   S. or D.

CLEMATIS

Apart from the well known climbing species (see p. 283) there are several herbaceous Clematis of bushy habit, which die down in winter. Most have small, blue flowers and rather attractive, divided foliage. Any good garden soil, sun or partial shade. Dress occasionally with hydrated lime. *C. recta* and its varieties and *C. heracleifolia* are worth growing.

2—4 f.   Summer   3 ft. sq.   S. or D.

*COREOPSIS Tickseed

Easily grown annuals and perennials for full sun and any soil which does not dry out in summer. Flowers usually yellow, round and daisy-like on branching stems. *C. grandiflora*, with single, 'Perry's Var.' semi-double and var. 'Badengold', with larger flowers, are all good for cutting, but need pea-stick sup-

Aquilegia Long spurred hybrids   Copyright Samuel Dobie & Son

30

port. 2½ ft. *C. verticillata*, 'Golden Shower', blooms all summer, is smaller (1—1½ ft.) with needle-like leaves and requires no staking.

1—2½ ft.　June—Sept.　1½ ft. sq. S. (sown in April) or side-shoots taken in autumn.

DELPHINIUM Perennial Larkspur

One of the most handsome garden plants, needing full sun and very rich soil. Protect dormant crowns against slugs early in year with weathered ashes or set poison bait (see p. 291). For superior spikes reduce shoots to three or four.

D. belladonna are small-growing forms, good for front of border, need no staking, and have mostly blue flowers. 'Naples', 'Wendy' and 'Blue Bees' are good varieties.

3 ft.　June—July　2½ ft. sq.　D.

Aster amellus – Michaelmas Daisy 'King George'

Cimicifuga racemosa　　　　　　　Copyright Ryder & Sons

D. x ruysii is a pink-flowered seedling, but new varieties are appearing with rosy and even red flowers. Heights usually 2—3 ft., flowering June—July.

The large flowered hybrids show a bewildering range of shades and mixtures of tones — usually blues — and vary in height from 4—7 ft. Each needs a ground area of approximately 2—3 ft. and are best grouped in threes. Increase named sorts by taking off the young basal shoots with a piece of the old rootstock in March, and root in a cold frame, dusting wounds with charcoal. Plants can also be raised from seed sown outside in spring, the Pacific Strain Hybrids producing excellent results.

4—7 ft.　June—July.　2—3 ft. sq.　C. D. S.

DICENTRA Syn. Dielytra, Bleeding Heart

Charming spring plants with dainty, Fern-like foliage and curiously-shaped, pendent flowers. Moist but well drained soil, protected from cutting winds, sun or partial shade. *D. eximia* makes a good edging subject, with drooping sprays of rosy-purple flowers. There is a white form *alba* and a larger form 'Bountiful'.

1—1½ ft.　　Freely in May and Sept. and intermittently between these months.　1 ft. sq.　D.

D. spectabilis. Arching sprays festooned with large, heart-shaped rosy-pink flowers with white tips; foliage very beautiful. *var. alba* is white.

2—4 ft.　May—June.　2 ft. sq.　D.

DICTAMNUS Burning Bush

Interesting and easily grown subjects, needing no disturbance for many years. All parts secrete an aromatic oil, particularly strong in the old flower spikes, which exude a volatile gas. On sultry evenings, holding a lighted match near them can set off a momentary flash, harmless to the plant. Flowers white or reddish, borne on spikes, leaves compound. *D. albus* (also known as *D. fraxinella*) is the type with white flowers, *var. purpureus*, purplish.

1½—2 ft.　June—July　2 ft. sq.　D. or S. (sown directly, after gathering)

*DORONICUM Leopard's Bane

Golden flowered, Daisy-like plants, blooming in spring but rather untidy later. If cut back after flowering they often throw an autumn crop. Moist but well drained soil, shaded from mid-

Centaurea montana

Dictamnus

Dicentra spectabilis

day sun. *D. piantagineum* var. 'Harpur Crewe' is the best, the blooms often 3 in. across on strong branching stems.

3—4 ft. April—May and again in Sept. 2 ft. sq. D.

*ECHINACEA Purple Cone-flower

Strong growing plant with rose or crimson-petalled Daisy flowers, with protruding brown or red central cone. Rich, well drained soil, moisture essential during growing season, and sun. *E. purpurea* varieties 'The King', wine-crimson with a mahogany coloured cone, 'White Lustre', white and 'Abendsonne', deep wine-red are the best.

2—2½ ft. Aug.—Sept. 2 ft. sq. D.

*ECHINOPS Globe Thistle

Easily cultivated, back of the border subjects, with spiny or lobed foliage, grey-green above and white beneath, and large, round, Thistle-like flowers. These are mostly blue. Sun or shade, most soils. *E. ritro* and its variety·'Taplow Blue' are both good the latter with deepest blue flowers. *E. horridus* has spiny leaves and slate-blue flowers.

3—5 ft. July—Aug. 2 ft. sq. D. or R.C.

*EREMURUS Foxtail Lily

Magnificent plants with broad, Yucca-like foliage and strikingly-tall spikes of flowers. Plant the octopus-like roots in October 10 in. deep in rich, well-drained soil, the centre of each resting on a bed of sand, with the thongs radiating outwards and slightly lower. Protect in winter with glass or bracken until established. Sheltered position, sun and occasional dressing of lime.

Species include *E. bungei*, bright yellow, with improved varieties such as 'Highdown Gold', and 'Dawn', deep pink florets on black stems, 2—3 ft.; *E. elwesii* is soft pink and 6—9 ft. high; *E. olgae*, white, 4 ft. and *E. robustus*, soft pink, 6—10 ft.

E. x *Shelford* is a fine race of garden origin with orange, buff, pink, pale yellow, pink and white flowers. 4½—6 ft.
Various.   June—July.   2 ft. sq.   D. or S.

*ERIGERON Fleabane

Mauve, Daisy-like flowers on branching stems, with small rough leaves and stems. Stake early with pea-sticks. Sun or partial shade; no particular cultural requirements. Useful for cutting, blooms intermittent May—Sept. Good named varieties include 'B. Ladhams', rosy-pink; 'Amos Perry', very large, deep mauve; 'Charity', soft pink; 'Darkest of All', deep violet; 'Gaiety', bright pink; 'Merstham Glory', deep mauve; 'Sincerity', light mauve.
1½—2 ft.   Al summer   1—2 ft. sq.   D. or S.C.

*ERYNGIUM Sea Holly

Steel-blue, Teazle-like flowers, blue stems and glaucous, prickly foliage. Stems and flowers frequently dried for winter decoration. With deep, rich, well drained soil, in full sun, they may remain undisturbed for years. An occasional dose of potash, especially kainit (2 oz. per sq. yd.) keeps plants healthy and improves colour. E. *agavifolium*, E. *pandanifolium* and E. *yuccaefolium* all have long, sword-shaped leaves several feet in height, flowers usually greenish, carried in large branching sprays, particularly fine in key positions. 4—6 ft.
Better known are the smaller-growing, larger-flowered E. x *oliveranium* hybrids, especially 'Violetta', with violet-blue stems and flower heads, 'Springhill Seedling', steel blue and var. *superbum*, light navy blue.
3—4 ft.   July—Sept.   3 ft. sq.   R.C. or S.
Slender growing species with much smaller flowers include E. *amethystinum*, E. *spinalba* and E. *planum*.
1—2 ft.   July—Sept.   2 ft. sq.   R.C. or S.

EUPATORIUM Hemp Agrimony

Suitable for a moist spot, producing flat-topped cluster of purplish or white flowers. Rather coarse and only suitable for rough corners. Sun. E. *cannabinum*, dull purple, E. *purpureum*, pale purple and E. *agaratoides*, dirty white. (2—4 ft.)
3—5 ft.   Aug.—Sept.   2 ft. sq.   D.

EUPHORBIA Spurge

Succulent plants with a poisonous milky sap, grown for early flowers and unusual foliage. Any soil, sun or partial shade.
The best border kinds are E. *wulfeni*, which being evergreen needs a warm, sheltered corner. Strong stems densely packed with oblong, bluish-green, somewhat hairy leaves, terminating in large heads of yellow-green flowers. 4 ft. May and June. S. or S.C. in early spring. E. *cyparissias* and E. *epithymoides* have small flowers, surrounded by bright gold bracts, impressive when massed.
1 ft.   April—May   2 ft. sq.   D.

FILIPENDULA Meadow Sweet

Spirea-like plants with pinnate or palmately-lobed leaves and terminal plumes of white, pink or red flowers. Particularly suited to the water garden. Sun or shade. F. *ulmaria* is our native 'Queen of the Meadows', found in damp ditches, with creamy flowers and handsome leaves. The double variety *flore-pleno* is particularly beautiful and var. *aurea* has gold-striped foliage. 2—3 ft. June.
Taller kinds include F. *camtschatica*, with fragrant, white flower plumes, var. *rosea*, pink, also F. *rubra*, deep peach and var. *venusta magnifica*, deep carmine.
4—8 ft.   June—July   2 ft. sq.   D. or S.

*GAILLARDIA Blanket Flower

Well known orange and yellow Daisy flowers, annual (see p. 133) and perennial. All appreciate a light, well drained soil with plenty of sunshine. Untidy in habit, need some support, e.g. pea-sticks. All the perennial kinds are derived from G. *aristata*. 'Burgundy' is rich wine red; 'Firebrand', red-orange; 'Mrs. H. Longster', large, golden with red centre; 'The King', red, tipped yellow; 'Wirral Flame', tangerine-red.
2 ft.   June—Nov.   1—2 ft. sq.   D.R.C. & S.

GALECA Goat's Rue

Members of the Sweet Pea family with soft green, pinnate leaves and spikes of small, white or blue flowers. Any soil, sun or light shade. G. *officinalis*, purplish blue, has produced varieties with lilac, mauve and white, white and double flowers.
3—4 ft.   June—July   3 ft. sq.   S. or D.

GAZANIA Treasure Flower

Brilliantly coloured Daisy-shaped flowers only opening in sunshine. Suitable for front of border, light, well drained soil. Leaves long and narrow, dark green and greenish-white beneath. Most from 6—12 in. high and flower continuously June—Oct. Planted out in May, about 1 ft. apart; not very hardy, so root side shoots in frames during August and leave there all winter. Colours range from white to yellow, orange, scarlet, tangerine and green, many with black markings and showing several tints in the same flower.
½—1 ft.   Summer   ¾ ft. sq.   S.C.

GERANIUM Crane's Bill

Useful for naturalising, especially in grassland in sun or semi-shade. Usually five-lobed, Buttercup-like leaves and branching stems festooned with small, open flowers. G. *endressii*, clear pink, flowers all summer, 9—12 in.; G. *pratense*, large, rich blue blooms, has varieties with blue and white, mauve, pink and purple flowers both single and double. 1½—2½ ft.; G. *psilostemon*, brilliant magenta with a black spot at the base of each petal. 2—3 ft.
Various   June—Aug.   2 ft. sq.   S. or D.

Centaurea macrocephala

GEUM Avens

Easily grown in most soils, blooming intermittently all summer. Sun or light shade. Best garden forms derived from a Chilean species *G. chiloense*, including 'Mrs. Bradshaw', brilliant orange-red flowers like semi-double roses on branching stems, and strawberry-like leaves; 'Fire Opal', single orange; 'Lady Stratheden', rich golden-yellow, double; 'Prince of Orange', bright orange and 'Red Wings', semi-double scarlet.

2 ft. Summer 2 ft. sq. S.D.

*GYPSOPHILA Chalk Plant

Chalk loving plants, succeeding in any deep, well drained soil. Full sun. Cloudy masses of small, white or pinkish flowers. Established plants make thick, Parsnip-like roots and cannot be transplanted. The type *G. paniculata*, with single white flowers, is raised from seed, but named and double varieties like 'Rosy Veil' and 'Bristol Fairy' have to be grafted on small seedlings of this species.

3 ft. (some smaller) June—Aug. 2—3 ft. sq. S. or Grafts.

*HELENIUM Sneezeweed

Indispensable plant for late summer and autumn work in the border. Any soil provided site is sunny. Pinching back in June reduces height and makes a more branching habit.

The leafy stems carry on branching heads quantities of yellow, bronze and red Daisy-like flowers. Representative varieties include 'Gold Fox', streaky-red-orange, 3½ ft.; 'Moerheim Beauty', brown to orange-red, 3½ ft.; 'Golden Youth', large, rich butter-yellow, 3 ft.; 'Gartensonne', golden 4 ft.; 'The Bishop', self yellow, 2 ft. and 'Wyndley', bushy habit, copper-orange, 2 ft.

2—4 ft. June—Sept. 2 ft. sq. D.

HELIANTHUS Sunflower

Somewhat coarse, but useful perennials for the back of the border. Divide periodically to avoid spreading. Any soil, but better under moist conditions and needing full sun. *H. atrorubens* (Syn. *H. sparsifolius*) has rough leaves, 6—8 ft. stems and handsome, single, bright yellow flowers. 'Gullick's Var' and * 'The Monarch' last weeks when cut. Lift tubers of latter in October and store like dahlias until May. *H. decapetalus* is the most useful for border work and perfectly hardy. Varieties include 'Capenoch Star', lemon yellow, 5 ft.; *flore pleno*, double gold, 4 ft.; 'Loddon Gold', rich gold with quilled petals; 'Soleil d'Or', sulphur yellow, petals fluted and quilled like a Cactus Dahlia, 4½ ft.; 'Triomphe de Gand', the best semi-double, 5 ft. and *H. rigidus* 'Miss Mellish', an old but good variety with smaller (3 in.) flowers, growing in a drier place than the others. 7 ft.

4—7 ft. Aug.—Oct. 3 ft. sq. D.

*HELIOPSIS Orange Sunflower

Sunflower-like perennials needing similar conditions to Helianthus, but general habit is smaller and flowers brighter. Resistant to drought but adaptable and thriving in moist ground.

Varieties of *H. scabra* include *incomparabilis*, with almost double, Zinnia-like flowers; 'Goldgefieder', full double, gold with green centres; 'Gold Greenheart', double lemon-yellow, emerald green at centre until fully open; 'Orange King', bright orange; 'Light of Loddon', single butter-yellow, 3 in. across; *patula* semi-double.

3—4 ft. July—Sept. 2 ft. sq. D. or S.C. in spring

HELLEBORUS Christmas and Lenten Rose

Invaluable for early flowers and long-lasting blooms — beautiful both in leaf and flower. Rich deep well drained soil, not liable to dry out, shade from midday sun. Associate well with Ferns, Bluebells and Foxgloves. *H. corsicus* is evergreen with deeply-cut, leathery leaves and clusters of nodding, Apple-green flowers, in March and April. 2 ft. *H. foetidus*, *H. viridis* and *H. x nigricors* have green flowers from Feb. to April. *H. niger*, the Christmas rose, has clean, white, saucer-shaped flowers, and varieties include 'Keesen Variety' and *maximus*, both finer than the species. 1—2 ft. Dec.—Feb. *H. orientalis* makes best border plant, flowers from Dec. until April, with nodding white, pink, red, crimson and spotted flowers.

2 ft. Dec.—April 1½ ft. sq. S.D.

HEMEROCALLIS Day Lily

Hardy and adaptable plants, suitable for almost any site or soil, sun or shade, a few even under bog conditions. Grassy,

Macleaya microcarpa

Hemerocallis 'Sandstone'

Heliopsis 'Orange King'

arching foliage, Lily-shaped flowers, lasting one day only, usually fragrant, mostly yellow and orange. New hybrids of British and American origin, however, show pink, red and brownish colours.

*Good garden forms are usually better for border work than the species. They include 'Margaret Perry', tangerine; 'Black Prince', ruby-purple; 'Hesperies', citron-yellow; 'Marcus' rich orange, overlaid bronze; 'Pink Lady', amber pink; 'The Doctor', deep red; 'Garnet Robe', deep blood-red and 'Royal Ruby', crimson.

3—4 ft.   July—Aug.   2 ft. sq.   D.

HEUCHERA Alumroot, Coral Bells

Front row plants with heart-shaped, rough leaves and slender spikes of small pink or red flowers. Unless frequently divided, preferably in spring, plants tend to die out.

*H. sanguinea has red flowers and somewhat hairy foliage; atrosanguinea, dark red; 'Huntsman', scarlet; 'Pearl Drops', almost white; 'Rhapsody', glowing pink; 'Red Spangles', rich crimson and 'Snowflakes', white.

1—1½ ft.   June—Sept.   1½ ft. sq.   D. or S. (variable results).

*HOSTA Syn. Funkia, Plantain Lily

Woodland plants needing moist soil and shade, with handsome leaves. Flowers funnel-shaped, white or mauve, on slender spikes. Types with green or glaucous leaves include *H. fortunei*, *H. glauca*, *H. plantaginea* and *H. ventricosa*. Variegated leaved sorts are *H. fortunei albopicta*, *H. undulata*, *H. ventricosa marginata* and *H. lancifolia var.* 'Thomas Hogg'.

1—2 ft.   May—June or Aug.—Sept.   1—2 ft. sq.   D. in spring.

INCARVILLEA Chinese Trumpet Flower

Plants of striking appearance, with large, rose, Gloxinia-like flowers and handsome pinnate leaves. Grow in a sheltered position in light sandy loam. Protect the first winter and mulch occasionally. *I. delavayi*, rosy-crimson, with 5 or 6 blooms on a stem is perhaps the best. *I. grandiflora* is shorter (1 ft.) with more rounded leaves but flowers are larger.

1—2 ft.   May—July   1 ft. sq.   S.

INULA

Showy plants with yellow or orange Daisy heads 2—4 in. across. Some only suitable for the wild garden but the following make useful border perennials. They like sun and grow readily in most soils. *I. ensifolia* var. 'Golden Beauty', golden-yellow, flowers 2 in. across, on a bushy plant, from June to Sept. *I. orientalis*, the best known, large, orange, finely petalled flowers 4—5 in. across and striking, dimpled leaves; *var. grandiflora*, is

35

a better form of preceding; *I. royleana*, deep orange, with long, drooping, rosy petals.

2—3 ft.   Summer   2 ft. sq.   D. or S.

*IRIS

A large and important family of diverse habit. Some, like the rhizomatous *I. germanica*, have broad leaves, need lime and full sun; *I. sibirica* has grassy foliage, dainty flowers, dislikes lime and needs moister soil; others prefer shade *(I. foetidissima)* or very moist soil or bog. For bog and aquatic types see p. 267.

I. germanica Flag Iris

For real success lift and divide every third or fourth year. Well drained but fertile soil, full sun and an occasional dressing of lime are main requirements. Countless varieties from white and bicoloured forms to light blues, mauves, purples, pinks, reds, browns and yellows. Typical are 'Aline', sky-blue; 'Amigo', deep blue and purple; 'Arabi-Pasha', intense royal blue; 'Arab

Liatris pycnostachya   Copyright R. & G. Cuthbert

Helianthus — perennial Sunflower

Chief', burnt orange; 'Arctic Snow', white; 'California Gold', deep golden; 'Chantilly', orchid-pink; 'Golden Hind', rich yellow; 'Great Lakes' clear blue; 'Gudrun', white and gold; 'Hester Prynne', coppery-red; 'Indiana Night', almost black; 'Louvois', velvety-brown and maroon; 'Melchoir', maroon; 'New Snow', pure white; 'Radiation', orchid pink and tangerine; 'Ranger', crimson; 'Sable', deep violet; 'Solid Mahogany', chestnut-red; 'St. Agnes', greyish-white, and 'Wabash', deep violet and white.

2½—4 ft.   June   1—1½ ft. sq.   D. in July

I. chamaeris and *I. pumila*

Need similar conditions to *I. germanica* and are early flowering (April) miniature forms of that species. Useful for front of the border, in white, yellow and blue shades, and should be planted about a foot apart.

I. sibirica

The Beardless Iris are moisture-loving, with thin grassy leaves and smaller flowers. May be left for years without division. Varieties include 'Perry's Blue', sky-blue; 'Emperor', deep violet; 'Roger Perry', Cambridge-blue; 'Marcus Perry', Oxford blue; 'Snow Queen', white.

2½—4 ft.   June   1½ ft. sq.   D.

Other Beardless Iris in this group are *I. aurea* 5 ft., golden-

Kniphofia and Artemisia

36

yellow flowers in June and July; *I. delavayi*, rich violet, 5 ft.; 'Margot Holmes', a striking hybrid, with cerise-purple flowers in June, 18 in. and *I. ochroleuca*, a late bloomer with broad, strap-like leaves and 5 ft. flower stems, carrying several large yellow and white flowers. June to July. All can be propagated by division.

KENTRANTHUS Spur Valerian

Suitable for dry, sunny spots, old walls, rough banks, etc. *K. ruber* has rosy-red flowers and there are also white and deep red varieties.

1½—3 ft.   Summer.   1 ft. sq.   S. sown outside in March.

KIRENGESHOMA Yellow Wax Bells

K. palmata is a beautiful shade plant from Japan, needing moist, rich soil. Leaves are Maple-shaped, grey-green and slightly woolly, flowers bell-shaped, waxen yellow, freely carried on branching stems.

2—3 ft.   Aug.—Oct.   2 ft. sq.   S. or D.

KNIPHOFIA Red Hot Poker; Torch Lily

Noble, grassy-leaved plants with conspicuous spikes of brilliant flowers. Sun, good drainage and an occasional mulch keeps plants happy for years in the same positions. Leaves evergreen. *K. caulescens* has Yucca-like foliage rising from a short, stout trunk. The flowers may be 4—5 ft. reddish salmon, paling to cream. Autumn flowering. *K. corallina* has closely set coral-red flowers on 3 ft. spikes June—August. *K. x erecta* has fiery-orange blossoms, the old flowers turning upwards as they age; an uncommon variety as less hardy than most and needs slight winter protection. 4 ft. Aug.—Sept.; **K. galpinii*, vivid flame, grows 2½ ft. only; *K. gracilis* is whitish and has varieties such as 'Buttercup'. Very narrow leaves, June—Aug. 2 ft.; **K. uvaria* is the parent of most garden forms with large, showy flower spikes. Varieties include 'Bee's Lemon', citron-yellow; 'John Benary', orange-red; 'Lord Roberts', bright red; 'Maid of Orleans', ivory-white'; 'Mount Etna', scarlet; 'Red Chief', bright red; 'Royal Standard', bright red and yellow; 'Primrose Beauty', and 'Yellow Hammer'.

3—5 ft.   Summer.   2—3 ft. sq.   D. or S.

LAMIUM Dead Nettle

The dwarf Dead Nettles with variegated foliage make good ground cover or edging plants. Tolerant of some shade and will live on poor soils but must be kept in bounds. *L. maculatum* has white stripes on the leaves and purplish flowers; *var. aureum* golden foliage.

Under 1 ft.   May—July.   1 ft. sq.   D.

LAVATERA Tree Mallow

L. olbia is a shrubby plant with Vine-like leaves, making a fine specimen in the border or isolated on a lawn. Profusely covered with rose-pink, Hollyhock-like flowers, from June until frosts. Will grow in dry soil but needs full sun. Prune back hard in spring and let it flower on the young wood. Renew every 3—4 years.

5—6 ft.   June—Oct.   5 ft. sq.   S. or Heel C. spring or July.

*LIATRIS Kansas Feather; Gay Feather

Unusual North American plant with spikes of stalk-less, tassel-like flowers of a curious cyclamen-purple shade, opening from top downwards. Leaves dark green, tapering and glossy. Prefers full sun and firm well drained soil. *L. callilepis, L. pycnostachya* and *L. scariosa* are all similar. Varieties include 'Sep-

Pyrethrum

tember Glory', with long flower spikes, and 'White Spire', white flowers.

2—4 ft.   Aug.—Oct.   1 ft. sq.   D. (spring) or S.

LIGULARIA

Handsome foliage perennials with mostly broad, heart-shaped leaves and branching spikes of yellow and orange flowers. Moist soil. *L. clivorum* has lower leaves up to 18 in. across on a vigorous plant, with 4—5 ft. reddish stems of bright orange, Daisy flowers. Varieties with larger blooms include 'Othello', with purplish foliage, 'Orange Queen' and 'Desdemona'.

L. veitchiana and *L. wilsoniana* are other good kinds; *L. japonica* has deeply cut leaves.

3—5 ft.   July—Sept.   3 t. sq.   D.

*LIMONIUM Sea Lavender

Also known as Statice, useful plants with cloudy sprays of minute flowers which can be dried as everlastings. Prefer full sun and light well drained soil. *L. incanum* and *L. latifolium* are the best known kinds; varieties from latter include 'Violetta', rich violet-blue; 'Chilwell Beauty' deep mauve and 'Blue Gown', light lavender.

2 ft.   July—Sept.   1½ ft. sq.   R. C.

LINDELOFIA

L. longiflora, a Himalayan plant with terminal clusters of rich blue, Forget-me-not-like flowers and dark green, hairy, narrow leaves.
1½ ft.   May—Aug.   1 ft. sq.   S. or D. (spring)

LINUM Flax

A genus of annuals (see p. 130) and perennials with light habit, small leaves, and dainty blossoms. Individual flowers are short-lived, but plants are prolific and provide a continuous show of bloom for many weeks. Flowers only open in sunshine, so an open position and light, well drained soil are essential. Named varieties of *L. narbonense* such as 'June Perfield', 'Heavenly Blue' and 'Six Hills Variety', all with rich blue flowers, make fine groups set about 9 in. apart in the front of the border.
1½ ft.   May—June   9 in. sq.   S. (sown outside April. Half ripe cuttings in July or careful division)

LOBELIA Cardinal Flower

A variable genus, but those suitable for the border all demand plenty of moisture and sun. The following should be treated as half-hardy. i.e. lifted in autumn and wintered in a cold frame. Plant 9 in. apart in a prominent position, possibly alongside silver foliaged subjects.
L. fulgens varieties include 'Queen Victoria', deep purple leaves and crimson flowers; 'Huntsman', scarlet; 'Purple King', purple; 'Rose Queen', 'The Bishop', salmon-pink. *L. cardinalis* is equally brilliant, but has green leaves. *L. syphilitica*, with blue or white flowers, is more suited to the water garden (see p. 271).
1—3 ft.   July—Sept.   1 ft. sq.   S.C. (July) S. (sown under glass in April)

LUPINUS Lupin

These deserve to be planted generously for their bright and early flowers come at a time when there is little else out in the border. *L. arboreus*, the Tree Lupin, grows 3—5 ft. high with branching stems carrying small, fragrant, yellow, mauve or white flowers.

L. polyphyllus includes the Russell Lupins, with long, sturdy spikes crowded with bright flowers. Succeed on all soils save the over rich or very chalky. For best effects plant in groups of single colours. Do not save seeds from blue varieties (the dominant colour), nor allow every spike to set as this shortens the life of the plant. Remove old flower heads on fading; a secondary crop of bloom often follows in late summer. Since hybrids are not long lived renew frequently from seed or increase named sorts by spring division. Discard old and woody growth, retaining only the small, fibrous-rooted pieces. Cuttings, taken with a piece of the old rootstock, can also be rooted in March in a cold frame.

Named varieties come in shades from soft pink to deep red, light and dark blue, yellow, violet and cream. Excellent, and very much cheaper stock can also be raised from seed sown outside in April or September. 'Apple Blossom', soft pink; 'Betty Astell', rose-pink; 'Blue Jacket', blue and white; 'Canary Bird' and 'Celandine', both yellow; 'Cherry Pie', cherry red; 'Commando', deep mauve and yellow; 'Cynthia Knight', violet and white; 'Elsie Waters', pink and white; 'Flaming June', orange; 'George Russell', clear pink; 'Heatherglow', wine-purple; 'Monkgate', blue and white; 'Nellie B. Allen', salmon-orange; 'Patricia of York', primrose; 'Thundercloud', dark violet and blue and 'York Minster' pale rose and cream.
2½—3 ft.   June—July.   2½ ft. sq.   S. D. or C.

LYCHNIS Campion

Easily grown plants and good perennials; sun or partial shade.

Euphorbia wulfeni

Doronicum 'Harpur Crewe'

Erigeron 'Elsie'

Kniphofia uvaria

L. chalcedonica, Maltese Cross, sends up stiff, brittle stems packed with tapering, hairy leaves and culminating in round heads of vivid scarlet flowers. 2–3 ft. June to Aug. There is a white and also a rather rare double form. *L. coronaria*, the Rose Campion, forms dense clumps of white woolly leaves and has branching stems with single, vivid magenta flowers. The best variety is 'Abbotswood Rose'.

2 ft.   July—Aug.   2 ft. sq.   D. or S.

L. x haageana is a hybrid race with scarlet, orange, crimson or buff flowers about 2 in. across. Full sun, not very hardy.

1 ft.   June—July.   1 ft. sq.   D.

LYSIMACHIA Loosestrife

Favouring damp conditions but fairly accommodating. Sun or semi-shade. Very suitable for the bog garden; *L. clethroides* and *L. punctata*, the one white, the other yellow, have flat, open blooms in whorls round a leafy tapering spike.

1½–3 ft.   June—Aug.   1½ ft. sq.   S. or D.

*LYTHRUM Purple Loosestrife

Of easy culture in moist soil and suitable for a woodland, setting or bog garden. Very vivid sage-like flowers, on slendery slightly curved spikes. Varieties from *L. salicaria* include 'Lad', Sackville' and 'Brightness'; both brilliant rose; 'The Beacon magenta-red and 'Robert', clear pink, only 2 ft.

2–4 ft.   June—Sept.   1½ ft. sq.   S.C.

MACLEAYA Syn. Bocconia; Plume Poppy

Stately plants with beautiful, heart-shaped; much cut leaves, silver on reverse. Flowers feathery, in dense, terminal panicles. Spreads by underground stems, but easily kept in check with the hoe. Good to mask unsightly objects. Sun or light shade. *M. cordata* is buff; var. 'Coral Plume', pinkish; *M. microcarpa*, copper-yellow.

5–7 ft.   July—Sept.   3 ft. sq.   Suckers or S.

MECONOPSIS Himalayan Poppy; Welsh Poppy

Essentially woodland plants, but suitable for borders with cool, well drained soil and some shade. Avoid drought in summer and waterlogging in winter. Usually propagated from seed. Stems and leaves are normally roughly hairy, attractively cut and the flowers 4-petalled and wide open like Poppies, those with blue shades being particularly beautiful. Plant 1–2 ft. apart.

BLUE SHADES

M. betonicifolia (syn. *M. baileyi*) is the most exciting, with glistening sky-blue flowers. Best grown from seed as a biennial, pinching out the flower stem the first season. 2–5 ft. June—July. *M. napaulensis* is satiny blue but also produces red, purple and occasionally white flowers. 4 ft. June. *M. quintuplinervia*, lavender-blue with fine bronze, hairy leaves. 1–1½ ft. May—June.

YELLOW SHADES

M. cambrica, The Welsh Poppy, has single clear yellow or orange flowers. There are double forms of each. Seeds itself freely. 1 ft. June—Sept. *M. integrifolia*, 1–1½ ft. rich yellow, July and *M. regia*, rich yellow with fine leaf rosettes, thickly covered with golden hairs. Dies after flowering. 4–5 ft. June—July.

MERTENSIA Virginian Cowslip

Likes a partially shaded, sheltered and damp situation and will often colonise under such conditions. Flowers turquoise blue, nodding, on arching sprays with blue-grey leaves. *M. virginica* is the best.

1–2 ft.   April—June   1 ft.   S. or D. after flowering.

MIMULUS Musk

Essentially plants for the waterside, but suitable for very damp soils af front of border. See also pp. 134 and 272.

MONARDA Bergamot

Square stemmed, aromatic foliaged plants with striking Dead-Nettle type flowers. A moist soil which never dries out is es-

d'Andre Chaudron', has jagged grey leaves and 2-foot spikes of Lavender-like flowers from June to Sept., leaves fragrant.

1—2 ft.   May—Sept.   1 ft. sq.   S.C.

OENOTHERA Evening Primrose

Perennial members of this family are usually low growing, unlike biennial forms. (See p. 139). They will flourish in practically any soil provided not waterlogged, in sun or light shade.

Meconopsis betonicifolia   Copyright Samuel Dobie & Son

Paeonies.   Copyright R. & G. Cuthbert

sential, in full sun or partial shade.

Varieties of *M. didyma* include 'Cambridge Scarlet', brilliant red; 'Mrs. Perry', crimson; 'Croftway Pink', rose-pink; 'Mahogany', deep red; *alba*, white; 'Perfield Crimson', crimson and 'Pale Ponticum', lavender-mauve.

2—3 ft.   June—Sept.   2 ft. sq.   D. or S.C.

MORINA Himalayan Whorlflower

M. longifolia has Thistle-like foliage and spikes of tubular flowers, red in the bud, paling to white, arranged in whorls around stem and protected by spiny bracts. Cover in winter with a pane of glass. Excessive wet sometimes causes rotting. Well drained soil, full sun and shelter.

2—3 ft.   June—July   1 ft. sq.   D. after flowering S. sown
as soon as ripe.

NEPETA Catmint

The common catmint *N. faasenii* (more usually known as *N. mussinii*) makes a useful edging plant, with its smooth silver-grey leaves and spikes of mauve Lavender-like flowers. Renew frequently as it does not persist long in heavy soils. Cut plants hard back after flowering for new shoots which root easily under cloches or in cold frames in July. 1 ft. *N. x 'Six Hills Giant'* is a taller (2 ft.) and more erect form and *N. grandiflora*, *'Souvenir

Best kinds are *O. speciosa*, a fine plant with large, white fragrant flowers from July to Sept.; *O. missouriensis* (syn. *macrocarpa*), a spreading species with reddish stems and funnel-shaped, 4-in wide, yellow flowers, makes a good front of the border plant, under a foot high. July—Aug.

O. fruticosa had twiggy, upright stems with large yellow flowers; 'Yellow River', 'William Cuthbertson' and *'youngii'* are improved forms.

9 in.—2 ft.   June—Autumn.   1 ft. sq.   S. or S.C.

OMPHALODES Blue-eyed Mary

O. verna has brilliant blue flowers and fresh looking, heart-shaped leaves. Of creeping habit, it makes a good ground cover neat trees.

6 in.   March—May   1 ft. sq.   D.

OROBUS Bitter Vetch

Neat bushy plants with Vetch-like flowers and leaves, often referred to *Lathyrus* or *Vicia*. All bloom in spring or early summer, none of them 'run' and they grow in any damp soil in sun or partial shade. *O. lathyroides* is blue; *O. vernus*, bright purple; *albus plenus*, double white, and *O. aurantiacus* (syn. *Vicia aurantia*), orange and yellow.

1½ ft.   May—June.   1 ft. sq.   S. or D.

*PAEONIA Paeony

Includes some of our most important and attractive border plants, with fine flowers which are often fragrant, and handsome cut foliage. Hardy, dependable and resistant to most pests and diseases Paeonies grow in practically any soil, in full sun or light shade. Blooms last longer in a cool situation but avoid an east position as the flowers come early, and may be damaged if a quick thaw follows an overnight frost.

There are many species and varieties, the best of the former being *P. mascula*, glossy leaves, single, rose-red, 2—3 ft. *P. mlokosewitschi*, single, soft yellow with coral stamens, very fine. 1½ ft.; *P. officinalis*, the old Cottage Paeony, with double red, rose and white flowers. 2—2½ ft.; *P. peregrina*, single scarlet. 3 ft.; *P. tenuifolia*, brilliant crimson, with finely cut, Fennel-like leaves. 1½ ft. and *P. wittmanniana*, bowl-shaped, cream, single, 3 ft.

Paeonia officinalis rubra

Russell Lupins at Kew

Paeonia peregrina

Most of the garden hybrids are derived from *P. lactiflora* and known as Chinese Paeonies; nearly all are scented.

DOUBLES

'Adolphe Rousseau', maroon; 'Bunker Hill' crimson; 'Cherry Hill', cherry-red; 'Canary', cream; 'Couronne d'Or', white; 'Felix Crousse', bright rose; 'General MacMahon', glowing crimson; 'Karl Rosenfield', dark wine-red; 'Mrs. Edward Harding', white; 'President Roosevelt', deep red and 'Wiesbaden', blush pink.

SINGLES

'Clairette', white; 'Bowl of Beauty', pale pink; 'Globe of Light', pure rose; 'Pink Delight', soft rose, passing to white; 'The Bride', pure white; 'The Moor', dark red; 'Victoria', deep crimson and 'Winston Churchill', rose pink.

2½—3½ ft.   June   2—3 ft. sq.   D.

See also p. 70.

*PAPAVER Poppy

Gay plants of easy culture, but untidy after flowering, therefore plant mid-way in the border, with something like Gypsophila coming along later. In well drained soil and a sunny position the plants are almost indestructible. For border work use varieties of *P. orientale* in clumps of one colour. Staking is necessary for most. 'Beauty of Livermore', blood-crimson; 'Cowichan', oxblood-red; 'Ethel Sweet', pure rose; 'Mahony', dark blood-red; 'Marcus Perry', bright orange-scarlet, late (July—Aug.), does not require staking; 'Mrs. Perry', soft salmon pink; 'Perry's White', 'Salmon Glow', double salmon-orange 'Stormtorch', fiery red and 'Watermelon', cherry-rose.

2—3 ft.   May—June.   2 ft. sq.   R.C. or S. (not reliable to colour)

*PENSTEMON Beard Tongue

Includes some useful summer and autumn plants but not all fully hardy or longlived. Sun and good drainage essential with winter protection in cold districts. Most root readily from cuttings, best taken in September in a cold frame and left all winter. *P. barbatus*. A hardy species with clustered spikes of coral-red, tabular flowers about an inch long, and smooth, narrow leaves. Var. 'Rose Elf' is particularly prolific with 10 or more spikes to a plant; *coccineus* is scarlet. 3 ft. June—Aug. *P. glaber* is the Blue Penstemon with dumpy spikes of bright blue flowers, pink and rose shades also available. 9 in.—2 ft. Aug. *P. heterophyllus* is also blue but varies from seed. Var. 'True Blue' can be propagated from cuttings. 1—1½ ft. *P. hybrida* includes the bedding Penstemons and such varieties as 'Southgate Gem' and 'Myddelton Gem', light crimson; 'Cherry Red', 'White Bedder' and 'Carnet', deep crimson.

2 ft.   July—Sept.   1—1½ ft. sq.   S.C.

PEROVSKIA Russian Sage

P. atriplicifolia grows like a shrubby Salvia with spikes of soft blue, Nepeta-like flowers and small, toothed silvery leaves. Very well drained soil and sunny, sheltered position.

3—4 ft.   Aug.—Sept.   3 ft. sq.   Heel C. in spring.

PHLOMIS Jerusalem Sage

Low, shrubby plants with silver, plush foliage and spikes with whorls of large yellow or mauve, Dead-Nettle flowers. A hot, dry position suits it best. *P. fruticosa* is yellow, also *P. samia*; *P. cashmeriana*, lilac-purple.

2—4 ft.   June—July   3—4 ft. sq.   S.C. in spring.

Monarda 'Croftway Pink'

Polemonium coeruleum   H. Smith

Papaver orientalis 'Marcus Perry'

*PHLOX

Particularly useful in the mixed border, being in character between the early summer and autumn displays. Needs some sun and well drained but permanently moist soil. Mulching about April prevents dryness at the roots. Although plants may be divided and also increased from soft cuttings, they should be propagated only from root cuttings, between Sept. and March. This is because of the danger from eelworm, a common pest in these plants.

Typical varieties, all derived from *P. paniculata*, are 'Aida', crimson with purple eye; 'Blue Boy', bluish-mauve; 'Cecil Hanbury', orange-salmon with carmine eye; 'Commander in Chief', crimson with dark red centres; 'Dresden China', shell-pink; 'Europa', white and carmine; 'Fanal', flame-red; 'Frau Ant. Buchner', large white; 'Le Mahdi', violet-blue; 'Leo Schlageter', scarlet-carmine; 'Newbird', rich crimson; 'Purple King', purple-violet; 'Salmon Glow', 'Sir John Falstaff', rich salmon and 'Symphony', strawberry-pink.

2—3 ft.   End July—Sept.   2 ft. sq.   R.C.

*PHYGELIUS Cape Fuchsia

P. capensis. Shrubby plant, something like Fuchsia, with candelabra heads of drooping, tubular, scarlet flowers and neat, smooth leaves. Provide a warm sheltered position in well drained soil. Top growth usually caught by frost and doubtfully hardy in very exposed situations.

4 ft.   Aug.   3 ft. sq.   S. (sown under glass) and C.

PHYSALIS Chinese Lantern; Cape Gooseberry

Flowers of little value but grown for the ornamental fruits which can be dried. See p. 280.

*PHYSOSTEGIA Obedient Plant

P. virginiana is called the Obedient Plant because the individual rosy-pink, Sage-like blossoms can be moved from side to side on the flower spike and remain as placed. The long tapering leaves are toothed. Any soil, including clay; sun or very light shade. Roots tend to roam, prevented either by thrusting slates around planting area or cutting out wanderers in spring with sharp spade. The var. 'Vivid' is the best form, bright rosy-purple; 'Rose Bouquet' is paler. There is also a white form.

2—3 ft.   Aug.—Sept.   2 ft. sq.   D.

PLATYCODON Balloon Flower

A Campanula-like flower, with petals joined and inflated in the bud stage, when they can be popped like a balloon. They open to a wide bell, 2 in. across — mostly blue, but sometimes white. Full sun and well drained soil. *P. grandiflorum* is the only species but there are semi-doubles and also a double form.

1—2 ft.   Aug.—Sept.   1 ft. sq   S. or D.

PODOPHYLLUM May Apple

Shade plants for rich, moist soil, having twin leaves and flowers which hang beneath these and later develop to large fruits. In *P. emodi* the leaves are marbled, flowers pale pink and fruits red. *P. peltatum* has green, glossy and wrinkled leaves, with white flowers and yellow apple-like fruits.

1—1½ ft.   April—May   1½ ft. sq.   D. or S.

POLEMONIUM Jacob's Ladder

P. coeruleum has dainty 5-lobed flowers on leafy stems, foliage pinnate like an Ash-leaf. Any soil except the very dry, sun or partial shade. The type is blue, a richer colour in *var. himalayanum* and there is also a white form. 'Blue Pearl' and 'Sapphire' are other improved varieties.

1—2½ ft.   May—July   1 ft. sq.   S. or D. in spring.

*POLYGONATUM Solomon's Seal See p. 202

Rudbeckia 'Golden Ball'　　　Copyright Samuel Dobie & Son　　Physostegia virginiana 'Rose Bouquet'

POLYGONUM Knotweed; Fleece Flower

A variable genus, some coarse and weedy, others useful in a moist or shady border. Best are *P. affine*, with spikes of pale pink flowers. 1½ ft. July—Sept. 1 ft. sq. *P. campanulatum* has simple oval leaves, whitish beneath and drooping sprays of pale pink, fragrant flowers. *Var. roseum* is a deeper pink; and *var. lichiangense*, creamy white.

2—3 ft. July—Oct. 2 ft. sq. D. spring or S.

POTENTILLA Cinquefoil

Good front row plants with Strawberry-like leaves and brilliant single flowers. Well drained but moist soil and full sun. *P. atrosanguinea* is reddish-purple but more frequently grown are varieties such as 'Gibson's Scarlet', brilliant scarlet; 'California', golden, semi-double; 'Monsieur Rouillard', double blood-red; 'Victor Lemoine', red-edged yellow and 'Yellow Queen', semi-double and silver leaved.

2 ft. June—Sept. 2 ft. sq. D. or S. sown outside in April.

*PRIMULA Primrose

Most members of this large family are more suitable for the bog or woodland garden than the border, yet Polyanthus particularly are so useful for their early flowers as to merit special consideration. Apart from a few named varieties, these can be raised according to colour groups — as in shades of pink, or blue, or yellow, bronze and white. Sow outside in May or June in a shady corner. Grow the seedlings along and in October place plants in flowering quarters. Lift again in May, divide and replant in a damp, shady spot for the summer. Rich cool soil at all times or the leaves flag.

1 ft. March—April 1 ft. sq. S. or D.

P. juliae and its hybrids, mostly very short stemmed, with wine-coloured blossoms, are also useful for their early flowers. Sparrows often tear petals off early primulas; cottoning seems the only sure remedy.

Under 1 ft. March—April 9 in. sq. S. or D.

PULMONARIA Lungwort

Plants with rough, hairy leaves and tubular flowers on short sprays suitable for the woodland garden or front of border. *P. angustifolia* has flowers which are pink at first then bright blue. 'Munstead Blue' is Gentian-blue and there is a red form *rubra*. The leaves of these are unspotted, whereas in *P. officinalis* they are heavily veined with white. This is the true Lungwort or Spotted Dog of gardens and has rosy flowers which develop to blue; *var. rubra* is blotting paper red.

1 ft. March—May 1 ft. sq. D.

43

PULSATILLA Pasque Flower

Also known as *Anemone pulsatilla*, these are variable plants with flowers in various shades of mauve and purple and white. Leaves deeply cut, silvery when young; flowers large, with prominent boss of yellow stamens. Resent disturbance and should be planted when very young. Deep well-drained soil and sun; not averse to lime.

1 ft. April 9 in. sq. S. or D. after flowering.

*PYRETHRUM Turfing Daisy

Well known plants, ideal for cutting. Pyrethrums are really Chrysanthemums, but since they need different cultural conditions are usually separated in grower's catalogues. Useful for early summer borders and, if cut down after blooming, frequently throw a second crop of flowers in the autumn. For cultural conditions see p. 23.

RANUNCULUS Buttercup

R. aconitifolius, with shiny, palmately-divided leaves and white Buttercup flowers, is at home in any place where the soil is perpetually moist. More attractive is the double form, also known as Fair Maids of France, the branching stems spangled with white rosettes.

½—1½ ft. May—June 1 ft. sq. D.

RHEUM See p. 273.

RODGERSIA See p. 273.

ROMNEYA Californian Tree Poppy

Magnificent perennials with fine, blue-grey leaves, somewhat leathery in texture and huge, fragrant, papery, white Poppy-like flowers. 4—5 in. across, filled with prominent golden stamens.

Deep but well drained soil, sunny situation, to best in a sheltered south-facing spot. Resent disturbance and are difficult to re-establish the slightest damage to the roots causing them to die. Best grown from seed in pots. Some winter protection necessary. *R. coulteri* and *R. trichocalyx* are very similar except that the latter has not such a pleasant scent.

4 ft. July—Aug. 6 ft. sq. R.C.

*RUDBECKIA Coneflower

Dependable autumn perennials, useful for cutting. Most soils, but best where moist. Full sun. The flowers often have a protruding central cone.

R. hybrida includes a number of varieties of doubtful parenthood, such as 'Goldquelle', deep yellow; backward pointing flowers, 5—6 ft.; 'Golden Ball', nearly double branching, deep yellow and *deamii*, grey-green foliage, very like *R. speciosa* (Black Eyed Susan) 2½ ft. *R. nitida*, yellow daisy flowers on stout stems, the rosy florets held back like a Cyclamen and with a green central cone. Var. 'Herbstsonne' is an improved variety. A back of the border plant. 6 ft. Aug.—Oct. 3 ft. sq. *R. speciosa* (Syn. *R. newmanii*), Black-eyed Susan, is a useful front row plant, golden flowers with black centres. Leaves narrow and rather rough. 'Sullivant's Variety' is an improved form with larger flowers. 2 ft. July—Oct. 2 ft. sq.

Propagation in all cases by spring cuttings or D.

SALVIA Sage

Requires plenty of sun and very well drained soil. Suitable for dry gardens, and easily raised from seed. *S. heamatodes*, with big, spreading branches of bluish-violet, funnel shaped flowers (June—Sept.) and *S. sclarea*, Clary, bluish-white, need frequent renewal. Aug. 3 ft. More permanent is *S. x superba* (syn. *S. virgata nemorosa*) with deep violet flowers and Sage green, aromatic leaves. 2—2½ ft. and its shorter form *compacta*, July—Aug. *S. uliginosa* is less hardy but blooms from Sept.—

Phlox for midsummer display Bakers of Codsall

Tiarella and Periwinkle

November with azure flowers on 4—5 ft. branching stems. Propagated by S.C., seed or D.

SANGUISORBA Burnet

Also known as Poteriums, with sprays of finger-like leaves and spikes of fluffy pink or cream flowers gathered at the tops of the stems like a bottle brush. Any soil. *S. canadensis* is white or pale pink; *S. obtusa*, bright pink.

2—3 ft. Summer 2 ft. sq. D. or S.

SAPONARIA Bouncing Bet

S. officinalis has smooth, opposite leaves and panicles of large rosy pink flowers. Double forms are best and may be white, pink or red. Inclined to spread. Any soil.

2 ft. Aug.—Oct. 1½ ft. sq. D. in spring.

Eremurus   Fisons Horticulture

Dwarf Michaelmas Daisies

*SCABIOSA Scabious

Graceful plants with dainty flowers, excellent for cutting. Full sun and light well drained soil essential; they like a little lime. Leave alone when well established. Never disturb in autumn.

Varieties of *S. caucasica* include 'Clive Greaves', rich mauve; 'Constancy', violet-blue; 'Imperial Purple', 'Miss Willmott', cream; 'Moerheim Blue', and 'Malcolm' light navy; 'Penhill Blue', soft blue; 'Souter's Violet', rich violet; 'Vincent', cobalt and 'Wanda', rich blue.

1½—2 ft. June—Sept. 1½ ft. sq. D. or C. with heel of old plant.

SEDUM Stonecrop

Mostly rock plants, but the following suitable for the herbaceous border. Any soil. See also p. 180. *S. maximum atropurpureum* has striking, crimson-purple, fleshy leaves and dull pink flowers. 2 ft. *S. spectabile* has stiff stems and leaves, the latter green and fleshy. In September the flat flower heads open, glistening pink, deeper coloured in 'Brilliant', 'Carmen' and 'Meteor'.

1—2 ft. Sept.—Oct. 1½ ft. sq. D. or S.C.

SENECIO

A very large genus, mostly weedy or only suited to the wild garden. *S. cineraria*, however, is worth growing for its finely cut, silver foliage which contrasts well with *Lobelia fulgens* and *Sedum maximum atropurpureum*. Not hardy in severe winters or exposed situations, but strikes readily from cuttings, which may be taken in late summer and kept in a cold frame all winter.

1—2 ft. Yellow flowers July—Sept. 1½ ft. sq. C.
See also p. 273 and Ligularia.

SIDALCEA Greek Mallow

Graceful, free flowering perennials for a mid-way position in the border. Group for effect. Flowers like small Hollyhocks; leaves deeply cut. Sun and a soil which will not dry out.

Varieties of *S. malvaeflora* are: 'Brilliant', carmine; 'Crimson Beauty', 'Croftway Red', clear, deep red; 'Dainty', pink and white; 'Elsie Heugh', satiny-pink; 'Listeri', pink with fringed petals; 'Pompadour', double scarlet; 'Rev. Page Roberts', light rosy-pink and 'Sussex Beauty', satiny pink.

2½—3 ft. July—Aug. 1½ ft. sq. D.

SISYRINCHIUM

S. striatum in leaf much resembles a Flag Iris, but the small pale yellowish-white flowers are closely packed on stiff spikes. Well drained soil, sunny position.

2 ft. June 1 ft. sq. S.

SMILACINA False Solomon's Seal

Very handsome plants with foliage like Solomon's Seal and feathery plumes of fragrant, creamy flowers. Moist soil and some shade. *S. racemosa* is the best.

2—2½ ft. May 1½ ft. sq. D.

*SOLIDAGO Golden Rod

Easily grown plants for massing, mostly with golden flowers. Any soil, sun or light shade. Good garden varieties are 'Leraft', 'Golden Wings', 'Goldenmosa', 'Leda', 'Lemore' and 'Lesdale'.

2½—3 ft. Aug.—Sept. 2 ft. sq. D.

STACHYS

S. lanata is the Lamb's Tongue or Donkey's Ears, with silvery plush-like leaves and stems, and spikes of purplish-rose flowers. Will grow in very poor soil.

1—1½ ft. July—Aug. 1 ft. sq. D.

*STOKESIA Stoke's Aster

S. laevis. Resembles a refined China Aster with rich lavender flowers on short sturdy stems. In character a long time. Practically any garden soil, sun or light shade. 'Blue Moon' and *praecox* are early varieties and there is a white form.

1—1½ ft.   July—Sept.   1½ ft. sq.   S.D.R.C.

THALICTRUM Meadow Rue

Chiefly valued for feathery sprays of flowers and dainty foliage. Useful for the back of the border or as 'dot' plants in a mid-way position. Any good, moist soil, sun or light shade. Stake taller varieties. *T. adiantifolium* has Maidenhair Fern-like foliage, the greenish-yellow flowers, of secondary importance, come in July and Aug. *T. dipterocarpum* is attractive, the slender branching stems spangled with lavender-mauve and yellow flowers. More exciting is 'Hewitt's Double', whose small mauve flowers cover the cobwebby branches like polka-dots. Good drainage and ever present moisture together with sunshine are essential; mulching is a great help in moisture retention.

2—5 ft.   June—Aug.   1½ ft. sq.   S. and offsets with
'Hewitt's Double.

T. flavum and *T. glaucum* are both yellow.

3—4 ft.   July   1½ ft. sq.   D.

THERMOPSIS

T. caroliniana and *T. montana* are bushy plants, with long spikes of bright yellow, Lupin-like flowers. Light soils, do well on chalk. Do not transplant well, except when young.

2 ft.   July   1 ft. sq.   S. or D.

TIARELLA Foam Flower

Ground cover plants, the leaves something like Heuchera but with bronze flushes on the upper surface. Small spikes of foamy white flowers. *T. wherryi* is a taller and better plant than *T. cordata*. Both will grow in deep shade.

1 ft.   April—June   1 ft. sq.   D.

A bio-generic cross between Heuchera and *Tiarella wherryi* has produced a plant 1—1½ ft. tall with rose-pink flowers. It is known as *Heucherella* 'Bridget Bloom'.

TOLMEIA Pick-a-back Plant; Youth on Age

T. menziesii. A shade plant, with rough Ivy-shaped leaves which from midsummer onwards produce young plants at the area where the leaf joins the leaf stalk. Flowers Heuchera-like, green and chocolate, in spikes. Often used as a house plant, but perfectly hardy in shady, well drained soil.

1½ ft.   April—May.   1 ft. sq.   Leaf C.

TRADESCANTIA Spiderwort

Adaptable plants of easy cultivation with three-petalled flowers — mostly blue — and decorative stamens. Leaves broad and Rush-like. In flower all summer. Varieties of *T. virginiana* include 'Iris Prichard', white with blue centre; 'Osprey', large white; 'Merlin', lavender-blue; 'Blue Stone', deep blue and *rubra*, purply-red. Any soil, sun or shade.

2 ft.   All summer   1½ ft. sq.   S. or D.

TRILLIUM Wake Robin; Trinity Flower

Shade plants with many parts — leaf segments, petals, sepals, etc. — in threes. Moist soil essential. Showy and well worth growing. *T. grandiflorum* is white; *T. erectum* red-purple.

1—1¼ ft.   May   1 ft. sq.   D. or S.

Delphinium 'Sutton's Mount Everest'   Sutton & Sons

Double Paeony 'Noemi Demay'   Copyright George Bunyard & Co.

Solidago 'Ballardii'

Scabiosa caucasica   Copyright R. & G. Cuthbert

*TROLLIUS Globe Flower

Moisture-loving perennials with round globe flowers of yellow or orange and Buttercup leaves. Ideal for water garden or damp border. 'Fire Globe', 'Goldquelle' and 'Sunburst', yellow are good forms.

2 ft.   May—June   1 ft. sq.   S. or D.

*VERATRUM False Hellebore

Aristocratic plants with noble foliage, leaves large and pleated, clasping the stems, flowers borne in showy panicles, white in *V. album* and green in *V. viride*. Moist soil and light shade.

3—4 ft.   July   1½ ft. sq.   D (spring) or S.

*VERBASCUM Mullein

Old-fashioned plants with large, often densely woolly leaves and strong branching spikes of flowers. Plenty of sun and good drainage. The majority are either biennials or poor perennials, so should be renewed frequently. V. 'Cotswold Queen', buff-terra-cotta. 4 ft.; 'Gainsborough', sulphur-yellow; 'Miss Willmott', white; 'Pink Domino', rosy-lilac and 'Boadicea', buff-rose are good garden forms.

4 ft.   June—July   3 ft. sq.   R.C.

V. thapsiforme, *V. phlomoides* and *V. bombyciferum* (syn. *V. broussa*) are all yellow flowered, the latter biennial, with heavily silvered plush-velvet stems and leaves. Usually these seed themselves naturally.

VERBENA

V. bonariensis is a tall plant with 3 in. heads of lavender-violet flowers on slender stems. The rootstock is very small so plants can be threaded amongst other types, such as Nepeta or dwarf Rudbeckias. Any good soil.

3—5 ft.   Summer and Autumn   1 ft. sq.   S.

VERONICA Speedwell

Mostly blue-flowered plants with neat spikes of flowers which must be massed to make a display. Good garden soil and full sunshine. Garden forms from *V. spicata* make best border plants. 'Blue Peter', deep blue; 'Barcarolle', deep rose-pink; 'Erica', orchid-purple; and 'Romily Purple', dark blue-violet.

1—2 ft.   July—Aug.   1 ft. sq.   D. in spring.

ZAUSCHNERIA Californian Fuchsia

Z. californica is a late flowering, front of the border plant with greyish leaves and tubular scarlet flowers. Only really satisfactory in very dry, sunny spots.

1—1¼ ft.   Sept.—Oct.   1 ft. sq.   S.C. or D.

47

Left: *Plan. The numbers refer to the key*

A plan for an

No. on Plan	Plant	Height in feet	Time of flowering	See Page No.
1	*Kniphofia caulescens*	5	Summer	37
2	*Delphinium* 'Pacific' strain	5½	June—July	31
3	*Rudbeckia* 'Herbstsonne'	5	July—October	44
4	*Campanula lactiflora* 'Loddon Anna'	5	May—July	29
5	*Echinops horridus*	5	July—August	32
6	*Delphinium* 'Hybrida'	5	June—July	31
7	*Aster* 'Eventide'	3½	September—October	29
8	*Althaea* (Hollyhock) red	6	July—September	27
9	*Helenium* 'Gartensonne'	4	June—September	34
10	*Aruncus sylvester*	4	June	29
11	*Salvia* x *superba*	3	July—August	44
12	*Iris sibirica* 'Emperor'	3	June	36
13	*Phlox* 'Dresden China'	2½	End July—September	42
14	*Paeony* 'Pink Delight'	2½	June	44
15	*Aconitum napellus*	3	June—July	25
16	*Phlox* 'Cecil Hanbury'	2½	End July—September	42
17	*Hemerocallis* 'Garnet Robe'	3	July—August	34

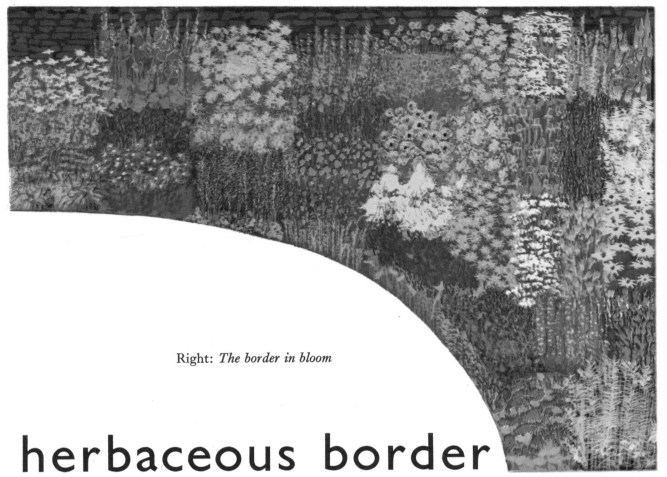

Right: *The border in bloom*

herbaceous border

No. on Plan	Plant	Height in feet	Time of flowering	See Page No.
18	*Sidalcea* 'Elsie Heugh'	2½	July—August	45
19	*Anthemis* 'Grallagh Gold'	2½	July—August	28
20	*Hemerocallis* 'Marcus'	3	July—August	35
21	*Scabiosa* 'Miss Willmott'	2½	June—September	45
22	*Erigeron* 'Merstham Glory'	2	All Summer	33
23	*Solidago* 'Leraft'	2½	August—September	45
24	*Papaver* 'Watermelon'	2½	May—June	41
25	*Heuchera* 'Rhapsody'	1½	June—September	35
26	*Aster* 'Margaret Rose'	9 in.	September—October	29
27	*Armeria* 'Bee's Ruby'	1½	Summer	29
28	*Verbascum* 'Boadicea'	3½	June—July	47
29	*Delphinium belladonna* 'Wendy'	2½	June—July	31
30	*Physostegia* 'Vivid'	2	August—September	42
31	*Erigeron* 'Darkest of All'	2	All Summer	33
32	*Catananche caerulea major*	2	June—August	30
33	*Dicentra eximia*	1	May and September	31
34	*Artemisia nutans* 'Silver Queen'	2	Late Summer	29

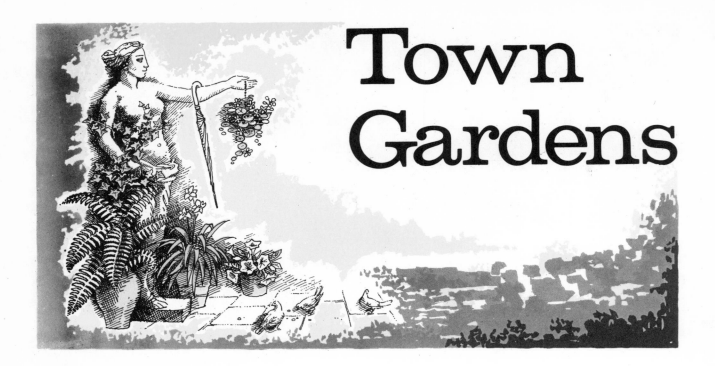

Town Gardens

Gardening in towns is often a real test of one's perseverance and ingenuity. Ideally a town garden can be a flourishing oasis in a desert of bricks and mortar. It is all a question of approaching the problem sensibly; of growing the right plants and overcoming certain difficulties peculiar to town gardening.

Broadly speaking, these are:

1. Lack of light.
2. Closed-in surrounds.
3. Air pollution.
4. Impoverished and usually acid soil.

BORROWING LIGHT

Light for plants is more than pleasant, it is absolutely essential. It provides the energy for the chlorophyll in the leaves to make sugar (the simplest plant food, manufactured from water and carbon dioxide), and without a sufficiency the plant merely 'ticks over'. It can keep its leaves going but has nothing to spare for flowers.

In the heart of an industrial area gardens are often small and restricted, or so shut in by the walls of other buildings that the general effect is rather dark and depressing. Under such conditions one must consider *house and garden together*, not separately. On a very small site the view looking in the direction of

Stone pedestal filled with Geraniums   By courtesy of Home Magazine

the house is just as important as the one looking away from it, so start planning from the far end of the plot, looking *towards the house*. This is contrary to normal procedure but absolutely essential with very small sites.

Many old houses have good lines and proportions; exploit these as far as possible and learn to mask the bad points.

Light may be 'borrowed' from a building by giving it a coat of light paint or distemper. Pastel colour washes are freely available. A pale grey, for example, looks most attractive with white paint on the doors and windows.

These washes can with advantage be extended to the surrounding walls. Besides brightening the garden they destroy the many pests which hibernate in the nooks and crevices left by bad pointing. Drainpipes in a conspicuous position should be painted to match.

An old wardrobe mirror in the garden is another ingenious way of borrowing light. Set behind a gay flower border it gives the impression of looking into another garden. Plants or shrubs can be planted near its edges to disguise it and a roofing board or shelf fixed over the top will protect the lustre.

THE SOIL

Once the house and walls have been cleaned, consideration should be given to the soil, which will probably be heavy and sour through years of neglect, and spoiled by mineral deposits of soot and other industrial waste materials.

The first essential is to test it for acidity (see p. 14). If the soil is markedly acid it is best to change it entirely in those areas where you hope to grow plants. Remove the old soil to a depth of 12 in., fork over the subsoil and introduce new loam, enriched with farmyard manure or compost. Areas for paving can be passed over, but the flower beds must have attention.

If this proves too difficult or expensive, cheaper methods of improvement must be adopted. Markedly acid soils will need heavy dressings of hydrated lime, up to $\frac{1}{2}$ lb. per sq.yd., using more for the heavier soils than the sandy types. But the ground must first be deeply dug and lightened, and its texture and food value improved. The best method is to work in plenty of really old farmyard manure or similar bulky organic material. Rotted straw, compost, spent hops, leafmould or broken down and moistened peat can be used instead, but remember that artificial fertilisers cannot solve the problem of soil improvement. They have their place later, but in these preliminary stages the texture of the soil is of prime importance.

Laying paving stones   Cement & Concrete Association

After digging and manuring, sprinkle lime on the surface and leave the ground to settle for a few weeks prior to planting.

A GREEN SURROUND

The boundaries of the garden — whether walls, fences or other buildings — should be covered with a living mantle of green. Wall shrubs and climbers take up less room than trees and do very well in towns. They also create a natural, neutral background and give an effect of depth.

Some of these plants are self-clinging like Virginia

Crazy paved path   Cement & Concrete Association

Small garden on an Edmonton estate

Concrete urns full of Geraniums

A corner of a town garden   Fisons Horticulture

A small suburban garden

Creeper and the Climbing Hydrangea, but most need ties or supports to keep them upright and tidy. These can be provided by the following methods.

1. *Make a trellis foundation*, fixing it several inches away from the wall, so that the fingers can reach the back for tying or cutting away plant material. Strips of unpainted, expanding plainwood trellis can be bought ready made, but this needs painting with Cuprinol or creosote before use to prevent rotting. If creosote is used the trellis must be left for a time to weather, as many plants cannot tolerate its fresh tarry fumes.

2. *Use horizontal straining wires.* These will be supported by galvanised wall eyes which must be screwed into the wall at intervals to take the strain and keep the wires level. Leave about 9 in. between each row. The plastic-covered types of wire are best as they do not rust. Secure plants to the wires by raffia, soft string, or the new twist types of plastic-covered wire.

3. *Plastic-covered wire trellis.* This is an admirable innovation, for ready made strips of various heights (from 3 to 6 ft.) and 6 ft. long can be bought, and either used against a fence or wall or pushed into the ground in a free standing position. Here they provide excellent support for small trained fruit trees. Advantages are that it does not rust and plant growths can be twisted in and out of the squares without need for ties. The plastic finish comes in green and white.

WALL PLANTS AND SHRUBS

The method of planting wall shrubs and climbers is described on p. 282. Remember to set plants a little away from the wall to avoid drought and to pay special attention to watering and mulching during the first season.

Quick Growing Coverage

If you want to cover the area as quickly as possible, resource should be made to climbing plants such as Nasturtiums, the golden-leaved Hop (*Humulus lupulus aureus*), the Cup and Saucer Plant (*Cobaea scandens*) or the Canary Creeper (*Tropaeolum peregrina*). Even Runner Beans can be used in an emergency and will provide a useful drape whilst more permanent plants are getting under way.

For Sunny Situations

Shrubs and climbers suitable for walls receiving a good deal of sunshine include *Cobaea scandens* and *Tropaeolum peregrina*, both annuals; Jasmines, Clematis, Ceanothus, Wistaria, Forsythia and many Roses, Brooms (*Cytisus*), Lavender, Hydrangeas and Figs will also succeed, or small trained fan or espalier

Colour in a confined space   Woodman & Son

Trellis and water in a town garden

fruit trees can be introduced. Peaches do well on a warm wall, even in a smoky atmosphere, provided the roots are kept cool and well nourished.

Shady Walls

Shrubs that prefer shade are very often evergreen. The Morello Cherry is usually a success on a shaded wall, but loses its leaves in winter. Others suitable for the town garden include Camellias, *Cotoneasters horizontalis* and *microphylla*, Ivies (Hedera), the Climbing Hydrangeas *(H. petiolaris* and *H. integerrima)*, Pyracanthas and Honeysuckles. These can all be tied to supports, except the Hydrangeas and Ivies, which are self-clinging.

OTHER PLANTS FOR TOWN GARDENS

As a general rule the plants likely to succeed best in towns are those with leathery or smooth leaves. A hairy surface attracts dust and so clogs the pores which cannot easily breathe or pass off water vapour. Plants from high altitudes are also unhappy in the smoky atmosphere of towns.

Nevertheless, many of the better known plants will thrive, including most spring bulbs and annuals, Geraniums, Petunias, Irises, Red Hot Pokers, Paeonies, Fuchsias, Tobacco Plants (Nicotiana), Buddleias, Dahlias, Anemones, Privet, Hostas, Lilacs, Weigelias and Spiraeas.

Periwinkles (Vinca), Ferns, Bluebells, Solomon's Seal (Polygonatum), Polyanthus and Japanese Anemones favour a shady border.

PLANNING

Having dealt with the soil and walls the next essential is to plan the garden features.

As with the larger garden a certain amount of open space must be left for sitting out and recreational purposes. Unfortunately, grass is a luxury in the small garden, and will not stand up to constant wear and tear. So use crazy-paving, York stones or even pebbles for the sitting out area and treat the grass as part of the flower garden. Strips of turf may be used to border the flower beds or small areas arranged each side of the central paved area, where it has a chance to flourish without being constantly trampled.

Try to place an interesting feature at the far end of the garden — perhaps a small rock garden, a summer-house, a raised flower bed or even a small tree; and consider the possibility of using different levels which somehow make a garden seem larger — a terrace or sunken garden, for example, joined by steps of stone or brick. A sundial, bird bath and attractive

Begonia semperflorens used for bedding in a town garden
Copyright R. & G. Cuthbert

way, and among ornamental plants the flowering Cherries *(Prunus erecta)*, and Robinias take up little room.

Window Boxes

Window boxes need not be restricted to window-sills for they are equally effective on the tops of porches, hooked on to sheds or supported on walls, where they may be arranged at different levels for informal effect. For details of planting and suitable choice of plants see p. 80. Herbs can also be planted in window boxes; Chives, Bay, Thyme, Sage and Marjoram do particularly well.

Tubs, Urns and Other Containers

These are useful for standing on hard-paved surfaces or concrete fringes, outside doors, on balconies, or at the top of a flight of steps. Tubs or urns planted with conifers or Rhododendrons can sometimes make a good screen in front of dustbins.

There are many types and shapes — of wood, concrete, fibreglass, earthenware, and metals, such as zinc; even old tree stumps can be hollowed out and planted. Bear in mind, however, the following points:

1. Adequate drainage is essential. Some receptacles have drainage holes, others can be drilled into the bottom of wooden tubs with a brace and bit. Make them between $\frac{1}{4}$ and $\frac{1}{2}$ in. wide. Cover the bases of *all* containers with about 2 in. of broken crocks, stones, weathered clinkers or similar drainage material. This in turn must be covered with moss or strips of turf laid grass-side downwards to prevent the finer soil

Tulips and Pansies in a town garden setting   Walter Blom & Son

garden furniture may also be included, provided they harmonise and fit in with the general scheme.

Paths can also lend colour to a garden. Patterned tiles are an integral part of Spanish and Moorish gardens and may be found suitable in some settings.

There is also no reason why trees should not be planted provided they are naturally small-growing. Apart from dwarf conifers and clipped trees like Bay and Box, most weeping trees can be kept in bounds. The exceptions are certain forms of native trees such as Beech, Ash and Willow. It *is* possible to obtain dwarf Weeping Willows — ask for *Salix caprea pendula* — but the others tend to grow very fast and very big. Always manageable, however, are weeping Cherries, weeping standard Roses and weeping Silver Birches. The last are particularly attractive with their silver trunks and soft green catkins.

Trees which grow in pyramidal fashion, after the lines of the Lombardy Poplar, are also economical on space. A cordon Apple or Pear tree develops this

A concrete fountain makes a good central feature
Cement & Concrete Association

54

Concrete containers, fountain and paving all lend variety to the garden

Cement & Concrete Association

particles (which go in next) from washing down and defeating their purpose.

2. The soil in containers needs constant renewal. If successfully planted, it will need changing fairly frequently. Some plants, however, can live for years in the same soil, enriched from time to time with a top dressing of compost or new soil mixture. You can also add plant nutrients by means of liquid feeds or powdered fertiliser. John Innes No. 1 Potting Compost (see p. 235) is suitable for most plants, but in the case of Rhododendrons, Azaleas, Camellias and similar lime-hating subjects a better formula is:

1 part fine sand
3 parts peat moss
1 part loam

To every bushel of the above add:
$1\frac{1}{2}$ oz. hoof and horn or blood meal
$\frac{3}{4}$ oz. sulphate of potash
$1\frac{1}{2}$ oz. superphosphate

3. Plants in containers require more water than those growing in the garden.

4. Because of their exposure to the elements they suffer more from excessive heat or cold. Move or protect them in extreme weather conditions.

5. Plants grown in containers suffer from the same pests and diseases as garden plants. Do not overlook them during routine pest checks.

6. Plants will not thrive if pot-bound but neither will evergreens (especially) succeed if planted in too large a container.

Trees & Shrubs

Trees and shrubs in the garden give permanence, shelter, shade, protection, privacy and colour throughout the year.

Trees are especially valuable both for their shape and beauty. Straight-trunked Lombardy Poplars are ideal for a formal setting, while for small gardens there are similar shapes in *Prunus amanogawa*, an upright growing Cherry, or the pyramidal forms of Robinia and many conifers. As canopies against the sun, there are utilitarian trees like Apple, variegated Acers, or purple Plums like *Prunus pissardi*. There are Weeping Willows for quiet water spots and Weeping Silver Birches for the lawn.

Carefully selected, shrubs can provide colour or flower all the year round. The sweet-smelling *Viburnum fragrans*, the weather-defying *Prunus subhirtella var. autumnalis* and the winter blooming *Jasminum nudiflorum* are adaptable enough for any garden. These are followed by a wealth of blossom — Daphnes, Witch-hazels, Winter Sweets, green-catkined Garrya and then Cherries, Magnolias and Rhododendrons — in all the colours of the rainbow. Lilacs, Roses and Philadelphus usher in the summer and after that come berry time, and the rich fiery and gold hues of autumn.

Nor is this all, for many shrubs and trees have beautiful bark, like the White Washed Bramble, the red and yellow-stemmed Cornus, the green and white striped Snake Barked Maple, and the satiny finish of many cherries — especially *Prunus serrula tibetica*, the chestnut patina of which gleams like mahogany in the wintery sunshine.

PLANTING

As a general rule deciduous trees and shrubs should be planted whilst in a leafless state, that is between September and March. Evergreens are usually moved about April, when new growth is starting.

Exceptions occur when the plants are put out from pots, for this does not disturb the roots, but neither deciduous or evergreens should be moved when the soil is ice-locked or covered with snow. New trees arriving in such weather should be heeled in with some dryish soil or sand in a shed until the weather breaks.

Initial preparation of the ground is more important than any after-care you can provide. Poor soil, doubled up or damaged roots and wrong siting can never be remedied later, so plant in good soil, deeply dug and manured, in a situation appropriate to the particular species.

Take out a planting hole seemingly well in excess of requirements and fork over the bottom soil. Add a little well rotted manure or compost and cover with a thin layer of soil, for manure must never touch the roots. Trim or remove any damaged roots of shrubs to be planted, and spread remainder well out in the planting hole, so that they radiate outwards and downwards from the centre; then return the soil, a little at a time. Set the tree firmly, to the level of the old planting mark, but do not be tempted to set the roots deeper under the mistaken impression that you will thus avoid staking. They will only remain in the cold subsoil longer than usual and have to make new surface feeding roots.

Planting trees is really a job for two people, one supporting the trunk whilst the other returns the soil. Tread down periodically as the work progresses and leave the soil slightly higher than the surrounding

Prunus amanogawa

Rhododendrons in a woodland setting

Cistus laurifolius

Magnolia soulangiana nigra

land. This will allow for normal subsidence so that eventually the ground will be on one level.

Evergreens are always lifted with a ball of soil surrounding the main root system. Do not break this, but if it seems dry at planting time, stand the plants in a bucket of water for an hour beforehand.

Young standard trees or top-heavy shrubs may need supports for a year or two until they become established. A stake of appropriate length, tapered to a point at one end and inserted in the ground during the planting (or very carefully afterwards) will make a suitable prop. Attach the tree to this with one of the patent ties on the market, or secure with strips of felt or flannel wrapped round the bark, and tied with soft tarred cord. The inner tube of a motor tyre cut into strips also makes good protective material for trees and prevents chafing.

After-care

Give the trees a good soaking if the ground seems dry at planting time. Use soft water for Rhododen-

drons, Kalmias and other calcifuges, otherwise tap water. Spray foliage of evergreens occasionally during the first summer.

Keep the soil clear of pernicious weeds and mulch round with moist peat, chopped bracken, leaves or spent hops to retain moisture and provide humus.

Avoid deep digging close to shrubs as this destroys the feeding roots which are usually near the surface; the hoe is the best tool for general work. Trees planted in grass should have rings of soil left round the trunk. Plant these with Narcissi and Crocus for spring and *Cyclamen neapolitanum* for autumn interest.

Newly planted shrubs often lift from the ground in a thaw, exposing the roots to the next frost. Tread these back firmly after each cold spell.

PRUNING

Pruning includes not only the cutting back or removal of sound branches but also the taking out of dead and diseased wood. The purpose in pruning flowering shrubs is to secure the maximum amount of good quality blooms, berrying shrubs to obtain well coloured fruits and ornamental trees to achieve balance, safety and shapeliness.

The Tools

Pruning unavoidably wounds the tissue and provides a possible source of disease infection. All cuts must therefore heal as rapidly as possible, so always use a sharp knife or secateurs and paint over any wounds exceeding $\frac{1}{2}$ in. diameter with white lead paint or one of the proprietary materials such as Medo (Murphy). You will need some or all of the following:
A Sharp Knife for small shoots and trimming rough cuts left by the saw. Prices vary according to weight and quality of steel. Get the best you can afford.
A Pruning Saw for getting between branches. Some have saws each side (of different cuts), others fold into a handle.
Secateurs. Buy a good easily-handled pair. The Rolcut has easily replaceable parts and good balance, whilst the Wilkinson Knife Cut Pruner effectively cuts shoots and branches up to $\frac{1}{2}$ in. diameter. The blades are rust-proof. For out-of-the-way branches use long arm loppers or for very thick branches the heavy weight Toggle Lopper.

General Pruning

Remove dead or diseased branches right back beyond the source of infection. Do it at any time of the year, and at the first sign of trouble.

Most trees should have an open centre, so that light can reach all the branches. Cut away any rubbing, crossing or badly placed branches, if possible during the winter months. Watch out for the dreaded Silver Leaf disease in ornamental Plums, Cherries, Almonds, Portuguese Laurel, Poplars and even Rhododendrons. Since this disease is active in winter, major operations in an affected district may have to be carried out during the summer (before mid-July).

Many shrubs benefit from being cut back occasionally. Take off the top to a shoot lower down on the branch. You may lose a season's flowering, but the result will be a better and more shapely shrub. Philadelphus, Lilac and Climbing Roses particularly benefit from this attention.

Pruning Deciduous Shrubs

After taking routine measures, pruning of deciduous shrubs and climbers will mainly be related to the season of flowering.
1. *Those which flower and fruit on the new wood.*

These bloom on wood made in the same calendar year and flower comparatively late in the season.

Examples: *Ceanothus*, 'Gloire de Versailles', *Tamarix pentandra*, *Clematis jackmannii*, *Hydrangea paniculata grandiflora*, *Buddleia variabilis* and its varieties, Leycesteria and many Spiraeas, especially the variety 'Anthony Waterer'.

Prune early in the year (February or March). Old shrubs which have grown large enough should be cut back really hard, to within an inch or so of the old wood; Buddleia and Clematis particularly benefit from this treatment. For smaller specimens remove the ends of the shoots.
2. *Those which flower early in the season on the wood they made the year before.*

Acacia dealbata   By courtesy of Home Magazine

Examples: *Jasminum nudiflorum*, *Prunus triloba*, Forsythia, *Clematis montana*, Weigelias and *Spiraea arguta*.

Prune these as soon as the blossoms have faded. The old flowering wood is either tipped (with small specimens) or taken back almost to the previous year's growth.
3. *Those flowering on old wood.*

Many of these require little or no pruning, for they flower on the same old timber year after year.

Examples: Azaleas, Cistus, Cotoneasters, Daphnes, Witch-hazels, Magnolias, *Cercis siliquastrum*, the Judas Tree, Hibiscus and Paeony.

Shorten these back, however, preferably in early spring, if they become too large or are damaged by frost. Always cut *just above* a shoot growing lower down on the branch, or take the branch right out at ground level or where it joins the trunk in the case of a tree.

Philadelphus 'Voie Lactée'

Syringa 'Marie Legrave'

4. *Those flowering in summer on wood of the previous year.*

These need little pruning beyond an occasional thinning of the branches, the removal of weak twigs and an occasional shortening back of leggy shoots.

Examples: Lilacs, Ribes, Philadelphus and some Spiraeas.

5. *Plants with Coloured Bark.*

Examples: Cornus (Dogwoods) with gold, red or violet stems, *Rubus flagelliflorus* and *R. biflorus*. Cut back almost to ground level in Feb.

6. *Evergreens.*

Evergreens hold their leaves all winter but refrain from making new shoots at that time. Pruning should

59

therefore coincide with the production of new growth, in most cases about April.

7. *Pruning Hedges*.

These should be pruned hard in early years to encourage thick growth at the bottom of the hedge. Once the stems run high and straggling they never thicken properly lower down.

Fully grown hedges are usually clipped in July or Aug. although they may be tackled earlier. Beech and Hornbeam should be pruned about the end of July or August.

Flowering hedges should be dealt with after blooms are finished. Privet growth can be retarded for several months by spraying after cutting with Hedgeset, a proprietary product (Fisons) which saves much time in the busy season.

Climbing plants on walls, like Ivy, should be clipped with the shears in April and long, loose shoots removed with the secateurs in August. Secateurs, not shears, should also be used on hedges made up from large-leaved plants like Laurels.

PROPAGATION

Trees and shrubs are increased by:
1. Seed; 2. Division, layers or cuttings; 3. Budding and grafting.

Seed

This method is slow and in some cases impossible for trees because many foreign species fail to produce seed until they are quite old. A number will not fruit at all in this country.

Shrubs are often more rapid and the method is extensively used for species of Cotoneasters, Roses, Berberis and other berried plants. Many trees and shrubs, however, have certain characteristics which are different from the type, such as doubling in the flowers, colour changes or foliage variegations. These cannot be reproduced from seed.

Tree and shrub seed varies considerably, some being very small, others large and tough coated. They may take years to germinate or come up almost immediately.

For details of sowing see p. 234.

Vegetative Reproduction

Practically the whole gamut of plant propagation is practised in one form or another on trees and shrubs. Cuttings, layers, grafting, budding, division, root-cuttings, air layering and tip layering are all used.

Details of the techniques in these different forms of propagation are described on p. 236.

Cercis siliquastrum

Catalpa bignonioides

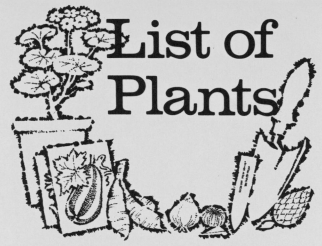

List of Plants

E. denotes Evergreen; D.Deciduous; R.C. Root cuttings; H.R.C. Half-ripe Cuttings; L. Layers; S. Seed; S.C. Soft Cuttings; Div. Division; Hard C. Hard Wood Cuttings.

ABELIA

Dainty shrubs, best against a sunny wall, with well drained soil. Flowers tubular, leaves deciduous or evergreen, small. The best are *A. chinensis*, D. pink and white, fragrant. July—Sept., 3—4 ft.; *A. floribunda*, E. rosy red, June—July, 3—5 ft.; *A. graebneriana*, D. pink and yellow, June—July, 8—10 ft.; and *A. triflora*, D. the hardiest, rosy-white, fragrant, June, 8—15 ft. Thin crowded shoots after flowering. H.R.C. July.

ABELIOPHYLLUM

A. distichum D. Slow-growing, winter flowering shrub, best in sheltered position. Erect shoots with 4-petalled, fragrant, white and orange flowers. Leaves like Forsythia. Jan.—April. 2—3 ft. No regular pruning. H.R.C. July.

ABUTILON See p. 282.

ACACIA Mimosa; Wattle

A large family of evergreen trees, mostly tender in Britain. *A. dealbata* is the hardiest and will live outside in sheltered districts. Ideal winter flowering plant for the cold greenhouse. Grey-green foliage and typical Mimosa flowers. Jan.—April. Makes a small tree 15—20 ft. No pruning. S. or H.R.C. July.

ACANTHOPANAX

Small deciduous trees with very prickly stems, leaves like Fatsia and clusters of purplish berries. No particular soil requirements or pruning. *A. pentaphyllus* and *A. ricinifolius*, the latter more showy, with white plumes of flower. 15—20 ft. S. or R.C.

ACER Maple

Mostly deciduous trees or shrubs, often with finely coloured foliage or bark, some assuming handsome autumnal tints. The majority like moist soil, a few even suited by swamp conditions.

Ornamental trees include *A. ginnala*, with vivid autumn colour, 15 ft.; *A. griseum*, the Paper-bark Maple, whose bark peels in long flakes to reveal the bright orange, newer bark within, 25 ft.; *A. grosseri*, with green and white striped bark, 20 ft.; *A. negundo variegatum*, with fine variegated foliage, 20 ft.; and *A. saccharinum pendulum*, weeping, 12—18 ft.

The Japanese varieties are mostly forms of *A. palmatum* and *A. japonicum* and include *palmatum atropurpureum*, crimson leaves; *dissectum palmatifidium*, finely dissected and a variegated form of the latter with green, cream and pink leaves. 3—10 ft. These are attractive in the rock garden. Open out centres of these trees occasionally and balance the branches by shortening. L. H.R.C. or S.

ACTINIDIA See p. 282.

AKEBIA See p. 283.

AMELANCHIER Juneberry, Snowy Mespilus

A. canadensis D. makes a small tree with green leaves and white Apple-blossom-like spring flowers, later followed by small red berries. Foliage red in autumn. Any soil, sun. April. 15—25 ft. Prune very little. L. or S. sown when fresh.

ANDROMEDA Bog Rosemary

A polifolia E. Good shade plant with Rosemary-like leaves and clusters of pinkish-white, Lily-of-the-Valley flowers. Hates lime. May—July. 1½ ft. No pruning. S. Runners or Div.

ARAUCARIA ARAUCANA E. Monkey Puzzle Tree

Well known conifer, with green stems and leaves like a prehistoric plant, imposing even in a small garden. Quite hardy, any moist, freely drained soil. Male and female cones borne on separate trees. 50 ft. in time but very slow growing. No pruning. S.

Aucuba japonica

Liquidamber styraciflua

ARBUTUS Strawberry Tree

A. unedo E. Attractive tree with neat, dark green leaves, white Lily-of-the-Valley flowers and bright red, round, Strawberry fruits. Winter blooming, often carrying flowers and berries at the same time. Any soil. *A. menziesii* has an attractive bark. 20 ft. No special pruning. L. (takes 2 years to root) S. or varieties budded or grafted on *A. unedo*.

ARTEMISIA

Small, mostly aromatic and often silver-leaved shrubs, suitable for shrubbery or herbaceous border. Flowers inconspicuous. Well drained soil; sun. *A. abrotanum*, E. Southernwood and *A. arborescens*, E. both have silver, feathery foliage. 3 ft. Cut back nearly to old wood in Feb. H.R.C.

Camellia williamsii hybrid   Copyright Samuel Dobie & Son

Arbutus unedo   Copyright R. & G. Cuthbert

Corylus avellana contorta   R. A. Malby

ATRIPLEX

A. halimus Tree Purslane. Low growing (3—5 ft.) semi-evergreen, with smooth, silvery leaves. Often used for seaside planting and not always hardy in bad winters inland. Rarely flowers. No special pruning. H.R.C.

AUCUBA

Often, although mistakenly, called Laurel; the true Laurel is *Laurus nobile*. Large, glossy leaves and scarlet berries. Male and female flowers on separate plants, so have one or two of the former amongst a batch of female if fruit is required. Will grow in dense shade and any soil; all are evergreen. Often used for hedging. Cultivated forms are derived from *A. japonica* which is plain green. *Var. crotonoides*, leaves mottled with gold; *maculata*, white variegated; *sulphurea*, leaves margined with yellow and *fructo-luteo*, yellow berries. 6—10 ft. April. No regular pruning except for hedging, when cut in April. H.R.C.

BAMBOOS

Hardy grasses, mostly evergreen, growing in any rich, loamy soil which does not dry out. Suitable for shade and also make good screen and enclosure plants. Hardy forms come in several families — Arundinaria, Phyllostachys, Pseudosasa and Sinarundinaria. No pruning. Propagate by division at end of April or May. Often sulk for a year but once established grow well. 2—18 ft., according to variety.

BERBERIS Barberry

Deciduous and evergreen shrubs with small leaves, prickly stems, usually golden flowers, red or black berries. Sun or shade, any except waterlogged soil. No regular pruning beyond occasional taking back to ground level of old stems, or reducing to strong shoot lower on branch. Prune evergreen forms in April; deciduous in Jan.

Good deciduous kinds are *B. aggregata*; *chitrea*; *x rubrostilla*; *thunbergii* and its coloured leaved form *var. atropurpurea*, and *wilsonae*. Heights 3—8 ft., all red fruited.

Chaeonomeles speciosa   Copyright R. & G. Cuthbert

Evergreens include *B. x stenophylla*, often used for hedging, free with yellow flowers in April, blue-black berries in autumn; *B. verraculosa, pruinosa, hookeri, candidula* and *gagnepainii*, all with blue-black berries, also *darwinii*, orange flowers and blue berries. Majority 8—10 ft. S. L.

BETULA Birch

Beautiful trees with delicate branches, small leaves, green catkins in spring and fine bark. Sun or shade, moist soils. *B. papyrifera* D. Paper or Canoe Birch has very white bark, which in *var. kenaica* is tinged with orange and brown. 30 ft. *B. pendula* is native Silver Birch which grows 20—40 ft.; its weeping form *youngii* ultimately makes a mushroom-headed tree — ideal as a lawn specimen. S. or grafts on *B. pendula*. No special pruning.

BUDDLEIA Butterfly Bush

Quick growing, free flowering shrubs in character in late summer. Any soil, preferably well drained and sun. Good seaside and town plant. *B. davidii* D. and its forms have fragrant, terminal spikes of mauve flowers. 'White Cloud' is white; 'Peace', white with orange centre; 'Royal Red', deep reddish-purple and 'Black Knight', deep navy. Prune hard back in Feb. 6—8 ft. in a season. June—Sept. Hard C.

B. alternifolia D. flowers on old wood so needs little pruning. Arching sprays covered with clusters of violet-purple flowers and small leaves. 6—12 ft. June. S.C.

B. globosa E. Orange Ball Tree. Holds its leaves in a mild winter. Flowers golden, in round balls. No regular pruning. June. 10—15 ft. Ripe cuttings in autumn.

BUXUS Box

Small-leaved evergreens which can be clipped to various shapes (topiary), made into a low hedge or allowed to grow into a tree. *B. sempervirens* the Common Box has various forms with variegated, broad and rounded leaves. From a bush to 20 ft. D.

CALLUNA

One of several genera of hardy heathers. E. See also Erica. Good ground cover plant and invaluable for winter flowers. Requires acid, rather moist, poor soil. If too rich plants become leggy, but clipping over in April keeps them low growing and compact. Propagate by Div. L. or H.R.C. For varieties see p. 66.

CALYCANTHUS Allspice

C. floridus D. Shrub or small tree with aromatic wood (especially when dried), reddish purple, spicy scented flowers and opposite, entire, dark green leaves. Any open soil, sun or partial shade. 6—10 ft. June—July. L.

CAMELLIA

Useful evergreens for lime-free soil with fine, showy flowers. Single, semi-double and double forms, C. *x williamsii* varieties particularly fine, especially 'Donation', semi-double, rose-pink; 'Cornish Snow', white single and 'Mary Christian', single pink. March—April. 4—10 ft.

C. japonica varieties include 'White Swan', white, single; *donckelarii*, red mottled white, semi-double; *nobilissima*, double white and 'Frau Minna Seidel', double pink. April—May. 4—20 ft. See also p. 286. Air layering, S.C. or grafts on *C. japonica*. No regular pruning.

CAMPSIS See p. 283. Propagated by R.C. and L.

CARPENTARIA

C. californica. Beautiful evergreen with clusters of fragrant, white flowers. Leaves tapering, felted beneath. Not over-hardy so must have a sheltered place. Rich, moist but well drained soil, light shade or sun. No regular pruning. June—July. 6—8 ft. S. or L.

CARYOPTERIS Blue Spiraea D.

Low-growing shrubs often used in herbaceous border. Autumn flowering, with clusters of deep lavender-blue or violet flowers on 2—4 ft. stems. Leaves grey-green, toothed and small. *C. x clandonensis* and *C. mastacanthus* are similar. Aug.—Oct. Cut back in Feb. leaving strong growths about 1 ft. high. S. or H.R.C.

CATALPA Indian Bean D.

C. bignonoides with green leaves and *var. aurea* with golden, are fine summer-flowering trees with Horse-chestnut-like flowers in bold spikes, fragrant, and large, Lime-shaped leaves. July. 20 ft. No pruning. S. or Ripe C.

CEANOTHUS See p. 283. Propagate from H.R.C. in pure sand in Aug. or Sept.; potted on as soon as possible.

CERATOSTIGMA C.

C. plumbaginoides 1 ft. and *C. willmottianum* 2—4 ft., are late flowering shrubs (Sept.—Nov.) with intensely blue flowers. Leaves small, turning red in autumn. Well drained, warm position. Often cut to ground in winter, otherwise prune back in spring to sound strong wood. Div. and S.C.

CERCIS D.

C. siliquastrum is the Judas Tree, with bunches of small, rosy, Pea-shaped flowers on the naked branches and sometimes even protruding from the black trunk. Leaves which follow are neat, smooth and rounded. Resents transplanting so plant out young. Any good soil with sunshine. Prune to shape. May. 10—15 ft. S.L. or S.C. from forced plants.

CHAENOMELES Japanese Quince D.

Well known shrubs, often called 'japonica', with spiny branches, small leaves, bright — usually red — flowers and yellowish

Cornus nuttalli

green, aromatic fruits, which can be used for jelly. Any soil, full sun or light shade; can be trained as a wall plant, of for hedging. Prune latter when blooms fade; established bushes just thin crowded stems; wall specimens shorten spurs back end of April.

C. speciosa is best known form with bright orange-scarlet flowers. Varieties have white, double rose, crimson and apple blossom-pink flowers. Var. 'Moerloesii' is pink and white. March—May. 6—10 ft. S. or L.

CHIMONANTHUS Winter Sweet D.

C. praecox (fragrans). One of the sweetest smelling plants, a single cut spray scenting a room. Blooms early (Feb.), unremarkable, yellowish-green and chocolate, bellshaped, studding the naked stems. Makes a small neat shrub with oval leaves. Best grown against a wall in sunny position and well drained soil. Spur back flowering shoots to within ½ in. of old wood, after flowering. 6—10 ft. L. in spring.

CHIONANTHUS Fringe Tree D.

C. retusa and *C. virginica* have sprays of 4-petalled, white, feathery, fragrant flowers, later followed by dark blue fruits. Make attractive small trees. Moist loam, sun. Little pruning. L. or S.; bought plants often budded or grafted on Ash seedlings.

CHOISYA E.

C. ternata Mexican Orange Flower. Useful shrub which will thrive in deepest shade, but flowers in sunny situation for months. Leaves 3-parted like Clover, shiny; flowers white, 5-petalled and fragrant. Well drained soil. No regular pruning. April onwards. 4—8 ft. S.C.

CISTUS Rock Rose E.

Small shrubs with aromatic foliage and showy, single Rose-like flowers. Very well drained soil and sunshine. Suitable for rock garden. No regular pruning. Need renewing fairly often from S. or H.R.C.

Species and varieties include *C. x cyprius*, large white flowers (3 in.) crimson blotch on each petal. Makes good hedge. June—July. 4—6 ft.; *C. ladaniferus*, gummy leaves and large, crimped white flowers with chocolate basal spots. May—June. 5 ft.; *C. laurifolius*, hardiest species, white with yellowish base, dark green, leathery leaves. 7 ft. May—June; *C. x purpureus*, reddish-purple. 4 ft. June—July; and C. x 'Silver Pink', a beautiful variety with clear pink flowers. June—July. 2½ ft.

CLEMATIS See also p. 283.

Propagate by S.L. H.R.C. July.

CLERODENDRON D.

All mentioned have fragrant flowers, but evil smelling leaves (when crushed). Protect from east winds and frosts. No regular pruning, well drained soil; sun or light shade. *C. bungei*, red flowers, large, heart-shaped leaves. Aug.—Sept. 3—5 ft.; *C. fargesii*, white with light blue berries in pink cups. Leaves purplish when young. July—Sept. 10 ft.; *C. trichotomum*, white with bright blue berries in red calyces. 10 ft. July—Sept. S., S.C., R.C.

COLUTEA Bladder Senna D.

Easily grown shrubs for sunshine and well drained soil. Small, yellow Pea-shaped flowers in bunches followed by bladder-like seed pods, which pop when pressed; leaves pinnate. Keep bushes free of weak shoots, cut back in Feb. almost to old wood. They flower on the young shoots. *C. arborescens* and its varieties most commonly grown. June—Oct. 12 ft. S. or H.R.C.

CORNUS Cornel; Dogwood D.

Small trees or shrubs with brightly coloured bark, handsome flowers and autumnal foliage tints. Moist soil in sun or shade. Unless required for bark (see p. 59) no regular pruning.

The most ornamental are *C. alba sibirica variegata*, with red stems and leaves margined in white, and *var. spaethii*, one of the best golden-variegated shrubs. Flowers white. June. 6—8 ft.

Of tree-like proportions are *C. florida*, with flowers (2 in. across) made up of small florets surrounded by 4 large bracts and its *var. rubra*, pink bracts. May. 10—20 ft.; *C. kousa*, large white flowers and fine autumn tints. May. 12—20 ft.; and *C. nuttallii*, cream bracts suffused pink. May. 20 ft. or more. *C. mas* is the Cornelian Cherry, with very early, yellow flowers. Feb. 6—10 ft. Ripe cuttings, L. S.

Deutzia · Copyright R. & G. Cuthbert

Cistus x purpureus

Good Shrubs: C. *bullata* D. 10—12 ft.; C. *salicifolia*, very narrow leaves 8—12 ft. semi-evergreen; C. *acuminata* D. 10—20 ft., all with red fruit.
Hedging Types: C. *simonsii* D.

CRATAEGUS Hawthorn D.

Small deciduous trees or hedging shrubs (known as Quick) with 5-petalled, Rose-like flowers, red haw fruits, small Oak-shaped leaves. Sun, any soil. Little pruning except for hedging kinds. See p. 247. C. *oxycantha* 'Paul's Scarlet' is double crimson; *plena*, double white; *rosea plena*, double pink. Also varieties with single flowers and one with variegated leaves. Ornamental kinds grafted on common Hawthorn.

CYTISUS Broom D.

Quick growing shrubs with green stems and small Pea-shaped

CORYLOPSIS Winter Hazel D.

C. *spicata* and C. *pauciflora* have fragrant, yellowish flowers with creamy bracts on naked wood. Leaves Hazel-like. Any moist soil, tolerant of shade. Thin crowded bushes. L (spring) or H.R.C. Mar. 4—6 ft. Div. or grafted on c. *avellana*.

CORYLUS Hazel D.

C. *avellana contorta*, a form of the common Hazel, with strangely contorted twigs and branches, and twisted stems. Attractive in spring when full of catkins. Feb.—Mar. 6—15 ft. C. *maxima atropurpurea* has large purplish-red leaves, effective in mixed shrubbery. Can be kept low by cutting, or runs up to 15 ft.

COTONEASTER D. and E.

Large family of shrubs or small trees, with neat foliage and frequently brilliant berries. Almost any soil or situation except waterlogged ground; sun or light shade. Best planted out when quite small. Some good hedging plants, others useful in mixed shrubbery or as lawn specimens. Clustered flowers are white, May and June; berries mostly scarlet but sometimes black or yellow. Little or no pruning except with hedging forms. See also p. 286. S. sown as soon as ripe or stratified, L. H.R.C. Bought plants also grafted on Hawthorn and other trees.
Tree Forms: C. *frigida* E; C. *lactea* E. 15 ft., both with red berries.

blossoms. Do best in poor, well drained soil and sunshine. Dislike root disturbance so must be planted out from pots when small. Avoid straggly appearance by pruning after flowering. Cut back stems almost into old wood. S. or H.R.C. Aug. C. *albus* is the Spanish White Broom; C. x *dallimorei*, pink and crimson; C. x *kewensis*, a drooping kind ideal for edge of rock garden, creamy-white, 6—12 in. C. *scoparius*, the Yellow Scotch Broom, has many varieties with differently coloured self and bicolour flowers. Mostly 6—12 ft., flowering May—June.

DAPHNE

Small, early flowering, usually fragrant shrubs. Moist but well drained soil, majority appreciating a little lime. Sun or partial shade; but keep roots moist in hot weather. No pruning. S. L. S. C. (some).
D. *mezereum* D. is best known and flowers on naked wood in Feb. Pale to deep pink, but also white varieties. Bright red berries. Full sun. Sometimes dies unaccountably when fully grown. 2—5 ft. D. *odora* E. Extremely fragrant, small leaves and bunches of pinkish flowers. Sheltered position and sun. Feb.—April. 3 ft. L. or H.R.C. D. *cneorum*, the Garland Flower, has pale pink or rosy flowers in terminal clusters, often hiding evergreen foliage. Spreading habit. 1 ft. May—June. C. *blagayana* is similar with creamy flowers. Partial shade. 1 ft. Mar.—April. Both useful for rock garden.

ELAEAGNUS Oleaster

Small group of shrubs with glistening foliage, often gold or silver. Flowers fragrant but rather small and insignificant. Poor soil usually brings out colour best. Sun. Prune to shape.

E. pungens aureo-variegata, and *E. aurea* both show gold variegations. *E. argentea*, D. is called the Silver Berry, leaves (on both sides) and berries being silvery. 6—8 ft. Propagation S. and Hard C.

Diervilla 'Van Houttei'   J. E. Downward

Erica 'Springwood White'   J. E. Downward

DESFONTAINEA E.

D. spinosa. Beautiful plant with small, Holly-like leaves and hanging, tubular, scarlet and yellow flowers (approx. 1½ in.). Moist but well drained soil, light shade. Only suitable for warmer districts. July—Oct. 6—10 ft. S.

DEUTZIA D.

Small shrubs with thin stems covered in early summer with bunches of small pink or white flowers. Partial shade, moist soil. When blooms fade thin out old or crowded shoots. Shortening back removes potential flowers. S.C. Hard and C. S. or Div.

D. gracilis. Slender white-flowered species which forces well in pots. There are pink and rose varieties. May—June. 3 ft. *D. x rosea* and *rosea carminea* are fine flowered forms 3 ft. with 'Pride of Rochester', good double white, 6—10 ft.

DIERVILLA Japanese Honeysuckle D.

Useful, low growing shrubs for a shady situation, also known as Weigelias. Do best in moist soil. Flowers tubular somewhat pendent, along the stems. Remove old branches or shoots occasionally. Ripe cuttings in autumn. Garden hybrids include 'Abel Carriere', soft rose; 'Bristol Ruby' and 'Newport Red', both ruby red; 'Mont Blanc', white; 'Conquête', pink, and 'Eva Rathke', deep crimson. *D. florida var. variegata* has bright golden leaf variegations and rose flowers. 3—5 ft. There is also a silver variegated variety.

EMBOTHRIUM Chilean Fire Bush

E. coccineum. Beautiful evergreen tree for favoured situations with dark green, glossy, oval-oblong leaves and brilliant scarlet flowers, which are narrowly tubular but bunched together, making a striking display. Dislikes lime, but does well in any good open soil. May—June. 20 ft. No pruning. Suckers or H.R.C. under glass.

ENKIANTHUS D.

E. campanulatus. Needs same conditions as Rhododendrons including lime-free soil. Flowers urn-shaped, greenish-yellow, veined with crimson, bunched on arching stems. Leaves smooth and glossy, soft green but brilliant red and orange in autumn. Prune to shape. May. 4—8 ft. L. S. or H.R.C.

ERICA E.

Plants similar in habit and uses to Calluna (see p. 63). A few will not tolerate lime, ideally suited by light sandy soil; sun. Tall, spring-flowering kinds require no pruning, beyond shortening back straggling shoots after flowering. Dwarf late summer and autumn kinds can be lightly clipped with shears in Feb. S. L. or S.C.

E. arborea, white, and *E. australis*, pink, are the Tree Heaths, with upright habit and masses of flowers. April—May. 5—10 ft. *E. carnea* has given rise to good garden kinds as 'King George V', pink, 'Springwood White' and 'Springwood Pink'. 9—12 in.

E. mediterranea superba makes a fine bush, 3—4 ft. with pink flowers Mar.—June. Also useful for hedging.

ESCALLONIA E.

Summer flowering plants for coastal or mild districts with small leaves and 5-petalled flowers. Recommended varieties for hedging are 'Apple Blossom', soft pink, 'C.F. Ball', rosy crimson, x *ingrami*, white. June—July.
Suitable for wall shrubs: 'Donard Star', rose-pink; 'Donard Brilliance', crimson; 'Pride of Donard', light red. 5—8 ft.; also *E. macrantha*, bright red, June—Sept. 6—10 ft.

EUCRYPHIA E.

E. glutinose has large, showy, white flowers with prominent gold stamens, something like Hypericum. Leaves Rose-like. Must be sheltered as leaves 'burn' in cold winds. Very free flowering. Acid soils most suitable, dislike lime. Mulch every year with moist peat for cool root run. No regular pruning; 8—20 ft. x *nymansay* is an improved form and will tolerate some lime. Aug. 10—20 ft. L. or H.R.C. in sandy peat in July.

EUONYMUS Spindle

Shrubs or small trees chiefly grown for bright fruits and autumn colouring. Some evergreen with shining, often markedly variegated foliage. Any good soil, including lime, preferably shaded from midday sun. No particular pruning, except when used for hedging. Flowers insignificant. *E. europaeus* D. has fine pink fruits with orange seeds; 'Brilliant' is an improved form, 5—7 ft.; *E. alatus* D. red seeds and corky wings on the bark. Both species show fine autumn tints. S. or H.R.C. or L.

E. japonicus E. makes a good close hedge. Foliage varieties include gold and silver variegated forms. 10 ft. *E. radicans* is a ground-hugging evergreen with many foliage forms including 'Silver Queen' and 'Silver Gem'. Under 1 ft. Evergreens S. H.R.C. or Hard C.

FATSIA E.

F. japonica. Often (but wrongly) called the Castor Oil Plant. Large, glossy, finger-cut leaves and clusters of creamy Ivy-like flowers followed by black berries. Semi-shade, moist soil. No pruning. Oct.—Nov. 7—10 ft. H.R.C. in bottom heat.

FORSYTHIA D.

Easily grown shrubs valued for early flowers, bell-shaped, 4-petalled and golden. Smooth oblong leaves follow blooms. H.R.C.

F. viridissima, greenish-yellow, 5—8 ft. and *F.* x *intermedia*, a hybrid from which good garden forms like 'Lynwood Gold', *spectablis* and *primulina* are obtained. 7—8 ft. Needs no pruning. *F. suspensa fortunei* is of drooping habit and needs pruning to check arching branches from rooting. Cut back to within one or two buds of old wood after flowering. 8—10 ft. Flowers appear Feb.—April.

FUCHSIA See p. 255 and p. 286.

GARRYA See p. 284.

GAULTHERIA

Evergreen shrubs for shaded, lime-free soils. Flowers white in long sprays like Lily-of-the-Valley. No regular pruning. H.R.C. in a cold frame. L. or S. *G. procumbens* has red berries. 6 in.; *G. forrestii*, porcelain-blue, 1—4 ft.; *G. cuneata*, white berries, 1 ft. All flower May—June.

GENISTA D.

Later flowering Brooms than Cytisus, with fragrant, golden flowers. Sunshine and light soil. Do not cut back into old wood. S. and H.R.C.

G. aethnensis, the Mount Etna Broom, makes a small tree up to 8 ft. July—Aug. Heavy branches often need support. *G. cine-*

Euonymus grandiflorus salicifolius
J. E. Downward

rea, June—July. 8 ft. *G. tinctoria flore pleno*, double, Pea-shaped flowers. Ground cover plant. June—July. 1 ft.

GINKO Maidenhair Tree D.

G. biloba. An interesting and curious tree, very slow growing with upright habit and light green leaves, yellow in autumn, shaped like leaflets of Maidenhair Fern. Any good soil, sun. Male and female flowers inconspicuous and on separate trees. Seeds edible. No pruning. S. 20—30 ft. eventually.

HALESIA Snowdrop Tree D.

H. carolina. Naked branches draped in spring with white, Snowdrop-like flowers. Leaves smooth, oval and toothed. Sun

Forsythia spectabile

Hydrangeas

or light shade, deep, well drained but moist soil. Makes a small tree. 20—25 ft. May—June. S. or L.

HAMAMELIS Witch Hazel D.

Fine winter-flowering shrubs or small trees, the naked wood covered with fragrant, narrow-petalled flowers resembling paper tassels. Leaves small, entire, oval. Moist soil, sun or light shade. S. L. or varieties sometimes grafted on *H. virginiana*. Only prune to preserve shape after flowering. *H. mollis*, Cowslip-scented, bright yellow flowers. Dec.—Feb. 10 ft.; *H. japonica*, pale yellow, 10 ft. Also some good garden forms such as *pallidiflora*, very large, soft yellow; 'Jelina', reddish; 'Hiltingbury', reddish-gold and *arborea*, golden yellow. Dec.—March.

HELIANTHEMUM Sun Rose See p. 176.

HIBISCUS Tree Hollyhock D.

H. syriacus. Good summer flowering shrub, with white, red, blue or bicolour Hollyhock-like flowers on 6—8 ft. bushes. Full sun or very light shade and well drained soil. 'Coeleste', deep blue, single; *coeruleus plenus*, double blue; 'Duc de Brabant', double red; 'Lady Stanley', double blush with maroon centre; 'William Smith', white single; 'Mauve Queen', single mauve and *rubus*, single red, are representative varieties. Aug.—Sept.H.R.C. L. or grafts on *H. syriacus*.

HIPPOPHAE Sea Buckthorn

H. rhamnoides. Tree or small shrub, with silver shoots and leaves, inconspicuous flowers and clusters of bright orange berries. Does particularly well near sea. Sunshine. No regular pruning. S. or L. June—July. 10—30 ft.

Paeony lutea Sheriff's var.

HOLODISCUS Rock Spiraea D.

H. discolor. Graceful late summer shrub with striking plumes of feathery white flowers and Spiraea-like leaves. Moist soil, sun or light shade. Prune to shape. H.R.C. July. 4—8 ft.

HYDRANGEA See p. 287 for climbing sorts.

Well known, dependable shrubs, remaining in flower for months. Moist soil and plenty of sun is essential for florist's types of *H. macrophylla.* These are often known as *hortensis* and include forms with white, pink, red, mauve and blue flowers. Many blue naturally but others may be helped by dressing the soil with one of the proprietary colourants or aluminium sulphate (4 oz. to 1 lb. according to size of the bush). All do better in sheltered place with some sort of background. Aug.—Nov. 2—5 ft. Remove old flower heads and worn out stems in late summer. H.R.C. Aug. in warmth or L. *H. paniculata* has large green leaves and dome-shaped heads of white flowers which gradually change to pink. In *var. grandiflora* these are sometimes 18 in. long and 12 in. across. July—Aug. 6—8 ft. Remove weak shoots in Feb. and shorten others by half. H.R.C.

HYPERICUM Rose of Sharon; St John's Wort

Evergreen shrubs for moist soil and shade. Trim over in Feb. Div. or H.R.C. struck in gentle heat Aug. Golden flowers and neat, glossy leaves. *H. calycinum* has large golden flowers like pincushions, 3 in. across. Good plant for north border, completely weed-proof. June—Sept. 1 ft. Taller Kinds: *H. hookerianum* 2 in. golden flowers. 3 ft. Aug.—Oct.; *leschenaultii* (syn. Rowallane Hybrid) large, saucer-shaped 2½ in. blooms July—Sept.; x *moserianum*, good ground cover plant, 1½—3 ft., also *patulum* var. 'Gold Cup', 3—4 ft., fine open flowers.

JASMINUM See p. 284.

KALMIA Calico Bush

K. latifolia. E. Rhododendron-like shrub with oval, glossy leaves and bunches of bright pink flowers like inverted umbrellas. Cultivate as for Rhododendron. May—June. 3—5 ft. No special pruning. S. or H.R.C.

KERRIA D.

K. japonica flore pleno. Shrub with small, Nettle-shaped leaves and round, golden, double flowers. Any soil but best against a wall or fence in full sunshine. Cut out old wood occasionally to encourage new shoots. S.C. or offshoots. April. 4—8 ft.

KOLWITZIA D.

K. amabilis. Small shrub with tubular flowers, pink and yellow, something like Diervilla. Leaves oval. Prune as for Diervilla. May—June. H.R.C. 3—6 ft.

LABURNUM D.

Small trees, flowering in spring, with hanging sprays of golden, Pea-shaped flowers. Do not plant near a pool as seeds can kill fish. Best garden plants are *L. alpinum* and vars. *vossii* and *watereri*, which have very large and long flower trusses. May—June. S. 10—20 ft.

LAVANDULA Lavender E.

Fragrant shrubs with silver foliage, and spikes of blue or purple flowers. Well drained soil, sun. Plants may be used as individuals, for edging purposes or as low hedges. Flowers for drying should be cut just before they are fully out, and old flower stalks removed late summer. Leave major pruning, however, until April. H.R.C.

Varieties of *L. spica* include *alba*, with white flowers, 'Munstead Dwarf', rich purple, 'Twickel Purple', deep dark purple, and *rosea*, pink. July—Aug. 1½—3 ft.

LAVATERA See p. 37.

LEYCESTERIA Patridge Berry

L. formosa, D. Quaint shrub with bright green hollow stems, heart-shaped leaves and drooping bunches of purple and white flowers. These are succeeded by reddish-purple, juicy berries. Useful in the wild garden or larger shrubbery. In March old stems can be cut almost to ground level. July—Sept. 6—8 ft. S.

LONICERA See p. 287.

MAGNOLIA

Beautiful small trees with waxy cup-shaped flowers. All require sheltered situation and deep, fertile, well drained soil. Partial shade suits some species but majority like sun. Mostly deciduous, but the fine wall shrub *M. grandiflora* is evergreen. See p. 284. Little pruning required and then only during growing season. Propagation L. (usually takes 2 years), Air layers, S. (sown directly after harvesting) and sometimes H.R.C. (with bottom heat).

M. denudata D. Lily Tree. Large, cup-shaped, pure white, fragrant flowers and attractive leaves. March—June. 6—20 ft.

M. kobus D. will grow on chalk soils and has creamy, 6-petalled flowers followed by Cucumber-like fruits with red seeds. April. 20 ft.

M. liliflora D. is particularly useful in a small garden as it grows very slowly. Flowers goblet-shaped, white inside and purplish-red outside; *var. nigra* has wine-coloured blooms. April—May. 10 ft.

M. obovata D. is lovely for a shady setting, having long, tapering leaves and fragrant, cup-shaped flowers (7—8 in. across), white with a central ring of crimson stamens. June—July. 10—30 ft.

Kerria japonica plena

Standard Rhododendrons

M. sieboldii D. *(syn. parviflora)*. Oval leaves, green above and white flecked beneath. Flowers white with claret stamens. May—June. 6—10 ft.

M. x soulangiana D. Recommended garden form, succeeding even in heavy clay soils Fine, goblet-shaped flowers, creamy (but often stained purplish on the outside) on black naked branches. Blooms when very young. Varieties include *brozzonii*, the largest white, shaded purple; *lennei*, rosy purple outside; *hammondii*, very narrow petals; and *alba superba*, almost white; April—June (when it flowers with the leaves). 6—30 ft.

M. stellata D. Very branched, slow growing shrub with a wealth of narrow-petalled (12—18) flowers, white, later tinged red, 3 in. across. Apt to be damaged by frosts. Include plenty of peat in soil. March—April. 10 ft.

M. wilsonii D. Beautiful plant with downward-hanging, cup-shaped flowers, white with rich red stamens, fragrant. Fruits 2—3 in. long, purplish pink. May—June. 6—20 ft.

MAHONIA E.

Often confused with Berberis (see p. 63.) but distinguished by compound leaves and absence of thorns. Some tolerate extreme shade and all mentioned are winter flowering. Any soil. Little pruning. L. S. Air layers.

M. aquifolium, the Oregon Grape, has glossy leaves and clusters of yellow flowers. Grows in complete shade but blooms more freely in sun. Feb.—May. 3—4 ft.

M. japonica (syn. bealei). Beautiful plant with showy sprays of fragrant, Primrose-yellow flowers at tops of branches. Leaves glossy, with 13 or so leaflets. Sun or partial shade, rich but well drained soil suit this species best. Feb.—March. 3—7 ft.

M. lomariifolia. Erect habit and fine, compound, leathery leaves. Flowers in terminal spikes, 4—10 in. fragrant, deep yellow. Fruits blue-black berries. Nov.—Dec. 8—12 ft.

MALUS Flowering Crab

Early flowering small trees, with coloured Apple-blossom flowers. Any except waterlogged soil, sunshine. Varietal forms, usually grafted or budded on Crab and Apple stocks, can be obtained in bush, half standard or standard sizes. Prune to shape and keep centre of tree open.

Among many representative garden forms are: x *atrosanguinea*, rich rose, leaves shining green; x *eleyi*, rich red flowers followed by crimson crab fruits, leaves reddish purple, one of best varieties; *floribunda*, rosy red gradually paling to almost white; *floribunda atrosanguinea*, deeper red. Good fruiting varieties are 'John Downie', conical, 1¼ in. long, bright orange and scarlet; 'Golden Hornet' and 'Transcendent', both yellow, and 'Dartmouth', reddish purple. Few feet up to 30 ft. in standards. April—May.

OLEARIA See p. 284.

OSMANTHUS See p. 285.

PAEONIA Paeony D.

The Tree Paeonies are deciduous shrubs with slender branches, large, showy, usually fragrant flowers and deeply cut, elegant foliage. They need a sheltered position in sun or light shade, in deep, fertile, yet well drained soil. Annual mulches improve quality of blooms. Little pruning beyond removal of old seed heads and sucker growths, for garden varieties are usually grafted on other species. (*P. lactiflora* or *P. officinalis*). May also be air and stem layered. May—June.

P. suffruticosa, Mountain or Tree Paeony, has branching habit and rose-pink or white flowers usually with a magenta blotch on the petals, and flowers 6 in. across. Varieties are multi-coloured, often with fringed petals. 6 ft.

P. lutea, golden-yellow, 4½ ft. has produced varieties such as *ludlowi*, with finely cut foliage; *chromatella*, soft yellow, and 'Sheriff's Variety', with larger flowers. *P. x smouthii*, deep ruby. 3 ft.

Pyracantha lalandii   H. Smith

PARROTIA D.

P. persica is a small tree with fine autumnal tints and short clusters of reddish flowers festooning naked branches in spring. Any good soil, sun or light shade. S. or L. 20—30 ft.

PASSIFLORA See p. 285.

PERNETTYA

P. mucronata, E. Low growing, richly coloured, fruiting shrubs with large berries, often the size of marbles. These may be white, pink, lilac, crimson, purple, magenta and almost black. Leaves small, tapering, glossy; flowers white. Rigid habit. Likes an acid soil but detests lime; sun. Plant several together to ensure fruiting. L. S. or H.R.C. in sandy peat or vermiculite in August. May—June. 3—5 ft.

PHILADELPHUS Mock Orange D.

Sweet scented, white-flowered, summer shrubs often known as syringa. Very adaptable, succeeding in most soils, sun or light shade. Remove old branches occasionally and to reduce height, cut out top to a vigorous shoot lower down. H.R.C.

Varieties from *P. coronarius* include 'Virginal', perhaps the best double white; 'Innocence', single white; 'Voie Lactee', also white; 'Enchantment', late double, and 'Norma', with scentless flowers; *aureus*, golden leaves, makes good hedging plant 3—8 ft.

Philadelphus grandiflorus   J. E. Downward

Pernettya mucronata hybrid   J. E. Downward

P. grandiflorus very erect and vigorous. 10—12 ft., also has scentless flowers. June—July.

PHLOMIS See p. 41.

PHYGELIUS See p. 42.

PIERIS E.
Beautiful shrubs requiring similar soil and conditions to Rhododendrons; all dislike sun. Mostly evergreen with white, showy sprays of Lily-of-the-Valley flowers. Leaves oblong, leathery and deep green; young foliage often brilliant scarlet like Poinsettias. Remove old blooms after flowering and prune to shape. H.R.C. in sandy soil in a cold frame in Aug.
P. floribunda, formosa and *japonica forrestii* are all good plants, with *formosa* slightly less hardy but flower clusters 4—6 in. long and wide, fragrant. April—May. 6—9 ft.

PIPTANTHUS Evergreen Laburnum E.
P. laburnifolius. Only hardy in sheltered situation, well drained soil, sun. Best grown against a wall. 3-parted leaves densely covered with short silver hairs. Flowers in clusters, bright yellow, Pea-shaped. Cut out old wood and shorten young shoots to half length in Feb. S. or Heel C. May—June. 8—10 ft.

POTENTILLA E.
P. fruticosa makes compact little bush 2—4 ft. high, covered practically all summer with yellow, Cinquefoil flowers. Leaves pinnate, divided into 5 or 7 leaflets. Varieties include 'Donard Gold', 'Moonlight' and *alba*, white. Well drained soil, full sun. H.R.C. Remove old wood occasionally.

PRUNUS
This family includes the ornamental Plums, Cherries, Almonds, Peaches and Laurels. All mentioned are hardy and suitable for any good garden soil. They flower better in sunshine although many are tolerant of some shade.
Prune only during growing season because of danger of Silver Leaf disease (see p. 291). Usually propagated by budding or grafting on suitable Plum or Cherry stocks, and can be had in bush or standard forms. Can sometimes be raised on own roots by air layers or from heel cuttings rooted in gentle heat.
Flowering Cherries D.
P. avium flore pleno, a double-flowered form of native wild Cherry. April—May. 12 ft. or 30—40 ft.
P. cerasus flore pleno, another good double white.
P. subhirtella, Rosebud Cherry. A beautiful bush (8—12 ft.) or can be grafted on *P. avium* to make a small tree (20—30 ft.). April. Flowers rose-pink, in clusters. Its *var. pendula* makes a weeping tree and *var. autumnalis* carries semi-double, pink blossoms from Nov. onwards.

Rhododendron 'Koster's Brilliant'

Pieris japonica forrestii

Philadelphus coronarius aurea

P. serrula tibetica. Tree with peeling bark. Flowers white, April.

Japanese Cherries D.

These bear clouds of single or double flowers in early spring, pink, white or red and one, 'Ukon', yellowish-green. 'Cheal's Weeping' has pendulous branches wreathed with double pink flowers; *yedonensis pendula*, white is also weeping; *amanogawa* (syn. *erecta*) has upright rather than spreading habit — like a Lombardy Poplar; flowers soft pink. These are all small growing kinds (approximately 15—20 ft.) but there are larger trees many with Japanese names, with correspondingly greater display of blossom.

Flowering Plums D.

Often have coloured foliage, as the small tree *P. pissardii* (correct name *P. cerasifera atropurpurea*), with deep purple leaves and rosy-pink flowers. This and other varieties also used as hedges or in mixed shrubbery. For details of former see p. 247. *P. cerasifera* is white.

Almonds and Peaches D.

The common Almond is *P. communis* and often flowers in Feb. Double form *rosea plena* is more attractive. 10—20 ft. *P. persica*, 'Russell's Red', and 'Clara Meyer', former double red, latter pink, are varieties of the common Peach, with attractive flowers in April. 'Wendle Weeping' is a pendent form with double pink blossoms; *foliis rubris* has deep crimson leaves all the year, rose-pink single flowers on naked branches in April, followed by edible, dark crimson Peaches. This variety comes true from seed, grows about 12 ft. high. Others vary between 10—20 ft. *P. triloba flore pleno* is a small shrub with slender branches, with double pink flowers in April, 7—9 ft.

Laurels E.

P. lusitanica Portuguese Laurel, a hardy evergreen with strongly scented racemes of creamy flowers in June, oval, polished leaves and sometimes dark purple berries. May be used for hedges or can develop to a small tree. 10—20 ft.

PUNICA See p. 285.

PYRACANTHA See p. 287.

RHODODENDRON

A large genus which includes Azaleas and Rhodoras; either deciduous or evergreen, and from almost prostrate habit to shrubs or tall trees. Chiefly valuable for brilliant and spectacular flowers, probably the brightest in the shrub world. Plants thrive best in a deep, cool and moist soil with plenty of humus. They do not like dryness at the roots or lime.

Being surface rooting they appreciate frequent mulches of moistened peat or leaf mould. They dislike strong sun, and often do best sheltered by other trees or hedges.

Old seed heads should be removed after flowering and since many garden forms are grafted on Cyclamen-coloured *ponticum*, watch for suckers from latter. Old neglected bushes can be cut back very hard (several feet from the ground) and will eventually break away to make better shaped plants. Naturally this entails some loss of flower for several seasons.

Evergreens May Flowering

Among the evergreen, larger-flowered Rhododendrons there are literally hundreds of species and varieties, but a representative collection in the various shades could include:

Yellow

'Butterfly', 'Dairymaid', 'Devonshire Cream', pale yellow, 'Idealist', 'Mrs Ashley Slocock', cream. 'Fabia', 'Unique', pale orange to orange salmon.

White

'Albatros', 'White Pearl', 'Loder's White'.

Pink

'Pink Pearl', 'Mrs G.W. Leak'.
'Betty Wormald' (dark eye).
'Cynthia'.
'Loderi' (a fine hybrid but not hardy everywhere).

Crimson and Red

'Unknown Warrior', 'David', 'King George', 'Cynthia'.

'Hino-mayo', clear bright pink; 'Hatsu-giri', rosy purple; 'Iro-hayama', soft pearly-pink.

Azalea pontica D. (also called *Rhododendron luteum*), vigorous species with clear yellow, fragrant flowers, up to 10 ft. and good autumn colouring — useful for massing in shrubberies.

RHUS Sumach D.

A small family with fine autumnal tints. All more or less poisonous, one species the famous Poison Ivy of America. Little pruning, except for *R. typhina*, which should be cut hard back in April.

R. cotinus, The Smoke Plant, has smoky-grey, feathery plumes of flowers and small, oval to round, smooth green leaves turning yellow in autumn. The variety *purpureus* has leaves which open crimson and turn purple. 6—10 ft. June. *R. cotinoides* (*Cotinus americanus*) has magnificent flowers and green leaves turning to flame, gold, red and yellow in autumn. 12 ft. June. Both plants like poor soil and a somewhat open position. H.R.C. root in a cold frame in July or plants may be layered. *R. typhina*, Stag's Horn Sumach. A distinct plant making a small tree with strange, black branches, covered with short hairs, large pinnate leaves changing colour in autumn, and knob-like clusters of dark crimson flowers. Late July. 10—15 ft. Root C.

Rhododendron 'Cynthia'   Copyright R. & G. Cuthbert

Cherry, showing beauty of bark

Deciduous Azaleas (A. mollis)

April flowering before the leaves develop. Not as sweetly scented as the Ghent hybrids but glorious colour range. 'Adriaan Koster', deep yellow; 'Koster's Brilliant', deep salmon; 'Clara Butt', deep pink; 'Mrs L.J. Endtz', clear yellow; 'Marmion', pale yellow; 'Spek's Orange', orange red; 'Frans Hals', deep red; 'Anthony Koster', yellow.

Knap-Hill Azaleas May Flowering

These are mostly hybrids raised by the late Anthony Waterer. 'Royal Lodge', deep red; 'Brazil', nasturtium-red; 'Farrall Yellow', chrome; 'Farrall Honey', flame-pink; 'Goldcrest', straw; 'Persil', white; 'Satan', blood-red; 'Pink Delight', carmine pink; 'Tunis', orange and red.

Ghent Hybrids D. Honeysuckle Azaleas, June flowering. Tubular, richly scented flowers opening as leaves are breaking. Colours clear and brilliant and leaves give vivid autumn display. *Coccinea speciosa*, salmon; 'Fritz Quihoui', vermilion; 'Mrs H. White', pink, white and yellow; 'William III', orange; 'Fanny', rose-magenta; 'Nancy Waterer', soft yellow;

Kurume Azaleas E. April—May. 1½ to several feet.

Dwarf evergreen plants with small, deep green leaves, the dense, spreading branches smothered with vivid flowers — magenta, rosy red, etc.; very useful in rock garden, window boxes or tubs.

RIBES Flowering Currant D.

Well known plants chiefly valued for early flowers and easy cultivation. Sun or shade. Ripe cuttings in late summer. *R. americanum*, yellowish flowers and crimson foliage tints in autumn. April. 5 ft. *R. sanguineum*, hanging racemes of pinkish flowers, better coloured in varieties *atrorubens*, 'Pulborough Scarlet', and 'King Edward VII'. March—April. 6—8 ft.

ROBINIA D.

Attractive small tree with fine pink Laburnum-like flowers and leaves. Branches brittle, so try to give wall or shrubbery protection. *R. hispida*, the Rose Acacia, has thick racemes of purplish-crimson flowers about 6 in. long. *R. kelseyi* is bright rose. May—June. 5—10 ft. Both trees stand fairly severe cutting and make sturdier plants on poor soil. Suckers, S. or grafts on *R. pseudoacacia*.

ROMNEYA See p. 44.

ROSA See p. 104 and p. 285.

ROSMARINUS Rosemary E.

Popular shrub with fragrant foliage and bright blue flowers. Likes full sun, very well drained soil; makes good seaside plant.

Shorten plants after flowering but never take back into old wood. H.R.C. outdoors in July or in a cold frame. *R. officinalis* has produced varieties with deeper coloured flowers, 'Corsican Blue' and 'Seven Seas', also an upright growing form 'Miss Jessop's Upright'. April—May. 4—6 ft.

RUBUS D.

R. deliciosus is the best of the ornamental brambles with white, 5-petalled, single flowers, 2 in. across, like wild roses. Sun, sandy well drained soil. Remove old branches occasionally.

R. biflorus is the White Washed Bramble with waxy white stems in winter. Cut hard back each spring. May. 3—4 ft. *R. thyrsoideus fl. pleno*, double white, is sometimes grown for its flowers. L.

RUSCUS Butcher's Broom E.

R. aculeatus is a prickly plant, tolerating shade, with bright red winter berries. Some plants single sexed, so purchase hermaphrodite specimens or introduce male amongst several female plants. Any ordinary soil. Thin out old wood occasionally. Div. or S.

SALIX Willow D.

S. caprea pendula is perhaps the smallest of the Weeping Willows, an attractive waterside tree. 7—8 ft. C. *S. purpurea pendula* is 8—15 ft. and *S. pendula* (syn. *babylonica*) 40—60 ft. Moist soil and sunshine. Hard C.

SANTOLINA Cotton Lavender E.

Aromatic, silvery-leaved shrubs, best in well drained soil and full sunshine. Useful for front row positions or between brightly coloured bedding or herbaceous plants. H.R.C. root easily in July. Trim old flowers with shears and cut hedges fairly closely in April. *S. chamaecyparissus*, leaves fragrant, flowers yellow, like Daisies without the outer florets. 1½—2 ft. *Var. viridis* has green foliage.

SCHIZOPHRAGMA See p. 287.

SENECIO E.

S. laxifolius and *S. greyii*, both very similar, are shrubby members of the Daisy family with bright yellow flowers and spreading branches of silver-grey, felted leaves and stems. Striking in groups at edge of border, especially contrasted with red-leaved shrubs (like *Berberis thunbergii* or *Prunus pissardii*). Rapid growing and happy in well drained soil, but sometimes 'burned' by frost. Like sun, do well in coastal districts. No special pruning. H.R.C. June—July. 3—4 ft.

SKIMMIA E.

S. japonica and *S. reevesiana*. Slow growing shrubs, male and female flowers on separate plants. Both needed for bright red, long-persisting berries which often coincide with next season's flowers. These are borne in terminal panicles and are dull white and fragrant. Well drained soil, not drying out in summer; sun. S. or H.R.C. April. 3—4 ft.

SOLANUM See p. 285.

SOPHORA D.

S. viciifolia (syn. *davidii*), a member of the Pea family, has pinnate leaves, spiny branches and racemes of blue and white Wistaria-like flowers. 4—5 ft. June. Sun, any good soil. C. with bottom heat. *S. tetraptera* E. makes elegant wall shrub or may be grown in open in warmer districts. Profuse sprays of deep golden, Pea-like flowers. Waxy leaves beautifully cut. May—June. 10—12 ft. No special pruning.

SORBUS D.

S. aucuparia is the Rowan or Mountain Ash, a small tree with white flowers, attractive leaves which usually change colour in autumn and scarlet berries. These can be made into jam. *Var. xanthocarpa* has yellow fruits, and *pendula* is of weeping habit.

Rubus thyrsoideus fl. pleno

Senecio greyii   J. E. Downward

May. 10—20 ft. Any soil, open position. No special pruning. S. or hybrid kinds can be grafted on the type.

SPARTIUM Spanish Broom D.

S. junceum is valuable because it flowers between seasons (June—Aug.) and carries stray blooms until the frosts. Green Rush-like stems, tiny leaves and sprays of large, bright yellow, fragrant Pea-shaped flowers. Straggling habit but will become bushy if old growth trimmed back each April. Sunshine, well drained soil. 9—12 ft. S. but should be raised in pots to avoid root disturbance at planting time.

SPIRAEA D.

Summer-flowering shrubs with groups of dainty flowers usually along branches. Leaves small. Sun or light shade, most soils. Pink kinds sometimes difficult and need careful placing. *S. bullata* is a dwarf (1½ ft.) with rosy-pink flowers in dense heads in July. Very bright. Remove old flower heads. *S. japonica* has magenta-pink blooms, but is chiefly passed over for the deeper-coloured variety 'Anthony Waterer'. 3—4 ft. July—Aug. *x vanhouttei* is a good white. June. 4—6 ft.; so is *x arguta*, the Bridal Wreath, with slender twigs and bunches of tiny florets. April. 6—8 ft. L. S. or late summer H.R.C.

STACHYURUS See p. 285.

STAPHYLEA D.

S. colchica. Spring flowering shrub with bunches of white flowers, individually like tiny Daffodils. Fruit an inflated capsule. Leaves opposite, toothed, usually 3-parted. Sheltered position, leafy soil, will also grow on lime. May. 5—8 ft. No regular pruning. S. or H.R.C.

STEWARTIA D.

Resemble Camellais with fine white flowers, in some kinds 2—3 in. across, appearing singly or in pairs in the leaf axils.

Foliage often colours well before falling in autumn. Plant with Azaleas and Hydrangeas as they like the same conditions. Protect from midday sun. Species include *koreana*, *pseudo-camellia* and *sinensis*; the first probably the best. Up to 30 ft. June—Aug. No special pruning. S. (which must be soaked before sowing) L. or Heel C. with bottom heat in sandy soil.

STYRAX Snowbell D.

Flowering trees with pendent, white, Snowdrop-like flowers and oval leaves. Blooms hang in rows from every twig and are most effective seen from below. Acid soil (no lime) rich in humus, protected from strong winds. No special pruning. S. L. or Heel C. in warmth. *S. japonica* is perhaps the best. 10—20 ft. June.

SYMPHORICARPUS Snowberry D.

Suitable for woodland or wild garden with oval, smooth leaves, inconspicuous flowers and laden branches of white, 'mothball' berries from Oct. onwards. *S. albus laevigatus* is best form. 7—10 ft. S.H.C.

SYRINGA Lilac D.

Popular shrubs with showy sprays of very fragrant flowers and smooth, heart-shaped leaves. Rich soil, damp in summer and a warm sheltered spot, but also tolerate lime. Light shade prevents rapid fading of blooms, but too much tends to inhibit flowering.

Prune to shape. Cut straggly specimens hard back in Nov. to make a new tree. Remove faded flowers to prevent seed formation. C. or L. are better than grafts, as suckers from the latter (if on common Lilac) are a nuisance.

Singles 12—15 ft. April flowering
'Etna', wine purple; 'Hugo Koster', slaty-blue; 'Candeur', creamy-white; 'Congo', rich red; 'Marie Legraye', white; 'Souvenir de Louis Spaeth', deep purple; 'Vestale', white; 'President Lincoln', pale lilac.

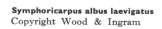

Symphoricarpus albus laevigatus
Copyright Wood & Ingram

Skimmia

J. E. Downward

Viburnum carlesii

Viburnum macrocephalum

Double Varieties 12—15 ft. April Flowering
'Edouard André', the best pink; 'Emile Gentil', blue purple; 'Charles Joly', dark reddish-purple; 'Edith Cavell', creamy yellow, opening to white; 'Mrs Edward Harding', purplish-red; 'Primrose', soft yellow; 'Olivier de Serres', pale mauve.

Some fine hybrid Lilacs raised in Ottawa are known as *S. prestoniae*. These have looser sprays of flowers and appear about a fortnight after the common Lilacs. They also make better shrubs in mixed border. Named varieties worth growing include 'Isabella', mallow-purple; 'Miranda', pink; 'Virgilia', lilac-magenta; 'Brilliant', rose and 'Desdemona', reddish-purple. May—June. 8—12 ft. *S. reflexa*, deep pink, is another good species but scentless 12 ft.

TAMARIX Tamarisk D.

Good seaside shrubs with bright green, feathery foliage and slender branches smothered with masses of rosy flowers, smelling of gingerbread. Full sun, any well drained soil. Ripe Hard C. in autumn.

T. pentandra should have old flowering wood cut back nearly to old growth in April. Bright rosy-pink flowers, very free. 12—15 ft. Aug.—Sept.

T. tetandra, spring flowering, so prune back when these are finished. Bright pink. 10—15 ft. May.

TRACHYCARPUS Chusan Palm E.

T. fortunei is the hardiest of the Palms and will even succeed in London in a sheltered spot. Protect young plants, however, during first years with leaves, straw or sacking in bad weather.

Makes a small tree with deeply cut, fan-shaped leaves, often $2\frac{1}{2}$ ft. long and $3\frac{1}{2}$ ft. wide. Trunk thicker at top than at base, covered with coarse black fibres and dead foliage of previous seasons. Flowers borne at top of tree in huge yellow panicles, something like Rhubarb. No pruning. Well drained soil, sun, and occasional mulch in spring. May. Very slow, but eventually 20—25 ft. S.

TRICUSPIDARIA Lantern Tree E.

T. hookerianum. Beautiful shrub or small tree, with dark green, oval leaves and brilliant sealing-wax scarlet flowers swinging on long red stems. Suitable for sheltered areas only and lime-free soils. No special pruning. May—Aug. 6—25 ft. S. or Heel C. in a frame in summer.

ULEX Gorse; Furze; Whin

Well known plants of heath and moor with dark green, prickly stems and leaves and golden Pea-shaped flowers. Useful for exposed positions or poor dry soils. *U. europaeus* is native species, but inferior to its double form *plenus*, which in a sunny position becomes a mass of gold. Cut old leggy plants hard back in April, otherwise leave alone. Feb.—May, but stray flowers all year. 4—6 ft. H.R.C. in a sandy soil in a frame.

VERONICA Speedwell

The shrubby Veronicas are particularly useful in seaside gardens where they flower for months. Give sheltered positions inland. Majority evergreen although they may lose leaves or even be cut back in a bad winter. Some used for hedging purposes. No regular pruning beyond thinning of occasional shoot and removal of spent flowers. Propagated by cuttings. *V. armstrongii* and *V. hulkeana* are perhaps best in the rock garden, the former has snake-like stems covered with tiny, old gold leaves and terminal heads of white, starry flowers 1—2 ft. July—Aug.; the latter, less hardy, has long (12 in.) branching sprays of rich blue flowers and small toothed leaves. May, June. 1—3 ft. *V. speciosa* has given rise to many garden forms with flowers in late summer. Small plants often give best effects. They provide dwarf plants (1—3 ft.) for bedding purposes. 'Alicia Amherst', royal purple; 'Autumn Glory', violet; *carnea*, rosy-white; 'Gloriosa', bright pink; 'La Seduisante', bright crimson and 'Midsummer Beauty', lavender are typical varieties.

Others grown chiefly for foliage are *V. elliptica*, with small, narrow, pointed leaves making a good hedge; *V. cupressoides* has narrow Cypress-like foliage and *V. brachysiphon* (syn. *V. traversii*) smooth, oval leaves and small white clusters of axillary flowers. This is one of the hardiest. 2—5 ft. July—Sept. S.C.

VIBURNUM

Important family of shrubs, more or less indifferent to soil conditions including lime, provided not waterlogged, or drying out in summer. Many noted for winter flowers. Remove old worn out branch occasionally, during the dormant season with deciduous kinds, in April with evergreens. Propagation various, according to species. S. H.R.C. Soft cuttings under belljar in July, grafting. *V. carlesii* D. forms rounded, bushy shrub with oval, toothed, felted leaves and rounded trusses of white, very sweet scented Daphne-like flowers in great profusion. Buds pinkish. Best in sheltered position. Often grafted on *V. lantana* but best on own roots. April—May. Hybrids from this are x *burkwodii*, taller than its parent (10 ft.), semi-evergreen and of loose habit with slightly smaller flower trusses. Makes good wall shrub, even on north walls. 'Park Farm Hybrid', E. has larger flowers and is shorter (4—6 ft.). V. x *carlocephalum*, D. has larger leaves than the type, more vigorous with flower clusters up to 5 in. across. Very fragrant. May. 4—8 ft. All these can be propagated from H.R.C.; old plants do not transplant well. *V. tomentosum*, 'Lanarth Variety', D. forms compact bush with horizontally-placed, arching branches, bearing flat clusters of large white flowers, carried in pairs, each about 4 in. across. Leaves wine-coloured in autumn. Other worthwhile forms from *V. tomentosum* are 'Rowallane Variety', *plicatum*, the Japanese Snowball, with balls of white flowers, and *mariesii*, with larger florets. All grow between 5 and 8 ft. and bloom in May.

V. macrocephalum, Chinese Snowball; Semi-E. Brittle, best grown before a wall. Flowers towards the end of May in showy 4—6 in. clusters, lasting several weeks. 6—8 ft. *V. opulus* D. Guelder Rose, has translucent red berries and Maple-shaped bright green leaves, handsomely tinted in autumn. Does well in light shade and will grow on chalk — var. *sterile* is the Snowball Tree with round hanging bunches of white flowers. 'Notcutt's Variety', an improved form of latter, has yellow berries like amber beads. May—June. 10—15 ft. H.R.C. L. and S.

V. tinus E. is a winter flowering species blooming freely from Nov. onwards in a sunny situation. Will also grow in considerable shade. Oval leaves something like those of Fuchsia. Any soil. 5—8 ft. H.R.C.

V. betulifolium D., a berrying plant, the former of upright habit and Birch-shaped leaves with clusters of white flowers, followed by branch-bending sprays of Redcurrant-like berries. June—July. 8—12 ft.

V. davidii E. is a ground-cover subject with oval, leathery white-veined leaves and bright turquoise berries. Plant several roots to ensure cross pollination. June. 2—3 ft.

V. fragrans D. is one of the most dependable winter flowering shrubs for light soils, blossoming from Oct. until May. Upright habit, leaves small, slightly reddish when young, flowers fragrant in small bunches at the ends of branches, first naked then leafy. Var. *x bodnantense* is a still better plant with longer (3 in.) rose-flecked flower trusses. May be grown in shade but takes a year or two to flower. 6—10 ft. H.R.C.

Another interesting Viburnum is *V. rhytidophyllum* E. with wrinkled leathery leaves, brown-felted underneath and whitish flowers in terminal heads. Makes a good windbreak shrub. May—June. 8—10 ft. *V. henryi*, E. has white flowers and first red then black berries. Foliage glossy and narrowly oval. June. 8—10 ft. H.R.C.

VINCA Periwinkle E.

Ground cover or trailing, soft-stemmed evergreens valuable for shady situations or between taller shrubs. Any soil. Prune to shape. Div. or S.C.

V. major variegata, an attractive trailing variegated plant, never seems to revert to green, rarely flowers. *V. minor*, 'Bowles Variety', is best of group with many large bright blue flowers from a compact plant. Never throws out runners. Other forms (which do run) include 'Miss Jekyll's White', *aureo variegata*, gold leaf variegations, *flore pleno*, double blue and *multiplex* double purple. April—May. 1 ft.

VITIS See p. 285.

WISTARIA See p. 286.

XANTHOCERAS

X. sorbifolium, D. is a small tree for shady or moist woodland conditions, with pinnate leaves made up of 9 to 17 sharply toothed leaflets. Flowers 5-petalled, each about, 1 in., white and carmine-red in bunches on spurs from branches and trunk. Spectacular when established, sometimes 6—8 in. long. Fruits like those of Horse-Chestnut, but with several seeds. No special pruning. S. or Root C. May. 10—20 ft.

YUCCA E.

Well known shrubs with stiff, sword-shaped leaves and erect spikes of showy creamy flowers. Prefer hot, dry positions, do well in towns or by sea. Solitary plants grown so as to view from all angles make most effective display. Stems lengthen over years until they rot at the base and fall. The tops, however, will root if trimmed and inserted in a warm frame in sand or vermiculite. Dwarf species can be divided, and offshoots from all species taken off and rooted. *Y. filamentosa* has slender, glaucous leaves,

Tamarisk

flower spike up to 5 ft., individual florets 2—3 in., nodding, yellowish-white. Var. *variegata*, leaves striped green and cream. July—Aug. 2—5 ft.

Y. gloriosa, Adam's Needle, has wider and spiny-tipped leaves from a short woody trunk. Flowers creamy. July—Sept. 8 ft. *Y. recurvifolia*, the hardiest species with recurving leaves having spiny tips. Flowers creamy. July—Sept. 8 ft.

ZENOBIA

Z. pulverulenta. Unjustly neglected deciduous or semi-evergreen shrub, 4—6 ft. high with small, shining, dark green leaves, oblong oval. Young shoots have curious bluish bloom. Sprays of pendent, Lily-of-the-Valley flowers in late June. Needs peaty soil or mulches of leaves or peat on light loam; semi-shade. Young plants can be easily forced. H.R.C. in gentle heat in July. Remove old flowering heads as they fade.

Window Boxes & Hanging Baskets

Window boxes and hanging baskets provide a quick means of bringing colour to rooms, houses, even to entire streets.

The containers are not difficult to plant and maintain but they do demand regular attention. If they have to be left for days unattended they will not be a success.

They are particularly appreciated in and suited to town gardens, but can of course be used in any area. Hanging baskets also make attractive features in garden rooms and greenhouses.

THE BOXES

The containers must be stoutly made as they have to carry a great deal of weight and are at all times exposed to the elements. They can be of wood — deal, oak or teak — of zinc, aluminium, concrete, or of such new man-made materials as fibreglass or plastocrete.

Ideally they have portable inside liners, made of metal, which can be taken out in a few seconds and replaced with others freshly planted.

Wood boxes should be made from a hard, durable material like oak or teak, though deal can give good service if the boxes are properly made and treated. The outside should be given an undercoating of lead paint with two coats of colour on top. The inside should not be painted, except perhaps for an inch at the top, just above the soil level. Painting with Cuprinol will protect, but do not creosote as it is poisonous to many plants.

Make up the box to the required size, using one inch timber. It should be at least 9 in. deep and for window use must be made an inch wider than the sill so that the front juts out slightly. When intended for wall hanging, stout iron brackets should be driven into the wall to act as supports. It is advisable to fix all window boxes so that they tip slightly backwards. This is a safety measure in bad weather and easily

Hanging basket with Ivy-leaved Geraniums
By courtesy of Home Magazine

arranged on a flat surface like a windowsill by pushing wedges under the front. Do be sure that all boxes are securely fixed, so as to avoid the possibility of accidents.

Drainage is important, particularly where the boxes are exposed to the elements. Standing water is detrimental to all plants save aquatics and drainage holes, bored at intervals in the bottom of the box, will guard against this danger.

On windowsills, however, they are not so essential; indeed good-neighbourliness is not fostered by water dripping on the heads of passers by! Two or three inches of broken crocks or rubble, such as stones or broken bricks, laid over the bottom, covered with leaves or pieces of turf turned grass-side downwards, provide excellent drainage even in a solid container. As a general rule a routine watering once a day is enough to keep the soil sufficiently moist. This, of course, is subject to its containing a certain amount of peat, a material which holds water and prevents rapid drying out. If portable liners are used, these can be removed and the plants well soaked away from the window.

SOIL

In towns, one either has the task of improving the soil or using a ready prepared compost such as the John Innes No. 1 Potting Compost.

Soil from the existing garden should be mixed with coarse sand and broken moist peat, together with fine bonemeal and general fertiliser. Make this up as follows:

1 part coarse sand
1 part moist peat or leaf-mould
2 parts garden soil or loam

To every box (length 3 ft.) add:

3 handfuls fine bonemeal
1 handful National Growmore, Clay's Fertiliser or any other general fertiliser.

Mix together and moisten sufficiently for the soil just to bind in the hand when squeezed. Fill the box (over the layer of crocks and leaves or turf) to within an inch of the top. Put in the plants, using a trowel and setting them firmly up to the old planting mark, and water them in.

SUITABLE PLANTS

Most of the plants suitable for window boxes are reasonably priced. As long as you do not put sun-loving subjects in a north window or shade plants in bright sunshine, and remember always to keep the

Hanging basket of Begonias   J. E. Downward

soil moist, a surprising variety of plants will succeed.

In some circumstances colour can be very important. Thus red blossoms will hardly show against a red brick wall or house, nor white blossoms before a whitewashed facade. Yellow blooms may shine like gold against a white background but will not always please against red. This is largely a matter of personal taste, but generally speaking, contrasts should be sought, i.e. combinations which are pleasing in themselves but do not detract from the general appearance of the house.

PLANT ASSOCIATIONS

Red Brick Walls
Use white with soft blues, lemons and a touch of lilac.

SUNNY ASPECTS

Spring
White Hyacinths and Forget-me-nots
Pink and white Daisies and bronze and cream Wallflowers
White Tulips and Grape-hyacinths

Summer
White Marguerites and mauvy pink trailing Geraniums
Mixed Stocks
Sweet Alyssum

SHADE

Spring
Polyanthus (mixed or one colour)
Narcissi (short kinds) and most bulbs

Summer
Campanulas
Candytuft
Violas and Fuchsias

Window boxes and hanging baskets   H. Smith

Grey Stone or Colour Wash
Use deep blues or purples, also bright reds and pinks.

SUNNY ASPECTS

Spring
Mixed Wallflowers
Pink Tulips and Forget-me-nots
Blue or pink Hyacinths

Summer
Mixed Petunias
Scarlet Geraniums and pink ivy-leaved types like Galilee with Calceolarias and Lobelia
Asters
Stocks

SHADE

Spring
Polyanthus
Various Primulas
Small evergreens

Summer
Fuchsias
Heliotropes
Begonias
Nasturtiums

Geraniums and other plants in hanging baskets and pots
Valerie Finnis

White Painted or Washed Walls
Use really bright colours with plenty of green, or pastel shades of pinks and mauves.

SUNNY ASPECTS

Spring
Golden Wallflowers and Forget-me-nots
Red Wallflowers and Daisies
Red and blue Hyacinths
Crocus
Cinerarias (for a short period)

Summer
Geraniums
Marigolds
Calceolarias
Tagetes
Petunias
Dwarf Chrysanthemums

Achimenes are good plants for hanging baskets

A brilliant window box display   Valerie Finnis

Geraniums in hanging baskets   H. Smith

SHADE

Spring	Summer
Polyanthus	Calceolarias
Ferns	Iceland Poppies and Ferns
Violas	Nasturtiums
Periwinkles	Creeping Jenny

In winter the emphasis will be on foliage, and many nurserymen sell little evergreen shrubs which can be planted from pots end September. Suitable subjects are clipped Box, shrubby Veronicas (especially the variegated kinds) Junipers, Euonymus and dwarf Piceas. These may be interplanted with Crocus or other small bulbs for early colour. It is also possible to purchase specially prepared Narcissi for planting outdoors to bloom around Christmas. These must be planted the day after delivery.

Town dwellers can also grow herbs in a window box. Use a small Bay tree as centre-piece and plant this round with Parsley, Thyme, Mint and Chives. These all do well provided the soil is not allowed to dry out.

Pot plants also keep a window box bright with flower. Fill an empty container with moist peat and plunge the pots in this. Water plants in the normal way.

CARE OF WINDOW BOXES

Normally tall-growing subjects are not desirable in front of a window, but where there is a good expanse of blank wall, wire netting or trellis can be

Fuchsias are excellent window box subjects

81

fixed behind the box, attached partly to the box and partly to the wall. Nasturtiums, Ivies, Canary Creeper *(Tropaeolum peregrina)* and other creepers can then be planted at the back of the box and trained to cover the trellis.

Constant watering packs the soil down hard, so loosen it occasionally with any small houseplant tool. It is only necessary to break the soil crust and leave it with a crumb-like structure.

You should neither let your plants become dry nor soak them so much that the soil becomes sodden. Casement windows should not be opened from the bottom (except for tending the plants) as draughts from behind will quickly ruin the plants.

The soil in the boxes should last 12—18 months, especially if a little liquid fertiliser is occasionally given to the plants when in flower.

If evergreens are used, sponge the foliage now and again with tepid water in which a little soft soap has been dissolved. This frees them of soot and grime. Even in summer a weekly syringe with clear water cleans and freshens the plants in a remarkable way.

Finally, remove dead leaves and flowers regularly, both to keep the boxes tidy and to encourage a succession of blooms.

HANGING BASKETS

Hanging Baskets were widely used in Victorian times and are now enjoying a revival. Although they may be used anywhere, they are particularly adapted to town gardens; hanging types are suitable for the adornment of porches or verandahs, and other kinds can be clipped on the side of a wall or door.

The chief drawback in use is the problem of watering, for being exposed on all sides they quickly dry out. Nor are they suited to very exposed or draughty situations. Supporting hooks and chains must also be strong and in an accessible position. The old wire-framed baskets lined with moss, which cannot adequately be watered from overhead, must be taken down and immersed in a bath of water for a few minutes, and then hung up to drain. Lining the basket with polythene reduces the frequency of this operation.

The framework of the basket may be made of various materials, such as galvanised, painted or plastic-covered wire, strips of wood nailed together, bamboo treated in similar fashion, or even terracotta pots with holes at intervals in the sides.

The usual procedure is to line the container with moss, pressing this firmly against the sides until there is about 1 in. on the bottom and slightly less towards the sides. Fill the basket with John Innes No. 1. Potting Compost and introduce the plants. Certain

trailing kinds such as *Campanula isophylla*, Lobelia, Creeping Jenny *(Lysimachia nummularia)*, or even small pieces of Asparagus Fern *(Asparagus sprengeri)* may be planted low down in the basket with their roots inside and the growths taken through the wires to the outside.

Some of the subjects used at the top may be of a trailing nature, but others should grow upright. Avoid tall plants which look straggly and are liable to break in the wind. When finished, the soil at the centre top should be lower than the sides, so that the moisture can penetrate during waterings.

This type of basket looks most attractive, but does need constant attention and watering. A more practical application for the busy person is to line the basket with polythene (instead of moss) and stand a saucer in the bottom. The saucer should contain a quantity of broken charcoal which will act as drainage and help to keep the soil sweet. Overhead watering will now be more effective as it will not drain through, but one must be careful not to overwater as standing moisture can cause root rot.

The usual plants seen in hanging baskets are Geraniums (Pelargoniums) of various kinds, especi-

Window box in Belgravia

J. E. Downward

Window box with Petunias and Lobelia

By courtesy of Home Magazine

Hanging basket of Fuchsia

J. E. Downward

ally the Ivy-leaved trailing sorts, Fuchsias, Petunias, blue Lobelia, Calceolarias and *Campanula isophylla* with blue, saucer-shaped flowers. Other plants which could be tried are Begonias, Stocks, French Marigolds, *Oxalis floribunda rosea*, variegated Nepeta, Bulbs and Ivies.

Bulbs & Corms

Under a general heading — BULBS — we usually include a number of plants which do not strictly fit into this category. A *true* bulbs is made up of thickened leaf modifications, as in the Lily or Onion, but there are others with underground storage organs which need similar cultural conditions, and so find themselves in the bulb grower's catalogue.

Thus CORMS, although similar in appearance, differ from bulbs in that they are solid right through, being made up of modified stems instead of leaves. Gladioli and Crocus are typical examples.

TUBERS are also thickened underground stems but have eyes or buds situated at various places to produce new shoots. They are also very variable in shape and size as in Ranunculus, *Anemone coronaria*, Cyclamen and tuberous Begonias.

Bulbs will grow anywhere, in town or country gardens, in woodlands, borders, grass, window boxes or even indoors. They are relatively inexpensive, and offer a wide range of shapes, scents and colours.

IN THE GARDEN

The hardier bulbs planted in a woodland or wild garden become virtually no-trouble plants. They seem to thrive on neglect, forming broad colonies with seeming indifference to soil types and situations.

Nevertheless, starvation conditions must in time reduce the quantity and quality of bloom, for the bulb is a storehouse and at the end of the season contains an embryo plant together with a reserve of food for next year's growth. When we buy bulbs they already contain the bloom or blooms for next season's display, so it is most important to purchase good bulbs from a reliable source.

When these have bloomed do not let them go on to seed, but water the foliage well in a dry season and from time to time manure the ground. One cannot too strongly condemn the current practice of knotting Daffodil leaves or reducing bulb foliage before it dies down naturally. A dry spring together with premature leaf reduction, are the main causes of so called 'blindness' in bulbs. Sufficient food must be available to ensure flowering in successive seasons and to this end the leaves must be left to complete their work.

An occasional mulch of really well rotted manure or compost works wonders with an old bulb colony, or the ground can be dressed with coarse bonemeal (4 oz. per sq.yd.) in autumn and watered when in leaf with dilute liquid manure.

GROWING BULBS OUTDOORS

Among the best types for geometrically designed beds are Hyacinths and Tulips. Their stiff, erect habit seems particularly suited to the regimentation and precise grouping we associate with formal bedding, whilst Hyacinths in particular are less subject to wind damage in window boxes and other exposed containers.

Where especially impressive displays are wanted choose solid, bright colours as in the early flowering Fosteriana Tulips and certain of the Darwins like 'Wm. Pitt' and 'Golden Hind', but for general use in suburban settings the softer shades often give more restful effects.

Tulips used for bedding purposes vary enormously in shapes and shades. In April we have the single and double early flowering sorts, followed by the

Crocus varieties
Walter Blom & Son

Mendel and Triumph strains which bloom a little earlier than the Cottage Tulips. The Darwins which follow these are perhaps the most popular, with good clean colours and erect habit, but in recent years Parrots, with variegated flowers of different colours, Lily types with reflexed petals, Bizarres and Breeders, both strikingly tinted, and the Viridifloras, whose flowers contain a good deal of green, have been much in demand both with gardeners and flower arrangers.

Various Narcissi can be used for bedding, although these are best associated with other flowers, such as Arabis and Forget-me-Nots. Bulbous Iris may be used in the same manner, growing through a thick under-carpeting of other plants, or Lilies in a woodland setting.

Very small beds can be made bright with De Caen or the St Brigid types of Anemones or the double flowered Turban and Giant French Ranunculus.

Plant outdoor bulbs with a trowel, but on no account leave them 'hanging' in a soil pocket. Special bulb trowels are obtainable with narrow blades which cut easily into the ground, and some of these have marked measurements for setting bulbs at the required depth. On very heavy soils it pays to sit the bulbs on a cushion of sand, or even to surround large loose-scaled types like *Fritillaria imperialis* and Lilies completely with a ½ in. sand layer.

For naturalising small areas of grass or woodland throw down bulbs at random and plant them where they fall. Lifting the turf and then replacing it leaves a neater finish but is laborious, though there is a bulb planter on the market which takes out a core of soil and turf, enabling the gardener to drop the bulb in the hole and then replace the turf.

On no account must the grass be cut before the leaves have turned yellow or ripened, normally about the end of June. This is one reason for grouping bulbs together in specific areas. A scythe (or shears, in the case of a small plot) makes the best cutting tool for the first cut; mowing will later restore the ground to a neater appearance.

Another good way of using bulbs is to plant them haphazardly in a rough piece of grassland to make an alpine lawn. Here native and foreign species of bulbs and flowers, such as Narcissi, Snowflakes (Leucojums), Crocus, Fritillarias, Geraniums (Cranesbills), Camassias and Kingcups (Calthas) may be allowed to colonise. This is an easy and labour-saving form of gardening, and one or two rough cuttings each season with an Allen or hand scythe will suffice.

Many Lilies are suited to woodland planting and also look well in association with Rhododendrons and Heathers. The following are fairly easy to grow and should be planted about the end of November,

Hyacinth 'Princess Irene'　　　　　Walter Blom & Sohn

Narcissus 'Snowball'　　　　　Walter Blom & Son

4–6 in. deep. In spring add another inch of soil and cover this with a thin layer of leaves or peat to keep the ground moist.

L. auratum, white with crimson or yellow spots and rays; *L. canadense*, clear yellow to deep orange; *L. henryi*, orange spotted; *L. martagon*, purple, white or pink; *L. pardalinum*, deep orange with maroon spots; *L. regale*, white, trumpet-shaped, sometimes flushed pink; *L. speciosum*, white with crimson spots; *L. tigrinum*, bright orange, spotted.

Leucojum aestivum
Copyright Ryder & Sons

BULB AND SPRING FLOWER COMBINATIONS FOR EARLY BEDDING

1. Tulip 'Queen of Bartigon' (rich pink) with Forget-me-Nots.
2. Blue Forget-me-Not studded with 'Golden Age' Tulip (Buttercup yellow).
3. A groundwork of yellow Alyssum studded with any Darwin or Cottage Tulip that is not yellow in colour.
4. Double Arabis interplanted with a Golden Trumpet Daffodil like 'King Alfred' or 'Lord Wellington'.
5. 'Mount Hood' (white trumpet) Daffodil and purple or mauve Aubrieta.
6. Very dark red Wallflowers with white and lemon yellow Tulips.
7. Blue and white Hyacinths edged with double pink Daisies.
8. Mass of pink and red shades of Wallflowers edged with double Arabis.
9. Bed of Polyanthus (blue shades) with a few white Tulips or 'Pheasant Eye' Narcissus.
10. Cottage or Darwin Tulips with Violas planted between.
11. White Narcissi with Forget-me-Nots planted between.
12. Aubrieta and white Tulips.
13. Parrot Tulips with a groundwork of Golden Alyssum.
14. White, cream and yellow Polyanthus interplanted with Tulips in bronze, apricot or yellow.
15. Pink, red or white double Daisies against a background of dark-coloured Tulips.
16. Double white Arabis and pink Tulips.
17. Evergreen, rosy-flowered Thrift (Armeria) with rosy Tulips.
18. Mauve Aubrieta, Golden Alyssum and white Tulips.

Sternbergia lutea

List of Plants

Bulbs Suitable for Naturalising in Grass and Woodland

Anemone apennina, A. blanda, A. nemorosa; Chionodoxa; Colchicum; *Crocus speciosus, C. tomasinianus, C. vernuus vars; Cyclamen neapolitanum; Endymion non-scriptus* (Bluebell); Eranthis (Winter Aconite); Erythronium (Dog's Tooth Violet); *Fritillaria meleagris;* Galanthus (Snowdrop); Muscari (Grape Hyacinth); Narcissus (various particularly *triandrus* and species); Ornithogalum (Star of Bethlehem);

Bulbs for the Rock Garden

Anemone apennina, A. blanda, A. fulgens, A. 'St Bavo'; Chionodoxa; Crocus, spring-flowering kinds, *C. speciosus;* Cyclamen; Eranthis; Erythronium; Galanthus (Snowdrop); *Iris danfordiae, I. histriodes, I. reticulata; Leucojum vernum* (Snowflake); Muscari; *Scilla sibirica;* Sternbergia; Tritelia (syn. Ipheion); Tulip (small flowered), *pulchella, kaufmanniana* hybrids, *fosteriana.*

Bulbs for Forcing and Pot Work

Hyacinths, large flowered, *H. cynthella,* and 'Roman'; Narcissi and Daffodils e.g. Helios, Golden Harvest, Cragford, King Alfred, Fortune etc; Tulips, especially Doubles and Cottage; Crocus; *Iris reticulata, I. danfordiae,* Spanish Vars.

ACHIMENES Hot Water Plant

Summer flowering, for the greenhouse or hanging baskets, with bright funnel-shaped flowers in shades of pink, purple, mauve and white. Plants are started in spring from dried off tubers, and set 1 to 1½ in. deep in boxes of sandy compost in a warm propagating frame or house. When growth starts plant several together in a pot or basket, pinching the first young shoots to induce bushy growth. Stake as necessary and dry off after flowering. Leave tubers in completely dry pots of soil all winter.

ACIDANTHERA

A. bicolor murielae should be grown like Gladioli, but start the corms in pots of sandy soil in April, turning these out carefully in a sunny, sheltered situation when the growths are a few inches high. Slow developers, often not blooming until Oct. Flowers pure white, with exceptionally long perianth tubes and a Plum-purple blotch at the base of each petal. Very fragrant. 2—3 ft.

AGAPANTHUS African Lily

Not really a bulb but usually included in growers' catalogues. Strong, strap-shaped leaves and showy umbels of blue, mauve or white flowers on 2—3 ft. stems. Hardy outside in warm situations. Often grown in tubs, put outside in summer and brought indoors for the winter. Keep fairly dry during the dormant season. *A. africanus* (syn. *umbellatus*) and *orientalis* are the main species. Plant in spring and feed occasionally in summer with liquid manure.

ALLIUM

The Ornamental Onions make attractive subjects for the border or rock garden. The majority need well drained soil and full sun. Small colonies should be planted 3 in. deep and about 12 in. apart. Several can be forced for the greenhouse, notably the golden-flowered *A. moly* which may also be used for naturalising and flowers May and June. 12 in.; also *A. neapolitanum,* white and green umbels of flowers. 18 in. Others are *A. caeruleum,* sky-blue, 1—2 ft.; *A. cyaneum,* turquoise-blue, 9—12 in.; *A. giganteum,* bright lilac, 3—4 ft.; *A. narcissiflorum,* pendulous, bell-shaped, pinkish-purple flowers on 12 in. stems; *A. karataviense,* large ball-like umbel (up to 1 ft. across) of whitish flowers; *A. siculum,* green and red hanging flowers on 3 ft. stems. Most bloom May—June.

AMARYLLIS Jersey Lily

A. belladonna does best in a warm, sheltered spot, as against a south facing house or greenhouse wall. Good drainage is essential and the plants, once established, should be left alone. Flowers appear without the leaves in Aug. or Sept., funnel-shaped, deep pink and fragrant, many on a stem. Leaves strap-shaped in spring; Var. 'Hathor' is white and 'Parkeri' deep pink. 1½—2 ft.

ANEMONE Wind Flower

All tuberous Anemones must be grown in full sun, in a rich but well drained soil. Tubers can be planted in autumn on light ground or during Feb. and March when it is heavy. Small monthly plantings ensure continuous cut blooms from the St Brigid types and except in warm light soils the tubers should be lifted and stored annually in June and July.

The most important of the tuberus kinds are *A. fulgens,* brilliant scarlet, 9—15 in.; *A. coronaria* which is the parent of several good strains such as St Brigid (mostly semi-double), De Caen or Giant French in a rich range of colours, and also of a number of named varieties with purple, red, crimson, mauve, white or pink flowers.

Anemones with rhizomatous roots are more tolerant of shade and any of the following are suitable for open patches in the shrubbery or a lightly shaded rock garden pocket. *A. apennina,* sky-blue on single 6 in. stems. This is the wild Anemone of

Group of spring flowers Walter Blom & Son

Grape Hyacinths (Muscari)   Copyright Fidlers of Reading

Acidanthera bicolor murielae   —   Copyright R. & G. Cuthbert

S. Europe and has given rise to white, pink and double forms. *A. blanda* needs full sun and is also deep blue. It comes to flower in Feb., before *A. apennina. A. nemorosa* is our native wild Anemone with single white blossoms on 6—8 in. stems. Varieties include several blue and a good double white. *A. ranunculoides*, also a native has yellow flowers. 8 in.

ANTHERICUM St Bernard's Lily
A. liliago. Summer border perennial which can be left in the ground. White, Lily-like flowers on 2 ft. stems; leaves Rush-like. Plant tubers 3—6 in. apart. Also suitable for wild garden.

ARISAEMA
Fascinating Arums with variously coloured flowers, mostly suited to moist soil and light shade. Mulch the ground now and again with moist peat and plant 3—4 in. deep. Leaves frequently 3-lobed or much divided.
A. candidissimum, spathe white-veined with pink and green, needs bog conditions; *A. dracontium*, Dragon Root, characterised by purplish spotted leaf stalks; flowers green; *A. triphyllum*, green with purple stripes. 1—2 ft.

ARUM
Includes the well known Lords and Ladies of the hedgerow. Flowers usually green with variously coloured stripes or flushes, followed by scarlet berries. Leaves arrow-shaped, smooth and deep green. *A. italicum var. marmoratum* has beautifully marbled green and white leaves, very useful in flower arranging. Plant in shade. 1 ft.

BABIANA
Require very warm situations outside (where the corms should be planted 6 in. deep), but highly suitable for pot work in a cool greenhouse. Plant corms in Nov. (6 to a 5 in. pot) and keep in a cold frame until they start to grow. Moved to the greenhouse, they should be well watered and gradually dried off when they begin to die down. Cup-shaped flowers frequently fragrant, in brilliant colours. 10—12 in.

BEGONIA See pp. 190 and 252.

BRODIAEA
Mostly from Western N. America, these summer-flowering corms are distinguished by umbels of tubular flowers and grassy leaves which disappear before the blossoms open. Full sun, protect with ashes in winter. *B. laxa, californica, pulchella* and *coronaria* all have blue flowers but *B. ida-maia*, the Californian Firecracker, less hardy, has scarlet flowers like short tubes — topped with yellowish green. General height 18 in.

BULBOCODIUM
B. vernum. Small bulbous plant suitable for alpine pans in the cool greenhouse or rock garden pockets. Flowers like small Colchicums, rosy-purple. March—April. 4 in. high. Plant Sept. 3 in. deep or 1 in. deep in pots.

CALOCHORTUS Mariposa Lily
Beautiful but not freely available plants with striking flowers, often several to a stem in a wide range of colours. Leaves narrow and grass-like. Seed takes about four years to come to bloom. Plant outside in Nov. or Feb., setting the bulbs on sand, in a sunny, sheltered position and 3 in. deep. They flower in June and July.

CAMASSIA Quamash
Hardy bulbous plants with many star-shaped flowers on prominent 2—3 ft. spikes. Leaves broadly strap-shaped. Suitable for naturalising or for the herbaceous border, the plants do best in a rather moist soil. Plant Sept. or Oct. about 4 ins. deep. The best blue-flowered species are *C. quamash* (syn.

Allium moly   Walter Blom & Son

situated at the fringe of the shrubbery or amongst shade-loving perennials. *C. autumnale* is the native species, with flowers about 2 in. long, with narrow, starry rosy-lilac segments. There are also white, purple and double forms in both shades.

C. byzantinum, *C. cilicum* and *C. speciosum* are other garden species and there are also some excellent varieties such as 'The Giant', 'Lilac Wonder', 'Water Lily' and *bornmulleri*.

CRINUM

Good for the base of a south facing wall, where they should be planted with part of the neck of the bulb out of the ground. Flowers very showy, several clustered at the top of a thick stem, hanging, funnel-shaped, pink or white. Leaves broadly strap-shaped. *C.* × *powellii* and its forms are the best. 2½—3 ft. July—Sept.

CROCOSMIA

Often called Montbretia, these are not generally hardy and are best lifted and stored like Gladioli in winter. Panicles of flowers and flat leaves arranged in a fan. Good soil and a sunny position. Varieties of *C.* × *crocosmiiflora* include 'His Majesty', orange and crimson; 'Star of the East', pale orange-yellow; 'Citronelle', lemon-yellow and 'Earlham Hybrids', in mixed shades. 2—3 ft. Aug.—Sept.

CROCUS

Very early flowering plants suitable for naturalising in grass and woodland, for forcing and pot work, also bedding purposes and in rock garden pockets. The majority favour full sun and well drained soil — including chalk. Plant 3—4 in. deep.

Careful selection can give blooms from late Aug. until April. The winter blossoms are particularly valuable and come in a wide range of colours although blooms are generally smaller than the large-flowered Dutch varieties. Some of the best varieties in each group, according to times of flowering, are:

Autumn Flowering

Late Aug.—Oct. Plant July.
C. specious, deep mauve to lavender, with var 'Oxonian' the deepest in colour; *C. byzantinus*, rich bluish-purple on outer parts, mauve in inner segments; *C. niveus*, white and yellow; *C. sativus*, mauve; *C. nudiflorus*, deep purple.

Winter Flowering

Dec.-mid-Feb. Plant Sept.—Oct.
C. aureus, rich orange; *C. chrysanthus* varieties, especially 'E. A. Bowles', yellow and bronze; 'Moonlight', sulphur-yellow; 'Snow Bunting', white, feathered lilac; 'Yellow Hammer', deep yellow; 'Blue Pearl', pale blue and 'Blue Bird', purplish-blue, margined white.

C. tomasinianus, very free flowering and seeds all over the place, bright mauve-lilac. Vars. 'Whitewell Purple' and 'Taplow Ruby' are improved forms. *C. laevigatus*, mauve.

Spring Flowering

Early Feb. — late March. Plant Sept.—Oct.
C. biflorus, white to lilac; *C. corsicus*, lilac-mauve; *C. sieberi* varieties, 'Violet Queen' and 'Bowles' White', and *C. versicolor*, white to purple.

Large Flowered Dutch Varieties

March—April. Plant Sept.—Oct. These are the best kinds for forcing and massing in grass.
White 'Joan of Arc', 'Kathleen Parlow' and 'Snowstorm'.
Deep Purple 'Negro Boy', *purpureus grandiflorus*, 'Remembrance' and 'The Bishop'.
Yellow 'Dutch Yellow'.
Pale Mauve 'Enchantress', 'Vanguard' and 'Queen of the Blues'.

esculenta) and *C. cusickii*. *C. leichtlinii* is more variable with white, cream, blue or purple flowers and there is also a form with double lemon-yellow blooms.

CARDIOCRINUM

C. giganteum (syn. *Lilium giganteum*). A magnificent woodland plant growing up to 10 ft. high, with up to 20 glistening white, fragrant, trumpet-shaped blooms on the leafy stems. Plant the large, dark green bulb with the tip at ground level in peaty Rhododendron soil. Dies after flowering but leaves several offsets which can be divided.

CHIONODOXA Glory of the Snow

Small bulbous plants for rock garden pockets, alpine pans, window boxes etc. Bright blue flowers in clusters on 6—8 in. stems. *C. luciliae* and *C. sardensis* are two good species. Plant early autumn 3 in. deep.

Chionodoxa luciliae has been crossed with *Scilla bifolia*, producing hybrids known as Chionoscillas, usually darker blue and taller than the parents.

COLCHICUM Naked Boys, Son before the Father

Often mistakenly called Autumn Crocus, but distinguished by large and rather coarse leaves on tall leafy stems. Best

Pale Mauve with Darker Stripes 'Striped Beauty', 'Cinderella' and 'Mikado'.

CYCLAMEN

Hardy outdoor Cyclamen are practically ground-cover plants, favouring semi-shaded situations as at the base of trees or in the rock garden. If carefully tended they will colonise to make large patches. Since the corms remain close to or just above the surface they are easily hoed up or disturbed by sharp tools, so hand weeding is essential. An occasional mulch of well rotted leaf-mould is beneficial, as is a sprinkling of bonemeal.

Flowers are mostly mauvish or pale pink but white forms are common. After flowering, the stems contract like a coiled spring to ripen the seeds, which are then scattered on the ground. To increase stock these should be gathered and sown in pots of leafy soil in a cold frame before planting them outdoors.

C. neapolitanum produces roots from its upper surface and must be planted 2—3 in. deep with the smooth, dome side of the corm downwards.

Autumn Flowering

C. neapolitanum, *C. europaeum* and *C. graecum*. The first is the hardiest.

Spring Flowering

C. orbiculatum and *var. coum* (the hardiest), *C. libanoticum* and *C. repandum*, all of which are equally suitable for alpine pans in cold districts or outside in mild areas.

DIERAMA Wand Flower

D. pulcherrimum, a beautiful plant for the herbaceous border with very thin, arching, 4—6 ft. stems carrying numerous bell-shaped, hanging flowers. Leaves sword-shaped. Flowers purple, mauve, wine-red and white. Aug. Plant 3 in. deep in Nov. in well drained soil and full sun.

ENDYMION Bluebell

Well known garden and woodland plants suitable for moist,

Crocus speciosus   Walter Blom & Son

shady situation. *E. non-scriptus* (syn. *Scilla nutans*) is our native Bluebell, but the Spanish counterpart *E. hispanicus* is much larger and better for garden work. Pink, white and deep blue varieties are available. May. Plant in autumn 4—5 in. deep.

ERANTHIS Winter Aconite

Early-flowering plants like large Buttercups with ruff collars of bright green leaves. Suitable for sun or shade. Plant soon after flowering, 3 in. deep, or Sept.—Oct. Best kinds for the garden are *E. x tubergenii* and 'Guinea Gold'. 3—5 in. Feb.—March.

ERYTHRONIUM Dog's Tooth Violet

Delightful little plants for sun or shade with backward-pointing petals and plain green or spotted leaves. Soil should be leafy and well drained. Plant bulbs in Sept. 3—4 in. deep. *E. dens-canis* prefers light shade, flowers variable from white and pink to deep Fuchsia-mauve with orange-red markings round the base. Leaves beautifully mottled. 6 in. March—April.

Colchicum 'Water Lily'   Walter Blom & Son

E. tuolumnense, golden-yellow flowers with pale green leaves. 1 ft. *E. hendersonii*, particularly beautiful foliage and pale lilac flowers with purple markings. 6 in. April. *E. revolutum*, white or pink flowers, leaves heavily mottled. 8 in. April—May.

EUCOMIS
E. comosa (syn. *punctata*), a curious plant with a small tuft of leaves, like a Pineapple, at the top of the flower stem and spikes of yellowish-green flowers. Leaves lanceolate, 2—3 ft.

colonies. Sun or light shade. Varieties have single or double flowers, also, in one case, yellow instead of green markings on the blossoms. *G. nivalis reginae-olgae* flowers in Oct. but most appear in Jan.—Feb.

GALTONIA
G. candicans (syn. *Hyacinthus candicans*). Fine border bulb with stout green stems 3—4 ft. high, carrying many pendulous, pure white, fragrant, bell-like flowers. Leaves strap-shaped.

Double Tulips   Walter Blom & Son

Anemone 'St. Brigid'   Copyright Samuel Dobie & Son

July—Aug. The large bulb should be planted 6—8 in. deep and protected with ashes in winter. Does best against a warm wall.

FRITILLARIA
A large family with many species, the following recommended for the garden.

F. imperialis, Crown Imperial. 4 ft. high plant, growing with strong stems terminating in a tuft of leaves like the top of a Pineapple. Flowers, large, showy and arranged in a circle round the stem, are usually orange, orange-scarlet or golden, but there are also varieties with double flowers and variegated leaves. A curious characteristic of the blooms is the presence of white nectaries, which look like unshed tears. Bulbs should be set 5—6 in. deep in July or Aug. and encased all round with sand. They like well drained but moist soil and full sun.

F. meleagris, Snake's Head. A pretty native for naturalising in grass or open woodland, with slender stems terminating in large, hanging, white or purple-chequered flowers. April. 12—15 in. Plant 3 in. deep in Sept. Sun or light shade and moist soil.

GALANTHUS Snowdrop
Well known spring flower with many uses in the garden. Bulbs should be planted in early autumn, about 3 in. deep, in

Likes sun and well drained soil and may be left years without disturbance. Plant Sept. or April, 6 in. deep.

GLADIOLUS
Most of the garden forms of this well known genus are of hybrid origin. Corms should be planted 3—4 in. deep from March until early May in full sunshine and well drained soil. If the latter is heavy, rest these on a little sand to prevent standing moisture and possible corm rot.

After flowering, the plants should be lifted, dried, cleaned and stored in a dry, frostproof place. Small cormlets (usually known as spawn) may be grown on in frames or small borders to produce new stock. Plants will require staking, especially with the large-flowered types. For cutting purposes gather when the bottom flowers are just opening.

Varieties are obtainable in white, yellow, orange, light and dark pink, scarlet, red, crimson, mauve and purple.

G. primulinus with hooded, pale yellow flowers has been hybridised with the large-flowered types to produce the Primulinus varieties, smaller and daintier than the latter, but also with hooded petals. Midget-flowered. Miniature-flowered and Small-flowered strains are also obtainable.

There is also a small race of early-flowering varieties often used for pot work or in small sunny borders. They include 'The Bride', pure white; 'Peach Blossom', shell-pink; 'Spitfire', salmon with violet spots and 'Nymph', white with crimson flecks. Height up to 2 ft. April—June.

HERMODACTYLUS Widow Iris
H. tuberosus (syn. *Iris tuberosa*). A hardy plant with strange, Iris-like flowers of greenish-yellow and blackish-purple. April—May. 1 ft. Warm, sunny position. Can also be forced in pots.

HYACINTHUS Hyacinth
Popular, fragrant plants for flowering outside in early spring. Suitable for bedding, window boxes, rock gardens etc. when they should be planted 3—4 in. deep and 6—8 in. apart about Oct. Sun and well drained soil. For details of forcing see p. 118.

White	'L'Innocence', 'Blom's Gem', 'Hoar Frost', 'Queen of the Whites'.
Yellow	'City of Haarlem', 'Yellow Hammer', 'Prince Henry'.
Pale Blue	'Delft Blue', 'Myosotis', 'Winston Churchill', 'Queen of the Blues'.
Deep Blue	'Purple King', 'King of the Blues', 'Ostara'.
Pink	'Pink Pearl', 'Princess Margaret', 'Lady Derby', 'Delight'.
Red	'La Victoire', 'Tubergen's Scarlet', 'John Bos'.

SPECIES HYACYNTHS
H. amethystinus for rock garden or pot work. Porcelain-blue. March—April. 8 in. There is also a white form.
H. azureus. Flowers densely clustered, deep azure-blue, 6—10 in. March—April. Plant both species 3 in. deep in autumn.

IPHEION
I. uniflorum (syn. *Triteleia* and *Brodiaea uniflora*). A charming hardy plant which deserves to be more widely grown. Grassy leaves and masses of single star-shaped, pale mauve fragrant flowers. March—April. Sun or light shade and well drained soil. Increases rapidly. Suitable for edging purposes and in the rock garden. 6—8 in.

IRIS
Dutch Irises make particularly fine cut flowers, coming into bloom before the Spanish Irises, in June, and growing about 2 ft. tall. Plant the bulbs in well drained soil and a sunny position about Oct. Lift and dry off after flowering. English Irises appreciate a moister position and bloom later (June—Aug.). These can remain in the ground.

DUTCH IRISES
Blue and Purple	'King Mauve', 'Saxe Blue', 'Wedgwood'.
Yellow	'Alaska', 'Golden Harvest', 'Lemon Queen'.
White	'Jeanne d'Arc', 'White Pearl'.

ENGLISH IRISES
Blue	'King of the Blues', 'The Giant'.
White	'Montblanc'.

SPANISH IRISES
Blue	'Hercules', 'Reconnaissance' (purple and bronze).
Yellow	'Cajanus'.
White	'King of the Whites', 'Queen Wilhelmina'.

Other Bulbous Irises
The following are suitable for the rock garden and alpine pans in a cool greenhouse. The majority favour sunshine and light, well drained soil; they do not take well to forcing. Plant early autumn.
I. danfordiae. Flowers bright yellow 2 in. across on 4 in. stems.

Sparaxis tricolor   Copyright Samuel Dobie & Son

Jan.—Feb.; *I. histrioides major*, deep blue, with yellow markings on 3 in. stems. A beautiful plant often flowering in mid-Jan.; *I. reticulata*, height 6—8 in. with violet-scented, deep blue flowers with yellow markings. Foliage grassy. Forms include 'Cantab', Cambridge blue; 'J.S. Dijt', reddish-purple; 'Krelagei', very similar and 'Harmony', deep sky-blue. Feb.—March.

By placing a sheet of glass over the plants just before they come to flower the blooms are protected from the weather.

Fleshy Rooted Irises
These require a heavy but well drained soil and full sun and must have a thorough baking period in summer, so are best protected after flowering by glass, raised on bricks to give good air circulation. Among the commonest species are *I. bucharica*, white and yellow, 12—18 in. and *I. vicaria*, bluish-white, 2 ft. Plant about Sept. to flower in April.
I. unguicularis (syn. *stylosa*). A delightful evergreen species which must be planted in light, well drained soil and a warm, sunny situation. Flowers lavender-blue with gold markings. Buds appear from Nov. to March and are invaluable for winter home decoration. 9—12 in.

IXIA Corn Lily
S. African corms producing dainty star-like flowers on thin, wiry stems. Not very hardy so protect with glass in winter,

Daffodils in spring　　　　Walter Blom & Son

Gladiolus nanus 'Nymph'　　Walter Blom & Son

grow in pots or lift and replant in March. Sandy, well drained soil with plenty of sun. *I. viridiflora* has sea-green flowers with a curious central blotch. Others are 'Azurea', violet with a darker centre; 'Bridesmaid', white and red; 'Hogarth', creamy-yellow with a purple centre; 'Vulcan', scarlet. Nurserymen also sell mixed varieties which give a good colour range.

LACHENALIA Cape Cowslip

Plant for the cool greenhouse, with a minimum winter temperature of 45°F. Pot 5 or 6 bulbs in a 5 inch pot of rich soil about July or Aug. for blooms in early spring. After flowering gradually withhold water and rest the bulbs until July when they can be restarted. *L. aloides* has tubular green flowers edged with red and yellow, about 20 or so on a stem. Leaves mottled with purple blotches. Var. 'Nelsonii', bright golden, is a form from this. March—April. *L. bulbifera* has plain green leaves and purple, green and yellow flowers. 1 ft.

LEUCOJUM Snowflake

Resemble overgrown Snowdrops, but with all the perianth segments of equal length (instead of three long ones and three short) and longer stems. They like a moist soil and do well amongst shrubs or in the wild garden. Useful for cutting. *L. vernum* is the Spring Snowflake and has one or two flowers on 8 in. stems. Feb.—March. *L. aestivum* Summer Snowflake blooms from mid-April onwards, with several flowers in a terminal umbel on 2 ft. stems. *L. autumnale* has white flowers tinged with pink on 8 in. stems in Sept., and needs a warmer position.

LILIUM Lily

The aristocrat of bulbous plants, varying tremendously in form, colour and habit. Some are very difficult to grow but others go on for years in the garden if happily situated. Suitable for pot work, sunny or shaded borders (according to variety) and valuable for cutting. The majority like a rich moisture-retentive soil.

Some Lilies, particularly the stem-rooting kinds such as *L. regale, speciosum, auratum* and *tigrinum*, need deeper planting, about 6 in. deep, or else set 4 in. deep and top-dressed with 2 in. or so of good leafy soil when they start to grow. Never allow bulbs to become dry and if for any reason they are lifted, cover with fairly dry peat moss. Planting takes place from mid-September although they may also be transplanted in April when they have just started to grow.

Madonna Lilies make secondary growths in autumn and must therefore be planted in Aug. with only about an inch of soil over the bulbs. This also applies to *L. x testaceum*.

L. longiflorum, auratum, speciosum, regale and *brownii* are good pot plants and should be set one to a 6 in. pot in John Innes No. 1. Potting Compost. Stem rooters must be kept low in the pot and gradually have the compost added as the plants grow. Cool greenhouse treatment suits them best.

MUSCARI Grape Hyacinth

Small bulbous plants for sun or light shade with clusters of blue or white flowers like small Grapes on the 6 in. stems. Foliage narrow, strap-shaped. Suitable for edging, as cut flowers or for alpine pans and in the rock garden.

Varieties 'Blue Pearl', 'Heavenly Blue' and the white *botryoides album* are all worth growing. April. *M. plumosum* flowers in May with curious mauve heads of plumy growth. 8 in.

NARCISSUS Daffodil

Plants with many uses and indispensable for early cut flowers. Plant bulbs outdoors between late Aug. and Nov., and cover with about twice their own depth of soil. Any good garden soil, possibly enriched from time to time with a dressing of bonemeal (4 oz. per sq. yd.) in sun or partial shade. Bulbs should be periodically lifted, divided and replanted or the blooms will become small.

There are a number of species and groups with hundreds of varieties. A few kinds of each are included here. Most of them flower in March and April.

Bulbocodium group *(N. bulbocodium)* — Hoop Petticoat Daffodil var. 'Peeping Tom'. Alpine meadows, rock and pot work. Expanded trumpet, small outer segments.

Cyclamineus group *(N. cyclamineus)*. Naturalising in grass, rock garden. Petal segments laid back, Cyclamen-like.

Jonquil group *(N. jonquilla, N. juncifolius)*. Naturalising. Several flowers on stem, very fragrant.

Poeticus group *(N. poeticus)* — Pheasant's Eye, Actaea, Queen of Narcissi. Wild and formal gardening. Mostly white, small cups, very fragrant.

Tazetta group *(N. tazetta)* — Cheerfulness, Cragford, Geranium, Soleil d'Or. Cutting, rock and formal gardening. Several flowers bunched on stem, very fragrant.

Triandrus group *(N. triandrus albus)* — Silver Chimes, Thalia. Forcing and rock garden. Several white flowers on stem, very fragrant.

Dwarf Trumpet group *(N. asturiensis* syn. *minima)*, *N. minor*. Rock garden. Miniature flowers.

Garden Forms

Large Trumpets: Beersheba, Golden Harvest, King Alfred, Mount Hood, Mrs. E.H. Krelage, Spellbinder, Vester Prince.
Medium Trumpets: Carlton, Fermay, Fortune, Mrs. R.O. Backhouse, Niphetos.
Short Trumpets: Blarney, Chinese White, Frigid.
Doubles: *albus plenus odoratus*, Camellia, Inglescombe, Snowball.

NERINE

Very beautiful S. African bulbs with umbels of rich pink flowers in autumn, best suited to pot or border culture in the greenhouse but *N. bowdenii* may be grown outside in a warm, well drained and sunny situation. Good cut blooms. *N. sarniensis* is the Guernsey Lily, 2 ft.; 'Fenwick's Variety', 'Hera' and 'Pink Beauty' are forms of *N. bowdenii*. 2—2½ ft. Sept.—Nov.

NOMOCHARIS

Allied to Lilies and plants for cool, moist positions in partial shade. Not always easy to grow. Flowers saucer-shaped, pink or white, often spotted with deeper pinks or purples. 2—3 ft. June—July.

ORNITHOGALUM

O. umbellatum is the Star of Bethlehem, a rapid spreader in shrubberies and grass, with clusters of white flowers striped with green. April—May. *O. thyrsoides*, the Chincherinchee, should be treated in the same way as Gladioli, planted 4 in. deep in April to flower in summer. 2 ft. *O. nutans* is another good species. 1½ ft. April—May. Flowers greenish. Light sandy soil suits all species.

RANUNCULUS

Brightly coloured plants of the Buttercup family. The claw-shaped tubers should be planted 2 in. deep on a little sand, claws downwards. Plant the Giant French kinds Feb.—March; Turban varieties, Nov.—March. Sun and moist soil when growing. Lift tubers in July and store until planting time. Good cut flowers. May—June. 12—18 in.

SCHIZOSTYLIS Kaffir Lily

S. coccinea has spikes of scarlet flowers on 1—2 ft. stems in late summer (Oct.). Likes a moist soil and a sheltered position, sun. 'Viscountess Byng' is soft pink.

SCILLA Squill

Closely allied to Chionodoxa and needing similar treatment outdoors. *S. sibirica* flowers March and April and grows about

Iris danfordiae Walter Blom & Son

Ixias Copyright Samuel Dobie & Son

4 in. tall with bright blue flowers. Suitable for pans or rock garden. There is also a white form. *S. tubergiana*, flowers pale blue with darker stripes down the petals. 4. in. *S. peruviana* flowers in May and June and has conical heads of blue, starry flowers on 6 – 12 in. stems. All Scillas should be planted in autumn, 3 in. deep. Sun or light shade. See also ENDYMION.

SPARAXIS Harlequin Flower

Vividly coloured flowers, similar to and needing the same treatment as Ixias. Flowers April or May, 15 – 18 in., blooms orange, red, pink and purple, with prominent dark throats.

STERNBERGIA

S. lutea is like a yellow Crocus and flowers Sept. — Nov. It needs very good drainage and full sun, as in the rock garden or a sheltered border. Plant the bulbs about 4 in. deep and leave undisturbed when happy. It will not flower well unless these get a good baking. 6 in.

TIGRIDIA Tiger Flower

Very beautiful but short-lived flowers, with cup-shaped perianth and three petal-like segments. Brilliant colours — orange, yellow, red, purple and white, often spotted with crimson. Plant in a warm, sheltered position, 4 in. deep on sand, in April. Plants bloom in Aug. and should be lifted in Oct., dried and stored away from frost in winter. Propagate as for Gladioli. 2 ft. Flowers often 4 in. across.

TULIPA Tulip

Much-prized garden flowers for window boxes, rock gardens, cut flowers, display beds or forcing. All require plenty of sunshine and well drained but rich soil. The following are representative of the various groups.

Early Single — Apricot Beauty, apricot; Brilliant Star, scarlet; De Wet, orange; Van der Neer, dark purple; Princess Margaret, pink; White Hawk, white.

Early Double — Golden King, yellow; Jan Steen, orange; Peach Blossom, rosy-pink; Scarlet Cardinal, scarlet; Snow Queen, white.

Mendel — Dreaming Maid, clover-pink; Her Grace, white with rosy edge; Orange Wonder, orange-scarlet; Sulphur Triumph, primrose-yellow.

Triumph — Aureol, cherry-red; Garden Party, pink and white; Korneforos, cerise; Makassa, canary-yellow; Reforma, butter-yellow.

Darwin — Clara Butt, bright rose; Glacier, creamy-white; Golden Hind, deep yellow; Niphetos, soft lemon-yellow; Noble, bright red; Queen Bartigon, rich salmon-rose; Queen of Night, deep maroon, almost black; William Pitt, crimson.

Lily-flowered — Capt. Fryatt, deep burgundy; China Pink, soft pink; Philemon, lemon; Queen of Sheba, rusty red; White Triumphator, pure white.

Parrot — Blue Parrot, mauve and lavender; Fantasy, pink and green; Opal Queen, blue and white; Red Parrot, deep scarlet and red; Sunshine, yellow.

Bizarre and Rembrandt — Absolon, yellow and mahogany; Montgomery, white and vermilion; Nymph, mahogany and purple.

Cottage — Belle Jaune, golden yellow; Groenland, green and rose; G.W. Leak, orange-red with white base; Marshal Haig, bright scarlet; *viridiflora praecox*, yellow and green.

Fosteriana — Mme. Lefeber (syn. Red Emperor), fiery red; *purissima*, white; Rockery Beauty, scarlet.

Kaufmanniana — Alfred Cortot, scarlet and black; Gluck, yellow and carmine; The First, white with yellow base.

Species — *persica*, yellow; *praestans*, orange-scarlet; *pulchella*, rosy-violet; *tarda*, yellow, white-tipped.

Tigridias　　　　　　　　H. Smith

Lilium speciosum roseum　　　　　　Walter Blom & Son

ZANTEDESCHIA Arum Lily

Z. aethiopica is the well known White Arum, with glossy, arrow-shaped leaves and gold and white flowers. Not normally hardy but a recent variety called 'Crowborough' will live outside in warmer areas. Needs a warm position, plenty of moisture in summer but best kept on the dry side in winter. 3 ft. Summer-flowering, or may be forced in pots to bloom around Easter.

Note: For bulbs growing in bowls see page 118

Gladioli 'Green Woodpecker'   Copyright Samuel Dobie & Son

Parrot Tulips   Copyright Fidlers of Reading

Chrysanthemums

As the Rose is to the western world, so for centuries the Chrysanthemum has been the flower of the east. We know the Chinese cultivated blooms in 500 B.C., and that the Japanese held Chrysanthemum shows in 900 A.D., but in fact they have always been loved in the Orient and now, in this century, seem set to be equally popular here.

The reasons are several. Chrysanthemums are easy to grow yet are hobbyist's flowers, for to obtain exhibition blooms calls for great skill and twelve months' care and attention. They also appear at a time when garden flowers are scarce, and are attractive and long lasting when cut. The blooms are fragrant and — greatest lure of all — there is always a chance that a new type or colour will arise. Many varieties originated in this way in amateurs' gardens.

The three main groups are INCURVED, INCURVING and REFLEXED.

Incurved varieties should have all their florets curved inwards, tightly and firmly in regular formation to make a globular-shaped bloom.

Incurving varieties should have breadth and depth in equal proportion and the florets incurved, but are not so tightly packed as the Incurved.

Reflexed blooms have florets that point outwards, the outside petals very often drooping. Some Reflexed varieties may have their inner florets curving inwards but they still remain in the reflexed class because the outer florets extend outwards and downwards.

For show purposes these three main groups are further sub-divided according to size of bloom. A prospective exhibitor should therefore consult the National Chrysanthemum Society's 'Classified Catalogue of Varieties' in order to avoid placing an exhibit in the wrong section.

Classification also depends on the time of year

Outdoor spray Chrysanthemum 'Bridal Robe'
Copyright R. & G. Cuthbert

a variety normally commences to flower. Thus 'Early Flowering Chrysanthemums' are those which bloom whilst growing in the open ground, without any attention, before Oct. 1st; 'Mid-Season' are October flowering varieties, and 'Late Flowering Chrysanthemums' November and December blooming.

Early Flowering Chrysanthemums spend most of their life in the open garden and are therefore very suitable for the amateur gardener with limited time.

Mid-Season and Late Chrysanthemums grow in pots all their lives. They stand outside for the summer months but must be taken into the greenhouse during the first week in Oct.

PROPAGATION

Named varieties of Chrysanthemums are usually started from cuttings — only occasionally are they reproduced from seed or by splitting up the old clumps.

Early Flowering Chrysanthemums

The old roots or stools are normally wintered in a cold frame, packed closely together in old potting compost, or a sand-peat mixture. During February young shoots emerge from the stools and are used for cuttings. For details of making and rooting these, see p. 238. It is usual to dip each cutting in a solution of insecticide before insertion in the rooting medium.

'Evelyn Bush', a white, incurving variety   Walter Blom & Son

Given a temperature of 50°F. the cuttings should be rooted in two to three weeks and should then be individually potted in 3 in. pots, using John Innes No. 1. Potting Compost. This compost should be just moist (i.e. in potting condition), so that it will not be necessary to water again for several days. This is very important. In order to obtain new root action it is advisable to raise the temperature 5°, giving slight shade from strong sunlight and a light overhead spray (with plain water) each day.

When the plants are established they should be placed where they will receive the maximum amount of light. Poor lighting conditions cause drawn plants. Ventilation is also important at this stage and plenty or air should be allowed on sunny days. The aim generally should be to keep temperatures between 40°F. (minimum night temperature) and 60°F. (maximum day temperature).

As the plants develop the pots will need spacing out at greater distances to avoid the effects of overcrowding. Watering must be regularly and carefully carried out, and prompt measures taken should Greenfly make an appearance.

About mid-April the young Chrysanthemums must be transferred, still in their pots, from the greenhouse to a cold frame for 'hardening off'. On mild or sunny days the frames should be fully ventilated, or, if the frame lights are easy to handle, they may be removed altogether.

On the other hand, if night frosts are expected it may be necessary not only to replace the lights but also to cover them with insulating material such as straw, old sacks, reed mats etc. Such material should of course be removed in the daytime. Three weeks in the cold frame should produce strong, sturdy plants, ready for planting outside during the first two weeks in May.

Soil Preparation for Outdoor Chrysanthemums

Chrysanthemums respond well to thorough soil preparation. The ground must be deeply dug during the autumn and incorporated with liberal quantities of organic matter (well rotted stable manure, compost, straw etc.). The soil may be left in rough condition during the winter, then forked over in March or April. Prior to this last cultivation, a base fertiliser dressing should be applied so that it may be worked into the top 6 in. of soil. The following will give good results:

Hoof and horn meal at 4 oz. per sq.yd.
Bone meal   „ 4 „ „ „
Sulphate of Potash   „ 2 „ „ „

PLANTING

Outdoor Chrysanthemums are most conveniently

Large cream variety   Copyright R. & G. Cuthbert

Large bronze variety   Copyright R. & G. Cuthbert

planted in rows, about 2 ft. apart, or a little more if space allows.

Plants may be spaced about 16 in. apart in the rows. As they have to be knocked out from pots, roots should be given a good watering the previous evening. Planting should be carried out carefully and firmly, using a trowel. In wet weather, the planter standing on a planting board avoids compacting the soil surface.

A 5 ft. bamboo cane should then be placed alongside each plant, and the first tie made immediately planting is finished. Chrysanthemum stems are very brittle so that tying goes on continuously, as and when necessary, throughout the growing season.

Water if required, and during drought periods give the plants an overhead spray in the evenings.

Feeding

About a month after planting, a general fertiliser may be applied. There are many proprietary Chrysanthemum fertilisers which must be used according to instructions, the important point being not to overfeed. Three or four applications, at three week intervals, are usually sufficient in a season.

STOPPING

The term 'stopping' refers to the removal of the growing point of the rooted cutting, in order to encourage growth of side shoots or 'breaks' earlier than under normal conditions. Some varieties break naturally, but a good Chrysanthemum catalogue will not only state if a variety *has* to be stopped, but also give the date *when* it should be practised. The usual time for stopping Early Chrysanthemums is about one week after planting out.

Rubellum Chrysanthemum 'Clara Curtis'

Large pink variety　　　Copyright R. & G. Cuthbert

Disbudding

The smaller buds clustered round the Crown Buds have to be removed to obtain one large flower per stem. 'Disbudding' must be carried out regularly, the smaller buds being removed very carefully, in order to avoid damaging the one retained. Side shoots lower down the stem should also be pinched out.

Rubellums and Koreans

Rubellum and Korean Chrysanthemums are hardy varieties, useful for cutting, which produce sprays of flowers and need no staking or disbudding. They can be grown alone or in the mixed border with Michaelmas Daisies and Phlox. Split the old roots each April or May and replant the pieces. This makes for more and better flowers.

The Windsor Hybrids, Otley and Cushion Chrysanthemums are all forms of Korean Chrysanthemums.

MID-SEASON AND LATE FLOWERING VARIETIES

After flowering, these are cut down and wintered in a cold greenhouse or frame in exactly the same way as the Early Flowering Varieties, except that they remain in their pots.

Between late December and early February these stools produce young shoots, which can be removed and treated as cuttings. Management is exactly the same as for the 'earlies', the rooted cuttings being transferred to 3 in. pots of John Innes No. 1 Potting Compost.

About the first week in April, the plants become potbound and are then repotted (using John Innes No. 2 Potting Compost) into 5 in. pots. Hardening off in cold frames will commence towards the end of April.

The final repotting, using 9 in. pots and John Innes No. 3 Potting Compost occurs from the middle of May onwards, according to the vigour of the variety. It is very important to make sure that the plants are firmly planted in these final pots.

Now the plants have to stand outside, so select a level site. The pots must not rest on soil, yet free drainage is required, so the ideal is to have a clean bed of ashes or shingle for the standing ground. Large plants can be protected against strong winds by tying the bamboo canes in the pots to a wire, about 3 ft. high, stretched tightly between two stout end posts.

Plants in pots very quickly become dry, so regular watering is essential. So is feeding, which should commence about six weeks after the final potting

After stopping, several side shoots will be produced, and the six strongest of these should be retained. For exhibition work some gardeners retain only three or four.

At the end of each shoot a flower bud will appear, known as the 'First Crown Bud'. If these shoots are stopped again, (by pinching out the growing points) no first crown buds will develop, but a crop of secondary side shoots will grow from the point of stopping and go on to make other terminal flower buds, known as 'Second Crown Buds'. The secondary side shoots will of course be thinned out so that only four to six second crown buds are allowed to develop. Should the side shoots not be removed the plant would go on to make a final tier of blooms, known as sprays, which are much smaller but often useful for border display.

Early Flowering Chrysanthemums need only a single stopping. Second Crown Buds are, however, frequently (but not invariably) required on Late Flowering Varieties.

101

and must continue fortnightly until colour starts to show in the flower buds.

Just before the first frosts are expected (early October), the plants should be removed to the greenhouse. Artificial heat will not be required at first, the aim being to keep temperatures around 50°F. Full ventilation will often be required during the daytime, but as winter comes on a little artificial heat may be needed.

Stopping and disbudding will again be necessary. Times of stopping and the advisability of flowering the plants on First or Second Crown Buds differs with varieties, but the following instructions are typical of those appearing in catalogues:

1. Natural break, First Crown.
   (allow the plant to break naturally and use First Crown Buds).
2. Stop April 20th for First Crown.
3. Natural break, Second Crown.
4. Stop May 1st and June 1st for Second Crown.

ALL-THE-YEAR-ROUND CHRYSANTHEMUMS

Chrysanthemums can be purchased in flower all the year round, not only in autumn, thanks to special cultural conditions, particularly in relation to light.

Chrysanthemums normally come to bloom when the hours of darkness lengthen, i.e. in autumn. By artificially anticipating such conditions (as by giving the plants 12 hours complete darkness in mid-summer), they are induced to 'put down' buds before those left untreated. These go on to produce early

'Leda', an early flowering variety   Copyright R. & G. Cuthbert
'Mrs Huggett', a large incurving exhibition Chrysanthemum
Copyright R. & G. Cuthbert

Sturdy shoot suitable for cuttings   By courtesy of Home Magazine

102

flowers. Similarly, plants can be retarded by giving them artificial light (i.e. extending the natural period of daylight) in the autumn. They will then only put down buds when conditions return to normal. By these methods, Chrysanthemum flowers can be obtained all the year round.

SOME VARIETIES OF CHRYSANTHEMUMS

Outdoor Kinds

EARLY FLOWERING Amy Shoesmith, beautiful pink; Bella, pink; Brumas, pure white; C.E. Morris, clear yellow; Enid Walters, pale pink; Ermine, snow-white; George McLeod, rich yellow; Goldcoast, rich yellow; Golden Rule, golden-yellow; Hope Valley, pale pink; Life Guard, deep crimson; Mauve Princess, mauve and silvery-pink; reflexed; Pennine Snow, pure white; Red Leader, glowing red; Silver Dollar, flushed purple; Summer Snow, white; Sylvia Riley, old rose; Topper, light bronze; Volcano, orange-bronze, spiky petals. Westfield Bronze, orange-bronze; Xenia Field, rose-pink.

RUBELLUMS Anna Hay, pastel shade of shell pink; Ann, Lady Brockett, pinky apricot; Duchess of Edinburgh, glowing red; Jessie Cooper, copper-red; Mary Stoker, soft canary-yellow; Paul Boissier, orange-bronze.

OTLEY KOREANS Amber Glory, deep golden yellow; Autumn Glow, reddish bronze; Christine, rosy-pink; Harvester, old gold, flushed orange; Rosina, petunia-rose; Sungold, deep golden, yellow.

WINDSOR HYBRIDS Ariel, bright red; Bardolph, light red, Celia, soft coral pink; Kate, lovely clear yellow; Oswald, terra-cotta; Viola, pure rose pink.

EARLY FLOWERING OUTDOOR POMPON Cameo, pure white; Fairy, strawberry-pink; Imp, deep glowing crimson; Kim, bright scarlet-bronze; Tommy Trout, deep amber; Trudie, delicate pale pink.

KOREANS Cattleya, rosy-mauve; Falstaff, rose; Floradora, fiery bronze; Hey-Day, rich cerise red; Immortelle, yellow and bronze; Vogue, rich copper; Wedding Day, glistening white.

DWARF LILLIPUT Bashful, bronze-red; Happy, bright yellow; Honeybird, orange-amber; Isis, rosy-pink; Pheasant, pale strawberry; Redbreast, glowing red.

Indoor Kinds

SINGLES AND ANEMONE-FLOWERED Broadacre, white-green centre; Cheerio, terracotta; Elspeth, mauve-pink, Anemone-flowered; Grace Land, white, Anemone-flowered; Orange Glory, orange; Peter Robinson, yellow; Robin, red; Zulu, deep crimson, green centre.

DOUBLES Alice Burgess, salmon, reflexed; Balcombe Perfection, amber-bronze; Bellona, deep pink, Christmas flowering; Blanche Poitevene, a good dwarf white for pot work; Chairman, deep yellow, Oct. flowering, large blooms; Christmas Wine, deep wine, reflexed, dwarf; Fanfare, deep pink, Christmas flowering; F.E. Morris, rosy-salmon, gold reverse; Fred Shoesmith, white, cream centre; Friendly Rival, yellow, Christmas flowering; Imperial Pink, pink, flowers at Christmas; Isabel, deep pink, incurved; Lancashire, yellow, ball-shaped, dwarf habit; Leader, rich orange-bronze, Oct. flowering; Loveliness, silvery pink, large flowers; Mary Alesworth, pale-pink; Mayford Crimson, red-crimson; Mayford Perfection, warm salmon, large; Mayford Supreme, yellow, good shape; October Dazzler, red; Patricia Hurst, lilac-pink; Perfection, white; Princess Anne, pink, tinted salmon; Rustic, chestnut bronze; Shirley Brilliant, deep crimson, Christmas flowering; Shirley Primrose, primrose; Susan Alesworth, deep pink with silver reverse; Teddy Doig, large crimson, incurving; Tom Purvis, crimson, gold reverse; The Favourite, splendid white, incurving; White Bellona, clear white, good for cutting; Winn Quinn, sulphur yellow; Worthing Success, beautiful pink; Yellow Fred Shoesmith, yellow.

PESTS AND DISEASES

The chief pests and diseases are: — Slugs, Aphis, Leaf-miner, Capsid Bug, Thrips, Eelworm, Verticillium Wilt, Septoria (Leaf Spot), Rust, Powdery Mildew and Botrytis.

'Sylvia Riley', rose-pink, early flowering
Walter Blom & Son

Roses

The Rose is deservedly the most prized of garden plants. It is of easy culture and suited to a wide variety of soils, with exquisitely shaped, often fragrant and delightfully coloured blooms, which continue flowering over a long period.

Fossil remains in Europe and American establish the existence of Roses millions of years back and they are mentioned in the writings of both Theophrastus and Pliny. Theophrastus indeed gave what must surely be the first comment on Rose pruning when he wrote — 'If a bush be cut or burnt over it bears better flowers, for if left to itself it grows luxuriantly and makes too much wood.'

The name Rose comes from *rhod*, meaning red. The Island of Rhodes received its name because of the quantities of Roses which grew wild on its rocky shores.

Both the Greeks and Romans used great quantities of Roses at their feasts and festivals; Nero is said to have spent four million sesterces (approximately £17,000) on Roses for a single festive occasion.

Small wonder that the early Fathers of the Church disapproved of the Rose, because of its pagan association. They would not allow it into their churches for many years, until, strangely enough, it became the emblem of the martyrs, the five petals representing the five wounds of Christ and the white Rose the virginity of Mary.

Roses were much used in England in the Middle Ages for adorning shrines, wreathing candles, as rents and in heraldry. The Tudor Rose of Britain is derived from the amalgamation of York and Lancaster after the Wars of the Roses, when:

'Henry VII did the Roses unite,

His own was the red, and his wife's the white.'

Most garden species were initially collected by explorers and varieties obtained from crossing these have been derived from many growers and sources. Apart from their value as garden plants the petals have been candied, made into jam, used for Rose Water, sugar, rosettes and of course oil and perfume.

GARDEN ROSES

Rosa gallica is the oldest Rose of European civilisation. The single flowers are pink or crimson and the plant reaches a height of 4 ft. *Rosa moschata*, the Musk Rose, is native to India and China and has large clusters of small cream flowers, the plant making a huge thicket of growth 15 ft. high.

From Asia Minor comes the Damask Rose *(Rosa damascena)* from which Attar of Roses is derived, with double pink to red flowers. These species, together with our own Dog Rose *(Rosa canina)* were the ancient Roses of Europe.

From China, in the 18th century, came *Rosa chinensis*, a red Rose which was perpetual flowering, from June to September. It was crossed and recrossed with the existing types, giving rise to the perpetual-flowering hybrid China Roses. One of these, known as 'Parson's Pink China' was crossed with 'Pink Autumn Damask' in 1817 and gave rise to the first of the Bourbon Roses, so called because this work was carried out on the French Island of

Bourbon. These were highly scented, flowered for a long time, and were really the first of that great class of Roses known as Hybrid Perpetuals.

Further hybridising between the Bourbons and the scented China Roses in the 19th century produced first the Noisettes, and then the very popular Tea Roses. These rather delicate Roses were then crossed with the more vigorous of Hybrid Perpetuals to produce that famous class of Roses known as the Hybrid Teas.

The early Hybrid Teas did not have the brilliant shades of yellow, orange and apricot that make our modern Roses so attractive, but in 1900 Pernet Ducher produced his famous 'Soleil d'Or' by crossing the Persian Yellow *(R. foetida)* with Hybrid Perpetuals. This outstanding introduction was used to improve the range of colours in the Hybrid Teas.

Mention must be made of one other species from China, *R. multiflora*, a vigorous plant that has a climbing habit and produces masses of small white, sweetly scented flowers. Dwarf seedlings of this Rose were crossed with *R. chinensis* and gave rise to the popular Polyantha Pompons such as 'Edith Cavell' and 'Coral Cluster'. Other seedlings, which retained the vigour of *R. multiflora* produced the Polyantha Climbers such as 'Paul's Scarlet Climber'. When Poulsen of Denmark crossed the Polyantha Pompons with the Hybrid Teas he developed an entirely new class of Roses. These were originally called Hybrid Polyantha but are now known as Floribundas.

R. wichuraiana, from Japan, also has a rambling habit and was crossed with *R. multiflora* and the Hybrid Teas to give the true ramblers like 'Dorothy Perkins' and 'American Pillar'.

Finally, there are the Climbing Teas. Owing to the mixed ancestry of the Hybrid Teas a variety

Hybrid Tea 'Ena Harkness'

Fisons Horticulture

Floribunda 'Evelyn Fison'   Samuel McGredy & Son

occasionally changes its habit from the bush form to that of a climber. It is really a climbing sport, and combines the useful climbing habit with the handsome blooms of the typical Hybrid Tea.

MAKING AND PLANTING A ROSE GARDEN

The construction of a Rose Garden involves the following: *(a)* Design; *(b)* Choice of varieties; *(c)* Preparation of the soil and planting.

Design will depend very much on available space and personal taste. It may vary from the simple bed of Hybrid Tea Roses surrounded by turf, to elaborate designs which include climbers and ramblers on walls or rustic arches and fences, together with uniform borders of Floribundas, standards and weeping standards, and several beds of Hybrid Teas. There is certainly more interest in a garden which contains several *types* as well as varieties of Roses.

Colour again is a matter of personal choice. Some prefer a galaxy of hues, but a few well chosen shades which blend well together are likely to create more pleasing effects.

As far as possible, choose an open, sunny site for the Rose garden and if a wall is to be used for climbers, make sure that new plants do not suffer from lack of water. A wall often effectively shields a plant from natural rain.

Before deciding on types and varieties, it is good policy to visit a Rose nursery and select plants when they are in flower. This is the only way to make quite certain that no mistake has been made when planning for specific colour effects.

Roses will grow successfully on a wide range of soils if the following points are borne in mind:

1. A very acid soil will require liming (see pH tests p. 14). A soil with a pH of 6.5 is ideal, but Roses will grow within a range of pH6—pH7.

2. During hot, dry summers Roses require ample supplies of water.

3. Waterlogging is very bad for them. In order to produce a soil of good texture — well drained but not drying out in summer, it is essential to cultivate deeply and incorporate large amounts of organic matter. This is true for both sandy and clay soils. Peat soils are acid and contain enough organic matter, but tend to be short of mineral nutrients and are often badly drained; they should be treated with lime and artificial fertilisers. Deep digging will improve the drainage but for severe waterlogging it may be necessary to construct special drains.

The term 'organic matter' refers to any decaying plant or animal residue e.g. spent hops, compost, farmyard manure, leafmould, grass mowings, peat etc. Having produced a soil of good texture with such materials it only remains to dress it with a base fertiliser at the recommended rates as follows:

Hoof and horn meal   4 oz. per sq.yd.
Bone meal   4 ,, ,,   ,,
Sulphate of potash   2 ,, ,,   ,,

Fork these materials into the top 6 in. of soil during October, when the soil is in good working condition. Planting is done in November, but if the weather is unsuitable when the Roses arrive, heel them into a trench and delay the task until the soil can be easily worked. It is possible to plant as late as March, but in such cases precautions must be taken against dryness at the roots if a drought occurs, as it often during May.

Before planting, the roots may need pruning to remove any damaged portions and extra long roots should be slightly shortened. Make the planting holes wide enough to accommodate the roots without having to bend or force them into position, and let

Floribunda 'Frensham'　　　　J. E. Downward

CULTIVATION OF ESTABLISHED ROSES

The culture of Roses falls under the following headings: pruning, feeding and control of pests and diseases.

PRUNING

Pruning methods will depend on the class of Rose concerned, but there are some general rules which apply to the *pruning of all Roses.*

1. Keep a constant look out for sucker growths from the base. Rose varieties budded on briar stocks frequently send up basal shoots, and if ignored, the plants eventually develop into large briar bushes, while the original varieties die of starvation.

Suckers may be recognised by their much smaller leaflets, usually seven in number, compared with five on most garden varieties. Safer still is to compare the general appearance of the leaves, stems and thorns of the variety with those of the suspected suckers. Do not cut the sucker off at ground level for this will only encourage further buds to develop below ground. Scrape the soil away with a trowel or spade until the point of origin between sucker and main stock is discovered, and tear off at this point.

2. Crossing and rubbing branches must never be tolerated. When this happens one or the other must be removed or shortened back to suitably placed bud.

3. All cuts must be made immediately *above an outward pointing bud.* This produces open centred,

the depth be such, that when the operation is completed, the union between stock and scion is *just below* ground level. Plant very firmly and if severe frost occurs during the winter, press back the soil after every thaw.

Planting distances depend on the type of Rose and variety. An average distance between Hybrid Teas is 18 in. but more vigorous ones, such as 'Peace', require 24 in. Floribundas may be planted at the same distances but vigorous climbers and ramblers trained on fences and walls must be allowed at least 6 ft. between individual plants.

Newly planted Roses should be hard pruned during the last week of March. With Hybrid Teas (whether bushes or standards) shorten back all strong shoots to about 4 in., cutting these *immediately above a bud.* Very weak, thin shoots should be removed entirely. Ramblers and climbers should be cut back to leave the strongest growths about 12 in. long.

Weeping Standards are Rambler Roses budded high up on tall briars and should be treated like any other rambler.

Hybrid Tea 'Milord'　　　　Samuel McGredy & Son

107

Hybrid Tea 'Helen Traubel'

Fisons Horticulture

shapely bushes with the main shoots growing outwards and upwards.

4. Remove all weak shoots, i.e. short, twiggy growths which will never produce good blooms.

5. Dead or diseased wood must always be eliminated.

After these main points have been dealt with, pruning should proceed as follows:

Teas and Hybrid Teas

Cut the remaining strong shoots back to about six buds during the last week in March. Trials have shown that for garden display relatively light pruning allows the bushes not only to produce earlier blooms, but in greater quantity. For show purposes cut back to three buds.

Winter pruning is practised by some growers. This results in earlier flowers, but is risky in very cold climates because hard frosts in Jan. and Feb. may damage the tops of the pruned shoots, which will have to be cut back again at the end of March.

Hybrid Perpetuals

Treat in the same way as Hybrid Teas, but as they are usually much more vigorous than the latter, prune less severely. Hard pruning on an already vigorous variety may induce such an amount of vegetative growth that the formation of flower buds is suppressed. Hybrid Perpetuals should be cut back to about eight buds, but if an embarrassing amount of wood and leaf is produced, a good method is to arch over the strongest shoots and peg their tips to the ground; flowers will then be produced all along the arched shoots.

Polyantha Pompons

Prune at the end of March in the same way as for Hybrid Teas, but cut strongest stems to about half their length.

Floribundas

Weak and old stems are removed completely and the young growth shortened by about one-third. Good side shoots can be cut back to half their length. Some modern Floribundas have a growth habit similar to the Hybrid Teas, and pruning methods will closely approach those advocated for that class.

Ramblers

A true rambler is one which produces many strong new growths from the base every summer, as in the case of 'Dorothy Perkins'. Pruning is carried out in late summer when flowering is over and entails the complete removal of all the old flowering stems at ground level, the new young shoots of the current season's growth being tied in to take their place.

Climbers

Unlike ramblers, all climbers have a permanent framework of old wood, the new growth at the end of each branch being called a 'leader'. 'Emily Grey' is a typical example.

Pruning is done in March, when the leaders are shortened by two-thirds *in the early life of the plant only*. This induces strong young branches which are required when a wall has to be covered. Older climbers only need the leaders tipped by about one-third of their length. Lateral shoots are shortened to four or five buds. As with the vigorous Hybrid Perpetuals, climbers produce more flowers if their branches are trained obliquely, or even horizontally. Upright training tends to encourage much growth at the top, with long lengths of bare, unsightly wood towards the base.

Floribunda 'Masquerade'   Fisons Horticulture

come almost non-existent if nothing is done to curb excess vigour. Training shoots towards the horizontal position will increase flower production, but if this is still unsatisfactory, prune in July instead of March.

FEEDING

To maintain soil fertility on established Rose beds, two distinct operations are carried out:

(a) Mulching.

(b) The application of fertilisers as top dressings.

A mulch is a layer of organic matter, 2—3 in. thick, which is spread over the soil about the middle of April, in order to conserve soil moisture. It may consist of leaf soil, rotted compost, spent hops, or well rotted straw. Old farmyard manure makes an excellent mulch for Roses as it not only adds organic matter to the soil but provides the three major plant nutrients—nitrogen, potash and phosphate. These three are needed in larger amounts than most elements, and, provided that regular mulching is carried out, are the only ones which need be applied separately as extras.

There are many proprietary fertilisers, which must always be used strictly according to the maker's instructions. The golden rule with artificial fertilisers is to use them 'little and often'. The number of times feeding is carried out will depend on the natural fertility of the soil and the condition of the plants, but it is usual to apply the first top dressing just before mulching. A second feed may be given in early June and a third and final one a month later. If you prefer to prepare your own fertiliser, the following may be mixed and applied at 4 oz. to the sq.yd.:

2 parts by weight superphosphate of lime

1 part   ,,   ,,   sulphate of potash

1 ,,   ,,   ,,   sulphate of ammonia

When farmyard manure is used for mulching it should only be necessary to apply one top dressing of fertiliser towards the end of June.

Plant nutrients in very dilute solutions can be absorbed into plants via their foliage and this fact has given rise to the cultural operation known as 'foliar feeding'. The form of the chemicals does not

Hybrid Tea 'Suspense'   Fisons Horticulture

Climbing Sports

These are really Hybrid Tea Roses, a variety of which will occasionally become extremely vigorous and adopt the habit of a climber. Pruning is the same as for ordinary climbers. A notorious example of an already vigorous Hybrid Tea adopting a climbing habit is that of 'Climbing Peace'. Flowering can be-

Good (extreme left) and bad pruning cuts   Rolcut Ltd

Standard Rose before and after pruning   Rolcut Ltd

Pruning bush Roses   Rolcut Ltd

matter a great deal provided that two points are borne in mind:

a) The salts must be completely soluble in water.
b) The solution must be very dilute, i.e. not more than half an ounce of salts to a gallon of water.

The following is a satisfactory mixture:

3 parts by weight urea
2 „ „ „ di-hydrogen ammonium phosphate
1 „ „ „ potassium nitrate

Spray in dull weather, at monthly intervals, beginning the first week in June. The number of sprays will depend on the state of the plants, but three applications are usually sufficient.

In some soils (particularly those with a high pH) or containing much lime, Rose bushes occasionally develop so-called trace element deficiencies. Chlorosis, or inter-veinal yellowing of the leaves, is a typical symptom, due to the plant being unable to obtain sufficient iron, manganese or magnesium — or possibly all three. These elements may be present in the soil but are rendered unavailable to the plant because they are in an insoluble form. Hence it is little use applying them as fertilisers as these too immediately become insoluble.

It is now possible to purchase complex substances known as Chelates or Sequestrenes to overcome this problem. These contain the trace elements in question, are watered onto the soil, and will soon enable the plant to recover its green leaves and healthy growth.

CONTROL OF PESTS AND DISEASES

The three major diseases of Roses are Mildew, Black Spot and Rust, whilst the insect pests likely to cause most trouble are: Aphis (Greenfly), Rose Leaf Hopper, caterpillars of the Rose Tortrix Moth, Thrips, Chafer Beetles and their grubs.

In connection with the routine management of Roses, remember that regular hoeing not only destroys weeds, but maintains an open soil, allowing both air and water to penetrate easily to the roots. Whilst everything possible may have been done to produce a soil which is moisture retentive you may still need to apply water during periods of drought. This is particularly important for newly planted Roses. Always water the soil thoroughly. Merely wetting the top 2 in. of soil is a waste of time, the water being quickly evaporated again during hot, sunny weather. Drenching the foliage whilst watering is also very beneficial to the plants. It not only washes the leaves clean of dust and grime, but will also discourage the breeding of Greenfly.

CHOOSING YOUR ROSES
A SELECT LIST OF HYBRID TEAS

WHITE AND CREAM	Ardelle	Message
	Bridal Robe	Virgo
	McGredy's Ivory	White Swan
LIGHT PINK	Ann Letts	Lady Sylvia
	First Love	Ophelia
	Grace de Monaco	Picture
	Helen Traubel	Tiffany
DEEP PINK	Ballet	Perfection
	Eden Rose	Show Girl
	June Park	Silver Lining
	Michèle Meilland	Stella
	Montezuma	The Doctor
RED	Baccarat	Fritz Thiedemann
	Brilliant	Karl Herbst
	Charles Mallerin	Lady Russon
	Crimson Glory	Vivian Leigh
	Dr F.G.Chandler	Walter Bentley
	Ena Harkness	William Harvey
YELLOW	Buccaneer	Grand'mère Jenny
	Fantasia	McGredy's Yellow
	Gertrude Gregory	Peace
	Gold Crown	Spek's Yellow
	Golden Dawn	Sutter's Gold

BICOLOR, RED AND YELLOW

	Charles Gregory	Miss Ireland
	Cleopatra	Sultane
	Gay Crusader	Suspense
	Huntsman	Tzigane

ORANGE, COPPER AND FLAME

	Beauté	
	Barbara Richards	Mary Wheatcroft
	Flaming Sunset	Mrs Sam McGredy
	Mark Sullivan	Opera
	Thais (Lady Elgin)	Signora

LAVENDER AND BLUE-GREY

	Grey Pearls	Prelude
	Lilac Time	Royal Tan
	Pigalle	Waltz Time

A SELECT LIST OF FLORIBUNDA ROSES

WHITE AND CREAM		
	Glacier	Ivory Fashion
	Iceberg	Mrs Jones
	Irene of Denmark	Yvonne Rabier
LIGHT PINK		
	Dainty Maid	Queen Elizabeth
	Fashion	Rudolph Timm
DEEP PINK		
	Bonnie Maid	Paddy McGredy
	Charming Maid	Pinocchio
	Jiminy Cricket	Vogue
RED		
	Alain	Karen Poulsen
	Ama	Moulin Rouge
	Frensham	Red Favourite
ORANGE-SCARLET		
	Firecracker	Orange Sensation
	Highlight	Orange Triumph
YELLOW		
	Allgold	Gold Marie
	Faust	Poly Prim
	Golden Fleece	Yellowhammer
BICOLORS, PINKS, YELLOWS AND RED		
	Alpine Glow	Fanfare
	Circus	Masquerade

Climber 'Mermaid' Fisons Horticulture

Hybrid Tea 'Symphonie'
Fisons Horticulture

Floribunda 'Queen Elizabeth'
Fisons Horticulture

CLIMBING AND RAMBLER ROSES
FOR TRAINING ON WALLS FACING EAST

Ards Rover, dark crimson
Caroline Testout, pink
Danse du Feu, fiery red
Dr W. van Fleet, soft pink
Mme Alfred Carrière, white
Paul's Scarlet Climber, scarlet
Paul's Lemon Pillar, lemon

FOR WALLS FACING NORTH

Alberic Barbier, cream
Allen Chandler, scarlet
Dr W. van Fleet, soft pink
Hugh Dickson, crimson
Mary Wallace, rosy-pink
Mme Alfred Carrière, white
Gloire de Dijon, creamy-yellow

FOR WALLS FACING SOUTH AND EAST

Albertine, salmon
Chaplin's Pink Climber
Crimson Shower, crimson
Elegance, clear yellow
Etoile de Hollande, scarlet crimson
Zephirine Drouhin, carmine pink
Golden Dawn, climbing, gold
New Dawn, soft pink
Mermaid, sulphur yellow
R. longicuspis, white
Wedding Day, white

STRONGLY SCENTED ROSES

Eden Rose, carmine and pink
Ena Harkness, crimson scarlet
Crimson Glory, deep crimson
Shot Silk, cerise, shaded salmon
Lady Sylvia, pink
President Hoover, orange yellow
Golden Dawn, bright yellow
Symphonie, deep pink

FRAGRANT ROSES GOOD FOR CUTTING

Ena Harkness, crimson-scarlet
First Love, pale pink
Golden Melody, pale cream
Lady Sylvia, flesh pink
Ophelia, pale salmon
Picture, clear pink
Signora, orange and pink
Virgo, white

ROSES FOR HEDGES
LOW HEDGES

Betty Prior, carmine
Dainty Bess, pink
Donald Prior, crimson-scarlet
Elsa Poulsen, rose-pink
Will Scarlet, bright red
Yvonne Rabier, white

TALLER HEDGES

Frensham, scarlet
Hugh Dickson, crimson
Moonlight, lemon-white
Peace, light yellow
Penelope, shell-pink
Penzance Briars
Rugosa Roses and hybrids
Queen Elizabeth, deep pink
Wilhelm, deep red, semi-double

SOME ATTRACTIVE ROSES FOR THE SHRUB BORDER

R.damascena — The Damask Rose and its varieties, pink
R.moyesii — dusty-scarlet
R.longicuspis — white
R.nitida — bright pink and red hips
R.moyesii — 'Nevada', seedling, single white,
R.omiensis — white, very prickly
R.primula — primrose-yellow, fragrant foliage
R.rubrifolia — purplish-pink, reddish foliage
R.spinosissima — 'Frühlingsgold', single yellow
R.xanthina — 'Canary Bird', single gold

ROSES FOR WEEPING STANDARDS

Alberic Barbier, creamy white
Crimson Shower, crimson
Dorothy Perkins, rosy-pink
François Juranville, salmon-pink
Léontine Gervais, salmon
Sander's White, large clusters

ROSES FOR ARCHES, PERGOLAS AND PILLARS

Albertine, salmon
Crimson Shower, semi-double
Dorothy Perkins, rosy-pink

Excelsa, rosy-crimson
Mary Wallace, bright pink
Sander's White, rosette-shaped

SOME ROSE RECIPES

To Dry Rose Petals (For sachets, pot pourri etc.)

Gather the petals of red, scented Roses and lay out thinly in boxes or between layers of muslin. Dry them quickly but never in the sun. Nor should they re-absorb moisture, so if placed outside during the day bring them into a dry place at night.

When dry and crisp to the touch, but still keeping their colour, place in a closed jar with fine, dry powdered salt. Stir daily and after a week or ten days, sift out the salt. Keep the petals in a closed airtight container until wanted.

Use alone or mixed with other herbs, dried separately, such as Lavender, Lemon Verbena, Rose Geranium etc. for pot pourri.

Pot pourri

2 oz. ground Orris root ⎫ Fixatives without which fra-
1 oz. gum benzoin ⎬ grance would not last
4 drops Attar of Roses ⎭ (if available or a little more of a synthetic Rose perfume)

3 oz. brown sugar
1 oz. brandy or pure alcohol
1 oz. whole Cloves
2 oz. allspice
1 oz. stick Cinnamon
2 quarts dried Rose petals

Grind the spices well together with a mortar and pestle; sift out the salt from the dried Rose petals and mix together in a large bowl with the dry ingredients. Cover the bowl and set aside for 3—4 weeks, stirring once a day. Fill the pot pourri jar, adding the Attar of Roses at the end, and stir together. If the mixture seems dry, add a little brandy. After 4—5 years repeat the addition of brandy and Rose essence, stir, and the fragrance will be revived.

CANDIED ROSE PETALS

Gather red, scented Rose petals on a sunny day. Cut off the white heels (which are bitter) and, using a camel hair brush, paint them over both sides with Rose-water (obtainable from chemists). Sprinkle with finely sieved castor sugar and leave in the sun to candy. Turn the petals frequently and occasionally sprinkle with Rose-water or sugar until they become crisp.

ROSE PETAL JELLY

Ingredients: Dried Rose Petals
Preserving Sugar
Apple or Gooseberry Jelly

Make Apple or Gooseberry Jelly by washing and slicing (but not peeling) the fruit, covering it with water and simmering slowly until it is reduced to a pulp. Strain through a jelly bag and allow one pint of juice to every pound of preserving sugar. Warm and stir until the sugar is dissolved and then put in as many Rose petals as the liquor will hold. Boil till the jelly sets and test on a cold plate in the usual way. When ready, strain and pot in hot jars.

ROSE PETAL JAM

16 or 18 full blown Roses (the large cabbage Roses are best for the purpose, but any fragrant garden variety will do. If the blooms are small, use twice as many).
3 lb. Preserving Sugar
Approximately 2½ pints of Water
4 Lemons

Make a syrup from the sugar and two pints of water, bringing this to the boil and allowing it to simmer gently for thirty minutes.

Strip the petals from the Roses and cut away the white base of each (where it joins the calyx).

Throw all the petals into a dish and just cover with boiling water. Press the petals down with a silver or wooden spoon so that each is thoroughly wetted.

When the syrup is ready add the Rose petals and water in which they are steeped, and stir and simmer the mixture again for a further thirty minutes. Keep the mixture moving or the petals will rise to the top and discolour.

After a further half-hour they should be tender and transparent, and then the juice of the Lemons can be added. The whole should now be boiled for another ten to fifteen minutes, or until the mixture sets after the normal tests.

WILD ROSE OR DOG ROSE JAM

Sort out ½ lb. Rose petals (Dog Roses are best) cutting off any damaged pieces, put into boiling water and boil well, then sieve and drain. Dry petals on a clean cloth and put on a dish. Sprinkle with ½ lb. castor sugar.

Make syrup with 1½ lb. sugar and half a cup of water. When thick pour into it juice of a Lemon and put in Rose petals. Boil once. Pour into a china bowl. When cold add one drop Attar of Roses. Mix well and pour into jars.

MARMALADE FROM ROSE HIPS

To every pound of hips allow half a pint of water; boil till the fruit is tender, then pass the pulp through a sieve to separate the seeds. To each pound of pulp add one pound of preserving sugar and boil until it jellies.

ROSE BAGS TO SCENT LINEN

Mix together dried Rose petals, Cloves, Lavender and a little Mace (the last three well pulverised). Place in little bags and use amongst linen.

Hybrid Tea 'Miss Ireland'　　　　　Fisons Horticulture

113

Dahlias

The chief value of Dahlias is their adaptability to most soils and readiness to produce flowers over a long period. They may be had in bloom from July until October with dwarf, medium or giant size blossoms (according to type), and a brilliance of colouring perhaps unsurpassed by any other plant. The variety is amazing, in shades of deep (almost black) crimson, scarlet, red and pink, to shades of lilac, mauve, primrose and white. The majority make good cut blooms.

SOIL AND SITE

Dahlias appreciate a sunny position, although they are remarkably tolerant of semi-shade. As they enjoy a moist, rich soil, no better preparation can be given than deep digging and the incorporation of very liberal quantities of well rotted animal dung.

If this is not available compost may be used instead, provided a soil dressing is forked into the surface before planting. The latter should consist of bonemeal and hoof and horn meal at 4 oz. of each per sq.yd. and sulphate of potash at 2 oz. per sq.yd.

PROPAGATION

Seed

This method is usually only employed for the single and dwarf bedding kinds. Naturally none of the varieties breed true to name — only to type — and it should be remembered that for hybridising and raising of new varieties propagation by seed is essential. The method of sowing in the greenhouse is exactly the same as for half-hardy annuals. (See p. 126.)

Cuttings

Dahlias produce underground storage organs, known as tubers, and the purchase of these early in the year provides an easy way of growing good plants.

About the first week in April the roots are placed in shallow boxes of moist peat or old potting soil. The tubers are barely covered, with the collars, i.e. the bases of the old stems, left exposed, because it is from this region that the new growths arise. Given

Pompon Dahlia 'Little Dirk'   Walter Blom & Son

Collerette Dahlia 'Vera Lynn'　　　Walter Blom & Son

adequate moisture and a temperature of 60°F., shoots suitable for making into cuttings will develop in two to three weeks' time. See p. 238 for details of the propagation and rooting of soft cuttings.

As the roots are easily damaged, cuttings are usually inserted individually into 3 in. pots and when growing freely are potted on into 5 in. pots, using John Innes No. 1 Potting Compost.

Dahlias need much more warmth than Chrysanthemums and temperatures should not fall below

Decorative Dahlia 'Mary Richards'　　　Walter Blom & Son

55°F. if good growth is to be maintained. Lightly spraying the foliage with clean water and damping down to obtain a fairly high humidity are important operations.

The Dahlia must never be subjected to even the lightest of frosts. The hardening-off period in a cold frame will not take place until the last ten days of May, after which the plants should be ready for setting out in the open garden from the first week in June.

Tubers

If no greenhouse is available, tubers can be planted out in a cold frame during early May. When shoots appear the tubers can be lifted and divided, making sure that each has at least one shoot. Dust any wounds with charcoal.

Should no cold frame be available the tubers can be planted (without division) in the open ground in early May. They should then be covered with 4 in. of soil and will grow quite successfully.

Pot Tubers

This is a particularly useful method for those with limited storage space. The tubers are much smaller than usual and derived from late rooted cuttings (taken in April or May). These are inserted singly in 3 in. pots and allowed to remain in the same receptacles *all the summer*. This starves the plants, which do not flower, but go on to produce small tubers. About October all top growth is shortened back and the pots stored on their sides in a frostproof place.

In the *following* March or April the plants are removed from their containers and either repotted and grown on (similar to cuttings) or else put outside and carefully labelled, about mid-April. Pot tubers are particularly useful in situations where the soil is light or poor as they offer more resistance than freshly rooted cuttings.

PLANTING

Most greenhouse raised plants are transferred from their pots to the open ground in late May or early June. Distances will vary according to the height of the variety, for whilst the dwarf bedders need only 18 in. between plants, the large decorative types will require 3 to 4 ft.

Large varieties will require individual stakes about 4–5 ft. in length and at least 1 in. square. All the plant shoots should be tied in separately to their stake in order to preserve an attractive appearance.

Stopping, or pinching out the growing point, is not essential but is sometimes practised to encourage

115

Small decorative Dahlia 'Musette'   Valerie Finnis

Decorative miniature Dahlia 'Dr Grainger'   J. E. Downward

earlier branching at a lower level. Thinning of shoots and disbudding are both unnecessary for ordinary garden display.

Lifting and Storing Tubers

It is wise to lift the tubers when the first frosts have damaged the foliage. Cut the stems down to 6 in. and place the tubers in a well ventilated shed for a few days to dry. It is very important that the neck region is thoroughly dried before storage as it is here that rotting often commences.

To maintain tubers in good condition they must be kept cool and dry, but *never* exposed to frost. Straw, peat, sand and newspaper may all be used to

Dwarf double mixed Dahlia 'Monarch'   J. E. Downward

Medium cactus Dahlia 'Top Affair'   Valerie Finnis

Decorative Dahlias 'Nocturne', 'Chinese Lantern', 'Dutch Gold', 'Piquant', 'Jersey Beauty'   J. E. Downward

Five kinds of decorative Dahlias   Copyright Samuel Dobie & Son

protect them from frost especially when they are kept in garden sheds or rooms. Under the bench in a greenhouse, (kept at about 40°F.) is another suitable position if not too damp. Dusting the tubers and the collar with sulphur is good protection against moulds.

TYPES OF DAHLIAS

Dahlias rival Chrysanthemums for variety of form, size of flower and size of plant, so that it is again necessary to have some form of classification if the gardener is interested in exhibiting. The handbook of the National Dahlia Society lists all varieties and states the section to which each belongs.

The following simplified classification gives some idea of the main characteristics and may help those who would like to know to which particular section their own Dahlias belong.

Single Dahlias

One row of ray florets. Central disc. e.g. 'Domingo', red blends; 'Frances', yellow bicolor.

Star Dahlias

Two or three rows of pointed ray petals. Central disc. Cup-shaped flower. e.g. 'White Star', white.

Anemone-Flowered Dahlias

One row of flattened ray florets. Centre-raised — Anemone-like. e.g. 'Comet', red; 'Deanna Durbin', yellow.

Collerette Dahlias

A collar of short florets surrounded by one or more rows of flat ray petals. e.g. 'Accuracy', orange and yellow; 'Gigolo', red and yellow; 'Florissant', purple and white; and 'Vera Lynn', pink and white.

Paeony-Flowered Dahlias

Two or more rows of flattened ray florets. Central disc. e.g. 'Bishop of Llandaff', red; 'Saladin', red.

Decorative Dahlias

Fully double flowers. No disc. Florets broad, more or less flat and pointed. e.g. 'Stuart Ogg', yellow; 'Whitehall', white; 'Daily Mail', orange; 'Mrs Hester Pope', purple, and 'Mary Richards', lavender blends.

Double Show and Fancy Dahlias

Fully double flowers. Globular shape. No disc. Over 3 in. Florets with incurved edges, tubular, short and blunt. e.g. 'Esmonde', yellow; 'Standard', red.

Pompon Dahlias

As above but flowers smaller than 3 in. e.g. 'Little Beeswing', red; 'White Raider', white; 'Little Dirk', pink.

Cactus Dahlias

Florets with edges outcurved for a part or whole of their length. Florets narrow, pointed, either straight or incurving. e.g. 'Forward Look', purple; 'Lavender Beauty'; 'Doris Day', red; 'Hoek's Yellow'; 'John Woolman', red blends; 'Frau O. Bracht', yellow and 'Pinkette', pink.

Dwarf Bedding Dahlias

Not usually more than 24 in. high. Flowers may be single, decorative, collarette, paeony-flowered or cactus. e.g. 'Princess Marie Jose', lilac; 'Morning Light', soft pink. Among these various classes the most popular are the decoratives, cactus and the pompons.

Pests

Earwigs, slugs, wireworms, capsid bugs, aphis.

Diseases

Leaf spot and the viruses: Streak, Mosaic and Spotted Wilt.

Gardening in Containers

Plants, and particularly house plants will grow practically anywhere provided they are given enough light and water and a growing medium which contains the essential food elements. Cultivation in containers is therefore a rewarding occupation both indoors and out.

GROWING BULBS IN BOWLS

Bulbs for forcing purposes should be of good quality — firm, solid and free from any suspicion of flabbiness, with the growing point intact and the bulbs showing no mildew stains or bruises. In the case of Darwin Tulips, the brown outer coat or tunic should be intact. Buy the 'specially prepared' forcing bulbs for Christmas flowering. Top grade Hyacinths are often 8–10 in. in circumference and Crocus corms 4 in. round at the widest point.

Containers

Bulbs can be grown in a wide range of containers; bowls, flower pots, pans (with holes in the bottom), fancy bulb jars, or, in the case of Crocus and some Narcissus, in bulb glasses or arranged on pebbles in a saucer of water.

Season

Bulbs may be planted from late August until early November, the earlier the better. Many kinds of Narcissi — and especially Jonquils — deteriorate if they are kept lying about too long.

Compost

Bulbs in fancy bowls are usually grown in bulb fibre, as this is clean to handle, retains the moisture and will not mark the bowls. It can be made up at home from horticultural peat or moss fibre, oyster shell and charcoal, or may be bought ready mixed, often with the addition of a little fertiliser. Fibre must be thoroughly moistened before planting.

Narcissi and Tulips raised in flower pots or pans with drainage holes can be given soil compost, either John Innes No. 1. Potting Compost or a home-made mix containing equal parts of peat, loam and coarse sand.

Loamless composts give excellent results if they are not allowed to get dry and I have also grown bulbs in brick rubble and vermiculite.

Planting

First crock flower pots, pans or boxes and place a few lumps or charcoal over the bottom of fancy bowls.

Half fill the bowl with moistened fibre and stand the bulbs closely together — but not touching — and pack more fibre between and around them with a wooden ladle or spoon handle. Hyacinths and Narcissi should have their noses protruding, and other types just covered.

After planting set the bulbs in a cool place to develop roots. This is *most* important. If they are forced along at this stage or stood in a warm cupboard or sunny place they may go 'blind', i.e. have no flowers.

Tulips in a Danish pottery bowl   Smallholder and Home Gardener

If a sheltered spot can be found outdoors, set the planted containers on a firm piece of ground, covering them with 6 in. of light soil, sand or ashes. To protect glazed bowl wrap them first in polythene or newspaper. Those without gardens should wrap each pot in black polythene, and store in the coldest place in the house: a cellar, stone-floored shed or attic.

After 8 or 9 weeks examine the bulbs. If they

Fern growing in a Birch log   By courtesy of Home Magazine

show about an inch of top white shoot with the bowl full of roots, place them in a light but cool place, such as the windowsill of a fireless room. Water frequently from now on and when the leaves are well out of the bulbs and the flower buds developing take them into the living room to flower.

Useful temperatures to remember when forcing Hyacinths and Crocus in particular are:

To develop roots		40°F.
„	„ foliage	50°F.
„	„ flowers	60°F. (or 70° for quick development)

SPECIAL CULTURAL TIPS

Striped, blue or white Crocus are the best for forcing.

Never stand bulbs in a draught or the leaves will turn yellow.

Stunted growth denotes poor roots. The bulbs were not long enough in the plunge bed.

If the flower spikes go brown at the tips or florets die off, it is an indication that the bulbs were too dry at some stage.

Failure of the flowers to open, bud withering or yellow-tipped leaves denote haphazard watering.

Bulb Vases

Narcissi and Hyacinths may simply be lodged in the rounded neck of special glass vases. The roots grow downwards and trail in the water. Smaller-sized receptacles may be used for sprouting Crocus or Acorns.

The water should almost, but not quite, touch the base of the bulbs (except Narcissi, which do not mind being wet). Use rain water for preference and drop a few pieces of charcoal in the glass to keep the former sweet. Darkness and a low temperature in the early days are again essential.

Danish Crocus Pots

These have holes round the sides and are made of terra-cotta. Fill with moist fibre, placing a corm so that its nose protrudes outwards at each hole as the work proceeds. Set several in the top of the container which must be kept wrapped in black polythene in a cool place for 6 or 8 weeks. Bring into the light and turn the bowl round daily so that all the corms have an equal share of light. Flowers and leaves will completely envelop the sides and top of the container, making a most attractive effect.

Larger containers are available, suitable for Tulips.

VARIETIES FOR FORCING

Hyacinths

Roman Hyacinths — planted in September, will flower at Christmas.

Large flowered Hyacinths 'Pink Pearl', 'John Bos', crimson, 'Yellowhammer', cream, 'L'Innocence', white, 'King of the Blues'.

Narcissi and Daffodils

Early (early February)
'Golden Harvest', 'Gloria', 'Fortune', 'Cragford', 'Lanarth'.
Late (mid-February)
'Rembrandt', 'Scarlet Elegance', 'Mrs Barclay', 'St Agnes'.
N.B. Specially prepared bulbs of 'Golden Harvest', 'Fortune' and 'Magnificence' can be purchased to flower *outside* in January.
For Growing on Pebbles
Narcissi 'Cragford', 'Cheerfulness', 'Geranium', 'L'Innocence'. Balance these on pebbles at the bottom of a bowl or saucer and keep water *just below* the bulb level. Crocuses also grow on pebbles.

Tulips

Any early or double varieties. Plant before October 15th.
Those marked (a) flower from the second week January, (b) middle to end January, (c) second week February, (d) last week February.
Singles 'Brilliant Star', scarlet (a); 'Keizerskroon', red and yellow (b); 'Mon Tresor', yellow (a); 'Pink Perfection', pink (b); 'Sunburst', gold and red (b); 'Violet Lady', purple and white (c); 'White Hawk' (b).
Doubles 'Golden King' (b); 'Murillo', pastel pink (c); 'Peach Blossom', rosy-pink (c); 'Rheingold', pale yellow (c); 'Scarlet Cardinal' (a); 'Snow Queen', white (c); 'Vuurbaak', bright scarlet (d).

OTHER BULBS FOR FORCING

Most other hardy bulbs dislike too much warmth, but you can grow them along slowly on a cold windowsill or in a garden frame, in pans or flower pots of soil.

If they get too warm or the soil dries out the bulbs will go blind.

Try small pans of the following:
Winter Aconite (Eranthis), golden Buttercup flowers set off by a frill of green leaves; Snowdrops, single and double; *Iris histrioides major*, deep blue flowers on 2 in. stems; *I. reticulata*, taller (6–9 in.) a pretty Oxford blue and the Cambridge blue 'Cantab'; baby trumpet Daffodils such as *minimus*, only 2 or 3 in. high, and *Narcissus triandrus*, the incomparably lovely white 'Angel's Tears'.

MINIATURE GARDENS

These are dealt with in the chapter on Rock Gardens. Here are some suitable subjects for planting:
Miniature Roses, Rhodohypoxis, dwarf conifers such as *Chamaecyparis pisifera pygmaea*, *Thuya occidentalis glabra* and *Cryptomeria japonica nana*, together with tiny bulbs like *Narcissus asturiensis* — a 2 in. Daffodil, Crocus and Scillas.

BOTTLE GARDENS

Nathaniel Ward, a London physician, discovered over a century ago that plants could survive under

Trough of Geraniums

Geraniums and Marguerites   Valerie Finnis

certain conditions for many years without artificial care and watering. He believed that mosses and ferns might exist for a hundred years without extra watering in a tightly sealed case.

One can grow quite a few house plants inside a glass container in this way. A carboy makes an excellent 'garden', although magnum champagne bottles, large brandy glasses, the glass top of a street lamp and even aquaria can also be used.

To make a carboy garden select one with white or very light glass and rinse it thoroughly. Now pour dryish soil through the opening so that a third of the bottle is filled, using John Innes No. 1. Potting Compost (without the fertilisers) but including a small quantity of crushed charcoal. Even better results can be obtained with the new loamless composts.

Small rooted cuttings, carefully washed, are dropped through the opening and planted with the aid of a dessert spoon and fork lashed to bamboo canes. They soon establish themselves in the moist humidity. Suitable plants are Fittonia, Selaginella, mosses of all kinds, Maranta species, Zebrina and little ferns, but even Dracaeanas and African Violets thrive in some instances. Use several plants with coloured leaves to provide variety.

Water can be introduced through a small piece of rubber tubing but if the carboy is corked it is rarely necessary.

African Violets and other house plants will also grow in a goldfish bowl. Place a little shingle at the base, cover with soil or loamless compost, plant in the usual way, and keep in a warm, light place.

FERN BALLS

An unusual method of growing ferns. The one generally used is *Davallia mariesii*, the Hare's Foot Fern, whose slender rhizomes are wound round a ball of Sphagnum Moss and tied to a compact shape with fine wire. During the dormant period the ball need only be kept just moist, but in spring it should be soaked in water and hung up in a moist atmosphere.

Subsequent waterings are performed in the same manner, by soaking. In due course the ball will break out into leaf, forming a living globe of green. The chief difficulty of this method lies in fastening the rhizomes in place without breaking them. The Japanese, however, are particularly adept at the practice and one can sometimes purchase fern balls ready prepared. Similarly animal, bird and human shapes can be purchased, made of wire frames, mossed and planted, which, given the same treatment, sprout fern fronds all round.

HANGING BOTTLES

This method is more suitable for plants of a slightly woody nature, such as Plectranthus, Fuchsia, small-growing and Ivy-leaved Pelargoniums, Coleus and even Garden Sage and Thyme.

The most convenient bottles are those used for light wines which have an inward-pointing, dome-shaped base. Make a hole in the bottom — about ¾ in. across in the centre of the dome — using a diamond or similar instrument. Since it has to hang, the bottle should have a pronounced rim at the neck, around which wire can be fastened. If not, push a piece of flexible wire through the bottle from the neck end and hook it round the base. Leave enough wire at the top to protrude for several inches and bend it over to form a hook.

Now half fill the bottle with light soil and push in a rooted cutting (more if there is room) of Plectranthus, Calceolaria etc., turn the container the right way up and hang it in a light position, as in a window. The plants eventually turn upwards all round the sides of the bottle. Plectranthus is particularly attractive treated in this way and flowers more freely than in pots, producing masses of Lavender-like spikes which remain in character all summer. Water, if required, is applied through the neck of the bottle.

GROWING WITHOUT SOIL

One of the best methods of growing Bromeliads (p. 190) is to use moss as a rooting medium. Pots, pieces of bark and even birch logs cut in half can be used as containers. With the last, bore a hole about 3 in. in diameter through the centre, put a small tin or cold-cream container into the base of the log and hold in place with clips; its purpose is to trap moisture and prevent damage to household furnishings.

Suitable plants for logs include ferns of all descriptions, bromeliads and the dwarf squat *Sansevieria hahni*, which has short green and white leaves arranged in rosettes. These may be packed tightly in place with a little soil and moss and then used flat on the table or hung against a wall (by fixing an eyelet pin or hook to the top). Apart from frequent sprayings, the plants require no feeding, although ferns may occasionally be given a short soaking.

Plant troughs, made of galvanised iron, wood, plastocrete, lead etc., also provide a method of soilless cultivation. This is described on p. 186.

Plectranthus growing out of the base of a bottle
By courtesy of Home Magazine

Plants growing in a carboy   By courtesy of Home Magazine

WINDOW BOXES, TUBS AND HANGING BASKETS

These are all forms of container gardening. For planting methods and suggestions for suitable material see p. 78.

STRAWBERRY BARRELS

This is an interesting method of growing Strawberries when space is limited. Each barrel takes up less than a square yard and yet can accommodate a couple of dozen plants.

Oak wine casks are best (creosote barrels can be poisonous) and should have holes, about 2½ in. across, bored at intervals round the sides. The average 40 gallon barrel will take three rows of these, approximately six in a row, the middle set being staggered between the others.

Set some form of conduit in the centre of the barrel to help watering, such as a section of 6 in. drainpipe, or flower pots piled up on each other, upside down, or a folded roll of wire netting stuffed with crocks or moss.

Cover the base of the tub with a 2 in. layer of stones or broken crocks, put the conduit in place and fill in with good garden soil enriched with well decayed manure or compost. Add a handful of bonemeal, but avoid lime.

As filling proceeds insert the Strawberry plants as you come to the holes. Push the leaves through from the inside, or the roots from the outside — whichever is easier — and pack them round firmly with soil. Fill the drainpipe (if used) with broken brick or clinker and water each layer as the work proceeds. Afterwards the pipe can be slipped out, leaving a porous core of brick which will allow for water to reach all parts of the tub.

Finally, plant half a dozen Strawberry roots at the top, and the barrel is complete.

Plants growing in a variety of containers
Smallholder and Home Gardener

The idea may be elaborated in a town garden by planting up with Petunias or Geraniums instead of Strawberries. Whitewashing the tub first gives a more attractive finish.

FRUIT TREES IN POTS

Years ago fruit trees in pots were a common feature of the larger estates, the aim being early fruits of superb quality. This was achieved by taking the pots into a cool greenhouse, about the end of February or March, thus giving them protection and a little extra warmth which encouraged early blossom and fruiting.

If you have a cool greenhouse which is empty at that time of year, you can try this method, or you can keep the pots standing in large saucers out of doors, or plunged in soil in the warmer weather.

Apples and Pears grown on dwarfing stocks go on for years in a 12 in. pot, but the method is also suitable for Cherries, Gages, Figs and Peaches. The idea is to keep small, compact trees with an open centre and uniformly placed branches.

Use good rich soil for compost, such as John Innes No. 3, or well rotted manure, loam, sand and peat. Plant trees in the normal way. Early in the year mix a little strawy manure and clay together with water and bind this round the top of each pot, to make a false rim about 2 in. high. They can then hold more water during the growing season and the manure in the straw gradually washes down to the roots. To encourage a good set of blossom, hand pollination with a rabbit's-tail or camel-hair brush is advisable under glass; outdoors, one can usually rely on the bees.

As soon as the fruit is set plenty of water must be provided and thinning practised to a reasonable crop. Feeding with liquid manure takes place weekly whilst the fruit is swelling, but ceases when it begins to colour.

After harvesting, the tree is taken outside and plunged in soil up to the rim in a sheltered, but partially shaded position. Summer pruning is necessary to keep the tree compact and prevent the production of over-strong shoots. In autumn the pot may be top-dressed with fresh potting soil. Occasionally it may be repotted entirely, best effected by laying the pot on its sides and gently hosing away most of the soil. This is then replaced by new compost without damage to the roots.

All winter the trees remain plunged in the garden, with a mulch of straw over the ground to prevent frost cracking the pots. In February they come inside to flower and fruit. It is, however, perfectly possible to fruit them if grown entirely outdoors. It depends entirely on the opportunities available.

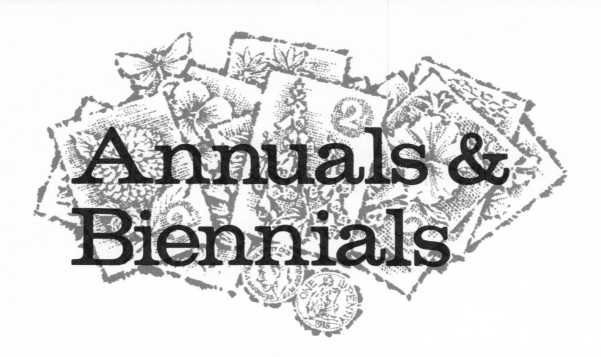

Annuals & Biennials

An ANNUAL is a plant which completes its life cycle — from the germinating seed through growth, flowering, seed time and harvest — and then dies, all within the space of twelve months. Many annuals make up for their brief life-span by a prodigality of blossom and brilliance of colouring unsurpassed by any other members of the Plant Kingdom.

They are easy to grow and cheap to buy, and for long flowering patches of brightness or as temporary stop-gaps whilst more permanent material is becoming established, they prove invaluable. They also develop quickly so that the returns are rapid, an important point in a new garden.

THEIR PLACE IN THE GARDEN

Annuals may be used in the garden in any of the following ways:

1. In a border devoted exclusively to plants of annual duration. Some of these will be sown *in situ*, the HARDY ANNUALS, other raised under glass and planted out as seedlings towards the end of May, the HALF-HARDY ANNUALS.
2. As part of a bedding scheme. Normally this means two crops, hardy annuals such as Forget-me-nots or Wallflowers (biennial) for a spring display, followed by half-hardy or hardy kinds (Petunias, Tagetes, Ageratums, etc.).
3. For bright colour patches in the mixed border.
4. As window box and hanging basket subjects.
5. To prolong interest in the rock garden, which is normally past its best in July.
6. For pot work in the home or greenhouse.
7. As cut flowers.

General Requirements

Annual plants are found in all parts of the world, but the brightest and gayest seem to be native either to South America or South Africa. A knowledge of its habitat often gives a clue to a plant's requirements and an open sunny position generally produces the best results.

Annual borders and display beds should accordingly be sited in an open position and away from trees or hedges which will 'draw' the stems. Contrary to a widely held belief, the plants *do not* do best in poor soil. When first class results are desired, therefore, the ground must be adequately dug — preferably in autumn — and have plenty of well rotted organic material incorporated.

The ground should be given time to settle down before planting, but if this is not possible it must be trodden to consolidate the surface layers. This operation entails shuffling across the newly dug soil with the feet close together. Rake afterwards to remove footmarks.

Before sowing or planting, dress the soil surface with superphosphate (2 oz. per sq.yd.) and rake this into the top few inches.

Into a border prepared exclusively for annuals, the hardy types will be sown direct and half-hardy ones planted out from pots and boxes as soon as the danger of frost is past. A considerable number of the same kind of plant will be needed to make a show, though it is not essential for each genus or race of plants to be the same colour. Very fine patchwork effects can be obtained by using mixed seed of Shirley Poppies or Petunias, for example, in one block, variously hued Eschscholtzias in another and so on.

Informal set-ups on the other hand — as amongst other plants in the shrubbery or herbaceous border

Nemophila insignis   W. J. Unwin Ltd

SOWING HARDY ANNUALS OUT OF DOORS

Three things are required for germination — moisture, air and warmth. Cold, water-logged or bone dry ground should therefore be avoided. Ideally the soil should be friable, so that it breaks down into small crumbs or particles, and moist. Spring is the best time although certain kinds may also be sown in autumn in order to produce larger plants.

Flowers for Cutting

Sow in straight drills, taken out with a hoe and using a line. Leave plenty of space between the rows and have the beds rather narrow (approximately 3 ft.) so that you can walk either side without trampling on the bed. Keep each kind together. The cut flower border should be away from the ornamental part of the garden and there are many suitable varieties. (See p. 281.)

For Garden Work – Spring Sowing

Seed for this purpose is sown directly into the ground where the plants are to grow. It is best to define the area for each variety or species beforehand, drawing this out with a stick or outlining it with sand.

Draw the shallow drills with a pointed stick or else broadcast the seed. In either case sow very thinly and lightly cover the seed with soil, using the head of the rake. Seedlings will need thinning twice — the first time to an inch apart, and later according to their ultimate height. Thus a plant 12 in. high should

— demand casual plantings. The new introductions should fit into the general scheme as regards height and colour and also comfortably fill their allotted space.

The best plan for formal bedding is to draw out a scheme on paper first, deciding on the main pattern and colour and arranging key positions for 'dot' plants, i.e. taller-growing subjects, such as standard Fuchsias, Eucalyptus, old Geranium plants which have grown on a leg, Grevilleas, Cannas or even annual grasses like the variegated Maize, planted at intervals in the bed to relieve the flatness.

Nemesia, dwarf compact hybrid

Petunias

125

Antirrhinums, semi-dwarf types Copyright Samuel Dobie & Son

eventually be thinned to 6 in., one of 18 in. to 9 in., and any 2 ft. or over left a foot or more from their neighbours. Support weak-stemmed varieties or those suffering from the effects of a gale with shrubby Pea-sticks. Label each patch or group of plants as they are sown.

Autumn Sowing

This method is always more or less a gamble, but if it comes off results in larger plants and earlier and finer flowers. Seed is sown where the plants are to flower from the end of August into September in an open, well drained yet protected situation. Plants will be 2–3 in. high by the time winter sets in.

Half-Hardy Annuals

These are annuals which are sensitive to frost and so either have to be sown outside when all danger of this is over (which would make them very late flowering) or else raised under glass in February or March and then planted out as seedlings towards the end of May or June. For details of method see p. 234.

Among the plants normally raised in this manner are annual Asters (Callistephus), Salvia, Ageratum, Lobelia, Zinnia, Nicotiana, Dahlias, Dimorphotheca, Ipomaea, Kochia, Stocks, Mesembryanthemums, Mimulus, Nemesia, Petunia, Tagetes, Salpiglossis and Venidium.

For Tender Annuals see Greenhouse Section.

Biennials

Biennials take two years to complete their life cycle, usually forming a rosette of leaves and strong rootstock the first season and then expending all their energies in one glorious burst of flowering the next.

The time of sowing is all important, for if this is too soon, the seedlings become over-large at planting time and often succumb to winter's cold. On the other hand biennials sown in late autumn will not make good plants by the following year, although they will certainly flower. June is the best month, with the plants raised in a convenient but out of the way spot and planted out in autumn.

Prepare the soil as recommended for annuals. Where the ground has been manured the previous autumn it will suffice to dress the soil with superphosphate (2 oz. per sq.yd.) and hoe this into the surface layers. Superphosphate stimulates an extensive root system, and is the quickest acting of the phosphatic fertilisers. On very acid soils basic slag may be used instead.

Reduce the soil to a fine level by constant raking and sow the seed thinly in drills. In general, sowing will be a little deeper in summer than spring, because of the greater risks of drying out. Large seeds should be covered with three to four times their own depth of soil, small seeds only lightly covered. Fresh seed, being more vigorous than old, may be set slightly deeper. Watering the ground may be necessary in dry weather, but only as a last resort as it tends to cake the soil surface.

After the seed has germinated the plants must either be thinned or pricked out into nursery beds, 12 to 15 in. apart with 6–9 in. between each.

HARDY ANNUALS

— sown where they are to flower, end of March or April, unless otherwise stated.
* denotes suitable for cutting
+ suitable for autumn sowing in the open
.X. may be grown in partial shade
R suitable for rock garden

ADONIS R
    Buttercup-like flowers and finely cut foliage.
A. aestivalis   Pheasant's Eye. Deep Crimson 1½ ft. June and July.
A. autumnalis   Red Camomile. Crimson with deep red eye 1–1½ ft. June—Sept.

ALYSSUM Sweet Alyssum R
    A. maritimum (Syn. *Lobularia maritima*). Ground cover plant

with small white flowers, honey scented and narrow grey foliage. Varieties with lilac and purplish flowers are available. 6—12 in. All summer.

AMARANTHUS* Love Lies Bleeding
A. caudatus. Long trailing tassels of flowers, almost cord-like. Blood-red, also white and pale green forms. Leaves pale green. Sow April.
A. hypochondriacus Prince's Feather. Leaves greenish-purple, flowers in erect spikes, dark-blood-red. 2—3 ft. Late summer.

ANCHUSA
A. capensis. A biennial which succeeds best treated as a hardy annual. Brilliant blue flowers, very free, something like Forget-me-nots. Good varieties include 'Blue Bird' and 'Bedding Bright Blue'. 1—1½ ft. Summer.

ANTIRRHINUM*
Sow seed in July for flowering the following year. See p. 132.

ATRIPLEX* Red Mountain Spinach
A. hortensis. Crimson leaves, useful in flower decoration. 4—5 ft.

BAERIA
B. coronaria (Syn. *Shortia californica*). Useful for edging, masses of golden Daisy-like flowers; finely cut foliage. 6—9 in.

BORAGO Borage
B. officinalis. Bright blue flowers; rough hairy leaves, useful for flavouring fruit drinks. 2 ft.

CALENDULA*+ Pot Marigold
C. officinalis. Well known plant, adaptable and easy in practically any soil or situation. Sow early March to May. Wide range of varieties with orange, yellow, sulphur, and double flowers. 1—2 ft. All summer. Recommended kinds: 'Surprise', pinkish-orange; 'Twilight', cream and 'Nova', a good single.

CALLIOPSIS See COREOPSIS

Aster, ostrich plumed variety 'Los Angeles'
Copyright Samuel Dobie & Son

CENTAUREA*+
C. cyanus Cornflower. Well known plant with blue, pink or white, maroon and purple flowers. Many of the colours have been fixed so that they come true from seed. There are also double forms, which have an extra row of florets making a larger flower head. 2 ft. A dwarf form, 'Jubilee Gem', may be used for edging purposes Guard against Aphis in the young growing tips. See p. 290.
C. moschata Sweet Sultan. + Excellent cut flowers with fragrant, silky flower heads of white, light and deep mauve, purple and yellow. Likes lime in the soil and plenty of sun. Cut flowers when very young. 2 ft.

Dimorphotheca or Star of the Veldt

Copyright Samuel Dobie & Son

Ursinia anethoides   W. J. Unwin Ltd

CHRYSANTHEMUM *

C. segetum Corn Marigold. Bright golden or ivory flowers. 1½ ft. Varieties 'Morning Star', 'Eastern Star' and 'Evening Star'.

C. coronarium Crown Daisy. Taller with yellow and white flowers. 'Golden Crown' is double; 'Golden Glory' is a well known florist's flower. 2—3 ft.

C. carinatum. Single and double flowers, the former banded in several colours. About 2 ft. Varieties: 'Pole Star', white, purple and yellow; 'Burridgeanum', crimson, white and yellow; 'John Bright', lemon yellow and purplish-brown; 'Eclipse', buff, brown and crimson; 'Torch', bronze and red with crimson or purple zones.

C. frutescens. See p. 253.

CLARKIA +

C. elegans. Autumn sown make twice the size (2—3 ft.) of spring sown plants (1—1½ ft.). Branching, pyramidal habit with long spikes of white, deep purple and various shades of pink flowers. Need early staking and plenty of sun. Sow Sept.—Oct. to flower May—June; or March—April to flower June—July. Single and double varieties available.

COLLINSIA .X.

Lilac and white flowers on slender spikes, in character for several weeks. 1 ft.

COLLOMIA +

Gilia-like flowers, cherry-red. Sun. Favoured by bees. 15—18 in.

CONVOLVULUS

C. tricolor. Dwarf plant with showy funnel-shaped flowers in blue, white and rose. Does well in poor soils. 1 ft. 'Crimson Monarch' is particularly bright, 1 ft. and 'Royal Marine', royal blue, 6—9 in.

C. major (Syn. *Ipomaea purpurea*). A climbing species which must have a sheltered position in sun. Rapid growing for trellis, fences, etc. Sow in May. Flowers blue, carmine, purple and white, usually obtained in mixed seed. July—Sept.

COREOPSIS * Tick-seed

C. tinctoria. Variable plants as regards colour and habit. Some are tall (up to 3 ft.) others dwarf (9 in.) the latter suitable for edging purposes, *atrosanguinea* has rich dark red flowers; *marmorata* is curiously marbled and striped; 2—3 ft.

C. drummondii has golden flowers with chestnut-brown centres. 18 in.

DELPHINIUM * .X. Larkspur

True Larkspurs are derived from two species (*D. ajacis* and *D. consolida*), are not fastidious but favour a well drained soil. Sown Aug.—Sept. in their flowering positions they will reach 5 ft. and come to bloom the following June, continuing for 8—10 weeks. Seed sown March or April produces smaller spikes and flowers from mid-July onwards. Varieties come in various blues, white, purple and pink flowers on branching stems. There are also dwarf varieties up to 1½ ft. tall.

Other Delphiniums raised from seed include the perennial kinds such as *D. belladonna* and *D. hybridum.* See p. 31.

ECHIUM Viper's Bugloss

E. plantagineum. A free flowering annual with bright blue flowers and rough leaves. Favoured by bees. Varieties; 'Blue Bedder', 'Bright Pink' and 'Bright Blue'. 1—2 ft.

EMILIA * Tassel Flower

E. flammea. Clusters of orange-scarlet, tassel-like flowers at the ends of the slender stems. 1½ ft.

ERINUS R

E. alpinus. Ideal for crevices in walls and similar well drained situations in sun. Does not appreciate transplanting, so place seed directly in crannies in walls or rock gardens. Usually flowers the second season. Mauve flowers on short spikes, also pink and white form. 5—6 in.

African Marigolds

Emilia flammea

W. J. Unwin Ltd

ESCHSCHOLTZIA * +R Californian Poppy

E. californica. Brilliant Poppy-shaped flowers in a wide range of colour with single or double blooms. Forms a fleshy tap root (so that it becomes perennial in warm situations) and glaucous, much cut foliage. Any well drained hot position.

Tall Varieties. Height 1 ft.

Alba, white; 'Aurora', creamy-pink; 'Fireglow', glowing orange, 'Golden Glory', 'Ramona', coppery rose; 'Orange Prince', bright orange; 'Orange King', brighter still and 'Mandarin', deep orange.

Dwarf Varieties. Height 6—8 in.

'Miniature Primrose', pale lemon; 'Carmine King', 'Fireflame', 'Golden Rod', 'Rose Queen'.

Double Varieties. Height about 9 in.

'Sutton's Scarlet Glow', 'Double Enchantress', 'Golden Glow', double golden, 1 ft.

EUPHORBIA .X.

E. heterophylla. Mexican Fire Plant. Forms a bushy plant with small orange-red flowers surrounded by green and scarlet blotched leaves. Start under glass in March for stronger plants. 2 ft.

E. marginata. Snow on the Mountain. Pretty plant with light green leaves variegated in white and whitish bracts. 2 ft.

GILIA

Easily grown plant with pincushion-like flower heads of lavender blue. These have black or golden throats in *G. tricolor.* 1—1½ ft. *G. x hybrida* is very varied in colour; yellow, orange, red, rose, purple and violet. 3—6 in. R.

GODETIA *

Something like Clarkia but larger and more showy flowers. Varieties from *G. grandiflora* have given rise to singles and doubles, also dwarf doubles (known as Azalea-flowered), particularly bright with stems 15—18 in. high, smothered with double cerise, crimson or salmon flowers. Suitable for window boxes, cutting, potwork and in the border. Some scented. Varieties: 'Celestial', lavender with black anthers, 1 ft.; 'Kelvedon Glory', rich salmon-pink, 'Sybil Sherwood', double rich salmon edged white, 15 in.; 'Pink Frills', full double; 'Crimson Glow', deep blood red, 1 ft.; 'Snowdrift', white and 'Sutton's Double White'; 'Rose', 'Cherry Red' and 'Mauve', all 2½ ft.

GRASSES

These are attractive in flower, useful for cutting and the majority dry well. The most popular are: *Agrostis nebulosa* Cloud grass; *Agrostis pulchella* Hair Grass; *Avena sterilis* Animated Oat; *Briza maxima* Quaking Grass; *Eragrostis* Love Grass; *Hordeum jubatum* Squirrel-tail Grass; *Lagurus ovatus* Hare's Tail Grass; *Coix lachryma-jobi* Job's Tears which should be started in heat and planted out in May. Has pearly-grey seeds which may be dried as beads.

GYPSOPHILA *

G. elegans is a branching, slender plant with grey leaves and stems and clouds of small white flowers. Used for market work. There is a rose-pink variety, *rosea* and 'Sutton's Crimson'. 1½ ft.

HELIANTHUS Sunflower

The Giant Sunflower grows 8 to 10 ft. high, too tall and

massive for many gardens. Varieties from this have produced a double orange and a fine dark-centred plant, banded with Chestnut-red and known as 'Sutton's Red', 6 ft. There are also singles in colours ranging from creamy white and primrose to orange (3—6 ft.) and miniature forms with black centres, 4 ft., of which 'Stella' is one of the best.

IBERIS R Candytuft
I. umbellata is a popular annual with clusters of white flowers; varieties are pink, deep rose, purple and lilac. Named sorts include 'Lilac Queen', 1 ft. *I. amara* 'White Spiral', 18 in., has spikes of pure white flowers.

IONOPSIDIUM .X. R Violet Cress
Carpeting plant with pale mauve flowers. Spreads freely but never invasive. 2 in.

LARKSPUR See DELPHINIUM

LATHYRUS See SWEET PEA

LAVATERA + Mallow
L. trimestris (Syn. *L. rosea*) is the only annual species of the family, making a branching plant 2—3 ft. high and across. Wide-open flowers of a delightful shade of pink. The best variety is 'Loveliness', deep rose, but there is also a white form and a carmine one 'Carmine Queen'. In flower all summer.

LAYIA +
L. elegans. A 'Daisy' plant with yellow flowers tipped with white; 1 ft.; grey-green, rather hairy foliage.

LIMNANTHES + R
L. douglasii. Very fragrant flowers, 1 in. in diameter, bright yellow with white edges. Shiny green foliage. 6 in.

LINARIA * Toad Flax
L. maroccana. Widely grown annual with variously coloured, Snapdragon flowers on slender stems. Group in patches of mixed colours for best effects. 12—15 in.

LINUM R Flax
L. grandiflorum var. rubrum. The Scarlet Flax is a brilliant annual with campanulate blooms of vivid scarlet, opening only in sunshine. 1—1¼ ft.

LUPINUS * Lupin
The annual Lupins are perhaps less spectacular than their perennial relatives but are nevertheless useful for the back of the annual border. Very accommodating in most soils and situations. White, blue, pink, yellow and bicolored. 1½—4 ft.

MALCOMIA * .X. Virginia Stock
M. maritima. Best sown Sept. for large flowering plants the following year, but can also be sown outside in March and April. Flowers white, pink, red and yellow. 6 in.

MATRICARIA *
Strong smelling plants related to Chrysanthemum with round double heads of flower. *M. eximia* 'Golden Ball' and 'Silver Ball', although perennial, are often used as edging subjects, from March-sown seed under glass. They have double yellow or white flowers respectively. *M. maritima* 'Bridal Robe' is annual and may be sown outside. It has dark green, cut foliage and double white flowers. 1 ft.

MENTZELIA
M. lindleyi (Syn. *Bartonia aurea*). A showy plant with large golden-yellow flowers, filled with golden stamens. Sow in full sun March or April, or raise under glass in Feb. and plant out as soon as big enough to handle. Full sun. 1½—2 ft.

MOLUCELLA * Bells of Ireland
M. laevis. The attractive seed pods are green and shell-like on long stems. Finer plants are obtained by sowing seed separately in small pots in March. May be dried for winter decoration when pods turn white. 1½—2 ft.

NASTURTIUM See TROPAEOLUM

NEMOPHILA + R .X.
Pretty plants of compact and often trailing habit, with wide-open flowers, lasting weeks in character. Sun or shade, moist cool soil. White, purple, claret, blue and white flowers. 6—8 in.

NIGELLA * .X. Love-in-a-Mist
N. damascena 'Miss Jekyll' is a favourite cottage garden plant, with blue flowers surrounded by feathery leaflets and attractive seed pods. Often colonises in a moist, half-shaded spot. There is a white form and one very dark blue. 1—1½ ft.; taller from autumn sown.

Double Godetia 'Sybil Sherwood' Copyright Fidlers of Reading

Coreopsis tinctora   Copyright Ryder & Sons

OMPHALODES + R Venus' Navelwort

O. linifolia Grey foliage, masses of small, white, Forget-me-not flowers. For edging, crazy-paving, and in pots in the cool greenhouse. 9—12 in.

PAPAVER * Poppy

P. rhoeas is the parent of the Shirley Poppy, which gives us some of our brightest annuals. Flowers in a wealth of pastel shades, from white to deep red, some bicolored, single, double and of a pompon nature. Very easily grown in any well drained soil and sun. 1—2 ft.
P. somniferum Opium Poppy has glaucous foliage and flowers 4—5 in. across, varying from pink, rose and purple to white. Garden forms often full double and others bicolored. 3 ft.
P. glaucum Tulip Poppy. Brilliant scarlet, Tulip-shaped. 15—20 in.
P. nudicaule Iceland Poppy. Although perennial, is usually treated as annual. Flowers bright yellow, orange, rose-pink and white on willowy stems. Good for cutting if treated as suggested on p. 279.

PHACELIA .X. R.

Bright blue, bell-shaped flowers. Blooms freely six weeks from sowing in the open ground in April. Favoured by bees.
P. campanularia useful for edging. 9 in. 'Blue Bonnet' is a good variety.
P. tanacetifolia, taller, 1—1½ ft.

RESEDA * .X. Mignonette

Grown for its fragrance. Smooth leaves, spikes of white, yellowish or red flowers. *R. odorata* creamy. 1—1½ ft. Varieties

'Crimson Giant', 'Machet Goliath Golden', 'Red Monarch' and 'Orange Queen'.

SAPONARIA * Soapwort

S. vaccaria has sprays of large pink flowers, excellent for cutting. There is a white form. 2 ft.

SCABIOSA * Scabious

S. atropurpurea Pincushion Flower; Mournful Widow. May be treated as biennial or hardy annual. Excellent cut flower with round 'pincushion' heads white, pink, scarlet, pale mauve, blue and maroon. Slender stems may require staking. Any good garden soil and plenty of sun. 2—3 ft.

TROPAEOLUM * .X. Nasturtium

Well known genus containing both climbing and dwarf varieties. Do well in poor stony soil and may be used for masking trellis, in window boxes, as border subjects and for pot work. Aphides are chief menace and must be dealt with early; spray with nicotine. See p. 290. Most garden forms derived from *T. majus.*
Tall Climbers. Usually singles, with bronze, scarlet, yellow creamy-white, blood-red and variously spotted flowers. Some have variegated foliage.
Semi-Tall. Include the Gleam hybrids — 'Scarlet Gleam', 'Golden Gleam', 'Primrose', 'Orange' and 'Salmon Gleam', all with showy, double flowers.
Dwarf Double. In a variety of shades, making compact, ball-shaped plants.
Single Dwarf. Also known as Tom Thumb. All shades, also variegated foliage forms. Ideal for window boxes.
T. peregrinum Canary Creeper. Delightful climber with small, fringed, bright yellow flowers and pretty, pale green leaves. Shade or sun. Rapid growth, flowers all summer.

HALF-HARDY ANNUALS

See also Greenhouse Section. Raise under glass and plant out when danger of frost is over.

AGERATUM R.

Masses of fluffy mauve flowers; plain green leaves, good for edging, in rock garden or as carpeter. Sun, any soil. 8—10 in. Varieties: 'Blue Riband', 'Capri', 'Little Blue Star'.

Double Sunflowers   Copyright Samuel Dobie & Son

ALONSOA Mask Flower

Sprays of scarlet flowers on $1\frac{1}{2}-2\frac{1}{2}$ ft. stems. Bright green leaves. Light soil, sun. *A. warscewiczii* and its forms are the best.

AMARANTHUS *

A. salicifolius Fountain Plant. Narrow foliage brilliantly coloured with orange, carmine and bronze. 3 ft. *A. tricolor splendens* Joseph's Coat is another good foliage plant with crimson, yellow and green leaves. $2-3$ ft.

ANAGALLIS R Pimpernel

Bright scarlet or Gentian-blue flowers which only open in sunshine. Suitable for edging. 6 in.

ANTIRRHINUM * Snapdragon

Sow in warm greenhouse or frame Feb.—April, prick out into boxes, harden off and plant out end of May or June. Appreciate sun and well drained soil. Varieties can be obtained in yellow, pink, red, scarlet, bronze, white, orange colours or mixed. For best results grow the scientifically raised F 1 Hybrid Varieties, which must be renewed annually from bought seed.

Varieties may be obtained as follows: tall ($3-4$ ft.); inter-

Cleome spinosa, Spider Plant

Brachycome iberidifolia, Swan River Daisy   W. J. Unwin Ltd

mediate ($2-2\frac{1}{2}$ ft.); dwarf ($1-1\frac{1}{2}$ ft.); and Tom Thumb (6 in.). Also Rust-resistant varieties. Rust i main scourge of Antirrhinums for which reason the plants — which are really perennial — are usually treated as annuals so as not to carry disease spores from one season to another.

ARCTOTIS * African Daisy

Brilliant Daisy flowers of white, pink, rich red, bronze orange, yellow, carmine and apricot on $12-15$ in. stems. Only really good in a hot, dry position. Foliage attractively cut, silvery grey. Plant out in May for blooms from June until autumn.

ASTERS * China .X.

Correct name *Callistephus chinensis*. Seed should be sown in March or April in shallow boxes, pricked off and planted out in May. In warm areas may also be sown outdoors the end of April or early May. Rich soil which remains moist, sun or light shade. The main types are Double, including 'Ostrich Plume', $1\frac{1}{2}$ ft.; Chrysanthemum flowered, 1 ft.; 'Comet', $1\frac{1}{2}$ ft., 'Powderpuff', 2 ft.; 'Pompon', 15 in. Single, 'Giant Single' (Madelaine). Tremendous colour range, from pure white, soft yellow, pink, scarlet, and various shades of blue and mauve.

BALSAM See Impatiens

BRACHYCOME R Swan River Daisy

A dry, sunny position suits this dwarf, Daisy-flowered annual

with lavender, mauve and white flowers. *B. iberidifolia* is the main species. $6-9$ in.

CARNATION (Dianthus) *

Seed should be sown of the Chabaud varieties in Jan. or Feb. These come to bloom in Aug. and can be carefully lifted and potted to continue flowering under glass for winter blossom. Singles and doubles. $1\frac{1}{2}$ ft.

Dianthus chinensis, Japanese Pink. Contains the group known as *heddewigii*, with showy flowers, often with fringed petals in a wide range of pinks, reds and whites, violets and yellow; both single and double. $1\frac{1}{2}$ ft.

CINERARIA

C. maritima (Syn. *Senecio maritima*). Grown for its fine silver foliage which contrasts well with other plants in summer bedding schemes. 1 ft.

CLEOME Spider Plant

C. spinosa. An elegant plant with spiny stems and leaves and

Dwarf Gaillardias, Comet strain

132

Kochia scoparia var. childsii   W. J. Unwin Ltd

large, showy clusters of pink and white flowers with protruding stigmas. 'Rose Queen' is a brighter pink. Any soil which does not dry out. 2—4 ft.

COBAEA See p. 284.

COSMOS * Cosmea

Early flowering strains of *C. bipinnatus* sown in March and put out in May, provide flowers for cutting all summer. Blooms like Coreopsis, about 5 in. across, rose-pink, crimson or white. 2½—3 ft.

DAHLIA * See also p. 114.

Many of the bedding Dahlias are raised annually from seed. They are started in gentle heat towards the end of March and pricked off singly when large enough to handle into 3 in. pots, moved again into 5 in. pots as growth progresses and planted out in their flowering positions the end of May or early June. Rich moist soil and full sun.

Types so treated include 'Coltness Hybrids', singles in many colours, 18 in.; 'Collarettes', which have a second series of petals

Salpiglossis 'Bolero'   Copyright Samuel Dobie & Son

on the ray florets, 3—5 ft.; 'Double Pompons', round, double flowers up to 3 in. across, 3 ft. and variety of dwarf and other hybrids in a wide range of colour. 2½—5 ft.

DIMORPHOTHECA * Star of the Veldt

D. aurantiaca. Slender branching annuals with delicately coloured flowers of apricot, lemon, white or orange. The outer ray florets of these often have vivid blue or purplish bases. Good cut flowers although the blooms close at night. 1 ft. Well drained soil, full sun.

FELICIA R

F. bergeriana Kingfisher Daisy. Brilliant blue, Daisy-like flowers with golden centres. Edging or rockery work. 6 in. Sun. Apt to close in dull weather.

GAILLARDIA * Blanket Flower

Sow under glass in March and plant out in May. In flower from July till autumn. Good for cutting. Blooms blood-red, chestnut-red and crimson, also bronze, yellow and a mixture of shades. 15 in.

GAZANIA Treasure Flower. See also p. 33.

Brilliant Daisy flowers in a wide range of extravagant colours. Although perennial, they are often treated as half-hardy annuals. Sun essential. 12—15 in.

GOMPHRENA * Globe Amaranth

Looks like a purple Clover, with large round 'everlasting' heads. Varieties have white, golden, pink and variegated flowers. 1½ ft. Plant out in May from March-sown seed.

HELICHRYSUM * Strawflower

Popular 'everlastings' with bronze, crimson and orange flowers which feel like straw. The round, globular heads should be gathered just before they are fully ripe. 1½—2½ ft.

HELIPTERUM *

Everlasting flowers usually soft pink, smaller and daintier than Helichrysum. Sometimes offered as Acroclinium or Rhodanthe. Raise under glass in March and plant out later or grow in pots. 15—18 in.

IMPATIENS Balsam

I. balsamina requires rich, moist soil and plenty of sun. Must have shelter from strong winds or grown in pots if the situation is too exposed. Sow in March and plant out in June. The 'Double Bush-flowered' forms are useful for the front of the border. The Camellia-flowered hybrids produce branching stems, packed with large, double Camellia-like flowers in shades of salmon, scarlet, violet and white. July—Aug. 1½ ft.

IPOMOEA Morning Glory

I. rubro-coerulea 'Heavenly Blue'. One of our most beautiful climbing plants with large trumpet-shaped flowers of sheer azure blue. The stems will climb up string or twiggy pea-sticks and although individual blooms only last a day, the plant remains in character for weeks. Germination may be assisted by chipping or soaking the seeds before sowing.

KOCHIA .X. Burning Bush

Grown for its foliage *K. scoparia tricophila* makes neat little bushes of brilliant green which turn scarlet and bronze at the tips in autumn. 2 ft. Can also be sown outside in May.

LIMONIUM * Sea Lavender; Statice

L. sinuatum although biennial is usually grown as a half-hardy annual. This well known plant with lavender, mauve, rose, white and even dark blue shades is a favourite for cutting and may be dried as an 'everlasting' for winter decoration. 1½—2 ft.

133

Ageratum

L. suvorowii is more delicate and best treated as a pot plant, although it can be planted out in sheltered situations. Sow in March and pot on as required until finally in 5—6 in. pots. The bright rose flowers are stalkless and completely pack the branching 1½ to 2 ft. spikes.

LOBELIA R

L. erinus. Dwarf edging or hanging basket flowers with a long season of bloom. Varieties include Sutton's 'Cambridge Blue', 'Dark Blue', 'Mauve' and 'Royal Purple'. There are also white forms. Seed is very small and *must* be sown thinly. Rich, well cultivated soil that does not dry out. 4—6 in.

L. pendula 'Sapphire' is a trailing variety especially useful for window boxes or hanging baskets. Deep blue with white eyes.

MATTHIOLA Stock

Fragrant plants of fine habit. Grow for cutting, border work (with others or by themselves) as pot plants or in window boxes. Must have rich well cultivated soil and never be short of moisture. They like a little lime and repay feeding with liquid manure.

M. bicornis Night Scented Stock is a hardy annual and may be sown outside in April where it is to flower. Blooms insignificant but fragrance delightful. 1 ft.

Brompton Stock * Sow in cold frames in July, pricking out into boxes or singly in 3 in. pots and plant in flowering quarters Sept. or early Oct.

Summer Flowering * Treated as half-hardy. Sow in March, prick off and plant out in May.

East Lothian * Autumn-flowering, sow early March.

Winter Flowering * or Beauty of Nice. Sow in June and prick off into small pots. Grow on in cold frames and bring into greenhouse end of Oct. or Nov. May also be sown in March and planted outside in May.

Stocks come in a wide range of pinks and blues and there are mauve and white forms.

MESEMBRYANTHEMUM R

M. criniflorum Livingstone Daisy. Forms a spreading mat with succulent, linear leaves and brilliant Daisy flowers. These may be cerise, scarlet, carmine, pink, orange and apricot but only open in bright weather. Good seaside plant and useful on rock banks and similar dry, sunny situations. Sow March and April and plant out in May. 4 in.

MIMULUS .X. Monkey Flower

These need a moist position, shaded from the midday sun. Most of the garden forms have come from *M. cupreus* and *M. luteus*, both perennial. Sow under glass in March and plant 9—12 in. apart. Flowers tubular, scarlet, crimson, orange, etc. often spotted and blotched with chocolate. 1 ft.

NEMESIA *

N. strumosa. Brilliant annuals of neat, compact habit in scarlet, crimson, light blue, lilac, bronze, orange, pink, white and primrose shades. Good for cutting. Need cool conditions when young, so beware of drought. Sow mid-March and plant out in May. 9—12 in.

NICOTIANA .X. Tobacco Plant

Sweet scented, tubular flowers on long, slender stems. Do not plant out until all risk of frost is over. Rich moist soil, sun or partial shade. Blooms open at night or in shadier situations. Flowers pink, red, crimson and white. 1—2½ ft.

NIEREMBERGIA R Cup Flower

N. coerulea (Syn. *hippomanica*). A bushy plant with small leaves, covered with flat, open Petunia-like flowers of Lavender-blue, and clear yellow centres. Although perennial the plant is best treated as half-hardy and sown in Feb., under glass for planting out in May. Very bright in the front of the border. Lifted plants can be kept in the greenhouse or frame for flowering next year. 6—9 in.

PENSTEMON *

Perennials of doubtful hardiness, reproduced by cuttings or from seed as half-hardy annuals. Sow in warmth in Feb. and March for flowers from Aug. onwards. Mixed shades or varieties which come true in white, pink and scarlet shades may be bought, also Sutton's 'Blue Gem' and 'Brilliant Blue' for named sorts with blue flowers. Many of the blooms are edged with contrasting shades. 2 ft. well drained soil, sun or partial shade.

PETUNIA R

The single bedding Petunia is one of our most valuable annuals, and in an open position will flower well the whole summer. It has innumerable uses for borders (alone or mixed with others), in hanging baskets and window boxes, in pockets in the rock garden or even for growing in holes in tubs after the manner of a strawberry barrel. Some sections are suitable for pot plants in the cool greenhouse, and if cut back, will break again and flower a second time. *Pot Plants*. Sow Feb. under glass and pot on gradually until a 5—6 in. pot is reached. John Innes Potting Compost is suitable. *Bedding Kinds*. Sow March under glass, prick off in boxes and plant out early June.

The following types are available:

1. *Large flowered*. Known as F_1 Hybrids; very vigorous with large flowers of pink, red, white, Primrose-yellow (e.g. var. 'Brass Band') and crimson. Pelleted seed is available from many growers — each seed wrapped round with fertiliser and insecticide, making for easy sowing and giving the plants a good start. 12—15 in.
2. *Single or Bedding*. Various colours. Varieties include 'Blue Bedder', 'Rose of Heaven', 'Violet Bedder', 'Red Ensign' (an F_1 Hybrid), 'Pink Satin' and 'Coral Satin'. 1—1¼ ft.
3. *Double*. Usually offered in mixed colours. Flowers large and fringed. 1 ft.

PHLOX R

P. drummondii. Long-lasting plants, suitable for window boxes and formal bedding, which like a rich soil and plenty of sun. Sow in heat in March and plant out end of May. Can also be used for pots sown Aug.—Sept. and potted on singly to flower in the greenhouse April or May.

The Grandiflora or Large Flowered types come in white, vermilion, crimson, many shades of pink and purple, often with contrasting 'eyes'. They grow 12—18 in. high. There are also dwarf races, very free flowering and compact. The best of these is 'Sutton's Beauty', available in many shades and growing about 6 in. 'Twinkle Dwarf Star' comprises another group with starry flowers of many shades. 6—9 in.

PORTULACA R Sun Plant

Can be treated as half-hardy or hardy annual. Carpet habit, 6—8 in. with cup-shaped flowers only opening in sunshine. Single and double forms available in white, soft yellow, rose and white, purple and scarlet. Useful for carpeting a hot, dry bank or growing in shallow containers.

RHODANTHE See HELIPTERUM

Tithonia rotundifolia 'Torch'   Copyright Samuel Dobie & Son

Venidiums   H. Smith

Arctotis, African Daisy   Copyright Samuel Dobie & Son

Sweet Scabious   W. J. Unwin Ltd

RICINUS Castor Oil Plant

Fine foliage plant for 'dot' work amongst bedding plants. Reaches 2—6 ft. in a season, with large, deeply cut leaves. There are varieties with bronze and purple foliage. Sow seeds singly in small pots in March, pot on and place outside in June.

RUDBECKIA * Coneflower

The Gloriosa Daisies have fine large flowers 3—4 in. across in late summer and autumn. These have rough leaves and stems and Daisy flowers with protruding centres and florets of bronze, orange, crimson or yellow; many showing beautifully contrasting zones of colour. Excellent for cutting. 2—3 ft. Sow under glass Feb. or March and plant out in May. The tetraploid hybrids are particularly fine and up to 7 in. across. Rich, moist soil and sun.

SALPIGLOSSIS

S. sinuata. Half-hardy annual with trumpet-shaped flowers on slender, branching stems, often beautifully veined with contrasting colours, the main shades being gold, yellow, crim-

Giant-flowered Pansy   Copyright Ryder & Sons

son, violet or blue. Many of these come true from seed. 'Sutton's Trumpet' is a particularly good strain. Seed should be sown late Feb. or March, pricked off in pots and put outside early June. Seed may also be sown outside end of April or May. Well drained soil and a sheltered, sunny situation. 2½—3 ft.

SALVIA

S. splendens is the Scarlet Sage, a fine, fiery red plant which blooms all summer. Good varieties are 'Blaze of Fire', 'Fireball' and 'Harbinger', all 1 ft.; also 'Dobie's Tom Thumb', 6—8 in., scarlet and salmon.

S. horminum * Blue Beard has deep violet-blue bracts which terminate its 1—1½ ft. stems. There is a pink bracted form called 'Pink Lady'. These may also be treated as hardy annuals.

S. patens has brilliant blue, Snapdragon-like flowers and soft grey foliage. It is a tender perennial best treated as a half-hardy annual. There is a pale blue form called 'Cambridge Blue'. 1½ ft.

S. farinacea has long spikes of deep blue Lavender-like flowers and silvery stems. 'Blue Bedder' is deeper in colour. 2—3 ft.

TAGETES African and French Marigolds

Well known plants with thick stems, rather unpleasant smelling foliage and single or double gold, yellow, orange or bronze flowers.

African Marigolds. Derived from *T. erecta*, and taller than their French counterparts. The double forms are particularly fine, with large globular heads, 6 in. across on branching stems. The F₁ Hybrids are magnificent, especially in the 'Climax' and 'Crackerjack' strains. 2½ ft.

French Marigolds. These are from *T. patula* and dwarfer than preceding with single or double flowers. Colours range from palest lemon to deep mahogany, many striped with several shades. 9 in.—2 ft. Sow early April and plant out early June, in rich soil with plenty of sun.

T. signata pamila. Dwarf forms which make dome-shaped plants covered with single flowers. 'Lulu', yellow and 'Ursula', orange. Useful for edging. 9 in.

TITHONIA * Mexican Sunflower

T. rotundifolia. Flowers resemble a single Dahlia with rich orange-red petals. Much branched 5—6 ft. and good for cutting. 'Torch' is a dwarfer variety. Any good soil, full sun.

URSINIA *

U. anethoides. Daisy-like flowers of vivid orange with central zone of Chestnut-red. 'Golden Bedder' is light orange 1 ft. '*pulchra*' is a dwarf, 6—8 in. bright orange. Full sun.

VENIDIUM * Monarch of the Veldt

V. fastuosum. A beautiful 'Daisy' with large flowers 4—5 in. across, vivid orange, with a purplish-black central zone. The foliage and stems have a dense covering of short white hairs. Hybrids from this show a wide range of colour, e.g. ivory, cream, yellow and straw all with deep black and maroon central zonings. Full sun and well drained soil. 2—3 ft.

VERBENA

Half-hardy perennials usually grown as half-hardy annuals. Useful bedding plants or for edging purposes and in window boxes. Many have fragrant flowers. June until the frosts.

The majority make compact, bushy plants 12—15 in. high, with rounded heads of small flowers, pink, red, mauve, rich blue, purple or white, mostly coming true from seed. There are several Large Flowered Strains and also a Dwarf one about 9 in. high.

Other types include 'Sweet Lavender', globe-shaped clusters of lavender-blue flowers 15—18 in.; 'Rose Vervain', rose-pink 12—15 in.; *V. bonariensis*, really perennial, with 3—4 ft. stems and rosy-purple flowers; also *V. rigida* (Syn. *venosa*), violet-purple. 1 ft.

Mesembryanthemum criniflorum

Rudbeckias   H. Smith

Zinnia, Giant Dahlia flowered   Copyright Samuel Dobie & Son

ZINNIA* Youth and Old Age

Good cut flowers which show a wide range of colour. Must have a rich soil and plenty of sunshine. Resent transplanting so prick off into pots and plant out in June without damaging roots. Sow under glass in April or May in open ground.

Giant Dahlia-Flowered. Robust 2—3 ft. plants with double blooms in a wide range of shades from pale lemon to orange, apricot, pink, red, crimson and purple. 'Mammoth' is another large flowered strain.

Chrysanthemum-flowered. This type includes 'Burpees Hybrid' with incurved petals like Chrysanthemums.

Lilliput. Dwarf plants 9—12 in. high, with fully double miniature flowers in the usual colour range.

BIENNIALS

Sow one year to flower the next.

BELLIS* R Daisy

B. perennis, well known plant which has given rise to larger flowered garden forms with single or double blooms. The latter are more showy and may be white, pink or crimson, others have quilled petals. 9—12 in. Cool, moist soil. Sow seed May or June, prick out in nursery beds and flowering positions in autumn. 'Sutton's Miniature' is the name given to a race of dwarfs (4 in.) with double flowers, suitable for the rock garden.

CAMPANULA* .X.

C. medium Canterbury Bell. Available in single, double and Cup and Saucer varieties, in white, pink, pale mauve and blue varieties. These come true from seed. Sow May and June and plant out in flowering positions early autumn. 2—3 ft.

Several perennial species also are often raised from seed, notably *C. persicifolia* and *C. carpatica,* the former 2—3 ft., the latter 6—12 in. Flowers blue or white.

CHEIRANTHUS* Wallflower

Indispensable for early display beds, easy to grow even in chalk soils. Very fragrant and colours vary from white, pink, red, yellow and bronze. Varieties of *C. cheiri* include 'Blood Red', 'Cloth of Gold', 'Eastern Queen', chamois changing to rosy-red; 'Fire King', orange-red; 'Golden Bedder'; 'Harbinger', bronze; 'Primrose Monarch'; 'Rose Queen'; 'Ruby Gem' and

Wallflowers   H. Smith

Double bush-flowered Balsam

'Vulcan', velvety crimson. 15—18 in. Mixed shades give excellent results.

A dwarf race known as 'Tom Thumb' is useful for windy places or in window boxes. Flowers crimson and yellow 6—9 in.

Sow May and June, prick out in showery weather 9 in. apart and place in flowering positions Sept. or Oct.

*C. x allionii** Siberian Wallflower.

Best treated as biennial. Sow July and Aug. where they are to flower. Blooms brilliant orange. 15 in.

DIANTHUS*

D. barbatus Sweet William. Well known plants with stiff, sturdy stems and crowded heads of fragrant, beautifully marked flowers. Sow seed in June or July or under glass in early March for full flower in July and Aug. 15—18 in. Can be bought to colour, e.g. 'Giant White', 'Scarlet Beauty', 'Pink Beauty' etc. or in variable strains such as 'Auricula-Eyed', 'Mixed' and 'Indian Carpet' dwarf. 6—12 in.

The hybrid 'Sweet Wivelsfield' 1½ ft. can be treated as annual if sown in March.

DIGITALIS* .X. Foxglove

Stately woodland plants, which can even be transplanted when in full bloom. *D. purpurea* is the best known with purplish or white, brown spotted flowers on 2—3 ft. spikes. Varieties also obtainable with apricot, rose, pink and cream flowers, some spotted, others plain; the Excelsior strain is particularly good. Sow May or June in a shady spot, transplant as soon as possible and plant out in autumn in their flowering positions.

GILIA

G. rubra Scarlet Gilia. Tall stems with finely cut leaves and terminating in several plumed spikes of scarlet flowers. Sow Sept. under glass, pot singly and put out in May. 3—4 ft.

HESPERIS* .X.

H. matronalis Sweet Rocket, Dame's Violet. Has fragrant, single, Honesty (Lunaria)-like flowers in spikes. Purple, white and mauve. Scent more noticeable at night. Sow May and June in flowering situations. 2—3 ft. *H. tristis* flowers cream, purple or brownish. Fragrant. 18 in.

ISATIS*

I. tinctoria Woad. The plant with which Ancient Britons used to paint their bodies. Showy sprays of small yellow flowers, stems yield a blue dye. Leaves entire. Any soil, sun or light shade. 2—3 ft.

LUNARIA* .X. Honesty

Chiefly grown for the fine silvery seed pods which are decorative in winter bouquets. *L. annua* (syn. *biennis*) has spikes of white or purple flowers May to July and heart-shaped leaves. Sow April or May for flowering the following year. Light shade. 1½—2 ft.

MYOSOTIS* R Forget-me-Not

Sow seed May or June and plant in flowering positions Sept. or Oct. To maintain stock from one year to another, lift old plants in May and shake them over a waste piece of

Bellis perennis　　　　　　Copyright Fidlers of Reading

Digitalis 'Excelsior' hybrids　　Copyright Samuel Dobie & Son

ground before putting on compost heap. This usually gives enough seedlings for bedding purposes. Colours include light and deep blue, white and pink. Varieties: 'Sutton's Royal Blue', 'Wraysbury Blue', 'Carmine King', 'Indigo Blue', 9—15 in. and 'Blue Ball', 6 in.

OENOTHERA .X. Evening Primrose

O. biennis. Chiefly valuable for its spires of night-scented, night-opening pale yellow flowers on leafy stems. Light shade, as amongst tall trees. Sow June and July. 2—4 ft. *O. trichocalyx,* grey-leaved, with pure white flowers which stay open all day. Very fragrant. 1½ ft.

ONOPORDON .X.

O. acanthium Giant Thistle. Only suitable for the back of the border or the wild garden, this has large, silver, spiny leaves on silvery 8—10 ft. stems. Flowers blue-purple. Sow May and June in flowering positions for blooms the following year.

POLYANTHUS* .X.

Plants of hybrid origin (*P. vulgaris* Primrose x *P. veris* Cowslip) with showy flowers of many shades. Although perennial they are often treated as biennials to obtain larger blooms.

Sow the seed Feb. or March in boxes of light, peaty or leafy soil. Prick off and keep in frames until mid-May, then plant outside in a cool shady situation. Plant in flowering positions in Oct. (in sun). Lift old plants when flowers are finished, split and plant in shade until the following Oct.

Seed can be obtained in blues, pinks and red, yellows, creams, bronze etc. Although variable these will come reasonably true. 12—15 in.

P. auricula * .X. Auriculas. Treat as Polyanthus but sow the seed later. They will stand more sun than the latter. Shades very striking and variable, often with several zones of colour in the same bloom. 6—9 in.

VERBASCUM Mullein

Noble plants with tall spikes of yellow, apricot, creamy-white or mauve flowers. The foliage is often silvery, due to a dense covering of short white hairs. Suitable for any well drained soil, in the open border, lightly shaded shrubbery or wild garden.

V. olympicum, sulphur-yellow, very striking, 6—9 ft. June.

V. bombyciferum, more commonly known as V. 'Broussa' is perhaps the most beautiful, the whole plant silvery. Even the lemon flowers peep through a cotton-wool-like covering. 5—6 ft. July—Aug.

V. phoeniceum is really perennial, but often grown as annual, with flowers in mauve, pink, purple and white. 2 ft.

VIOLA* .X. R Pansies and Violas

Although they often persist for years, Violas and Pansies are best treated as biennials, setting the seed in June and July for flowering the following year. Sow in cool, moist soil, either in a frame (where conditions are more readily controlled) or in a shaded spot in the garden. Prick out 6 in. apart when large enough to handle, preferably in showery weather; rows 12 in. apart. Place in flowering positions in Sept. or Oct.

Although this is the best method, Pansies for summer flowering can also be sown under glass in March, pricked off in boxes and planted out early May. Alternatively, sow thinly where they are to flower in March or April. Keep the old flowers removed and grow in moist soil in light shade.

Giant Flowered Varieties and Winter Flowering Pansies come in many shades and colours. There are also named varieties.

Violas are similar to Pansies, but more tufted in habit, with smaller flowers; the blooms also are usually self coloured.

Varieties: 'Maggie Mott', very old blue form; 'Arkwright Ruby'; 'Yellow Bedder', 'Irish Molly', greenish-yellow; 'Jackanapes', small yellow and brown and many others. 6—8 in. All summer.

139

Lawns

A lawn is one of the most important features in a garden, attractive at all times and providing a pleasant foil for the surrounding flowers and trees. Sometimes it is also a recreational area, in which case it comes in for a considerable amount of wear and tear. In any case, the lawn mower constantly removes part of its surface, and when one realises that approximately 12 in. of grass is taken each year from the average lawn, it is scarcely surprising that some of these are not as green and flourishing as they might be.

Grass is a plant — just as much as any other in the garden and so needs feeding and watering and certain routine attentions.

Lawns can be made by one of the following methods:

SEED

This is slower than turfing but less expensive. It also gives the best results. Start by levelling the ground and digging it over to a depth of one spit. On very heavy land it may be advisable to drain the land first and then double dig it. Do not, however, mix the subsoil with the topsoil. Ideally, the digging should be done in autumn and the ground left rough until spring; then raked and hoed regularly throughout the summer to rid it of weeds and make all firm and level.

Sow early September (for best results) or April, using a good quality seed, free from Ryegrass. Only in hard playing areas should one include Rye in the mixture.

To ensure even distribution divide the lawn up into yard strips — using tape stretched across both ways. Dress the ground with Growmore fertiliser (2–4 oz. per sq.yd.) a week before sowing and rake

Lawn, Clare College, Cambridge

A garden in Kent H. Smith

Lawn and flower beds Fisons Horticulture

Lawn and rock garden J. E. Downward

J. E. Downward

it in. Apply the grass seed ($1\frac{1}{2}$–2 oz. per sq.yd.), gently rake in, but do not roll, and protect with cotton against birds.

When the new grass is about 2 in. high, lightly roll the surface on a dry day and a few days later cut with a scythe or a sharp mower (the blades set very high). As time goes by gradually reduce blades to a $\frac{1}{2}$ in. cut.

TURF

Prepare the ground as for seeding and make sure the surface is firm and level. Sprinkle Growmore (2–4 oz. per sq.yd.) on the surface and start laying the turves in one corner, working diagonally across the site. They should alternate with one another like bricks in a wall. Always face the way you are going and stand on a board over the turf you have just laid. Turves should be laid between October and February.

After laying, a top dressing of sandy compost may be applied (2–3 lb. per sq.yd.) to fill the cracks. Brush this in. Mow, lightly at first, gradually reducing height of cutting blades.

PLANTING ROOTS

This is a comparatively new method and involves planting small tufts of a particular variety of grass at regular intervals. A form of Creeping Bent (*Agrostis stolonifera*) is used and may be bought ready for planting. Make sure that it is green at time of purchase.

After preparing the soil by digging, manuring and raking, plant the roots in rows, using a line to ensure straightness. The tufts are set in a trench with soil returned to the centre so that the offsets protrude from each end like whiskers. The plants are placed 12 in. apart.

Advantages of this type of lawn are its resilient and hardwearing nature and permanent greenness; also it does not require as much mowing. It is not, however, suitable for sports greens although it will flourish under trees and bushes.

CARE OF ESTABLISHED LAWNS

Lawns require feeding, weeding, cutting, raking, aerating and sometimes watering. A routine programme should therefore follow along these lines:

End of March or April

Rake with a wire rake and apply a compound fertiliser (such as Growmore) at the rate of 4 oz. per sq.yd. If you are troubled by weeds buy a combined fertiliser and weedkiller e.g. Fison's Evergreen.

Mid-June

Repeat the fertiliser dose to keep the grass green and healthy for the rest of the growing season.

Laying turves. Note how the operator 'breaks' the joints
Fisons Horticulture

Autumn (late August and September)

Rake the grass thoroughly with a wire rake to pull out dead roots, etc. Spike the area (see p. 143) and apply an autumn turf dressing (2 oz. per sq.yd.), containing phosphate and potash but very little nitrogen.

Where the physical condition of the lawn is poor, denoted by weak or sparse grass, bad drainage and moss, it may be greatly improved by a top dressing of compost:

> 6 parts sharp sand
> 3 parts screened loam soil
> 1 part moist fine peat.

Apply this at the rate of 3 lb. per sq.yd. and work into the surface with a stiff brush. More loam may be included on very light soil.

LAWN TOOLS

Wire Rake

Choose one with long, springy tines that will pull out debris and dead grass. Use several times a year. *Do not* rake during frost or drought periods.

Pulling out matted growth, dead roots etc. with a wire rake. Do not rake lawn during frost or drought
Fisons Horticulture

Mower

Ideally, grass should be mown twice a week in summer. Motor mowers are easier to use but a good hand machine usually gives a better finish. There are also battery and electrically operated mowers. Always buy the best model you can afford and keep the grass box on whenever possible.

Shears

Essential for edge trimming; a pair of long handled shears save bending.

Watering

Sometimes necessary during droughts. A sprinkler at the end of a garden hose is best.

Spiking

Spiking with a fork helps to prevent soil compaction and encourages grass roots to grow freely. You may use either —

1. *A Garden Fork*, inserted 4–6 in. into turf and withdrawn without prising surface. Repeat at intervals of 3 in. all over lawn.

2. *Hollow-tine Fork*. These have hollow prongs and so remove a core of soil each time the fork is inserted. Repeat at intervals of 4 in. and sweep up cores on completion.

3. *Spiking Machines*. These are of various types and easy to manage.

Spreaders

Useful to give quick and even distribution of fertiliser, seed etc, available in several sizes. With the Quillot Spreader, for example, a hopper is fed with the material and the machine pushed (on two wheels) up and down the lawn. Distribution is governed by specially cut metering grooves in a roller beneath the hopper.

Rollers

Rarely needed on good lawns and do more harm than good. The only exception is when turf lifts after frost. Even then a light roller (not more than 2 cwt.) only should be used.

Weeding

Certain hormone compounds, such as M.C.P.A., 2:4-D and 2:4:5-T are harmless to grass but deadly to weeds. These can be applied, if required, between April and September.

a) Mixed with water from a watering can or sprayer.
b) From an aerosol applicator.
c) Mixed with fertiliser (e.g. Fison's Evergreen).

General rules to observe when using selective weedkillers are:

Only apply on a calm day, as drip may affect the flower borders.

Do not apply during a drought and don't mow the lawn for at least a day after application.

Don't apply selective weedkillers to new lawns for at least 3 months.

Wash out all equipment very thoroughly after use. Preferably keep a separate can for the purpose.

Apply during fine, warm weather when growth is active (between spring and early autumn), and water in if rain does not fall within 48 hours.

Don't use compost made from treated mowings until at least 6 months later.

Lawn Pests and Diseases: See p. 294.

A distributor spreads powdered fertiliser and/or selective weedkiller quickly and efficiently   Fisons Horticulture

Spiking the lawn to prevent soil compaction. Insert prongs 4–6 in. deep
Fisons Horticulture

Sweet Peas

The original Sweet Pea, *Lathyrus odoratus*, was a much smaller plant than any variety we know today, having two lavender-blue and reddish-purple blooms to a stem. It was also extremely sweetly scented. Hybrids were later produced with waved margins, (Spencer Sweet Peas), and with three, four and then five flowers to a stem, in a wide range of shades and colours.

CULTIVATION

Sweet Peas are raised annually from seed. Prefer-

'Gertrude Tingay'   J. E. Downward

ably these should be sown under glass, potted on when large enough to handle and later planted in their flowering positions. They may also be sown directly into the open ground, at the end of February or March, but unless the soil is exceptionally good and the weather mild results are uncertain.

Normal procedure is as follows:

1. Sow mid-September to early October, singly in pots, or 1½ in. apart and 1 in. deep in boxes of John Innes No. 1 Potting Compost. Keep in closed cold frames and water after sowing. No further moisture should be given until germination takes place. Now remove the lights and give as much air as possible. Stretch cotton or Scaraweb across the top if bird damage is expected, and only replace lights in torrential rains or heavy frosts. Nip out the tops when three pairs of leaves are showing. This makes for strong new basal growths, one or more of which will later be selected to carry next season's flowers. A week or so later pot plants singly in 3 in. pots and leave in cold frame until early March.

Harden off and plant out according to district and weather conditions — normally between the end of February and early March.

2. Sow in shallow boxes January—February, and place in the cool greenhouse. After germination remove the seedlings to a cold frame to harden off. Plant out at the first favourable opportunity.

The Soil

Sweet Peas thrive in most soils and districts but make better plants in deep, cool, rich but well drained soil. The roots go far down, so the soil should be dug as deeply as possible and adequately manured. If rotted manure is unobtainable use compost, or apply fertiliser thus:

On heavy land

4 oz. Basic Slag plus 2 oz. Kainit to each sq.yd. in autumn.

On light land

4 oz. Superphosphate plus 1 oz. sulphate of potash to each sq.yd. in spring, two weeks before planting.

Staking

This is a very necessary part of cultivation. Use stout posts (7–10 ft. high) or sturdy Bamboo canes of the same length. Stagger these in double or single rows 15–18 in. apart. Ties of string or wire can be strung across for additional support. Stakes are frequently put in with the plants, which are set 6–8 in. apart in the rows. Shake out the roots if wound round pots, when gardening on light soils, but leave the soil ball intact when plants go into heavy clay.

Tie the plants to the stakes and in three or four weeks remove all but two of the side shoots. Pinch out side shoots or laterals which appear on these. Eventually only one — the strongest shoot — should be left and trained upwards.

All ties should be very loose and made with soft string, raffia or fillis. The Growmore Mesh panels also make excellent supports for Sweet Peas, the shoots being simply wound in and out of the squares.

Cuthbertson hybrids   J. E. Downward

Picking should proceed regularly. Never let the old blooms remain on the plant or they will go on to seed and slow down flower production.

Watering is not advocated unless it can be very thorough and repeated as necessary, but spraying with a lawn sprinkler keeps the plants cool. Mulching the surface with peat, compost or decayed manure also conserves water in the ground.

If growth goes on beyond the capacity of the stakes, the stem can be carefully untied and 'kneed'. The loosened stem is taken upright for a short distance, then run along the string or wire horizontally, and finally sent upwards again, several feet away from the root.

Fertilisers

If the ground was well prepared prior to planting, extra fertilisers are unnecessary. Liquid manures may be used at weekly intervals if the soil seems to need it, but only diluted. Soft stems and foliage induced by overfeeding fall easy prey to streak and other diseases.

SOME GOOD VARIETIES

White and Cream Varieties

'Cream Delight', one of best creams; 'Cream Frills', cream; 'Ecstasy', blush-pink on white; 'Ice Cream', fragrant, delicate cream, frilled; 'Mount Everest', pure white, frilled standards; 'Ryder's Picotee Cream', cream, edged with pink; 'Ryder's Picotee White', frilled white, edged pink; 'Swan Lake', the best white; 'Tell Tale', white, with broad, rosy, picotee edge, fragrant; 'Valerie', white, frilled.

Pink and Red Varieties

'Carlotta', rich carmine; 'Cheerfulness', deep cerise; 'Clansman', mahogany-crimson; 'Elizabeth Arden', rich salmon-rose; 'Flamingo', orange-scarlet, shaded cerise; 'Goring', rosy-red, waved; 'King's Rhapsody', rich scarlet; 'Margaret Rose', rose-pink; 'Monty', deep clear pink; 'Mrs R. Bolton', rich rose-pink on white ground; 'Percy Izzard', cherry-red, with a white blotch; 'Piccadilly', rich salmon-pink; 'Pinkie', clear rose-pink; 'Princess Elizabeth', salmon-pink; 'Royal Rose', rose-red; 'Welcome', deep scarlet, sunproof; 'Winston Churchill', bright crimson, frilled and waved.

Blue and Purple Varieties

'Ambition', fragrant, rich lavender; 'Blue Shadows', clear light blue, suffused deeper blue; 'Capri', light blue; 'Ebony', blue-black; 'Elizabeth Taylor', clear mauve, frilled; 'Gertrude Tingay', deep lavender, very fragrant; 'Pall Mall', rosy-mauve, frilled and scented; 'Royal Mauve', rich mauve; 'Stylish', mid-blue; 'Velvet Knight', fragrant, rich deep blue, petals ruffled.

Fruit

The hardy fruit trees and bushes most generally found in our gardens tolerate a wide variety of soil types — hence their popularity in Britain, Northern Europe, North America and even in the cooler parts of the Southern Hemisphere.

Cultural difficulties may occur when the soil is poorly drained, for under wet conditions none of these trees or bushes really prosper. Very chalky soils, too, may cause trouble after the plants have become established. Nor are seacoast districts ideal, especially for tree fruits where these are exposed to wind-blown spray, or underground effects of salt water.

FEEDING AND GENERAL CULTIVATION

All fruits require annual feeding in order to give of their best. This can be achieved in two ways, by mulching, i.e. using organic matter from the compost heap, or by applying artificial or inorganic fertilisers, especially those containing nitrogen and potash (such as Sulphate of Ammonia and Sulphate of Potash). Hoeing the soil around fruit trees and bushes is of course essential to control weeds.

ON BUYING FRUIT TREES

1. Obtain grown plants from a reliable source, preferably from a fruit nurseryman whose soil is something like your own and whose main concern is to raise healthy stock, true to name or type. These plants usually carry a certificate saying that they have reached the required standards set by the Ministry of Agriculture.
2. Plant out healthy trees and bushes in *well prepared* ground. This means paying particular attention to removing perennial weeds such as Couch Grass and Bindweed, and is far more important than heavy manuring of the soil.

SOFT FRUITS
BLACK CURRANTS

These are produced from cuttings (see Propagation p. 238) and may be planted during the dormant season. Good spacing is needed between each bush, 4–5 ft. apart each way.

Fruit is carried on young wood and this must be replaced gradually by pruning away most of the old fruited wood close to ground level each

Blackcurrant 'Goliath'

146

Raspberry 'Malling Exploit'   H. Smith

year. There is no need to tip the remaining shoots.

Black currants require heavy feeding and therefore appreciate a good layer of compost or a manure mulch annually, together with a dressing of Sulphate of Potash (2 oz. per sq.yd.). Sun or partial shade.

Varieties

'Amos Black' (late). 'Black Bunch', 'Blacksmith', 'Boskoop Giant', 'Cotswold Cross', 'September Black' and 'Westwick Choice'.

Sulphur-shy Varieties (Sulphur sprays should never be used stronger than 2% strength.)
'Goliath', 'Nigger', 'Wellington'.

H. Smith

Likely Troubles Aphides, Big Bud Mite, Die Back, Reversion Disease.

RED CURRANTS AND WHITE CURRANTS

Both require similar treatment, and prefer an open, sunny position with shelter from strong winds. The most usual shape is an open bush produced on a short leg or stem.

Propagation again is by hardwood cuttings taken in autumn. Plant bushes 5 ft. apart. Apply Sulphate of Potash at 1–2 oz. per sq.yd. around each bush, lightly fork in and apply a mulch of stable manure or compost to the soil surface afterwards.

Fruit is produced on old wood. The aim of pruning, therefore, should be to prevent overcrowding of shoots by removing unwanted wood. Cut back leaders to 6 in. if strong, or less if weak, and spur back side shoots to about half an inch.

Major pests are Aphis and Gooseberry Sawfly larvae, whilst diseases to be guarded against are American Gooseberry Mildew and Dieback of shoots. The appropriate treatment is given under Pests and Diseases (p. 293).

Varieties

Red Currants 'Earliest of Fourlands', 'Fay's Prolific', 'Laxton's No. 1', 'Laxton's Perfection', 'Prince Albert', 'Red Lake', 'Wilson's Long Bunch' (late).

White Currants 'White Dutch', 'White Versailles'.

GOOSEBERRIES

Highly popular and easily grown berries. A well drained medium loam soil provides ideal conditions for many years of cropping.

Gooseberries may be obtained as young bushes, or as single-stem cordons, the latter being ideal for use on supports in a row along a fence or wall.

Planting should be carried out from end October to early March. Leave 5 ft. between each bush and each row. Single-stem cordons need be spaced only 2 ft. apart in the row.

Cultivation consists of hoeing, applying Sulphate of Potash as 1 oz. per sq.yd. during March, followed by a mulch of straw or compost during April.

Established bushes will require pruning, preferably late winter. Keep the centre of the bush open, lightly tip the ends of the main shoots and shorten all side growths to four or five buds. A single cordon should have the extension growth on the main stem shortened by about one-third and the side growths treated as before.

It may be necessary to protect the bushes in winter against damage from birds. Cotton thread is the best deterrent.

Varieties

Variety	Season	Remarks
Keepsake	Early	Green berries
Careless	Mid-season	Pale green berries
Golden Drop	Mid-season	Yellow berries
Good dessert variety.		
Leveller	Mid-season	Large greenish-yellow berries.
Whinham's Industry	Mid-season	Large dark-red berries. Vigorous.
Cousens Seedling	Late	Yellow berries. Rather spreading bush habit.

Pests Aphis. Gooseberry Sawfly Larvae (spray or dust with B.H.C. when first seen).

Diseases American Gooseberry Mildew is the most serious. (Spray with Washing Soda ½ lb. in 3 galls. water plus a soft soap spreader during May.)

RASPBERRIES

The Raspberry, a fruit indigenous to the British Isles, grows in the form of single canes which shoot up annually from the base of the plant, the fruit being borne on short laterals of the current season which grow out from the main stem.

Healthy canes are planted 18 in. apart in rows, allowing 6 ft. between each row, the planting being done in suitable conditions between November and February. Only shallow planting is necessary, the upper roots just below the soil surface. Cut down these newly planted canes to about 12 in. from the ground in March. This will produce strong canes from each plant, to bear fruit the following summer. A post and wire support will be required to tie the canes to when fully grown.

In the autumn cut down all canes that have borne fruit to ground level. Remove all weak young shoots. Cut off the tips of the canes in February.

A mulch of compost or grass cuttings alongside the rows in May is beneficial to the plants; supplement by Sulphate of Potash at 1–2 oz. per sq.yd.

Varieties

'Lloyd George', 'Malling Enterprise', 'Malling Exploit', 'Malling Jewel', 'Malling Promise', 'Norfolk Giant'.

Likely Troubles Aphides, Raspberry Beetle larvae, Mosaic Virus, Cane Spot.

LOGANBERRIES AND BLACKBERRIES

The Loganberry is a useful plant, productive and pleasantly flavoured. It is self-fertile, with the fruits, which are larger than Raspberries, carried on lateral shoots arising from vigorous canes. Owing to the length of the shoots a strong post and wire support is required to hold the fruiting canes. Plants must be kept in bounds by reducing the number of canes to

Strawberries   Copyright R. & G. Cuthbert

Raspberry 'Malling Promise'   Copyright Wood & Ingram

those few which can be adequately trained within the available space.

The topmost supporting wire should be 6 ft. from the ground, with two wires below this at 3 ft. and 5 ft. from soil level. Loganberry plants should be planted 8 ft. apart, and the canes trained fanwise on to the supporting wires. No fruit will be produced the first year, but in the second season lateral shoots will appear which bear flowers and fruits. At the same time new young canes will grow from the base of the plant. Tie these together and keep upright in the centre of the fan until the end of the season; then cut the fruited canes to ground level. Untie the young shoots and train to a similar fan shape to replace the previous ones.

Place a mulch of organic material around the plants early in the summer. Loganberries like plenty of sun and a sheltered position and are propagated by Tip Layers.

Common pests are Raspberry Beetle and Aphis. Cane Spot is also a troublesome disease.

Blackberries require similar treatment and conditions and will do better than Loganberries on a stiffer soil. Propagation by Tip Layers.

Varieties of Logan and Hybrid Berry
Loganberry 'Bauer Thornless Loganberry', 'Boysenberry' (darker than Loganberry and more acid) 'Newberry', 'Phenomenal Berry', and 'Youngberry'.
Blackberry 'Bedford Giant', 'Himalaya Giant', 'John Innes', 'Merton Thornless' and 'Parsley-leaved Blackberry'.

STRAWBERRIES

Both the small wild Strawberry and the larger cultivated form of this fruit have their place in the garden. The Wild Strawberry of Europe is *Fragaria vesca* and has been used as a garden plant since about 1200 A.D.

A popular variation in form is the French Alpine Strawberry with a succession of flowers and fruits well on into the autumn. They can be raised from seed, planted 12 in. apart, and being small and compact are useful for the edge of a border beside a path. Typical varieties are 'Cresta' and 'Baron Solemacher'.

A further development from the Wild Strawberry is the Perpetual Strawberry, which has larger fruits, produced in the summer, followed by runners. If stopped at the first plantlet, further crops will be produced in the autumn.

Typical varieties are 'St Fiacre' and 'Sans Rivale'.

The cultivated Strawberry is the result of hybridising between *Fragaria chiloensis* and *Fragaria virginiana* and is probably the most popular of all the soft fruits. Given good drainage and plenty of humus it will thrive on a wide range of soils. Runners from healthy stock plants may be used to produce new plants by pegging down the plantlets formed on these into the surrounding soil. The new plants are planted out when rooted during the summer in order that they may become well established before winter.

Owing to possible virus disease infection, a Strawberry plant should be limited to a life of three years, and then replaced by young healthy stock.

Gooseberry 'Careless'

Typical varieties are 'Royal Sovereign', 'Talisman', 'Huxley Giant' and 'Cambridge Favourite'.

Common Pests of the Strawberry are Aphis, Red Spider Mite, Tarsonemid Mite and Strawberry Rhynchites. Common diseases are Mildew, Botrytis.

TREE FRUITS

APPLE

Apples have a long and fascinating history. They were grown by the early Britons, and Glastonbury was known as the 'Apple Orchard' because of the quantities of fruit grown there prior to the Roman invasion. The apples of the past also had intriguing names — Quarrenders, Quinches, No-pips, Tom Urns, Pigs' Noses, Flesh and Blood, Leather-hides (Shakespeare mentions these), Jack Tars, Buff Coats, Masters' Apples and Ducks' Bills.

One of the oldest known varieties is the Costard Apple, which were apparently sold at Oxford in 1296 for a shilling a hundred. Pippins too were popular, the term pippin or 'pepin' meaning an apple propagated from seed, as opposed to the usual method of budding on to a rootstock. Cooking apples appear to have been originally small and immature green fruits of any variety, but the old English Codling was cultivated as a distinct variety in Elizabethan times.

Our choice of varieties today is more limited, but the quality of modern culinary and dessert types is excellent. All Apple trees nowadays are produced by budding or grafting on to a suitable rootstock, and years of research now make it possible to produce trees of known size, shape and performance suitable for varied growing conditions. The correct combination of the tree form and corresponding rootstock enables the gardener to grow the right tree in the right place. The following table will help to show this relationship.

ROOTSTOCK	HABIT	FORM OF TREE
East Malling XVI	Vigorous	Full standard (trunk 6 ft. high)
East Malling XII	Vigorous	Half-standard (trunk 4—5 ft.)
East Malling II	Mod. Vigorous	Bush (trunk 2½ to 3 ft. high)
East Malling VII	Semidwarfing	Cordon, Espalier (trained forms) Dwarf Pyramid.
East Malling IX	Very dwarfing	Dwarf Pyramid (trained forms)

Small trees can be trained to various shapes as follows:

Cordon. Grown on single stem and planted 2 ft. 6 in. apart at angle of 45 deg. This encourages fruiting all along stems.

Espalier. Branches trained horizontally from trunk. Makes good edging tree.

Pyramid. Bush-type with little trunk. Branche skep conveniently low for ease in picking and spraying.

Planting young Strawberries in September. A line makes for straight rows
Fisons Horticulture

A hole is taken out with a trowel   Fisons Horticulture

The plant is firmed round with the hand   Fisons Horticulture

Family Tree. Three or five varieties grafted on same tree, and selected for similar size, as good pollinators to each other and to provide succession.

The vigour of the established tree is largely determined by the rootstock on which it is grown, and this in turn is affected by the condition of the soil. Very dwarf trees on E.M.IX stock may hardly grow at all in a poor soil, so a less dwarfing rootstock will be required under such conditions.

Cultivation

A wide range of soil types suit this fruit though it will not tolerate badly drained and waterlogged conditions. A high sunshine record and a rainfall of 20–25 in. per annum are important factors in determining the quality of fruit and in selecting the area for planting. In regions of heavy rainfall, cooking varieties are more likely to be successful.

Plant dwarf bush and trained forms of trees in soil which has been previously cultivated, in open weather between October and March — the earlier the better. During the first few seasons give the soil around each tree a mulch of compost or manure.

Manuring Requirements

Inorganic fertilisers for Apples consist of annual applications (usually during February or March) of Sulphate of Ammonia (1 oz. per sq.yd.), Sulphate of Potash (1 oz. per sq.yd.) and every three years Superphosphate of Lime (2–3 oz. per sq.yd.). Many trees in garden suffer through insufficient supplies of potash, so important in the ripening processes of both the fruit and the woody tree shoots.

PRUNING ESTABLISHED TREES

Half Standard and Bush Forms. – Winter Pruning

Maintain an open centre in the tree. Lightly tip the main leading shoots when young and shorten all lateral side shoots to about half their length. Later the leaders can be left uncut. Remove awkwardly placed or crossing branches and cut out any dead or diseased wood.

Special Trained Trees e.g. Cordons and Espaliers

Summer. At the end of July shorten current season's growth (of all side shoots) arising from existing spur systems, to within one or two leaves from the base. This operation will seem rather drastic but is most effective in forming new fruit buds close to the main stem. It is a modified form of Lorette pruning.
Winter. Reduce the main stems of mature cordons and espaliers by shortening previous season's growth to a convenient length or height during the dormant winter season.

Dwarf Pyramid

Summer. Shorten all side shoots to about five leaves from the base at the end of July, pruning to a downward pointing bud.
Winter. Reduce previous season's main stem growth by one half its length.

HARVESTING

Dessert varieties should only be gathered when ready to leave the tree at a touch (usually from September onwards) and be stored in a cool airy place.

DESSERT APPLES

VARIETY	SEASON OF USE	REMARKS
American Mother	Oct. – mid-Jan.	High quality. Characteristic flavour. Crops regularly. Blossoms late, often avoiding spring frosts.
Charles Ross	Sept. – Nov.	Very large fruit of good flavour. Will grow well on chalky loam soils.
Cox's Orange Pippin	Oct. – Dec.	Ideal for cordon. Not easy to grow on heavy soils. Excellent flavour.

Eight varieties of Eating Apples J. E. Downward

CULINARY APPLES

Arthur Turner	July—Oct.	One of best early culinary apples. Good flavour. Attractive pink blossom.
Belle de Boskoop	Oct.—March	Extensively grown in Holland. Best on good soils.
Bramley's Seedling	Oct.—March	The best all purpose culinary apple. Requires to be grown as a dwarf bush in small garden. Particularly requires pollinating variety: e.g. James Grieve.
Lane's Prince Albert	Nov.—Feb.	An old favourite especially suited to small gardens on account of compact growth and regular cropping.
Rev. W. Wilks	Sept.—Dec.	Large pale fruits. Cooks frothily; excellent for baked apples. Compact tree.
Wagener	Oct.—June	An old American variety. Ripens to golden yellow with carmine flush.

SPRAY CALENDAR FOR APPLES

STAGE	APPROX. DATE IN S. ENGLAND	SPRAY MATERIALS	PEST OR DISEASE
Dormant	Dec.—end Jan.	Tar Oil	Aphis and caterpillar eggs
		Winter wash	Moss and lichen Aphis
Early Pink Bud	End April-early May	B.H.C.+ +Lime Sulphur or Captan	Caterpillar Capsid Bud Apple Scab

VARIETY	SEASON OF USE	REMARKS
Egremont Russet	Oct.—Dec.	Regular cropper. Good pollinator for Cox's Orange Pippin. Compact growth.
Ellison's Orange Pippin	Sept.—Oct.	Very juicy — slight aniseed flavour.
James Grieve	Sept.	A pollinating variety useful when cross pollinaton is necessary to ensure fruiting in certain other varieties. Ideal for cordon.
Laxton's Fortune	Sept.	
Laxton's Superb	Jan.—March	Good flavour. Trees liable to biennial bearing.
Lord Lambourne	Oct.—Nov.	Excellent flavour. Easy to grow where Cox will not.
Worcester Pearmain	Sept.	A pollinating variety useful when cross pollination is necessary to ensure fruiting in certain other varieties.

Apple 'Tydeman's Early Worcester' Valerie Finnis

Apple 'Lane's Prince Albert'   J. E. Downward

this to occur. Nevertheless, an intelligent eye to the choice of situation, aspect and shelter, will overcome many of these difficulties.

The Pear is not exacting as to soil, provided this is properly drained, but prefers a heavy loam to a light one. Propagation is by budding in summer or grafting in spring on to one of the Quince rootstocks, of which Quince A and B produce vigorous trees, while Quince C produces trees of moderate vigour. Some varieties will not grow well on Quince, and the grower has to graft these on to seedling Pear rootstocks or adopt the practice of double-working on to Quince, with an intermediate piece from a compatible variety, in order to overcome this difficulty.

TYPE OF TREE

Where a number of varieties are required, the sunny side of a wall or of a wooden fence are ideal sites. For most varieties the open bush shape or the pyramid are quite satisfactory and when these are produced on Quince stock moderate sized trees of good capabilities will result. Since Pears spur up well and naturally in forming fruit buds, they are ideally suited for training as cordons (both oblique and upright) and as espaliers. In planting these forms remember to keep the budding union or knuckle (visible at the base of the stem) a few inches above soil level, otherwise scion-rooting will result, and any dwarfing effect by the rootstock will be lost.

Plums, Peaches and Pears   Valerie Finnis

Fruitlet	Three weeks later	Lime Sulphur	Apple Scab
Midsummer	Last week in June to end of first week in July	Derris	Codling Moth Red Spider Mite
Petal Fall	Mid-end of May	B.H.C. + Lime Sulphur	Apple Sawfly Apple Scab

Warning
1. Although B.H.C. preparations are non-poisonous they should not be used on fruits or vegetables within three weeks of picking or cutting.
2. Certain Apples such as Cox's Orange Pippin are 'sulphur shy'. Instead of lime sulphur use either Captan or Dispersible Sulphur.

PEAR

The growing of good quality Pears presents a challenge to the gardener. Firstly, most varieties will not produce a good crop unless a suitable pollinating variety is also at hand: secondly, for the woody shoots to ripen well in summer good sunshine and warm weather are desirable: thirdly, for the fruit buds to develop in spring a cold rest period is necessary in winter. Our winters are often too mild for

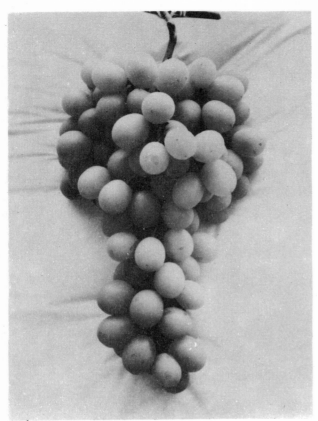

Grape 'Muscat of Alexandria'   H. Smith

Victoria Plums   H. Smith

CULTIVATION AND MANURING

The requirements of Pears are similar to those of Apples. Regular dressings of compost should be made to maintain regular growth, best applied as a mulch in spring and forked into the soil the following winter.

Nitrogen is most needed when trees produce plenty of blossom but little annual extension growth. Potash is less important than for Apples but should not be neglected. The following fertilisers should provide adequate feeding if applied annually in the late winter or early spring:

$\frac{3}{4}$ oz. sulphate of ammonia or nitro-chalk ⎫
2 oz. superphosphate of lime (once every three ⎬ per
                                years) ⎬ sq.
$\frac{1}{2}$ oz. sulphate of potash ⎭ yd.

PRUNING

Half Standard and Bush Forms – Winter Pruning

The general remarks for Apples apply equally to Pears, although Pears will stand harder cutting of the lateral shoots. Any dead or diseased wood (particularly wood with shrivelled or papery bark, (a symptom of canker disease) should be cut out completely and burnt.

Cordon and Espalier – Summer and Winter Pruning

The same directions as for trained Apple trees apply. Because Pears generally produce an abundant supply of short fruit spurs, such trees lend themselves to the close form of spur pruning.

Dwarf Pyramid

Prune as for Apple.

Varieties

Pears flower earlier than Apples — an indication of their probable Eastern origin. Some varieties are shy croppers by nature, whereas others fruit only too freely. All varieties (whether self-sterile or self-fertile) are improved by interplanting with other Pears to allow and encourage cross pollination by insects at blossom time. It is therefore wise (this applies to all kinds of tree fruits) to consult pollination tables before making a decision as to choice of varieties for the garden. The Pear tree next door may not be the right mate for yours!

Harvesting

The dessert quality of Pears is often spoilt if the fruit is allowed to ripen on the tree; a mealy flavour is usually an indication of this. Early and mid-season varieties must be picked before the green base colour has turned yellow. William Pears should still show the green background colour, though these may also have a slight flush, if they are to mature properly.

One test for picking is to lift the Pear from the

vertical to the horizontal. If the stalk breaks cleanly from the spur without pulling, the fruit is ready. Sound and undamaged fruit of late varieties may be stored in a dark cool cellar or similar place (temperature 40–50°F.).

DESSERT VARIETIES

Variety	Season	Harvest
Conference	Oct.—Nov.	End Sept.
Doyenne du Comice	Oct.—Nov.	Early Oct.
Dr. Jules Guyot	End Aug.	Mid-Aug.
Durondeau	Oct.—Nov.	End Sept.
Marguerite Marillat	Mid—end Sept.	Sept.
William's Bom Chretien	Sept.	End Sept.

CULINARY VARIETIES

Variety	Season	Harvest
Bellisime d'Hiver	Oct.—March	Early Oct.
Beurre Claireau	Nov.—Dec.	End Sept.
Catillac	Oct.—April	Early Oct.
Fertility	Sept.—Oct.	Early Sept.
Laxton's Superb	Aug.	Mid-Aug.
Pitmaston Duchess	Oct.—Nov.	End Sept.

SPRAY CALENDAR FOR PEARS

Blossom Bud Stage	Approx. date in S. England	Spray Materials	Pest or Disease
Dormant	Dec.—end Jan.	Tar Oil Winter Wash	Aphis, Sucker, Moss, Lichen on bark
Bud-burst	End March	Captan B.H.C.	Pear Scab, Aphis and caterpillar
Green Cluster	Mid—April	Captan B.H.C.	Pear Scab Pear Ridge
Petal Fall	Mid—May	Captan	Pear Scab

Note

Tar Oil Wash in usually only necessary once every two or three years. If Red Spider Mite has been a problem in previous years, add chlorobenzide to Captan spray at petal-fall stage.

QUINCE

The Quince, a type of wild Pear, is for use in tarts and preserves — especially Marmalade. A few slices added to an Apple tart will greatly improve the flavour and is worth growing for this alone.

A good loam soil with plenty of available moisture suits the tree. It is generally grown as an open bush type, planted during the normal dormant season.

Little pruning is required except the removal of dead, diseased or overcrowded branches during winter. A proportion of old wood should be cut back on old trees.

Quinces should ripen thoroughly on the tree and normally hang until mid-October. They should not, however, be exposed to frost. Pick fruits on a dry day and because of their powerful aroma store apart from other fruit in a dry frostproof place. In this way, the fruit will keep for two or three months.

Varieties

Pear-shaped Quince. A tree of great antiquity, beautiful in flower, with Pear-like fruits.

Bereczki. Very large Pear-shaped golden fruit and highly ornamental flowers. Makes a vigorous tree which crops early.

MEDLAR

Another uncommon fruit of great antiquity. The finest fruit comes from trees grown on a moist, loamy soil, but Medlars can be grown on a wide variety of soil types.

Several stocks can be used, but site and soil usually determine the type. In moist soils Medlars should be grafted or budded on Quince rootstock, whereas in dry places they are best worked on White Thorn rootstock.

Trees are obtainable as bush or standard shapes. A mulch of manure or compost applied as fruits are forming will improve size and quality.

Little pruning is necessary except the removal of dead or overcrowded branches in the centre.

The ideal time to pick Medlars is on a sunny day in November when the fruit is quite dry. After about a fortnight stored in a frostproof place, the fruit softens and becomes yellow, when it may be eaten or used for jelly or for making a sauce for game.

Varieties

The Dutch. A tree of weeping, decorative habit bearing large fruit.

The Nottingham. Small fruit but of good flavour. Less decorative than the Dutch as a tree but more compact and upright in habit.

The Royal. Smaller fruit than the Dutch, but well flavoured and a good cropper.

Pear 'Conference'   H. Smith

STONE FRUITS

PLUMS

Plums are happy in most soils, provided these are well cultivated, free of pernicious weeds and moist but not waterlogged. The ideal is good deep loam with a moderate amount of clay. Like all stone fruits, they benefit by the addition of lime to the soil. An annual mulch of farmyard manure or compost is recommended, and during the season following a heavy crop nitro-chalk should be forked into the soil around the trees in February at about ½ oz. per sq.yd. Sulphate of Potash (also at ½ oz. per sq.yd.) will prove beneficial and should be applied at the same time, especially on light or gravelly soils. In general, however, Plum trees have a greater need for nitrogen than for potash.

Shelter from cold winds proves helpful since there

Cherries 'Emperor Francis'   Copyright George Bunyard & Co

Apples and Pears, as pruning cuts will heal more readily at that time.

Probably the most important disease of Plums is Silver Leaf (see page 291) a fungus disease, the spores of which obtain entry via broken branches and exposed pruning cuts during autumn and winter. There is no effective cure once a tree has become badly infected, but precautions include pruning in summer and protecting all cuts with ordinary paint, or,

Plum 'Early Czar'   Valerie Finnis

are few pollinating insects about during the blossom period.

Rootstock and Propagation

Plums are raised by budding during the summer on to selected rootstocks such as Common Plum, Common Mussel and Myrobolan B. All these eventually make vigorous trees, requiring adequate space.

Types of Tree

Since they tend to be vigorous, Plums are probably most conveniently grown as open-headed, half-standard trees. These will have a clean stem 4–5 ft. high before branching. This form will accommodate both upright varieties and also those with a weeping habit. Little pruning is necessary once the framework of branches has been formed, and this is done before the tree is purchased. The complete removal of dead or diseased wood, overcrowded or crossing branches is all that is normally required. This should be done in the summer months, contrary to the treatment of

Mixed fruit from the garden   Valerie Finnis

Trained Peach tree on a south wall　　　Valerie Finnis

better still, a proprietary pruning compound suitable for this purpose.

In order to reduce the vigour of established trees root pruning may also occasionally be necessary. This entails cutting a soil trench around the tree a short distance from its base and sawing off all the roots thus exposed. This is a winter job when the tree is in a dormant condition.

Varieties

Some useful Plums giving a succession of fruit.

VARIETY	SEASON OF USE	REMARKS
Czar	Early Aug.	Culinary.
Early Laxton	July	Dessert or Culinary Warwickshire Drooper near-by to aid pollination.
Early Transparent Gage	Mid-Aug.	Dessert. Self-fertile.
Marjorie's Seedling	Oct.	Culinary or Dessert. Self-fertile.
Rivers Early	End July Early Aug.	Culinary.
Victoria	Late Aug. Early Sept.	Culinary or dessert. A good pollinator for other varieties. Self-fertile.
Warwickshire Drooper	Late Sept.	Culinary or Dessert, Self-fertile.

Spray Calendar

BLOSSOM-BUD STAGE	APPROX. DATE IN S.ENGLAND	MATERIALS	PEST OR DISEASE
Dormant	Dec. mid-Jan.	Tar Oil Winter Wash	Aphis eggs
or later	Dec. mid-Feb.	D.N.C. Petroleum Wash	Aphis eggs, caterpillar, Red spider
Post-blossom	Mid-May (about 10th —20th)	Derris or B.H.C.	Plum Sawfly caterpillars, Red spider

DAMSONS

The cultivation and treatment of Damsons is similar to that for Plums. Some varieties come true from their own suckers, thus simplifying propagation, but most Damson trees are produced by budding on to rootstocks similar to those for Plums.

Owing to their stiff, dense, twiggy growth, Damsons make admirable trees for planting as windbreaks or shelter belts of moderate height.

Varieties

VARIETY	SEASON	REMARKS
Farleigh Damson	Mid-Sept.	Culinary
Merry Weather	Sept. — Oct.	Culinary
Shropshire or Prune Damson }	Mid-Sept.	Culinary

CHERRIES

There are two broad divisions of Cherries, the sweet and the acid.

The Sweet Cherry, sometimes called the Mazzard Cherry, has been selected and improved from the wild *Prunus avium*. The acid Cherry has been de-

Peaches　　　H. Smith

veloped from the wild *Prunus cerasus*. So-called Duke Cherries are intermediate in character between sweet and sour, and are believed to be hybrids between the two species.

Cultivation

Cultivation of the sweet Cherry is somewhat restricted by soil conditions. A light loam on a well drained, gravelly or chalky subsoil, in a loam locality which is free from spring frosts, provides an ideal site and climate. All varieties eventually make vigorous trees which may be of bush or half standard or standard form.

Propagation of such trees is usually by budding on to a selected Mazzard rootstock. Planting is done in early winter and requires plenty of space, for in orchard practice standard Cherries have to be planted as much as 50 ft. apart, and bush types at least 20 ft. apart. Another disadvantage of the sweet Cherry for garden use is the fact that you will need at least two varieties, since they are self-sterile and require a suitable pollinator in order to set fruit. Add to that the thought of havoc by birds and you may well say no!

The sour or acid Cherry, however, is a more feasible proposition. This type flourishes on many different soils and is hardier than the Sweet Cherry; indeed it will even prosper on a north-facing wall. In the small garden it can be grown as a bush type in the open, or as a fan, trained on a wall. A further advantage is that the two commonly grown varieties are both self-fertile and will therefore produce crops even as isolated trees.

Such trees require very little feeding, at least until they carry a crop, when a little bonemeal and a light dressing of sulphate of ammonia in spring will maintain sufficient wood growth.

Pruning

The acid Cherries fruit only on the young growth and must therefore be encouraged to produce new shoots from established branches. Without removing the leaders (and hence the flower buds) young shoots can be stimulated by cutting back a few selected branches each year.

Sweet Cherries require little or no pruning beyond the removal of dead, diseased, damaged, or unwanted centrally placed wood.

Troubles

The chief pests of Cherries are caterpillars, Cherry Fruit Moths and Cherry Fruit Flies. Bacterial canker is one of the most serious diseases, some varieties being particularly susceptible. To prevent infection, which occurs exclusively through wounds, paint cut surfaces. This will also minimise the risk of infection by Silver Leaf Disease.

Cordon Pear trees are planted at an angle of 45°
Copyright Laxton Bros

A fruit hedge

Varieties

Sweet Cherries. Pollination tables should be consulted before making a choice of sweet Cherry varieties, or advice sought from your nurseryman. The following are examples of coupled varieties: i.e. those which when planted together will assist each other in pollination.

Early Rivers with Bigarreau Schrecken
Frogmore Early with Governor Wood
Roundel Heart with Bigarreau Napoleon
Elton Heart with Victoria Black

Acid Cherries. These are reasonably self-fertile, so no problem of pollination arises, particularly with Morello and Kentish Red, the two most widely available varieties.

PEACHES AND NECTARINES

Several differences are found among the fruits of these varieties, the most important being the colour of the flesh, which may be white or yellow, and in the attachment of the stone to the flesh ('free-stone' or 'cling stone').

Cultivation

The Nectarine is similar to the Peach in cultivation and appearance, except that the skin of the fruit is hairless. Most varieties of both fruits are reasonably self-fertile, although difficulties in fruit setting do arise in some seasons owing to cold winds and consequent lack of pollinating insects at flowering time. Because they flower early, trees do best in a warm frost-free site, and a south-facing wall in a garden will usually provide suitable conditions. Trees should be purchased trained in a fan-shape, the initial propagation being by budding on to one of the Plum rootstocks (although seedling Peach stocks are sometimes used).

The aim in the first few years after budding is to build up a shapely tree by pruning and training to produce the fan framework.

When planting, a well drained soil is required with a high lime content. If this condition is not initially present, it can be gradually produced by the addition of lime or old mortar rubble.

Guard against drought, especially in early years, by an occasional watering and annual mulches of rotted manure or compost.

Pruning

The pruning of established fan-shaped trees consists of removing from the existing laterals (during the early summer), all new small side shoots, *except one at the base of each lateral growth.* The growth at the tip of these remaining laterals is cut back to four leaves.

In late summer or winter, the laterals are spaced out and tied evenly on supporting wires so that they are 5 or 6 in. apart.

If large fruits are required, the young fruits must be thinned, i.e. reduced in number, at an early stage of development. In dry summers Peach and Nectarine trees growing against a wall benefit from generous watering, particularly during the early swelling of the fruitlets soon after flowering. If this is followed by the application of a layer of organic manure or compost as a mulch on the soil, so much the better.

Varieties

PEACH

VARIETY	SEASON	REMARKS
Amsden June	Mid-July	Hardy, one of best early Peaches for outdoor growth
Duke of York	Mid-July	Large fruits of good flavour
Peregrine	Early Aug.	Very hardy and fertile. Probably the best for the small garden
Rochester	Mid-Aug.	Good size and quality

NECTARINE

VARIETY	SEASON	REMARKS
Early Rivers	Mid-July	Good early variety
Lord Napier	Early Aug.	
Pineapple	Early Sept.	Flesh has distinct pineapple flavour. Needs more shelter outside, as is rather tender

Apricots   Colour Library International

Grapes   Valerie Finnis

SPRAY CALENDAR for OUTDOOR PEACHES and NECTARINES

STAGE	APPROX. DATE	SPRAY MATERIALS	PEST AND DISEASE
Bud-burst	Mid-Feb.	B.H.C. plus Lime Sulphur	Aphis and Peach-leaf Curl Disease

APRICOTS

The Apricot will thrive in a good, well drained soil which has a high lime content, and is best suited by a warm, sunny wall facing south. Alternatively, it may be grown in a large greenhouse, for it flowers very early in the year. It is not generally happy in very light sandy soil. In Southern England and the Midlands it can be regarded as an outdoor fruit, but farther north is best grown under glass.

The most suitable form of tree is a dwarf fan-shape, trained on supporting wires against a wall. Propagation is by budding in July or August on to a Plum rootstock.

The best time to plant is during October, in soil previously prepared by the addition of rubble to improve drainage and a dressing of bonemeal.

Remember that the wall against which it is planted should be high enough for the ultimate development of the tree — about 10 ft. Spread out the branches after planting so that the outside branches are brought almost horizontal. This will help the centre to develop more quickly.

One reason why Apricots sometimes fail to fruit is because they lack attention at blossom time. Being self-fertile the flowers can be fertilised by their own pollen, but, as with Peaches there are often cold winds at flowering time and few pollinating insects. This difficulty can be overcome by touching the flowers with a soft brush or piece of cotton wool tied to a stick. If there are drying winds at this time, a light spraying with water during the day will also help the blossoms to set. Roots may also dry out in early spring. Copious watering at this time will prevent the dropping of immature fruits.

Pruning

A golden rule in Apricot cultivation is to spare the knife or secateurs as much as possible, and to control the growth by pinching out the tips of shoots during the summer when they are soft and green. Only the minimum of cutting back should then be necessary in autumn.

Pinch out tips of lateral shoots in May, when they are about 3 in. long. A few weeks later all subsequent growths on these lateral shoots should be pinched back to one leaf to form spurs. Apricots carry fruit on spurs formed on previous year's growth, and this spur formation has to be encouraged artificially in this manner.

Figs and Mulberries   Valerie Finnis

Where growths are required for extension purposes, or to fill spaces on the wall, they should be tied into position while still pliable.

Fruit thinning may be necessary on established, heavily laden trees. Apart from this, and the summer pruning already described, little cultural attention is necessary.

Feeding an Apricot tree will depend on its requirements, but should be sparing, as lush growth is detrimental to fruiting. Most trees, however, benefit from a little sulphate of potash applied in February at 1 oz. per sq.yd.

Varieties

Hemskirk	End July — early Aug.
New Large Early	End July — early Aug.
Moorpark	End Aug. and Sept.

Pests and diseases are similar to those of the Peach and Nectarine. Occasionally the caterpillars of certain moths feed on the leaves during the summer, but can be controlled by timely applications of D.D.T.

FIGS

Compared with most other hardy fruits, Figs are not easy to grow in this country, particularly out of doors. Although an established tree may eventually produce an abundance of immature fruits, these almost always seem to shrivel and drop off. This is the tendency unless conditions encourage short-jointed annual growths, about 12 in. long, which must ripen thoroughly before winter.

To this end fan-trained trees are most useful, grown against a south or south-west facing wall where the maximum amount of sunlight, warmth and shelter are available. The common Fig will, in Mediterranean lands, produce two crops a year without pollination or seed formation. Only one crop, at best, can be secured from wall trees grown out of doors in this country.

Cultivation

Propagation is usually by cuttings or suckers from established trees, and growing trees in pots can be purchased ready for planting. Figs will flourish in a wide variety of soils, but cannot tolerate bad drainage. A good loam, to which a little lime and wood ashes have been added, will make an ideal planting site at the foot of a suitable wall. In order to prevent excessive growth some form of root restriction is necessary. This can be achieved by using paving slabs placed vertically as a lining to the sides of the planting site, with one or two placed flat at the bottom. Corrugated asbestos sheeting will also serve for this purpose.

Alternatively, the plant can be put in good soil in a 10-in. diameter pot or tub, and will produce good fruit without ever becoming a large tree.

Figs against walls should be planted in March, with horizontal wires stretched at 12 in. intervals on the wall behind the tree. When the tree has settled, secure the various shoots by tying to these wires, the outer shoots being placed as near horizontal as possible. This will lay the foundation of the fan tree. Water should be given during the summer, and a mulch of compost spread over the soil surface. New shoots can be tied to wires as they develop, allowing plenty of room for sunlight to penetrate and warm the wall.

Pruning

In this country the Fig flowers in May, the flowers being produced inside a Pear-shaped object which subsequently enlarges and becomes the fruit (harvested the following year). Thus the outdoor Fig bears its fruits on the tips of well ripened shoots produced during the *previous summer*. Such young fruits require protection from frost during the winter, by drapes of sacking or hessian, which must be removed during the first warm days of spring.

Pruning should be delayed until late March in case some shoots have suffered frost damage. The aim is to keep up a succession of young shoots from the main branches of the fan, and at the same time to cut out surplus, worn out branches and any damaged or overcrowded shoots.

Varieties

The fruits should begin to ripen about mid-August and will continue during September. They should be able to ripen on the tree. Two recommended varieties are: Brown Turkey and White Marseilles.

The Fig is little troubled by pests and diseases and does not need a spraying programme. Grey mould fungus may attack the young shoots and fruits in summer, but prompt removal and burning of infected shoots or fruits quickly controls this trouble.

GRAPES

Although in Britain Grapes are often considered to be greenhouse plants, there are many varieties which lend themselves to outdoor cultivation — with perhaps some temporary protection to assist the ripening of the fruit.

The Vine will thrive on many different soils as long as the chosen site is well drained and the rainfall not excessive. Propagation is usually effected by cuttings or buds. Cuttings can be made in the winter from pieces of ripe wood, about 8 in. long, taken from the current year's growth. The lower buds are removed, the cuttings inserted in the ground to half their depth in a nursery row, then transplanted to a permanent position the following autumn.

Buds taken from similar wood are prepared in late winter by cutting stems into 1-in. pieces each with an active bud in the middle. These pieces can then be placed horizontally on the soil surface in a box of compost, buds uppermost, and kept in a warm greenhouse until the buds, or 'eyes' as they are called, are well rooted. They can then be potted on as individual plants and will be ready for planting out during the following dormant season.

The following method is as successful as any for outdoor cultivation. On a sheltered border, preferably facing south or west, Vines of a suitable variety are planted in a row, 6 ft. apart, when the soil is in good condition during the winter, then cut hard back to within a few inches of ground level. A horizontal wire should be erected along the length of the row about 4 ft. above ground level, and an upright cane placed beside each plant. As growth commences in

Strawing Strawberries   A Shell photograph

Kentish Cob or 'Lambert's Filbert'   Copyright Laxton Bros

Quinces

spring and early summer, the shoots are tied to the cane and allowed to continue vertically throughout the season. In the autumn the strongest of these is selected, bent over *horizontally* and tied in to the supporting wire. The remaining shoots are cut hard back to within one bud from the base. The first fruiting rod is thus established on each plant.

During the following summer, large Tomato-type cloches are placed over the row, and the side shoots which develop from these will each form a fruit bunch at a short distance from the main rod. These are allowed to grow on to make three or four leaves beyond the bunch and then stopped: i.e. the growing points are pinched out. By this time the shoots will have grown through the tops of the cloches, but this will not matter, for the fruit bunches will remain under the glass, which will help them to ripen.

At the end of the season, after picking, the fruiting rod is untied from the wire and cut out completely close to the plant. The strongest of the new long growths is then bent down and tied to the wire in replacement, and the remainder cut out near the base of the plant. The cloche protection remains in position to ripen the wood of the new rod during bursts of sunshine on warm autumn days.

Varieties of Grape Suitable for Outdoor Cultivation

'Black Hamburgh'	Mid-season	Black. Large berries. Vigorous growth
'Brandt'	Early	Black, small berries. Growth moderate
'Royal Muscadine'	Early	White. Small berries.

COBNUT AND FILBERT

These are both varieties of the Hazel Nut, *Corylus avellana*, a common plant of woods and hedgerows. Although still found in gardens, they are no longer grown on a commercial scale, mainly due to their slowness in cropping and because of the competition from other shelled nuts from abroad.

The nuts are best grown as bushes, with five or six shoots springing from the base. They will thrive in sunny, open positions in gravelly soil or rough stony ground overlying a clay sub-soil. Plant bushes 10–15 ft. apart either in late autumn or early spring. Mulch with manure or compost and give a dressing of sulphate of potash at the rate of 1 oz. per sq.yd. Then cut back main shoots to three or four buds from the ground to a bud pointing outwards. This will encourage the development of tall main shoots which later carry the nut-bearing lateral growths.

Nuts flower early and depend largely upon the wind for fertilisation. The catkins, which comprise many flowers grouped closely together, occur on the bush separately, as male and female. The male cat-

163

kins, long and yellow with a rather mealy appearance, are carried on the previous season's wood. The female catkins are small, pink, like small brushes and are generally found on older wood. Delay cutting vigorous wood, therefore, until *after male flowers have shed their pollen*. Each year, about mid-March, remove some of the oldest wood, cutting back if possible to a catkin a few inches from the base of the shoot. Leave small twiggy growths from previous year's wood intact, for these bear the fruit. Prune in August by cutting back vigorous new side shoots to about half their length, or break them, leaving the ends hanging.

The nuts are harvested towards the end of September, being left on the bushes until the husks are completely brown. Lay them out in single layers in a dry place for some time before storing. This will greatly reduce the chance of their becoming mouldy.

Varieties

'Ashford', a round and thin shelled nut of good flavour; 'Kentish Cob', sometimes known as 'Lambert's Filbert'. Large and of good flavour.

WALNUT

The majority of mature Walnut trees in England are of seedling origin and produce nuts of inferior quality. Those imported from France are of a higher standard and propagated vegetatively from named varieties by grafting or budding.

A rather heavy, loam soil with a good lime content and good drainage is ideal for Walnuts. A sheltered site is essential, since only a few degrees of frost will destroy the young leaves and flowers. Trees may be of bush or standard type, with more than one planted if possible. The trees carry male and female catkins, and they are self-fertile, but these often develop at different times. A single tree may therefore produce few nuts.

Once the head of a bush or standard tree has been formed, little pruning is required beyond the removal of dead wood and crossing branches in winter, cuts being covered with a protective paint. Hard pruning will only result in excessive wood growth instead of fruiting spurs.

The ripe nuts are ready in late September or early October.

Varieties: 'Mayette'; 'Meylanaise'; 'Northdown Clawnut'; 'Parisienne'.

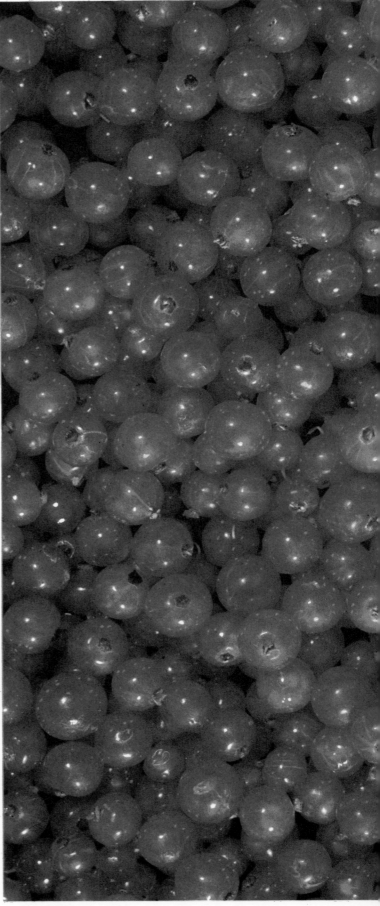

Red currants

The Fragrant Garden

Fragrance in the garden may come from flowers, fruits, leaves or even roots. Usually, however, it fits into one of the following categories:

1. *Direct Scent.* As with Lilies and Hyacinths, when it is wafted on the air.

2. *Secondary Scents.* Only apparent when some change takes place in the plant, as for example with grass — which hardly smells at all when growing. Yet cut grass or hay is very strongly scented. Certain Viburnums and Dogwoods only smell when the leaves fall. Woodruff is another example.

3. *Indirect Scent.* Fragrance only noticeable when leaves or root (sometimes stems) are bruised: e.g. Scented-leaved Geraniums, Southernwood and most herbs.

Early in the year many shrubs are redolent with strong perfume. The honey-scented *Mahonia bealii* is one of the best evergreens in this respect, and blooms with the green and chocolate flowered Winter Sweet *(Chimonanthus fragrans)*. All the Daphnes are sweetly scented, especially *D. odora*, whilst the distinctive fragrance of Lilacs is well known. There are also the Viburnums, especially *V. carlesii*, *V. carlocephalum* and *V. fragrans*.

June and July are the supreme months of fragrance of sweet scented Lavender, heady perfume from the Bean field — and in our gardens Lilies, Iris, Pinks — and summer's own flower — the Rose.

Sweet Peas, old-fashioned Clove Carnations, Sweet Williams and Mignonette are other blossoms for the scented garden, and among herbaceous perennials, Paeonies, the scarlet-flowered Bergamot (Monarda) and Sweet Rocket *(Hesperis matronalis)*.

There are annuals and biennials which can be raised from seed, such as Wallflowers, Stocks, Sweet

Centaurea imperialis, Sweet Sultan   Copyright R. & G. Cuthbert

Lilium speciosum   R. A. Malby

Sultan and Nicotianas. At dusk, the Night Scented Stock becomes almost overpowering with its penetrating sweetness. Evening Primroses, Jasmines and Honeysuckles are others which seem to have a more marked scent in the evening.

Even in the lawn fragrance is possible, especially if you plant a Chamomile Lawn *(Anthemis nobilis)*. The plants may be put in 9 in. apart or seed sown thinly over raked soil.

Some Scented Shrubs

Azaleas, Bay *(Laurus nobilis)*, *Berberis darwinii*, *Buddleia globosa*, *Chimonanthus fragrans* (Wintersweet), *Choisya ternata*, *Erica australis*, Hamamelis (Witch Hazel), Lavender (Lavendula sp.), Lilacs (Syringa), *Lippia citriodora* (Verbena), *Loniceras*, Myrtle (Myrtus), *Osmanthus delavayi*, Philadelphus (Mock Orange Blossom), Portugal Laurel *(Prunus lusitanica)*, Ribes (Flowering Currant), Rosemary (Rosmarinus sp.), Southernwood (Artemisia), *Viburnum carlesii*, *V. fragrans*, *Wistaria venusta*.

Fragrant Perennials

Hesperis, Irises, Lily of the Valley *(Convallaria majalis)*, *Monarda didyma*, Paeonies, *Phlomis fruticosa*, Pinks and Border Carnations, *Tussilago fragrans* (Winter Heliotrope).

Sweet Scented Annuals and Biennials

Abronia, *Alyssum maritimum*, Calendula, Dianthus, Evening Primrose (Oenothera), *Limnanthes douglasii*, Mignonette (Reseda), Nicotiana, Night Scented Stock *(Matthiola bicornis)*, Stocks (Matthiola), Sweet Sultan (Centaurea), Wallflowers (Chieranthus).

Fragrance in the Greenhouse

Carnations, *Cyclamen persicum*, Chrysanthemums, *Exacum affine*, Genista, Geraniums (Pelargonium sp.), Heliotrope, *Jasminum polyanthum*, Stephanotis.

Nicotiana affinis, Night Scented Tobacco Plant
Copyright R. & G. Cuthbert

Bulbs with Fragrance

Acidanthera, Freesias, Hyacinths, Lilies, Narcissi, Tulips.

The Water Garden

Acorus calamus (Sweet Flag), *Aponogeton distachyus* (Water Hawthorn), *Nymphaea odorata*, Water Mint *(Mentha aquatica)*.

Lawns

Chamomile *(Anthemis nobilis)*, Thyme *(Thymus serpyllum)*.

Vegetable garden

Beans, Fennel, Marjoram, Mint, Parsley, Sage, Tarragon.

SOME FRAGRANT FANCIES

Lavender Bottles

Take long-stemmed Lavender (just before it starts to drop) and use an uneven number of pairs (e.g. 18, 22, 26). Tie the heads tightly together with narrow ribbon and bend the stems back over the flower heads. Thread the ribbon in and out pairs of stalks until all the blossom is hidden. Wrap round stems and finish with a bow.

Marigold Petals

Dry the flowers and rub away the petals. Store these in a dry bottle and use a pinch to flavour soups and stews.

Candied Parsley

Dissolve two teaspoonfuls of gum arabic crystals in rosewater. This may take 2—3 days in a warm room. Paint the solution with a fine brush all over tiny sprays of Parsley. Dredge with castor sugar and dry on a cake rack. Store in a non-airtight cardboard box, and use for decoration.

Japanese Chrysanthemum Salad

Wash in several waters about 20 Chrysanthemum flowers, blanch in lemon or salt water, drain and wipe dry with a cloth. Mix them well in a salad composed of Potatoes, Artichoke bases, Shrimps and Capers. Arrange in a dish and decorate with hard-boiled eggs and Beetroot. Sprinkle with paprika.

Pomander

Take a thin-skinned Orange and stud with Cloves except for bands at each quarter wide enough to take a piece of ribbon or tinsel. A bodkin is useful to make the holes. Now roll the Orange in equal parts of ground Cinnamon and Orris Root. Rub it well in and store in greaseproof paper in a warm dry atmosphere. It should be dry and ready in 5 to 6 weeks. Dust off surplus powder, fasten ribbon round the bands and hang in the wardrobe.

Lavender Water *(Old Recipe Book circa 1813)*

1 quart spirits of wine	$\frac{1}{4}$ oz. essence of ambergris
$\frac{1}{2}$ oz. Oil of Lavender	Musk.
$\frac{1}{4}$ oz. Essence of Bergamot	

Shake all together and leave several months.

Moth Destroyer

2 oz. Dried Rosemary	1 oz. Dried Tansy
2 oz. Dried Mint	1 oz. Dried Thyme

Mix well together and store in airtight box. Scatter amongst blankets, furs etc. and no moth will go near them.

Rock Gardens

Transferring the dainty plants of alpine meadows and slopes into the garden calls for some ingenuity in reproducing the conditions to which they are accustomed. In their native habitats they remain dormant for months beneath a thick covering of snow. With the spring thaw and sunshine they are forced rapidly into growth. Standing water never remains long in their vicinity and after flowering they receive a good baking, which ripens the bulbs or roots.

Conditions are very different in our gardens. Mild winters maintain the green growth longer than usual so that the effects of wind and frost are more keenly felt, whilst winter wet and the sulphurous deposits of industry pollute the air and together take great toll of the more delicate species.

Nevertheless, there are plenty of hardy, dependable and beautiful rock plants which, with a little care, will grow happily for many years.

SITUATION

Try to site the rock garden in a position sheltered from draughts or strong spring winds. It should be in full light and sunshine for most of the day.
AVOID:
Waterlogged, or damp and airless areas.
A position between two houses or similar draughty spots.
The vicinity of trees.

TYPES OF ROCK

You do not need an elaborate rock garden to grow rock plants. Many will grow in simple raised beds (provided these are well drained), in dry walls made of stones or bricks, or even in old sinks or miniature gardens.

The best material is a fairly soft stone that will absorb moisture, encouraging plants to cling to it and yet not be soft enough to come to pieces in frosty weather.

Local stone, if available, is the cheapest and some are most attractive. Several kinds of artificial stone are also obtainable, which can be weathered to pleasing shades by painting them over with iron sulphate.

Whatever the type of rock, make sure to get it in fairly large pieces (preferably 2–3 ft. in length and nearly as broad); with good-sized pockets or beds between. These look much more effective than many little rocks.

Start at the bottom of the rock garden, bedding some of the largest pieces fairly deeply in the ground to resemble a natural outcrop. Keep lines of stratification, if well marked, horizontal. All rocks should tilt slightly backwards so that rain runs down to the roots of the plants. Pockets for plants should be 12–18 in. deep and filled with good soil containing plenty of drainage material such as coarse sand or rock chippings. Keep a supply of granite or rock chippings handy to top dress the soil after planting, particularly for moraine plants, like the Kabschia Saxifrages, Androsaces, Sempervivums and many Campanulas.

Compost for soil pockets will vary a little according to the type of plants. Those which tolerate lime may be given:

2 parts by bulk good fibrous loam
1 part ,, ,, leaf-soil or peat

1 part by bulk coarse sand
½ part   „   „   rotted manure, or
½ part   „   „   limestone chippings, or
                    mortar-rubble
Dusting of bonemeal

and the acid loving calcifuges:

1 part by bulk good loam
1 part   „   „   coarse sand
1 part   „   „   rotted leaf-soil or peat

After the ground floor row of rocks and beds, add more rocks and pockets, the latter ranging from 6 in. to 3 ft. Do not make the slope too steep or the plants may dry out in summer. A pool or series of pools add interest to the rock garden and may be built as

CARE OF PLANTS

Most alpines are planted in spring or autumn, although pot-grown specimens can be put out at any time provided they are watered in dry weather. Do not overcrowd them, especially the mat-forming types, which quickly cover a wide area and may smother choice but slower-growing species.

Plant firmly, without disturbing the roots, using a trowel. Cover the surface with ½ in. granite chippings or gravel to keep the soil moist and prevent dampness round the collars. After frost, gently press newly planted specimens back into the soil.

Remove weeds as they appear, and from time to time lightly prick the soil with a two-pronged fork

An attractive rock garden

Onosma taurica

Saxifraga jenkinsii

the work proceeds, the excavations from these helping to raise the general level. There are on the market various pumps which enable the same water to be used over and over again to form waterfalls or fountains.

Grass or crazy-paving can both be linked with the rock garden, depending on the amount of space available and what you are prepared to spend.

or even an old carving fork. Water as necessary and remove old flowers to discourage seeding. Cut back trailing plants like Aubrieta and Arabis to keep shape compact and encourage new shoots.

In autumn top dress the plants with ½ in. of the original compost plus a little more sand, working this round the crowns with the fingers. Remove dead leaves, etc., from moraine plants and renew drainage chippings if necessary. Alpine-cloches or panes of glass (set on bricks) will protect delicate plants from excessive wet and cold. Label all plants and wage continuous war on pests — especially slugs.

The Alpine House

Early-flowering plants can be grown better in an alpine house than out of doors. They are grown in pots or pans and kept in frames for most of the year, usually coming into the house in batches just before they come to flower. The house need not be large and normally requires no artificial heating, except occasionally in dank or foggy weather. It should

By courtesy of Home Magazine

have a central path and raised benches each side covered with pea-sized shingle. Since light is all important these benches should be close to the glass, and whenever possible doors and vents should be wide open.

You can also use a large frame for the same purpose or even make a rock garden (complete with stones and soil) in a deep frame, covering this with glass between November and March.

Dry Walls

Dry walls provide a pleasant and inexpensive means of growing rock plants. They can link two levels of a garden, extend the garden area by allowing for 'upright' flower growing and often display trailing plants to better advantage. Materials may consist of small pieces of Portland stone, fragments of sandstone or limestone rocks, old house bricks or concrete blocks.

When used as a retaining wall the bottom layer of bricks or stones should be sunk a little below the soil surface and tipped back slightly; but the tops must be level or the whole wall will be out of alignment. When using natural stone select wide, large pieces for the foundation. Concrete is not normally used except to bind the lower course of bricks, or in difficult positions, as when the wall has to be linked with a flight of steps.

Run some excavated soil (or compost of equal parts loam, peat and sand) over the bottom layer of bricks and continue with the next course. Leave occasional spaces (4–6 in.) between the bricks to take plants. Keep each line level but with a slight backward slope or 'batter' to attract moisture, about 2 in. (between front and back) for walls up to 3 ft., and 3 in. for anything higher. Occasionally set an oblong piece of rock endways into the bank to give additional support.

Turn out the plants from pots; pack the roots (make sure they are damp) tightly with compost, force into the crevice, push the next stone to this and carry on in similar fashion. Pack the soil behind with a rammer to strengthen the bank and to prevent roots hanging in an air pocket. Finish off the top of the wall with slabs of paving stone, or cover with 9–12 in. soil and plant.

Dry walls can also serve as boundaries between features: e.g. dividing the flower and vegetable gardens. Naturally these are wider as they are freestanding and usually built up from either side with stones or bricks which tip slightly towards the centre. Work plenty of soil between the sections and leave top surface unplanted until soil has had time to settle.

The following plants are suitable for dry walls:
Aubrieta, *Alyssum saxatile*, Arabis, Armeria, Androsace, Campanula vars, Cerastium, Dianthus, Erinus, Gypsophila (dwarf kinds), Helianthemum, Iberis, Onosma, Saxifraga vars, Sedum, Sempervivum.

MINIATURE AND SINK GARDENS

The main requisites for these types of container are good drainage, plenty of moisture during the growing season, abundant light and slight protection (for certain plants only) during the depth of winter.

Sink gardens are usually kept out of doors, raised on brick piers for convenient viewing and tending. Old stone sinks from cottage kitchens are ideal for the purpose, but several firms make concrete sinks which are almost as attractive.

Site these in an open, sunny, yet sheltered position, setting the sinks on a firm foundation, tilting (very slightly) towards the drainage hole, which should be protected against blocking with strips of wire netting, overlaid with small stones or crocks. The base of the container can also be covered with crocks, overlaid with a thin layer of roughage (grass roots, leaves, peat fibre, etc.) before adding the compost.

For general purposes the following compost is satisfactory for practically all plants:

    1 part by bulk good quality sifted loam
    1   ,,   ,,   ,,   silver sand
    1   ,,   ,,   ,,   decayed leafmould or peat
    1   ,,   ,,   ,,   rubble or granite chippings

A rock and stream garden

Acid soil subjects such as dwarf Rhododendrons, Gentians and Heathers, need twice the amount of peat. For succulents such as Sempervivums, Saxifrages and Cacti, add one part broken lump charcoal to basic mixture.

Fill the sink nearly brimful of compost, placing suitable pieces of rock in position and planting the pockets as work proceeds. Building up the back or sides with soil and rocks adds height, but plant these only with subjects which will tolerate dry conditions: e.g. Sempervivums, Sedums and Saxifrages. All plants must be naturally small growing, not small pieces of rampant alpines.

Miniature gardens can be made in fancy bowls, old cake or pie dishes (painted outside) or any small

A sink garden

Designed by Anne Ashberry for Mullard Ltd

portable receptacle. The deeper these are, the more soil they contain and the greater the scope, but as with sinks, drainage must first be provided, then the soil and rocks.

Miniature gardens, which with imagination can be diminutive versions of a proper garden, are normally kept indoors in a light place, as in a window. The foliage will need frequent syringings to keep it free from dust, and the whole garden can be placed outside during the summer.

For children's gardens attractive displays can be made by using wild plant material. Moss, sprouting Acorns, Beech Nuts or Horse Chestnuts, small Ferns, Primroses and Violets look most effective and last a year or two in a cool light place, if watered regularly. A Cactus Garden is also worth while. Keep the compost light and use slow-growing species. For details of these see p. 274.

Dwarf forms useful for miniature and sink gardens:

Alyssum, *Andromeda polifolia compacta*, Androsace vars, Arenaria vars, *Asperula nitida, Asplenium ruta-muraria,* Campanula, Dianthus, Draba, Dryas, Erinus vars, Erodium, *Gentiana verna, Globularia bellidifolia,* Helxine, Ionopsidium, *Iris cristata, Linaria alpina, Mentha requieni, Morisia hypogaea, Oxalis adenophylla, Phlox douglasii* and *P. subulata, Polygala chamaebuxus, Raoulia australis* and *R. glabra, Rhodohypoxis baurii* and *R. platypetala,* Rosa — miniature species and varieties derived from *R. roulettii* and *R. pumila, Salix repens,* Saxifraga — Aizoon or encrusted vars, also Kabschia and Burseriana groups, Sedum — dwarf kinds, *Sempervivum arachnoideum standsfieldii, Silene acaulis, Sisyrinchium bermudianum, Veronica rupestris nana, Wahlenbergia pumilia.*

The following dwarf conifers are also suitable. They are all slow growing, the majority not more than 18 in. high:

Chamaecyparis lawsoniana ellwoodii, C. lawsoniana lutea nana, C. obtusa ericoides, C. obtusa caespitora, C. obtusa tetragona minima, C. pisifera nana, C. pisifera plumosa aurea; Cryptomeria japonica elegans bandai-sugi; Juniperus communis compressa, J. sabina tamariscifolia, J. coxii; Picea albertiana; Thuya orientalis rosedalis compacta.

In addition one may introduce any small bulbs such as Crocus, Cyclamen, Muscari, Narcissi, Scilla, Snowdrops, etc.

Erigeron mucronatus

Saxifraga grisebachii

List of Plants

ACANTHOLIMON Prickly Thrift

Plants form dense cluster of spiny evergreen foliage, flowers something like Statice, various shades of pink. Needs very hot, dry position. *A. venustum* is best. 5 in. July. Cuttings or division.

ACHILLEA Milfoil; Yarrow

Aromatic plants, mat-forming, with white or silvery foliage and flat heads of flowers. Sun, well drained soil. *A. ageratifolia*, white flowers and foliage. 4 in.; *A. clavenae*, white, 6 in. and its variety 'King Edward', deep cream, 6 in.; *A. tomentosa*, deep yellow, woolly leaves, 9 in.; *A. umbellata*, white, silvery foliage, 6 in. May—Aug. Division.

AETHIONEMA Lebanon Candytuft

Attractive, free-flowering plants for hot places on scree or in wall crevices. Full sun, like lime. Best is 'Warley Rose', deep pink. May—July. 6 in. Cuttings.

ALYSSUM Madwort; Gold Dust

A. saxatile, very accommodating rock plant. Bright golden flowers appear with and make good companions for Aubrieta. Leaves silvery. Full sun. var. *plenum*, double, and 'Dudley Neville', soft yellow, are others worth growing. 6—8 in. April—June. Cuttings.

ANDROSACE Rock Jasmine

Some members of this large family are difficult; but accommodating in any well drained soil, sun or partial shade is *A. sarmentosa*, with Cowslip-like heads of rosy-pink flowers on 6 in. stems. Hairy leaves form close rosettes. Increases readily by means of runners, *var. chumbyi* is deeper colour. May—June. Layers or division.

ANEMONE Windflower

Large family (see also p. 88), some suitable for rock garden. All like lime and can be propagated from seed sown as soon as ripe. *A. fulgens*, bright scarlet, likes sun; *A. nemorosa*, white or pink, woodland plant; *A. magellanica major* is soft yellow, also likes sun. 10 in. Spring.

ANTHEMIS Dwarf Marguerite; Chamomile

Mostly herbaceous plants (see p. 28) but *A. bierbersteinii*, with golden Daisy flowers on 6 in. stems and silver leaves is good for well drained soil in full sun. Summer. Division.

ARABIS Rock Cress

Easily grown plants with silvery leaves and usually white flowers. *A. albida plena* is best double white; 'Rosabelle' is soft pink and *A. aubrietioides*, lilac-pink, 4 in. Sun or partial shade. Spring. Cuttings.

ARMERIA Thrift

Good seaside plants with evergreen tufts of grassy foliage and round ball heads of flowers. Full sun. *A. caespitosa* 'Roger Bevan', 2 in. deep pink, is best. Divisions treated as cuttings, or seed (which will not come true). May—June.

ARNEBIA Prophet Flower

Good for dry places. Yellow flowers with five dark spots when first open, disappearing with age. *A. echinoides* flowers in summer. 9 in. Seed or heel cuttings.

ASPERULA Woodruff

Mat-forming, with mostly pink flowers, those mentioned liking full sun. *A. hirta*, 2 in.; *A. pontica*, deeper in colour, 2 in. spring and summer. *A. odorata* is native Woodruff, suitable for damp, shady spots. Dried foliage very fragrant. Division.

ASTILBE False Goat's Beard

A. chinensis pumila, deep rosy-purple and *A. simplicifolia*, pinkish with dark, crinkled leaves are suitable for damp spots

near rock pool or stream. Shade from midday sun. 6—9 in.
Aug.—Sept. Division.

AUBRIETA Purple Rock Cress

Indispensable spring flowering, easily grown plants in various
shades of mauve, purple and crimson. Also a good variegated
form. After flowering cut plants hard back. Summer cuttings.

CALAMINTHA Calamint

C. grandiflora, a fragrant plant with spikes of purplish flowers
in summer. 6 in. Needs hot, dry place. Seeds and cutting or
division.

CAMPANULA Bell Flower

A large family, many useful for late summer flowers in rock
garden. Majority blue, propagated from cuttings in spring or
in some cases by division or seed. Easy, provided soil does not
dry out. *C. arvatica*, 2 in. with star-shaped, lavender flowers and
its white form *alba*, both for scree. *C. carpatica*, cup-shaped
flowers on 6—18 in. stems in various shades of blue and white;
C. garganica 2 in. white or light blue; *C. portenschlagiana* 4 in.
blue; *C. pulla* 4 in. deep violet. Also many named varieties and
forms stocked by nurserymen.

CASSIOPE

Plants for acid soils, stems tightly packed with scale-like
leaves, and delicate white, individual flowers like Lily-of-the-
Valley on thread-like stems. Semi-shade, will not tolerate
drought. *C. lycopodioides*, evergreen, 1½ in. and *C. tetragona*,
1 ft. are both recommended. April—May. Division or layers,
but propagation not easy.

CERASTIUM Snow in Summer

White flowers, silver foliage, May—July. Rather rampant.
Division.

CERATOSTIGMA

C. plumbaginoides, the hardy Plumbago, with bright blue
flowers on 6 in. stems Sept.—Oct. Leaves turn reddish in
autumn. Inclined to spread. Division.

CODONOPSIS

Very beautiful plants with hanging, bell-shaped flowers
marked inside with various colours. Grow well up in rock
garden to display inside of blooms. *C. ovata*, china-blue and
C. clematidea, greyish-blue are equally attractive. Summer.
9—12 in. Seed.

DIANTHUS Pink

Summer-flowering plants for full sun and well drained soil.
All like lime. See also p. 204 for details of cultivation, and
propagation. *D. alpinus*, *D. deltoides*, *D. neglectus* are all good
species. Good garden hybrids are 'Mars' and 'Little Jock'.

DODECATHEON Shooting Star; American Cowslip

Plants for cool, moist, lightly shaded situation in leafy soil.
Petals fall back from stamens like Cyclamen, hence common
name. *D. media*, rosy-pink, 12 in.; *D. hendersonii*, dark purple
to rose, 8 in. May—June. Seed.

Campanula carpatica   Copyright Ryder & Sons

Veronica bidwillii

174

Muscari praecox alba

EPIMEDIUM Barrenwort

Attractive chocolate-mottled foliage on wiry stems, which often remains all winter and dainty spikes of flowers in early spring. Makes dense cover which prevents weeds. Shade, leafy soil. Division. *E. alpinum*, 6 in. flowers yellow and crimson; *E. pinnatum*, yellow, 8—12 in. *E. youngianum niveum*, white, 6 in. and *E. youngianum roseum*, mauvy-rose, 6 in.

ERIGERON Fleabane

E. mucronatus (syn. *karvinskianus*), scrambling plant with small pink and white Daisies in flower all summer. Suitable for planting by stone steps or trailing over rock bank. Likes sun. *E. pinnatisectus*, violet-purple flowers about an inch across. 4—8 in. high, much cut leaves. Seed.

ERINUS

Charming little plant, best in rock crevices or on old walls. Slender 3—4 in. flower spikes, summer. Best kinds are *E. alpinus* 'Dr Hanele', crimson; 'Mrs Charles Boyle', rose-pink, *alba*, white, and the type plant, mauve. Seed.

ERIOGONUM Sulphur Plant

Silver, plush-like foliage and crowded, showy heads of fragrant flowers. Not always hardy, but surviving in well drained positions, especially when protected with a sheet of glass in winter. *E. umbellatum*, soft yellow, 9 in. Late summer. Seed.

ERODIUM Heron's Bill

Plants for sunny, dry place with finely cut, silvery foliage and delicate, Geranium-like flowers. *E. chamaedryoides roseum*, pink and red tinged foliage, 2 in.; *E. chrysanthum*, silvery leaves and lemon flowers, 6 in. and *E. guttatum*, white with dark spots. Summer. Seed or cuttings.

GENTIANA Gentian

Much loved, but sometimes difficult plants with trumpet-shaped flowers, often intense blue. *G. acaulis*, the Swiss Bell Gentian, is one of loveliest, but unpredictable. Water if necessary in spring to secure flowers later. Succeeds in many soils including lime or clay. Deep blue trumpets on 3 in. stems in spring. Near relatives are *G. kochiana* and *G. clusii*.

Autumn-flowering Gentians include *G. farreri*, Cambridge-blue blossoms on **3** in. stems. Likes leafmould and peat in soil. *G. septemfida*, more adaptable, has clusters of deep blue blossoms on **6** in. leafy steems in late summer. *G. sino-ornata*, brilliant blue, **3** in. and *G. lagodechiana*, deep blue, **6** in. are other late summer kinds, whilst the brilliant British *G. verna* flowers in spring, likes moist soil. **2** in. Division or Seed.

GERANIUM Crane's Bill

Mostly too tall and weedy for rock garden, but in sunny, open spot, the following useful for summer flowers: *G. argenteum*, pale pink, silver foliage, **3** in.; *G. cinereum*, large open flowers, pink or white, **3** in.; *G. sanguineum lancastriense*, pink with deep veining, **3** in. Seed or cuttings.

HELIANTHEMUM Rock or Sun Rose

Shrubby plants for bold groupings over rocks. Easily grown and free-flowering for almost any soil provided site sunny. Like chalk. *H. vulgare nummularium* has given rise to varieties in white, pink, rose, red, orange, yellow and bronze colourings, many double. Cut back occasionally to preserve shape. **6—9** in. July. Cuttings.

IBERIS Candytuft

Easily grown plants, sun lovers, propagated from cuttings. *I. gibraltarica*, evergreen, with straggly, short-jointed branches and showy heads of white flowers. **1** ft. *I. sempervirens* 'Little Gem' **6** in. also white. Spring.

Rhodohypoxis baurii

Dwarf shrubs, Juniper communis compressa and Chamaecyparis obtusa pisifera nana

GYPSOPHILA Chalk Plant

G. cerastioides, pink-lined white flowers, together with *G. repens rosea* and *G. repens fratensis*, both pink, are dainty, mat-forming types of the large Gypsophila. Full sun, well drained soil. Seed or cuttings. July.

HABERLEA

One of best rock plants for north aspect, where it may be planted sideways in rock crevice so that leaf rosettes do not touch soil. Water if necessary in dry weather. Leaves tufted, rather wrinkled, flowers very free. Division. *H. ferdinandi-coburgi*, **4** in., flowers trumpet-shaped, pale to deep lilac; *H. rhodopensis*, lilac-blue and its variety *virginalis*, white. All bloom in spring.

Saxifraga burseriana

IRIS

Among smaller members of this family, following are suitable for pockets in full sun or partial shade. Propagation by division in July. All spring-flowering.
I. chamaeiris, all colours except pink and red; sun, like lime, 6 in.
I. cristata, lilac-blue, moist, leafy soil 4—6 in.
I. gracilipes, mauvy-pink, partial shade, leafy soil. 6 in.
I. innominata, orange-yellow, leafy soil, sun, no lime. 9 in.
I. pumila, colours and conditions as for. *I. chamaeiris*.
I. tenax, lavender-mauve, leafy soil, no lime, sun. 12 in.

LEONTOPODIUM Edelweiss

Famous Swiss alpine plant with greyish-woolly foliage and flannel-like, whitish flowers. *L. alpinum* likes well drained soil, sun; moraine treatment prevents damage from winter wet. 6 in. Summer. Division.

LEWISIA Bitter-root

Beautiful summer-flowering plants with umbels of wide, starry flowers on small stems and rosettes of oblong leaves. Plenty of sun, good drainage; west-facing position suits them well. Some protection in winter extends life. No lime. *L. howellii* and *L. tweedyi* are perhaps best species and have given rise to hybrids with cream, apricot, pink and red flowers. Approx. 6 in. July—Aug. Division or seed.

LINARIA Toadflax

L. alpina and its varieties *alba* and *rosea*, violet, white and rose respectively, make pretty compact clumps in rock garden, bloom from early summer until autumn. Full sun, any good soil. Seed.

LINUM Flax

Attractive, round, brilliant flowers only opening in sun. Well drained soil. *L. narbonense*, 2 ft. deep blue, has given rise to good varieties such as 'Peto's Variety' and 'June Perfield'. L. × 'Gemmel's Hybrid' is yellow. 10 in. also *L. flavum*, golden. 12 in. Cuttings.

LITHOSPERMUM Gromwell

Brilliant blue, tubular flowers, on spreading clumps of greyish foliage. Best are 'Grace Ward', 6 in. Gentian-blue and 'Heavenly Blue', bright blue. Both detest lime, flower in high summer. Cuttings.

MIMULUS Musk

Attractive plants for moister parts of rock garden or near water. See p. 272 for cultivation and other details.

MORISIA

M. monantha (syn. *M. hypogaea*). Scree plant with yellow flowers on 1 in. hummocks of pinnate leaves. Spring. Seed, division or root cuttings.

OENOTHERA Evening Primrose

Rock garden species flower freely in summer, but tend to spread. All require well drained soil, full sun. *O. acaulis* is biennial, white fading to pink; *O. caespitosa*, white flowers, 6 in., *O. fremontii*, yellow, 4 in. and *O. riparia*, with smaller yellow flowers, 6 in. are all useful. Summer. Seed or cuttings.

OMPHALODES Navel-wort

Sprays of bright blue Forget-me-not flowers, only happy in deep shade. Seed and division. *O. cappadocica* is the best. May. 6 in.

ONOSMA

Plants for dryish, well drained soils, full sun. Hairy, lanceolate leaves and sprays of nodding, tubular flowers. *O. albo-roseum*, white changing with age to pink; *O. tauricum*, soft yellow, both 6 in. Early summer. Seed or cuttings.

OXALIS Wood Sorrel

Avoid many of smaller members which can become pernicious weeds. All have divided leaves and wide open flowers. Following require well drained soil and sheltered nook. *O. adenophylla*, grey-green, crinkled leaves and soft lilac flowers, 2 in.; *O. enneaphylla*, white to deep pink. Spring flowering. Likes some shade as does *O. magellanica*, white, 1 in. spring. *O. floribunda rosea* flowers from May until frosts if in full sun, very gay with deep pink flowers. 6—9 in. Division of bulbils.

Erigonium umbellatum

PENSTEMON

Dwarf forms usually very bushy, almost shrubby, and covered with summer flowers. Hot, dry, well drained situations.
P. scouleri is one of best with deep lavender-blue tubular flowers on 9 in. stems. Others are *P. menziesii*, lilac, 3 in.; *P. roezlii* 'Weald Beacon', deep red 6 in.; *P. rupicola*, crimson, 2 in. and *P. heterophyllus* 'True Blue', clear blue, 9 in. Seed, division or cuttings.

PHLOX Rock Flame

Among the finest and easiest of rock plants, making sheets of colour in spring, trailing over rock or peeping from dry wall. Can also be interplanted between stones in crazy-paving. Trim back after flowering. Practically any soil; full sun. Most kinds evergreen and studded with wide open flowers May—July.
P. amoena, dusty pink, 6 in.; *P. douglasii*, white, pink and lavender, 1 in.; *P. subulata*, lavender, pink, red and white. Vars. 'Betty', 'Camla', 'G. F. Wilson', 'The Bride' and 'Vivid' are among best.

PHYTEUMA

P. comosum. Quaint plant with congested heads of bottle-shaped flowers of lilac-blue. 3 in. Spring. Good drainage and plenty of sun. Seed.

Primula marginata 'Linda Pope'   H. Smith

Erigeron pinnatisectus

A sink garden full of Sempervivums   By courtesy of Home Magazine

POTENTILLA Cinquefoil

Flowers like the Strawberry, in character for a long time. Shrubby ones best, especially *P. fruticosa* and its varieties with white to deep yellow flowers on 1 to 2 ft. bushes and silvery cut leaves. *P. nitida*, white, blooms in spring. 3 in. also *P. eriocarpa*, yellow, 2 in. Seed or cuttings.

PRIMULA Primrose

Very large family, majority happiest in cool, moist soil, shaded from hot sun. Some more suited to bog garden (see p. 272) but others need good drainage. Among useful kinds are *P. marginata* and its varieties, especially 'Linda Pope', blue and lavender, 3—4 in. March—April; *P. juliana* hybrids, crimson to purple-magenta and white. 2 in. very early spring; *P. rubra*, crimson, 3 in.; the Auricula hybrids, *P. forrestii*, yellow with orange eye, May—June, 6—9 in.; the double Primroses in all colours; *P. allionii*, rose, mauve or white, March—April, 1 in.

PULSATILLA Pasque Flower

Beautiful plants with showy flowers at Easter, handsome silvery seed heads later, and silvery downy leaves and stems. Syn. *Anemone pulsatilla*. Well drained positions, sun. Like lime. *P. vulgaris* varies from white, violet, red, pink, and purple; Var. 'Budapest', particularly fine in various shades of blue. 6—12 in. *P. alpina sulphurea*, clear yellow, 12—18 in. Seed sown as soon as gathered.

RAMONDA

Beautiful rock plants, with deep violet flowers like Saintpaulias. Cultivation as for Haberlea. Grow in shade. *M. myconi*, lavender, pink or white in spring. 2 in. Division or seed.

SAPONARIA Soapwort

S. ocymoides, trailing habit, rose-pink flowers May—June, something like small Pinks. Double form superior. 4 in. Seed or cuttings.

SAXIFRAGA Rockfoil

Important family for rock garden, with dwarf hummocks of tightly packed leaves and masses of pink, red, white or yellow flowers. Majority like well drained position with dry conditions round collar in winter, so are well adapted to screes or sink gardens. All like lime and are spring or early summer flowering. Division or cuttings.
The main divisions are:
1. *Silver or Encrusted*
Like gritty soil and have tiny, compact rosettes of leaves, usually silver. Flowers rise from these in spires. *S. aizoon*, 6 in.; *S. cochlearis*, 4—6 in.; *S. cotyledon*, 18 in.; *S. lingulata*, 12 in. and *S. longifolia*, 18 in. and their varieties, particularly the lovely 'Tumbling Waters' are in this group.

Rock plants can be effective whether used sparsely or massed. Left, Primula forrestii; right, two levels of the garden linked by a dry wall.

Phlox 'Betty'

2. *Kabschias*

These are the Cushion Saxifrages, 1—2 in. high, silver with short-stemmed flowers. Dislike winter wet, so protect with alpine cloche or pane of glass. Included here are *S. x. irvingii* and the *S. burseriana* hybrids, often grown in pans for the alpine house. Must have top dressing of granite or lime chippings over soil.

3. *Englerias*

These are the Bell Saxifrages, with silver rosettes of foliage and hairy stems to the flowers. *S. grisebachii*, crimson and pink, 6 in. is one of the most striking. Best suited to the alpine house.

4. *Mossy*

These are easiest to grow and do well in light shade. Resemble tufts of moss with showy white, pink or red flowers on 6—9 in. stems. 'James Bremner', white, is one of the best; 'Sir D. Haig' is dark crimson.

5. *Miscellaneous*

S. oppositifolia has prostrate wiry stems and stemless flowers, mostly red. Likes leafy soil and northern aspect. 1 in. *S. umbrosa* is well known 'London Pride', with small pink flowers, rounded leaves. 6—9 n.

SEDUM Stonecrop

Another useful genus with numerous species and varieties. Easily grown, suitable for all rock gardens. *S. spathulifolium* 'Capa Blanca' with white, down-covered leaves and yellow flowers is one of best. 3 in. Division.

SEMPERVIVUM Houseleek

Useful for hot, dry places, forming ground-hugging rosettes of overlapping leaves. Flowers secondary to foliage. Division. *S. arachnoideum* is covered with fine hairs like cobwebs. *S. tectorum ornatum*, Apple-green and scarlet foliage; *S. calcareum* 'Mrs Guiseppi', light green and brown and 'Malby's Hybrid' mahogany, are all attractive.

Ramonda 'Natalie' H. Smith

Phyteuma comosum

Penstemon 'Weald Beacon'

Lithospermum 'Grace Ward'

SISYRINCHIUM Satin-flower; Blue-eyed Grass

S. bermudianum, Rush-like foliage 5—6 in. high, violet-blue flowers. *S. californicum*, yellow. Summer, sun. Seed or division.

SOLDANELLA

Fringed, bell-like flowers on slender stalks and round fleshy leaves. Slugs menace young plants so protect with glass against winter wet. *S. alpina*, bluish-mauve, 3 in.; *S. montana*, lavender, 3 in. Spring. Division and seed.

THYMUS Thyme

Mat-forming, suitable for growing between crazy-paving and similar hot, dry places. In *T. serpyllum* and its varieties, flowers (pink to scarlet) have scented foliage. 1 in. Division.

TUNICA

T. saxifraga flore pleno 'Rosette'. Beautiful rosy-pink, double-flowered plant with grassy leaves and Gypsophila-like blossoms. Well drained situation. 3 in. Summer. Cuttings.

VERONICA Speedwell

Spiky flowers, lanceolate leaves; herbaceous and shrubby. Well drained soil and sun. Division, cuttings or seed.
Herbaceous sorts:
V. armena, blue, 4 in. spring; *V. catarractae*, white, 4 in. summer; *V. prostrata*, (syn. *ruprestris*) blue, pink or white, 4 in. summer; *V. spicata* 'Crater Lake Blue', deep blue, 9 in. summer.
Shrubs:
V. bidwellii, white with pink lines, 6 in.; *V. buchananii*, white.

VIOLA

For moist soil and partial shade many of the dwarf hybrids are useful. *V. cornuta* and *V. gracilis*, both about 4 in., and their varieties come in wide range of colours. Seed, cuttings.

ZAUSCHNERIA Californian Fuchsia See p. 47.

There are also many small bulbs and shrubs suitable for the rock garden: see appropriate chapters. Also a number of Dwarf Conifers of which the following are perhaps the most easily obtainable.

Arborvitae	*Thuya occidentalis ericoides*
	— orientalis minima
Cedar	*Cedrus libani nana*
Japanese Cedar	*Cryptomeria japonica vilmoriniana*
Cypress	*Chamaecyparis obtusa caespitosa*
	— — juniperoides
	— — pisifera nana
	— lawsoniana nana
Douglas Fir	*Pseudotsuga taxifolia pumila*
Silver Fir	*Abies balsamea hudsonia*
Spruce	*Picea abies gregoryana*
	— mariana nana
Pine	*Pinus sylvestris beauvronensis*
Yew	*Taxus baccata compacta*
	— — pygmaea

Viola 'Ardrossan Gem'   H. Smith

Sempervivum schlepanii rubrifolium

Sedum spathulifolium 'Capa Blanca'

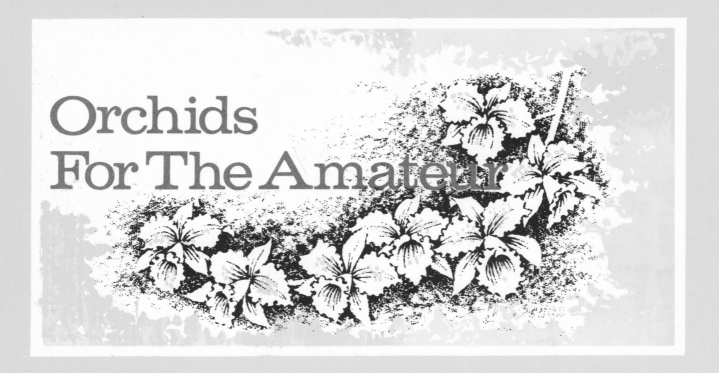

Orchids For The Amateur

Orchids are often considered luxury flowers, probably because so many are very expensive and difficult to cultivate. Nevertheless, there are a number of beautiful kinds which can be easily managed by the amateur, requiring only cool house treatment. They are neither difficult nor demanding in their requirements, and thrive happily in an average summer temperature of 60°F., and 50°—55°F. in winter.

Kinds to Grow

The easiest types to start with are any of the Cymbidiums — with long, arching spikes of blossoms which make good cut and corsage flowers; Odontoglossums, which also bear long spikes, and the Paphiopedilums, often known as Cypripediums or Slipper Orchids, because the large solitary flowers have their lower petals converted to striking, inflated, moccasin-shaped pouches.

Potting and Composts

The best time for potting is between March and May, and the general rule is to use as small a pot as possible. *Never* 'over-pot' an Orchid.

Many Orchids make pseudo-bulbs: i.e. green bulb-like structures which stick up above the soil, from which the leaves and flower stems emanate. Fresh pseudo-bulbs are produced each year by the sides of the old ones. When repotting, the older pseudo-bulbs (with attached rhizomes and roots) should be removed. Most plants of this type can stay two or three years in the same pot, provided a little of the top compost is taken out annually and replaced with fresh material.

Potting

Use clean pots, but, because Orchids have few roots, fill these for a third of their depth with broken crocks and lump charcoal. Cymbidiums, having larger roots than most, require only normal crocking. Trim the plants, removing old pseudo-bulbs and any

Dendrobium phalaenopsis

Cypripedium faireanum   Copyright R. & G. Cuthbert

Cypripedium pubescens   W. & R. Perry

dead portions, place a little compost in the pots and fit the plant in position, adding more compost to fill the pot and make it firm. Finally, dibble a few pieces of live Sphagnum Moss in the top compost, where it can grow and form a green carpet over the pot surface.

Compost for Odontoglossums

Equal parts fibrous peat or Osmunda fibre (which can be bought ready for use)
Sphagnum Moss
A little crushed crock to keep the compost open.

Compost for Cymbidiums and Paphiopedilums

1 part Osmunda fibre
1 part Sphagnum Moss
3 parts lime-free loam
A little brick rubble or crushed crocks.

Compost for Dendrobiums

2 parts Osmunda fibre
1 part peat
Crushed crocks or sand

Watering and Cultivation

Plants should not be watered for three or four days after repotting.

Aim to keep the compost moist throughout the year (but never sodden) for kinds which keep on growing, like the Slipper Orchids. Others only need water when growth and roots are active (in the case of Cymbidiums all the year round), but those with pseudo-bulbs rest for two or three months after flowering, during which time they require very little water.

Overhead spraying in summer with soft water provides a humid atmosphere and prevents Red Spider attacks. Shading should be provided in sunny weather and air given whenever possible.

Varieties

Varieties of Orchids are legion, but the following can be particularly recommended for the beginner with a small garden and greenhouse.

Paphiopedilum faireanum. A Slipper Orchid for a cool house with white and purple flowers, suffused dull brown and green. These last for weeks in character. *P. insigne*, very varied.

Dendrobium phalaenopsis. A beautiful Orchid with soft rose petals and dark-purplish-red lips.

Dendrobium densiflorum. This fine Orchid carries long, dense, pendulous trusses of rich yellow flowers with orange centres.

Cypripedium pubescens. A hardy Slipper Orchid for a sheltered corner of the rock garden. It has yellowish-green, purple striped petals and sepals and a pale yellow pouch with purple markings. Flowers May and June. Other kinds are *C. acaule*, *C. parviflorum* and *C. reginae* (Syn. *spectabile*).

Cymbidium. Cymbidiums must be kept growing all the year and have long sprays of dainty flowers. There are many varieties with green, pink, cream, brown and variously coloured blossoms, and they flower freely during the winter and early spring.

House Plants

The cultivation of house plants gives pleasure not only to gardeners, but to many whose outdoor activities are necessarily restricted, such as elderly people, invalids, flat dwellers and office workers.

House plants — like those in the garden and greenhouse — have certain basic needs, and these must be met as fully as possible according to available conditions. The choice of material will also be dictated by the aspect and size of room, for it is as useless to place tropical subjects in a fireless north room as to grow ferns in a south window. It is also good policy to start with fairly hardy and foolproof plants like Ivies, Tradescantia and Sansevieria before embarking on the more exotic types.

In order to grow house plants successfully the following factors must be considered:

LIGHT

Sunlight provides the energy which enables the green leaf to make food, so plants must receive plenty of light. The exceptions are the *natural shade plants* which can be damaged by too much sunlight.

During the winter months, all house plants should be given a window position, although naturally they should not be exposed to draughts or frost. In spring and summer they may be moved around more freely, and the shade lovers — like Ferns, Begonias and Fuchsias — put into less sunny windows or farther back into the room.

WATERING

Over-watering is a far more common fault than under-watering. A parched and drooping specimen can soon be revived, but persistent overwatering causes yellow foliage, leaf drop, root rot and sour soil.

Plastic pots require less water than the porous clay or terra-cotta types. Plastic is impermeable and on an average only requires one watering for every four given the other types.

Other points to remember are that compost containing peat retains moisture, whereas sandy soils scarcely hold water at all; that plants in full growth require more water than those in the juvenile or dormant stage; and that Cacti and Succulents never need as much watering as other plants.

Use soft water whenever possible and at room temperature. Large pot bound plants of Azaleas, Chlorophytums and Kentias should be watered by the immersion method. Stand them in a pail of water and leave until the bubbles of air cease to rise from the top. Stand to drain and return to their usual place.

Weight tells you a great deal about the plant's requirements. A heavy pot is usually quite wet, a moderately heavy one moist and a light one dry. In any case water adequately when this seems necessary. Plants must never stand in water all the time (unless they are semi-aquatic), so drain off the surplus moisture after an hour or so.

Philodendron scandens   Fisons Horticulture

HUMIDITY

House plants miss the humidity which naturally surrounds them when they grow outdoors. Indoor lighting and heating have a tendency to absorb moisture, and this greatly affects the plants, speeding up transpiration so that brittle dead patches often appear on the leaves. In bad cases these shrivel and fall; this is particularly the case with fleshy-leaved subjects like Peperomias and African Violets.

Humidity can be provided by any of the following means:

1. Plunge pots (Azaleas and Heathers especially) in large fancy pots packed with moist peat. Keep the latter damp.

2. Stand pots on trays or saucers containing about an inch of Pea-sized shingle. Keep a little water in the bottom of these, but *below* the pots so that the plants do not rest in water.

3. Syringe the foliage frequently with a mist-like spray of soft water. Use an old scent spray or one of the special aerosol types obtainable from Garden Centres and stores.

4. Occasionally rinse the foliage of tough-leaved plants like Ivies under a gentle stream from a running tap. Hold the pot on its side to avoid wetting the soil.

5. Large-leaved plants, e.g. Monstera, Ficus and Philodendrons, should be kept clean by wiping the foliage (once a month) with damp cotton wool. This should be dipped in water containing either a few drops of milk or Volck oil (which makes the leaves shine).

6. Bowls of water placed on or near radiators create a moist atmosphere. They can be filled with cut greenery for attractive effects.

7. Grouping several plants in a container, and packing them round with moist peat, not only presents a more attractive picture than a collection of pots, but makes for better plant growth. Put an inch layer of broken crocks or shingle over the bottom and keep the peat moist.

FEEDING

The John Innes Potting Composts contain all the nutrients required for healthy growth for some months after potting, but extra feeding is necessary later to keep pace with the new growth.

There are various methods:

1. By natural liquid feeds: e.g. a bag of soot or sheep-manure suspended in water for several months. The resultant liquid is diluted to the colour of pale tea and used weekly.

Sansevieria   E. Lyall

2. Solid fertilisers (usually in tablet form) pushed into the soil.

3. Liquid feeds of a proprietary nature, scientifically blended to supply the needs of the plant. These are usually diluted and given during the growing and flowering season.

AIR AND TEMPERATURE

Fresh air is essential to plants, and changing the atmosphere by opening the window *or* door, or using an air extractor, helps to combat disease. Draughts, however, can be fatal, so avoid a cross current of air (between an open door and window) and stop up cracks in window frames if delicate plants are to be grown on the sill.

Certain temperature fluctuations are unavoidable, but most plants do not require very warm conditions. The minimum winter temperature for the hardier types is 45°F. with 60°F. for the more delicate kinds.

SOME COMMON CAUSES OF FAILURE

1. *Gas.* Very few plants will tolerate gas. The leaves turn yellow and fall off and the plants ultimately decline. Some of the most resistant kinds are Aspidistra, Ivy, *Philodendron scandens* and Sansevieria.

2. *Draughts.* Avoid these at all costs.

3. *Over-Feeding.* Although a little stimulant helps the growing plant it must not be overdone or the leaves will become soft and flaccid and subject to pest and disease. Never apply fertilisers during the dormant season.

4. *Over-Watering.* This is a common cause of death. Do not be misled into believing a plant wants water because the leaves are limp. Over-exposure to sun or waterlogging can cause this symptom as well as dryness.

5. *Soil Exhaustion.* Leaving plants indefinitely in the same container results in progressive decline. Renew plants and/or occasionally.

6. *Scorching.* Proximity to fires or hot air will cause yellowing and leaf-drop.

7. *Pests and Diseases.* The main pests are Greenfly, Red Spider, Thrips, Scale Insects, Leaf Miners, White Fly and Ants; the worst diseases Root Rot (caused by over-watering), Mildew and Shothole Disease. The last shows as small dead or discoloured spots on the leaves. Moisture on the foliage in cold damp weather sometimes starts the trouble. See also chapter on Pests and Diseases.

GROWING PLANTS WITHOUT SOIL

A surprising number of plants can be grown in little or no soil and seem to manage happily with

Sansevieria, Ferns and Peperomia magnoliaefolia growing in moss in a log covered box

Smallholder and Home Gardener

Tradescantia, Begonia rex, Dracaena and Ctenanthe opperheimiana

African Violet

Smallholder and Home Gardener

a minimum of attention. We grow Epiphytes under fairly natural conditions by fixing an old tree branch in a flower pot and wiring the plants (their roots packed in damp Sphagnum Moss) at appropriate intervals. The Moss in turn is hidden by pieces of bark, also wired in place.

The plants that do best under these conditions are Stag-Horn Ferns (Platycerium) and Bromeliads — especially the Pineapple-like types such as Aechmeas and Nidulariums. Many Bromeliads have cupped leaf bases capable of collecting considerable quantities of water, and these natural reservoirs should always be kept filled. Frequent overhead spraying with tepid water is also beneficial.

Plants can also be grown without soil in troughs, by using Vermiculite. One type is particularly suitable, having a false bottom perforated with holes like a colander. Standing about an inch from the base of the galvanised steel container, this provides a convenient form of drainage.

The trough is filled with moist Vermiculite and the plants — washed free of soil — planted in posi-

tion. Water is provided through a special funnel at one corner and carried straight down to the base of the box. One should *never* water from the top but always by this sub-irrigation method. Water about once a fortnight.

As for feeding, fertiliser-impregnated material can be obtained which usually lasts several months; or liquid feeds can be provided via the water.

Strangely enough most plants grow more luxuriantly than when in soil, for the loose rooting medium seems to suit them. We have tried Hyacinths, Tulips, Daffodils, Pelargoniums, Primulas, Cyclamen, practically every kind of greenhouse plant (except Sansevieria and Cacti which find it too wet), Begonias, Schizanthus, Saintpaulias (which do particularly well) and a wide variety of herbs.

Soilless cultivation is worth trying, for it is clean and easy to handle, does away with the need for mixing composts, cannot carry soil pests and diseases, and since the plants grow as well (and in some cases better) than in soil it provides more latitude for the inexperienced.

BONSAI

The Japanese art of growing dwarf trees in pots is known as Bonsai. The aim is to produce faithful replicas in miniature of forest giants, the stunting being brought about by a combination of root restriction and feeding, and systematic pruning of roots and shoots.

Seed is sown in wire or wicker baskets of soil and the young plants allowed to grow on until their roots protrude through the container. These are then shortened and the operation repeated periodically, as necessary.

Simultaneously, unwanted buds and shoots are rubbed out, the weaker branches being retained in preference to the stronger. If any of these become too active and yet must be kept, they are weighted with stones. This lowers the branches and restricts the flow of sap — another dwarfing device. In course of years the trees develop all the outward characteristics of normal specimens, but on a reduced scale, the miniatures measuring 12 to 20 in. high and 3 to 4 in. in girth.

The containers or dishes used for specimen trees are about 1½ in. high with drainage holes in the bottom (or 'eyes' as the Japanese call them). These have either to be crocked or covered with fine mesh lids (known to the Japanese as 'eyelids') before the soil is put in place.

Good results can be obtained from pulverised clay soil, which should be sifted and mixed with soft sand or pulverised limestone, the amount varying with the trees; evergreens require about 50 per cent, flowering and deciduous plants 20 per cent. For the latter about 10 per cent of decayed leaf-mould is also added to the compost.

Contrary to popular belief, Bonsai trees are not house plants and do best when grown in a semi-shaded outdoor position most of the year. Prune them regularly in spring, and in summer nip off any seemingly vigorous buds. This all helps to check growth. Acers and other deciduous trees should be severely trimmed in February and their shoots constantly pinched back in summer.

Dwarf trees should not be repotted in large pots or pans. To keep them dwarf it is necessary to restrain the roots.

The soil may be changed every 3–5 years, using the same dish or one very slightly larger. Cut away over-vigorous roots in February or March.

Water as required and syringe the foliage at frequent intervals.

Begonia masoniana

Aechmea rhodocyanea

Fisons Horticulture

List of Plants

ACALYPHA

A. wilkesiana Beefsteak Plant

A temporary house plant grown for its vividly coloured leaves, which are mottled with red and crimson on a coppery-green background. They are oval-heart-shaped, but varieties vary in colour and form. Treat as for Codiaeum. Propagated from cuttings.

AECHMEA Air-Pine

Members of the Pineapple family with large stiff and incurving rosettes of leaves. They have little root and can withstand drought. The leaves taper to a funnel in the centre, into which soft water should be poured freely in summer, less frequently in winter. Keep away from strong sunlight and give a warmer position than most house plants (about 60°F. in winter). Compost 3 parts loam to 1 each fibrous peat and coarse sand.

A. rhodocyanea has silver foliage with horizontal grey stripes and showy spikes of pink and blue flowers, maintaining their character for months. *A. fulgens* has blue flowers and red calyces and Olive-green leaves. *A. macracantha* wine-red foliage. Propagated by offsets.

AEONIUM

Fleshy-leaved plants, forming rosettes. Some species have no stalks, others have stout stems and look like little trees. Some kinds die after flowering. *A. tabulaeforme* and *A. cooperi* are representative of the family, the former being stalkless and the latter a stemmed kind. Sandy soil and fairly cool conditions. Propagated from offsets.

AGLAONEMA

Compact plants with oblong, slender leaves, often variegated in cream or yellow. Allergic to fumes and should be kept almost dry in winter.

A. commutatum, *A. pictum* and *A. 'pseudo-bracteatum'* are all good foliage plants. Propagated from seeds or cuttings taken in bottom heat.

ANTHURIUM Flamingo Plant

A. scherzerianum. Flowers palette-shaped, brilliant scarlet and thick and shiny with a showy, yellowish spathe. Leaves oblong-lanceolate, dark green. Needs a warm, even temperature, good drainage and humidity. Compost, Osmunda fibre or Sphagnum Moss 6 parts, to 1 part leaf-soil with a little silver sand and charcoal. Propagated by division.

APHELANDRA

A. squarrosa var. Louisae. Favourite house plant with showy, zebra-striped leaves and four-sided spikes of yellow flowers. Plants often fail because grown in too cold a situation. Require

Cissus antarctica, Kangaroo Vine　　　　Keith Luxford

rich soil compost and careful watering, also plenty of light. Propagated from soft cuttings taken in bottom heat. Stopped plants make bushy specimens. Temp. 60°F. is ideal.

ARAUCARIA

A. excelsa Norfolk Island Pine. A small evergreen tree, with branches radiating outwards from the stem and covered with small, needle leaves. Slow growing but tolerant of cool conditions. John Innes Compost. Should be top-dressed occasionally, which creates less root disturbance than repotting. Does not mind shade. Usually raised from fresh seed sown in warmth, or air-layers.

ARDISIA Coral Berry

A. crispa (syn. *A. crenulata*). Delightful little shrub which holds its scarlet berries for months (in a greenhouse over a year). These often appear with the flowers for next season's berries and are always borne in whorls round the stems. Blossoms white. Leaves small and leathery with crinkled edges. Semi-shade and acid soil. Grow in fairly small pots. Propagation, seed sown early

Begonia 'Rajah'

Bonsai, Juniperus sargentii Copyright Samuel Dobie & Son

in year in warmth or cuttings. Temp. around 45°F. suits the plants.

ASPARAGUS

A. plumosus nanus. The Asparagus Fern, and *A. sprengeri*. Two well known foliage plants, the cut fronds of which are used for bouquets, etc., whilst the plants themselves make good pot subjects. John Innes Compost and large pots. Sometimes specimens can be kept for years. Grow well in a shady situation and are almost hardy. Over-watering or too much heat causes the leaves to drop. Seed or division.

Pinus thunbergii var. corticosa Copyright Samuel Dobie & Son

ASPIDISTRA Bar-room Plant; Cannon-Ball Plant; Cast Iron Plant

Old Victorian favourite which tolerates extremes of temperature, gas and poor lighting. Dark green, oblong leaves and insignificant flowers. *A. elatior* is the type, but there are also variegated forms. Leaves should be washed occasionally. Dislikes strong sun. Can be put outside for the summer months. Propagated by division.

BEGONIA

A very large family containing both ornamental foliage and flowering plants. Many of the latter are in great demand for greenhouse and garden decoration.

Most of the fine foliaged forms are native to tropical and sub-tropical forests, and thus need shelter from strong sunlight. The compost should be free from lime and containing a fair proportion of rotted leafmould and sand. They are intolerant of gas fumes and should not be over-watered. Soft water is preferable.

Propagation is usually by leaf-cuttings, although some of the taller growing species and varieties can be increased from stem cuttings, struck with bottom heat.

B. rex. These have leaves marbled and coloured in most beautiful shades of red, pink, pearl-grey and green. Many named sorts can be obtained, such as 'Silver Queen', 'Hoar Frost', 'La Pasqual', 'Helene Teupel' and 'King Henry'.

Other foliage species include *B. masoniana*, the Iron Cross Begonia, with curious leaf markings; *B. rajah*; *B. haageana* (which grows tall and leggy); *B. metallica*, *B. manicata*, *B. masculata* and *B. serratifolia*. Many have red undersides to the foliage. The last two kinds and *B. haageana* can be increased from stem cuttings.

Christmas Begonias and other varieties of *B. semperflorens* are characterised by masses of small pink or red flowers which carry on for months. Easily reproduced from cuttings and like a sunny windowsill.

BELOPERONE Shrimp Plant

B. guttata. Free flowering plant with pink, Nettle-like flowers having very conspicuous, reddish bracts and small, oblong leaves. Plants need a light, well drained soil and should be fed at intervals during the growing season. Keep fairly dry and cool in winter. Prune back to shape after flowering and propagate from spring cuttings. Leaves drop if over-watered.

BILBERGIA Queen's Tears

Easily grown plants with long, narrow, rather stiff leaves and sprays of pendent flowers in spring. These are violet and green with showy pink bracts. Any good soil. Propagated by division. Water carefully in winter.

BROMELIADS Air-Pines

The Air-Pines are mostly native to the tropical rain forests, where they grow in holes and niches on taller trees, drawing their nourishment from collected organic matter — such as fallen leaves — and watered by atmospheric moisture. Most of them require warm temperatures but are not difficult if carefully watered.

See Bilbergia, Aechmea, Cryptanthus, Nidularium and Vriesia.

CACTUS See p. 274.

CALADIUM

Beautiful foliage plants, heart-shaped and variously coloured. Some are green and white, others heavily suffused with red, but all are of delicate texture and almost transparent. Give plenty of light but shade from strong sun, also water freely in growing season. Dry off in their pots at end of summer and start again in a warm greenhouse in early spring. Tuberous subjects. 'Candidum' is one of the most attractive with almost white leaves.

CALATHEA

Attractive foliage plants with fine markings and tuberous roots. Do not grow in too strong a light or leaves will curl. These need humidity, so plunge pots in damp peat or stand them on a gravel tray, kept constantly moist. Temperature should not drop below 50 °F. Rich, well drained soil. *C. insignis*, leaves two shades of green, purple undersides; *C. picturata*, silver and green with maroon undersides; *C. zebrina*, leaves striped in two shades of green. Propagated by division.

CHLOROPHYTUM Spider Plant; Grass Lily

C. comosum variegatum. Grassy plants, green and white striped, with long narrow leaves and masses of baby plants at the ends of long pendulous yellow runners. Flowers small and white. Good house plant for sun or light shade, needs regular feeding. Propagate from runners.

CISSUS Kangaroo Vine

C. antarctica. Tough evergreen climber with long, heart-shaped, serrated leaves. Do not over-water, especially in winter. Plenty of light in winter, but avoid strong sun in summer. Propagate from cuttings. *C. striata* is a finer leaved and more elegant species with 3 to 5 lobed leaves.

CODIAEUM Croton

Shrubby plants forming a slender trunk, with variously shaped and variegated leaves. These are very variable, sometimes long and narrow, in other varieties Aspidistra-like or shaped like those of the Oak. Colouring varies from deep red-purple, to green and yellow — or red, yellow, green and cream on different leaves on the same plant.

Crotons appreciate a warm, constant temperature so succeed well with central heating, especially when stood on a gravel tray to maintain humidity. Plenty of light during growing season and sufficient food. Compost — loam, leaf and sand in equal proportions. Keep plants in small pots at all times. Cuttings not easy but will sometimes root with hormone assistance and bottom heat. They are best inserted in shingle or Sphagnum Moss instead of compost, but must be potted immediately they root.

CRYPTANTHUS

Practically rootless plants with rosettes of crisp, crinkly-edged leaves. *C. bivittatus* is the commonest species with brownish-pink foliage which has cream stripes. Colour alters according to the intensity of the light. Plants grow well packed in moss between pieces of bark or in tree stumps. They like humidity but not too much water at the roots. Division.

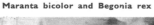

Maranta bicolor and Begonia rex

Neoregelia carolinae tricolor, an unusual and striking house plant

Valerie Finnis

CTENANTHE Never-Never Plant
C. oppenheimiana has oblong leaves about 5 in. long, banded with cream, dark and light green, purple underneath. Strong sunlight curls leaves. Grows from a rhizome which can be divided. Acid, peaty soil in shallow, well crocked containers gives the best results.

CYANOTIS Pussy Ears
Somewhat resembles Tradescantia, but with reddish, downy, fleshy leaves and blue flowers. *C. kewensis* is the best species, and makes a good hanging plant for the front of a bowl. Propagated by division. Shelter from strong sun, but otherwise give plenty of light. Well drained soil.

DIEFFENBACHIA Dumb Cane and Mother-in-Law Plant
D. picta. An imposing plant with fat stems like Sugar-cane and large green and white spotted leaves. Eating the stem produces swelling in the throat preventing speech for 24 hours — hence the English name. Warm, moist, semi-shady position in light rich but well drained soil. Suitable for central heating. Plenty of water in summer. Propagated from stem or soft cuttings rooted with bottom heat.

DRACAENA Corn Plant
D. fragrans and *D. deremensis.* Plants something like Crotons in habit, or Aspidistras raised on stems. Tolerate gas and shade better than most plants and temperatures down to 50°F. in winter. A rich soil containing plenty of peat and leaf-mould with some bonemeal is essential for good foliage and habit. *D. fragrans* is green, but varieties have striped, green and gold leaves. *D. deremensis* is also striped. Propagated from cuttings. *D. godseffiana*, Gold Dust Dracaena, one of the most popular; a low branching plant with oval leaves, thickly spotted with gold.

ELETTARIA Cardamom
E. cardamomum. Cardamom seed (used in curries) comes from this plant, which has a creeping, fleshy rootstock and wide, tightly packed, oblong leaves about a foot high. When handled they smell of Cinnamon. John Innes Potting Compost with fairly dry conditions in winter and protection from strong light are main cultural requirements. Fairly hardy. Propagated by division.

EUPHORBIA Poinsettia
E. pulcherrima. Plants usually discarded when flowers finished, but can be kept another year by gradually drying off after blooming, cutting back reasonably hard in April and watering to encourage new shoots. These may be rooted as cuttings (after dusting the cut with charcoal) or allowed to grow on. Mainly attractive for scarlet bracts which contrast well with soft green leaves. *E. splendens* is the Crown of Thorns, with scarlet flowers on spiny branches continuing throughout the year. Suitable for a centrally heated home.

FATSHEDERA

Garden cross between Aralia (Fatsia) and Ivy (Hedera) showing characteristics of each. *F. lizei* can be tied to trellis as a climber in a cool position. The variegated form is more attractive but slower growing. Sponge leaves occasionally. Keep fairly dry in winter. John Innes Potting Compost. Propagation, spring or summer cuttings in bottom heat.

FICUS Rubber Plant

Good foliage plants with milky sap. Can be acclimatised to full sun but usually grows best in semi-shade. John Innes Compost, with plants kept in comparatively small pots. Over-watering causes leaf drop. Sponge foliage occasionally and feed or top-dress if colour looks pale.

F. elastica decora is best type, together with its slower-growing variegated form. Propagated from air layers (taking 6—9 months) or stem cuttings rooted with bottom heat. *F. pumila* (syn. *F. repens*) is the Creeping Fig, a small leaved self-clinging plant; *F. radicans variegata* has small, variegated leaves on short-jointed stems, often used with other plants in mixed containers.

FITTONIA

Foliage plants with soft, oval, bright green leaves having conspicuous white veins in *F. argyroneura* and red veins in *F. verschaffeltii*. Flowers in spikes, greenish. Shade and a warm, moist atmosphere essential. Syringe overhead occasionally. Avoid draughts and grow in well drained pots of sandy-peaty soil. Propagated from cuttings.

GREVILLEA Silk Oak

G. robusta. Small tree with feathery, deeply-cut leaves frequently used as a 'dot' subject amongst bedding plants. Sun or shade. John Innes Potting Compost. Keep fairly dry in winter. Feed older plants in summer. Easily grown and raised from Feb. sown seed.

HEDERA Ivy

Large family of easily grown, climbing plants with smooth leaves, many attractively mottled and marbled. Ivies stand cooler conditions and more shade than most house plants, but often refuse to cling to freshly limed walls. All need plenty of water in summer but rather less in winter. Foliage should be sprayed or washed occasionally. Cuttings in Aug. root quickly under glass or polythene, or the variegated types may be layered in small pots of John Innes Compost.

H. helix is the English Ivy, small-leaved, with many varieties; *cristata* has curly-edged leaves; *marmorata* is marbled in grey, green and white; *canariensis* is characterised by large green leaves; 'Gloire de Marengo' is also large, but variegated in cream and green; 'Golden Jubilee' has small leaves, gold-centred with a green margin; 'Glacier' is silver-grey, and there are many others.

HELXINE Mind Your Own Business; Babies' Tears

H. soleirolii. Prostrate growing plant with tiny green, golden, or silver leaves; suitable for carpeting the soil, growing under greenhouse staging, or for trailing down over pots, drainpipes or other receptacles. Spray frequently and keep out of bright sun. Propagate from division. Any soil.

HOYA See p. 251.

IMPATIENS See p. 256.

MARANTA Prayer Plant

Stocky little plants with bright green, oval leaves variously spotted. *M. leuconeura var. kerchoveana*, foliage 5 in. by 3 in., red blotches when young but developing to maroon, on dark

Air Pines growing on an old tree branch

Bonsai, Dwarf Azalea

green leaves, *var. massangeana*, veins white, undersides of leaves reddish.

Shade-loving plants, needing well drained soil, made up from Sphagnum, sand, charcoal and leafmould with a little loam. They dislike lime. Very little water in winter. Leaves tip down at night, hence the popular name. Warm room plant. Propagate by division.

MONSTERA Swiss Cheese Plant

M. deliciosa. Handsome climbing plant, with very large leaves incised and cut like a Gruyère cheese. Likes warmth and plenty of water in summer. Large plants should be fed regularly and will then produce Mushroom-coloured, Arum-like flowers. These take 12 months to develop to green, Pine-shaped edible fruits. Early spring cuttings or layers.

NEOREGELIA

N. carolinae tricolor is a beautiful Air-Pine with its long narrow leaves arranged in rosettes. These are mostly green but have the centres splashed with cream and pink. The blue flowers arise from the centres of the rosettes. A mature plant may be 20 in. or more across. Water with soft water, filling the central 'vase' formed by the foliage. *N. spectabilis* is the Painted Fingernail Plant, green leaves tipped with red, Ash-grey beneath and banded in brown. Cultivation as for Aechmea. Propagate by offsets.

NEPETA Ground Ivy; Jill on the Ground

N. hederacea var. variegata. A handsome plant for hanging baskets or trailing over pots and troughs, with rounded, crinkly-edged leaves, which are green with white centres. Long leafy runners are produced on healthy plant. Moist soil and shade from very bright sunshine. Type plant is native to Britain but its variegated form is not hardy. Propagate by cuttings or division.

NIDULARIUM

N. innocentii. Very similar to Neoregelia, with rosettes of narrow dark green leaves, flushed with purple and bright crimson flowers. Cultivate as for Aechmea.

OPLISMENUS Basket Grass

Hanging plant something like Tradescantia but with grassy leaves in pink, white, green and violet stripes. Likes a fairly light position and well drained soil. Should be frequently renewed as old plants grow straggly. Cuttings and layers. *O. hirtellus variegatus* is the variety most commonly grown.

PEPEROMIA Pepper Elder

Chiefly grown for their variously coloured, fleshy leaves, these are dwarf plants with spikes of flowers, sometimes fragrant. Warmth, light soil and semi-shade. Small pots essential. *P. glabella* has green leaves; *P. sandersii* (syn. *P. argyreia*) heart-shaped, fleshy leaves, silvery green with white lines; *P. magnoliaefolia*, cream edged; *P. caperata*, leaves green and so corrugated that they appear to be pleated. Propagate by leaf cuttings.

PHILODENDRON Heart-leaf Philodendron

P. scandens. Fine climbing plant with plain green, shiny heart-shaped leaves. Keep out of bright sunshine. Best grown on moss or bark or Osmunda fibre, kept moist by spraying. Compost — leafmould, old Sphagnum, coarse sand and old potting soil in equal parts with a little rotted manure or bonemeal. There is a variegated form.

Larger leaved species are obtainable of which *P. bipinnatifidum* and *P. elegans* are perhaps the most widely grown. Propagated by layers or cuttings struck with bottom heat.

PILEA Aluminium Plant; Friendship Plant

P. cadierei. Low growing plant with shiny leaves, oval-oblong in shape and chequered with green and silver. It should be

Grevillea robusta   Copyright Samuel Dobie & Son

House plants in a variety of containers
Smallholder and Home Gardener

Syngonium vellozianum, Goose-foot
Smallholder and Home Gardener

RHOICISSUS Grape Ivy

R. rhomboidea. An evergreen climber with shining, 3-lobed, toothed leaves. Needs warmer conditions than Cissus but similar cultural conditions. Spring cuttings.

SAINTPAULIA African Violet

One of the few house plants grown primarily for the flowers, which have evolved from the small washy blue blossoms of the type species *(S. ionantha)* to varieties with single and double, pink, white, light blue, deep mauve, purple and even bicolour forms. Small, rounded plush-like leaves set off the flowers admirably and under the right conditions plants remain in bloom for months. They require a moist soil and humid atmosphere, coupled with fresh air in summer, but no draughts and plenty of warmth (average 60°F.) at all times. If plants are too cold the flowers drop.

Grow in plenty of light. Water falling on leaves in winter or whilst sun is shining will give rise to brown spots. An acid compost is best, made up from well rotted leaf-soil or peat, a little charcoal, sand, rotted Sphagnum and a little decayed cow-manure. Propagated from leaf-cuttings struck in Vermiculite or sand (they will also root in water) and helped by bottom heat.

SANSEVIERIA Mother-in-Law's Sharp Tongue; Bow String Hemp

Perhaps the most accommodating of all house plants, with-standing neglect, cold, heat and draughts, provided that they are not over-watered. Fairly stiff soil with some sand and charcoal. Last for years and only rarely need repotting. Wash the leaves occasionally. *S. trifasciata laurentii* grows 2—3 ft. tall and has yellow stripes running down the stiff, sharp, lance-shaped leaves. *S. cylindrica*, round, Rush-like leaves in two shades of green. *S. hahnii*, Bird's Nest Hemp. Forms a dense rosette only a few inches high in two shades of green. Propagate by division or leaf cuttings.

SAXIFRAGA Aaron's Beard; Mother-of-Thousands

S. sarmentosa var. tricolor. Hanging plant with round,

stopped frequently to induce a bushy shape. John Innes Compost and small pots. Very hardy. Propagated from cuttings. *P. muscosa* Artillery Plant. Very small leaves on short branching stems and tiny flowers which 'explode' their pollen when dry.

PLATYCERIUM Stag-horn Fern; Elkhorn

P. bifurcata. A true Fern, suitable for high temperatures. There are two kinds of leaves, one brown and rounded, the other green, forked like a pair of horns, which carries the spores. Usually grown on a piece of wood or bark, which may be hung up in a light (but sunless) situation. Here it often lasts years, growing steadily. If planted in pots use Sphagnum Moss and peat in equal parts. Syringe frequently and soak occasionally. Division.

PLECTRANTHUS

Herbaceous plants with trailing stems, well clothed with rounded, crenate leaves and spikes of attractive blue flowers. These look something like Lavender.

Better blooms can be obtained by growing the plant in a hanging bottle (see p. 121) placed in a good light. *P. oertendahli* is the commonest species. John Innes Potting Compost. Plenty of water in summer. Plants should be frequently renewed from soft cuttings.

RHODEO Boat Lily

R. discolor. A relation of Tradescantia with long, narrow, very fleshy leaves, green above and purple below, which rise in pairs from a purplish stem. Flowers boat-shaped, white and green, in the leaf axils. John Innes Compost and shade from strong sun. Plenty of moisture in summer. Cuttings.

Pegging down Scindapsus to make a compact plant
Smallholder and Home Gardener

195

crinkly-edged, small leaves in pink, green and cream. Continuously throws out runners, with a series of baby plants suspended from them. Flowers pale pink. John Innes Potting Compost. Keep fairly dry and warm in winter; cool in summer. Propagate from runners.

SCINDAPSUS Ivy Arum; Joseph's Coat
S. aureus. Climbing plants with heart-shaped leaves of shining green with streaks of yellow. Treat as for *Philodendron scandens.* Hates draughts and lime in the soil. Stop frequently to make a bushy plant. Varieties 'Golden Queen' and 'Marble Queen' with more yellow and white respectively on the foliage. Propagate from layers.

SETCREASEA Purple Heart
S. purpurea. A plant related to Tradescantia but of upright habit, with long narrow leaves about 6 in. long and veined magenta flowers. Both stems and foliage are a deep Plum purple. The stems are very brittle and need frequent stopping to induce a bushy habit. Needs plenty of light but not direct sunlight. John Innes Compost. Renew frequently from cuttings.

SPARRMANNIA African Hemp
S. africana. An evergreen, small tree with hairy leaves resembling those of the Lime tree. Bunches of showy white flowers with masses of stamens appear in late winter and spring. Rich, well drained soil. Feed in summer. Prune back periodically. Needs plenty of light. Cuttings root in water.

SPATHIPHYLLUM Lily of Peace
S. wallisii. A plant of the Arum family with white flowers which are green at first, and oblong, shiny, rather pointed leaves. Warm, moist position in shade. Keep fairly dry in winter but give plenty of water and food during the growing season. General height approximately 1 ft. Soil should be slightly acid, 2 parts loam to 1 each of peat or leaf-mould and sharp sand and ½ part rotted manure. A little superphosphate may be sprinkled over the mixture. Propagate by division or freshly gathered seed.

SYNGONIUM Goose Foot
S. vellozianum. Resembles Scindapsus and needs similar treatment. Grows well when trained up a moss-filled cone of wire netting. Leaves 3—5 fingered, like a goose's foot, in two shades of green. Will grow in a poor light. Feed and water well during the growing season. *S. podophyllum* is very similar. Cuttings soon root in bottom heat.

TRADESCANTIA Wandering Jew
Well known plant of creeping or trailing habit, with jointed stems and thin leaves. Flowers variously coloured — cream, pink, reddish and mauve but never very exciting. Variegated foliaged forms are best but need a good light to bring out the colours. All Tradescantias should be renewed frequently; pieces of growth root easily in water or sandy soil. *T. fluminensis* is green, but there are varieties with silver and gold variegations, also with reddish, mauve, pink and cream striations.
T. blossfeldiana has very hairy leaves, green above and purple beneath.

VRIESIA
Plants similar to Neoregelia, with strap-shaped leaves, arranged in rosettes, often attractively marked. Flower spikes are larger, the blooms mostly yellow. Cultivate as for Aechmea.
V. fenestralis, V. saundersii and *V. splendens* are all in commerce.

ZEBRINA
Extremely popular house plant, often confused with Tradescantia. The leaves and stems are much more fleshy, however, and larger in all their parts. They are also extremely brittle. Constant renewal advisable. The best variety is *Z. pendula var. quadricolor* which has leaves striped with white, purple and two shades of green; the undersides silvery-purple. Good light essential or colours fade. Treatment and propagation as for Tradescantia.

Mixed house plants Fisons Horticulture

TEMPORARY HOUSE PLANTS

During the winter a number of greenhouse subjects may be accommodated as temporary house plants.

In most instances plants used for indoor bloom like slightly acid conditions. Watering them with hard water builds up a lime content (often shown by a white rim on the flower pots). Use soft water, therefore, whenever possible, warmed to room temperature. The liquid obtained after thawing out a refrigerator can be used in the absence of rain water, or tap water may be softened by adding one teaspoonful of ammonium carbonate to every quart.

The following table suggests the best treatment for the most commonly grown types.

Name	English Name	Position	Watering	Special Tips
AZALEA A. indica	Indian Azalea	Keep cool and in a good light	Usually grown in peat which must be kept constantly moist. Stand the pot in a bowl of water for half an hour, then drain. Syringe the foliage with a fine spray of soft water to prevent leaf-drop.	Plunging the pot in a larger container and packing moist peat between the two keeps the soil moist and cuts down watering.
CYCLAMEN	Sow Bread	Keep cool and in a good light. Between 50°—55°F is ideal.	Over-watering is the chief cause of failure. To revive a jaded plant, stand the pot on a small basin in a bowl of boiling water. Do not let the water touch the pot. Leave for one hour. The steam revives the plant.	Pull out dead leaves of flowers instead of cutting them. Never let water touch the corm. Keep out of draughts.
ERICA	Cape Heather	Keep cool.	Water when required. Dislikes hard water. Never allow plant to dry out.	Spray the foliage daily or the leaves will fall. Discard when finished.
HYDRANGEA		Keep in a light window.	Very thirsty plant and in a warm place may need soaking *twice* a day.	Immerse the flower heads occasionally in lukewarm water to revive them. Use lime-free compost.
PRIMULA P. obconica P. malacoides		Cool and airy. Good light.	Water from below by standing the pot in a saucer of water.	Perhaps the easiest of all house plants, often flowering for months on end. Discard when finished.
SENECIO S. cruentus	Cineraria	Must be kept cool (45°—50°F) and out of strong sunlight.	Do not overwater but keep soil just moist at all times.	Subject to Aphides. Liquid feed once a week helps the blooms. Throw away when flowers are finished.
SOLANUM S. capsicastrum	Winter Cherry	Keep cool in a very good light.	Syringe leaves occasionally. Water as required.	Too much warmth and lack of air causes leaves to drop. A pinch of Epsom Salts (Magnesium sulphate) helps to retain the foliage. Feed occasionally.
ZONAL PELAR- GONIUM	Geranium	Very light window with sun.	Do not over water.	Very easy plant but must not get too cold.

Ferns & Shade Plants

A certain amount of shade in the garden is not necessarily a disadvantage. Many of the world's most beautiful plants cannot tolerate an excessive amount of sunshine. The natural shade-loving species, therefore, form the basis of our plantings in those areas which receive little or no sun.

For a site that is *shady and damp* there are many fine plants, but very few for the *shady dry areas*. It is therefore important to keep the top surface permanently moist, creating a spongy, humus-type soil such as is found in natural woodland; ideal conditions for growing a wide range of attractive plants. Among the most important of these are the Hardy Ferns.

Ferns used to be much more appreciated than they are today. Their lacy foliage and graceful fronds gave great pleasure to the Victorians, who frequently constructed grottos (both outdoors and under glass) in order to display them to better advantage. In such congenial spots, the plants developed to a size and beauty hardly conceivable to present-day gardeners. Books were written about them, nurseries specialised exclusively in ferns, catalogues were published, shows were organised, societies were formed and keen competition existed both on amateur and professional levels.

For the modern gardener the greatest attributes of Hardy Ferns are their permanency and undemanding nature. They flourish undisturbed for years, benefiting only from an annual removal of the previous year's fronds and an occasional top-dressing with sifted peat, leaf-mould and wood ash.

CULTIVATION

The site should not only be protected from strong sunshine, but also sheltered from cold spring winds

Onoclea sensibilis   R. A. Malby

Matteuccia struthiopteria

which may damage the tender young fronds. Drought, (especially winter dryness) is the greatest enemy and probably the major cause of failure.

Careful preparation of the soil before planting is essential. In their natural state ferns grow in a spongy carpet of rotted leaf humus that has accumulated through the years. The soil therefore should be deeply dug and a liberal supply of retentive organic material — such as garden compost, peat or peat moss litter, spent hops or well rotted leaves — should be introduced in the top layers. Later, as the plants become established, frequent top-dressing with any of these materials will help to maintain moisture and supply natural plant food. Never apply artificial fertilisers in any form. These quickly react on the plants, which grow luxuriantly for a time, but ultimately turn brown and die.

An occasional dressing of mature wood ash, however, is beneficial, whilst an annual application of old soot will improve the size and colour of the fronds.

Planting and divisional propagation of hardy ferns is best carried out during the dormant period, normally between mid-October and March. Small specimens can be moved with care at other seasons, but never disturb any fern whilst the new fronds are unfurling, since the young stems are very brittle and easily damaged.

The following Hardy Ferns are particularly recommended:

ADIANTUM Maidenhair — *A. capellus-veneris*, Hardy Maidenhair; *A. pedatum*, North American Maidenhair; *A. venustum*, Hayward's Maidenhair.

ASPLENIUM Spleenwort — *A. adiantum nigrum*, Black Spleenwort; *A. fontanum*, Rock Spleenwort; *A. ruta-muraria*, Wall Rue; *A. trichomanes*, Maidenhair Spleenwort.

ATHYRIUM Lady Fern — *A. filix femina*.

BLECHNUM Hard Fern — *B. spicant*.

CETERACH Scale Fern — *C. officinarum*.

CRYPTOGRAMMA Parsley Fern — *C. crispa*.

CYSTOPTERIS Bladder Fern — *C. fragilis: C. montana*, Mountain Bladder Fern; *C. regia*, Alpine Bladder Fern.

DRYOPTERIS — *D. filix mas.*, Male Fern; *D. aemula*, Hay-scented Fern; *D. disjuncta*, Oak Fern; *D. hexagonophera*, Beech Fern; *D. thelypteris*, Marsh Buckler Fern.

MATTEUCCIA Ostrich Fern — *M. struthiopteris*.

ONOCLEA Sensitive Fern — *O. sensibilis*.

OSMUNDA Royal Fern; Flowering Fern — *O. regalis; O. cinnamomia*, Cinnamon Fern; *O. claytonia*, Clayton's Fern.

PHYLLITIS (SCOLOPENDRIUM) — *P. vulgare*, Hart's Tongue Fern.

T. H. Everett

Phyllitis vulgare crispum   J. E. Downward

POLYPODIUM Adder's Fern — *P. vulgare*.

POLYSTICHUM Shield Fern — *P. setigerum* (syn. *P. angulare*); *P. acrostichoides*, N. American Christmas Fern; *P. lonchites*, Holly Fern.

WOODSIA Mountain Fern — *W. alpina; W. ilvensis; W. obtusa*.

WOODWARDIA Chain Fern — *W. areolata*, Veined Chain Fern; *W. virginica*, Virginian Chain Fern.

SHADE LOVING PLANTS

Apart from ferns there is a wide range of bulbous and herbaceous plants which will grow in partially shaded positions. The majority of these either flower early in the year, before a dense canopy of leaves develops and shades the area, e.g. Bluebells and Anemones, or the plants make and store their food at this time so that the blooms are produced in summer or spring.

Shrubs for shady positions are more fully discussed on p. 286 but the following low growing evergreen and deciduous plants are ideal for bringing variety and colour to these sunless spots.

ACONITUM See p. 25.

ACTAEA Baneberry; Cohosh
Attractive spikes of small white flowers in spring and clusters of berries in autumn. *A. alba* is the White Baneberry of North America, with deeply cut leaves and fringed white flowers which give place in autumn to white berries. *A. rubra*, the American Red Baneberry, has white flowers and scarlet berries. 18 in. May—June.

ADENOPHORA See p. 25.

AJUGA See p. 26.

ANEMONE *nemorosa* See p. 89.

AQUILEGIA See p. 28.

ARISAEMA See p. 89.

ARISARUM.
A. proboscideum Mouse-tail Arum. A quaint ground-cover plant with glossy, heart-shaped leaves and olive-green and white flowers. These are inflated to a pouch and have a brown mouse-like tail. Ordinary woodland soil or a sand, loam and peat-moss compost. 3—5 in. May—June.

ARUM See p. 89.

ASARUM
Excellent ground cover plants which defeat all weeds. The flowers are very curious, dark mauve or purple, resin-scented, with three long tails and long-stalked, kidney-shaped leaves. Spreads quickly. *A. caudatum*, 9 in. July; *A. europaeum*, 6 in. June and *A. virginianum*, 6 in. May. *A. shuttleworthii*, red, and *A. s. album*, white, are the best forms.

BERGENIA See p. 29

BRUNNERA *macrophylla* See p. 29.

CAMPANULA *glomerata; lactiflora; latiloba; trachelium.* See p. 29.

CIMICIFUGA See p. 30.

CLAYTONIA Spring Beauty
Dwarf plants bearing loose heads of attractive rose-coloured flowers in spring. Grow well in moist shady pockets in the rock garden or peaty soil under tall trees. *C. caroliniana*, rose, 14 in. April; *C. virginica*, pink, 14 in. March.

Vinca minor H. Smith

CLINTONIA
Small growing members of the Lily family with broad shining leaves and scrambling underground runners; flowers borne in umbels on long shining stems. *C. andrewsiana* has clusters of deep rose, bell-shaped flowers in June, followed by blue berries in the autumn. 1½ ft. *C. uniflora*, the Californian Queencup, has Lily-of-the-Valley-like leaves and drooping white flowers, succeeded by blue berries. 6 in.

CONVALLARIA Lily-of-the-Valley
This universal favourite delights in any moist retentive soil which can readily be penetrated by its fibrous roots. *C. majalis* is the ordinary Lily-of-the-Valley, but more gardenworthy are the varieties 'major' or 'Fortin's Giant', both with larger flowers and longer stalks; *var. rosea* has pink flowers; *var. variegata* has the leaves striped with gold and *var. prolificans* double flowers April—May.

CYCLAMEN See p. 91.

DENTARIA Coral Root
D. bulbifera
Uncommon native plant with pale purple flowers like the Milkmaid (Cardamine). In summer small dark buds grow on the upper parts of the stems which, when ripe, fall off to produce new plants. *D. diphylla* is the Pepper Root with edible roots, strawberry-like leaves and white flowers which turn pink with age. 1—1½ ft. June.

Trillium grandiflorum   H. Smith

DICENTRA See p. 31.

DIGITALIS Foxglove

In addition to the ordinary woodland Foxglove *D. purpurea* there are a number of attractive species suitable for the shady border. All grow in ordinary garden soil provided it contains sufficient organic material to prevent drying out in summer. *D. grandiflora* has long, narrow stem-clasping leaves and large flowers, pale yellow blotched with brown. *D. lutea*, the Straw Foxglove, has densely-flowered racemes of small Primrose-yellow blooms, and *D. thapsi* red and mauve spotted flowers, with long, oval leaves, somewhat wavy at the edges.

DODECATHEON Shooting Star

A family of beautiful plants for cool, shady positions. They have reflexed petals (like the Cyclamen) in white, rose, red or purple, usually several in stalkless umbel. *D. media*, which grows about 18 in., is the best for English gardens; *var. album* is white, 16 in.; *var. violaceum*, violet, 18 in.; *var. grandiflorum*, rose with a white base, 18 in. April—May. Leaves are oblong and smooth.

EOMECON Dawn Poppy

E. chionanthum. Leaves heart-shaped, crinkled at the edges, pale grey-green on long stems from a creeping rootstock. Poppy-like flowers milk-white and about 1½ in. across 1—1½ ft. May—June.

EPIMEDIUM See p. 175.

ERYTHRONIUM See p. 91.

GAULTHERIA Wintergreen

G. procumbens is the most decorative member of a large family of dwarf evergreen shrubs. The small, white, bell-shaped flowers are produced in midsummer and are followed in autumn by bright red berries. The foliage assumes fine chocolate-brown autumnal tints. 6—8 in. July—Aug.

GENTIANA Gentian

G. asclepiadea Willow Gentian. This sturdy species has long arching stems of dark tubular flowers; *var. alba*, the White Milkweed Gentian, has white flowers. Both require a rich moist vegetable soil. 1½ ft.

HELLEBORUS See p. 34.

HEMEROCALLIS See p. 34.

HOSTA (Syn. Funkia) Plantain Lily

Grown chiefly for their foliage, these are shade-loving subjects. In a dappled light the leaves assume greater size and better colours, although more flowers are produced in a better light. All species and varieties effective when interplanted with tall growing ferns.

H. fortunei from Japan grows 18—24 in. with pale lilac flowers and bluish-green leaves; *var. albopicta*, yellowish leaves edged with green; *H. albomarginata*, white-margined leaves; *H. lancifolia*, narrow, lance-shaped foliage and pale lilac flowers. 2 ft. and *H. ventricosa var. marginata* green leaves splashed with white and dark lavender flowers. Aug.—Sept.

IRIS foetidissima See p. 280.

KIRENGESHOMA Yellow Wax Bells

K. palmata A beautiful perennial requiring the same soil and location as the Male Fern. It has palmately lobed leaves and many large, nodding, yellow, bell-shaped, waxen flowers on each slender stem. 3½ ft. Sept.

LAMIUM See p. 37.

LILIUM See p. 86.

Maianthemum bifolium and Hasta fortunei   Valerie Finnis

LYSIMACHIA See p. 39.

MAIANTHEMUM
M. bifolium. A little plant which soon forms a dense mat in a cool, shady, moist (but not wet) position. Flowers white and fragrant, not unlike Lily-of-the-Valley. The smooth, heart-shaped leaves come in pairs. 8 in. May.

MECONOPSIS
The three species here mentioned are well adapted to shady or woodland conditions. They like shelter from rough winds, which are apt to damage the flowers, and rich soil. Avoid stagnant water which rots the crowns.
M. betonicifolia (syn. *M. baileyi*) The Blue Poppy. One of our most beautiful hardy plants, growing 3 ft. or more in height with large, four-petalled, satiny-blue flowers. Best treated as a biennial and raised every year from fresh seed, which should be sown as soon as gathered. Pick out flower buds in first season to encourage good flower crowns for the second season. 4—5 ft. June.
M. integrifolia from Tibet has large yellow flowers on leafy stems. 2½—3 ft. July.
M. napaulensis (M. wallichii). This has stiff, upright, leafy stems and intense sky-blue flowers. There are also red, purple and white forms. 4—6 ft. July.

MERTENSIA
M. virginica (Syn. *Pulmonaria virginica*) Virginian Cowslip. The best of the family for woodland or shade planting. Drooping heads of blue, Forget-me-not-like flowers and soft, bluish-grey leaves. Foliage turns yellow early in the summer, so interplant with plants like *Polypodium vulgare* to avoid bare patches. 1½—2 ft. May.

OMPHALODES *cappadocica* See p. 177.

OROBUS See p. 40.

PACHYSANDRA
P. terminalis. An evergreen, semi-woody plant with diamond-shaped leaves and greenish-white flowers, tinged with purple. One of the few plants able to succeed in dry shade. 'Silver Edge' is a variegated form. 12 in. June.

PODOPHYLLUM See p. 42.

POLYGONATUM Solomon's Seal; David's Harp
Well known plant for naturalising in woodland or copse. *P. multiflorum* has solitary, nodding white flowers on leafy arching stems. There is a double form. *P. flore-pleno* and a variegated variety *striatum.* 1½—2 ft. June.

PRIMULA Primrose
P. vulgaris Common Primrose. A plant that should not be overlooked in any shady border planting. It is particularly beautiful when allowed to naturalise itself in congenial surroundings. The plant has given rise to many varieties, some of which have double flowers in a wide range of colours, including mauve and green.

PULMONARIA See p. 43.

RODGERSIA Bronze-leaf
Superb ornamental plants from the Orient, suitable for sunny moist borders or light shade. *R. aesculifolia* has glossy bronze, crinkled foliage, like a large Horse Chestnut, and spikes of fragrant pinky-white flowers. 3 ft. July. *R. pinnata.* Flowers borne in large, much branched panicles of a pleasing soft rosy-pink shade. 4 ft. July. *R. tabularis.* Leaves like round plates,

Arisarum vulgare

Lily of the Valley

on thick, bristly stems and handsome sprays of creamy-white flowers. 3 ft. July—Aug.

SCILLA (Bluebell) See p. 91.

THALICTRUM Meadow Rue
T. aquilegiifolium. Spreading heads of soft purple flowers and pinnately divided leaves; *var. album* has pure white flowers and 'Dwarf Purple', purple fluffy blooms. 2—3 ft.

TIARELLA See p. 46.

TOLMEIA See p. 46.

TRICYRTIS Toad Lily
Striking members of the Lily family which thrive in a light shaded position in a mixture of moist, peaty loam and leaf-mould. Must be protected with a covering of leaves during severe weather.
T. hirta. Leafy stems and dark green foliage, the open bell-shaped flowers being white in colour and freely spotted with purple. They appear in bunches, from the leaf axils. The form *variegata* has finely marked and striated foliage, and the earlier flowering variety *nigra* has darker flowers.
T. macropoda. Stems smooth and flushed with rosy-bronze; flowers large and erect, greenish-yellow, spotted with purple inside. 1½—2 ft.

TRILLIUM See p. 46.

Eomecon chionanthum, Dawn Poppy

UVULARIA North American Bell-Flower
U. grandiflora, Merry Bells. A graceful perennial related to Solomon's Seal, with dainty yellow flowers which droop gracefully from the tips of the slender stems. Succeeds between dwarf ferns or in a moist shady pocket in the rock garden. 6—18 in. May—June.

VINCA Periwinkle
All the hardy Periwinkles make excellent ground cover plants for banks and shady places under trees.
V. minor is the common Periwinkle of the English wayside and should only be planted where it cannot smother other plants. Many of its varieties, however, are more refined in their habits and make excellent companions for the taller growing subjects.
Var. alba and 'Mrs Botfield' varieties are the best white flowered forms; 'Bowles' Variety' has large, deep sky-blue flowers, whilst *atropurpurea* is deep purple. *Var. argenteo variegata* has silvery foliage. May—June.

VIOLA Violet
A few Viola species are useful for planting in shady places, especially:
V. cucullata. A charming, free flowering North American species with violet-coloured flowers and large heart-shaped leaves. 9. in. May—June.
V. labradorica, with attractive, dark purplish-green foliage and small lilac-blue flowers with short spurs. 4 in. June—July.
V. papilionacea, the Butterfly Violet, which has large white flowers with violet centres; var. *alba,* pure white, 6 in. June; *V. pedata,* Bird's Foot Violet, flowers about an inch wide, light violet with darker coloured veins. 4 in. May—June.

203

Carnations

Carnations and Pinks belong to the large family of Dianthus, some being alpines, others more suitable for the border. Sweet Williams are useful biennials belonging to this family, whilst Carnations give us some of our earliest cut flowers.

Three main groups are recognised in this country:

Perpetual Flowering

The Florist's Carnations, grown under glass, with stiff stems and compact variously coloured flowers.

Chabaud Carnations

Grown as annuals for summer bedding purposes, similar in appearance and habit to perpetuals, but less perfectly finished. They, too, come in a wide range of colours, and provide useful cut blooms.

Border Carnations

The oldest and only hardy group of Carnations, directly derived from the species *Dianthus caryophyllus*. The symmetrical blooms are with broad flat petals, sweetly scented and show a wide range of colours.

Mixed varieties are probably the most useful, but various sub-divisions are recognised by exhibitors.

1. *Selfs.* Flowers all of one colour. 'Bookham Grand', crimson, 'Consul' apricot; 'Edenside White', white; Greyling', grey; 'Mary Murray', yellow; 'Ripton Rose', pink, and 'Royal Mail', scarlet.

2. *White Ground Fancies.* White flowers, marked, striped and striated with contrasting colours. 'Bookham Lad', 'Kathleen Galbally', and 'Lucy Bertram'.

3. *Yellow Ground Fancies.* Very similar to 2., but the basic colour is pale yellow, apricot, buff or orange. 'Aurora', 'Bookham Fancy' and 'Catherine Glover'.

4. *Other Fancies.* Backgrounds other than white or yellow. 'Afton Water', pink and rose; 'Harmony', grey and cerise, and 'Sussex Fancy', pink and red.

5. *Cloves.* Characterised by their rich and fragrant aroma. Scent is the deciding factor in this division. 'Crimson Clove', 'Lavender Clove', 'Merlin Clove', 'Ripston Clove', and 'Ripston Pimpernel'.

6. *Picotees.* Very similar to 2 and 3 except that the colour contrast is confined to the petal margins. There should be no trace of colour elsewhere. 'Eva Humphries', 'Firefly' and 'Perfection'.

7. *Flakes and Bizarres.* Flakes have a pure white background, with a broad contrasting colour at the petal edge which runs down into the petal. Bizarres are similar except that two or more colours appear on the glistening white background. 'Harmony', 'Pink Bizarre' and 'Sussex Fancy'.

PINKS

Pinks are smaller than Carnations, with a neater, more tufted habit and shorter stems.

The most important are the Mrs Sinkins group, hardy, free flowering and very fragrant.

Laced Pinks have double white flowers, traced *all round* the petals with a broad band of contrasting

Perpetual flowering Carnations   H. Smith

shade. Bicolor Show Pinks are again white with a blotch of contrasting colour at the base of the petals.

Among the most popular varieties are:
'Dad's Favourite', white ground laced with pink; 'fimbriata', white, fringed petals, very fragrant; 'Inchmery', pale pink; 'Mrs Sinkins', the old-fashioned white; 'Paddington', pink, dark eye; 'Pink Mrs Sinkins', pink with dark eye; 'Sam Barlow', nearly black, and white; 'White Ladies', white.

Other groups raised include the Allwoodii, Allwood's Show Pink, Imperial Pinks, London Pinks and Allwood's Golden Hybrids. These have many varieties in a wide range of markings and patternings.

CULTIVATION

All the Dianthus family like open, well drained soil and appreciate lime. On very wet ground they should be planted on raised beds (3–4 in. above the surrounding level), so that roots are comparatively dry in winter.

Plant Border Carnations in spring or autumn; rooted layers are normally put in their flowering positions in late September and October, and plants from pots in April or May. The ground must be firm.

Allow 15–18 in. between plants and put them in with a trowel. Do not cover stems with soil, and stake the plants later. Water occasionally with dilute soot water and give a top dressing of bonemeal (2 oz. per sq.yd.) every two or three years.

The Allwoodii Pinks can be kept stocky and compact by pinching out the growing tips in autumn. Do this when the cutting or layer is established, leaving five or six pairs of leaves. Side shoots break out from these and make a bushier plant.

Growing in Pots

Perpetual Flowering Carnations need a light, airy greenhouse, not necessarily heated, although protection from frost induces a longer flowering season.

The young rooted layers (or plants) must be potted on gradually in different sized pots, commencing in autumn with a 3-in. moving this to a 6-in. or placing two plants in an 8-in. pot. Crock the containers and use John Innes No. 1 Potting Compost for the first potting and No. 2 for the second. Pot firmly, without disturbing the soil ball, and do not water for a day or so. Then, water as required and never let the soil dry out. Since growth is upright, the pots can be fairly close. Keep a watchful eye for Greenfly.

As the flower buds appear in May, artificial feeds may be given fortnightly, using a proprietary fertiliser or weak liquid manure. Disbud, if large flowers are required, to one flower per stem.

Keep Carnations on the dry side in winter, but do not let the soil become bone dry. When water is given, pour it into the side of the pot — and *not* all over the foliage.

Propagation

Carnations and Pinks can be propagated by seed, layers or cuttings.

Seed. Sow thinly in spring in garden pans or seed boxes of John Innes Seed Compost. Barely cover with soil, and keep under glass until germination. Bottom heat is unnecessary. Transplant early, 3 in. apart each way, in boxes. Grow on in pots, or leave in boxes and plant out in Autumn.

Layers. Taken July–August and rooted in very sandy

A colourful display of Carnations   J. E. Downward

soil. For details of method see p. 237.

Cuttings and Pipings. Cuttings are taken from young tips of adult plants in June or early July. The pieces should be about 3 in. long, cut off cleanly just below a joint, with two or three of the bottom pairs of leaves also removed. Insert in pots or frames of very sandy soil. Pure sand or vermiculite can also be used as rooting media, but if so employed cuttings must be potted up directly they root. Keep the frame or cloche fairly close until rooting takes place.

Pinks are usually reproduced from pipings, taken in June and July, obtained by gripping the top bunch of leaves on a non-flowering side shoot and giving it a pull. The piping comes out cleanly, and after the lowest pair of leaves has been removed should be inserted in sandy soil in a frame in a shady part of the garden. They root in about 6 weeks.

Although most Pinks root readily from cuttings or pipings, Carnations are not always so amenable, but rooted cuttings are nearly always successful.

Troubles

Common Greenfly, Earwigs, Thrips, Ants (which encourage Greenfly), Red Spider and Rust.

Vegetables

Manures and fertilisers are essential for the growth of good vegetables. Since nitrogen, phosphate and potash are removed from the soil in large quantities by vegetables, they must be replaced regularly to maintain soil fertility. Generally speaking, the soil will not become deficient in these if animal manures and compost are used in conjunction with the artificial fertilisers.

Because different types of vegetables have different food requirements, it is customary to group together those which need similar soil conditions. Thus, Potatoes respond well on freshly manured soil, but fresh animal manure would cause distorted and forked roots of Carrot, Parsnip and Beet. The legumes (Peas and Beans) do not need dressings of nitrogen, whilst brassicas require a high lime content.

For the vegetable plot to be maintained in a balanced state of fertility, no one group of plants should occupy the same piece of ground two years in succession. This means carrying out a system of crop rotation, which also ensures that a soil pest or disease peculiar to one crop is not allowed to increase uncontrollably.

The diagram opposite shows a suggested three-year rotation, the arrows indicating its direction. The Peas and Beans should be widely spaced rows to allow for the intercropping of the Onions, Leeks, etc.

During the growing season it is most important to hoe the ground between crops, not only to control weeds, but also to keep the surface soil open to allow the easy penetration of air and water.

In the cultivation notes it will be seen that some crops are raised in a heated greenhouse. In these cases it is essential that the plants be transferred to a cold frame about ten days before planting in the

Exhibition Longpod Broad Bean   H. Smith

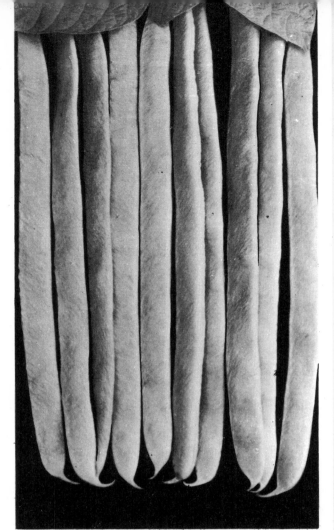

Runner Bean 'Prizewinner'   H. Smith

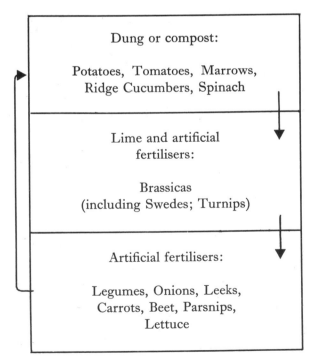

Dung or compost:

Potatoes, Tomatoes, Marrows, Ridge Cucumbers, Spinach

Lime and artificial fertilisers:

Brassicas
(including Swedes; Turnips)

Artificial fertilisers:

Legumes, Onions, Leeks, Carrots, Beet, Parsnips, Lettuce

open plot. This is the 'hardening off' period when the plants are subjected to a gradual lowering of temperatures prior to going in the open ground

THE COMMON VEGETABLES

FOR SOWING DATES AND VARIETIES SEE PAGE 217

Beans – Broad

Dig soil in autumn for spring sowings. Apply a general fertiliser and fork into top 6 in. of soil, breaking surface down to a good tilth. November sowings can be made on land cleared of Potatoes. Pinch out tops of plants when Black Aphis is seen (see p. 291). Make repeated pickings of the Beans while tender.

Beans – French or Dwarf

Because they are not hardy, do not sow French Beans outside before mid-May. Earlier crops may be had by sowing in a heated greenhouse in mid-April, hardening the plants off in a cold frame, and transplanting to the main plot in mid-May, but giving plants the protection of cloches. Alternatively, the plants can be grown on in pots in the greenhouse to obtain the earliest pickings. For this work choose an early forcing variety such as 'Lightning'.

Beans – Haricot (Wax Pod or Butter Beans)

These Beans grow well on ground which has been previously dug and opened up with liberal amounts of organic matter. A light soil suits them best, but they will grow successfully on heavy well-drained land. As pods turn brown, pull up the plants and hang in a dry, airy place. When dry remove seeds from pods and store in jars.

Beans – Runner

Best grown in double rows, allowing 8 ft. between each double row. The ground should be well supplied with organic matter to retain moisture. Bean poles, bamboo canes or strings may be arranged so that plants can climb and support themselves.

Alternatively, the Beans can be grown without stakes by pinching out the growing points and repeating as necessary. A new variety, 'Hammond's Dwarf Scarlet', is the first non-climbing Runner Bean and needs no supports. Spraying in the evening with plain water will encourage the setting of the pods.

Pick the Beans regularly before the seeds start swelling, and when plants reach tops of supports pinch out growing points.

Beet

A deeply cultivated light soil is best, but good roots may be obtained on other soils provided fresh animal manure is avoided within a few months of sowing the seed. Freshly manured ground will produce

207

forked and coarse roots. A general artificial fertiliser containing nitrogen, phosphate and potash may be applied and forked into surface of soil when breaking it down to a good tilth.

Apart from hoeing, the only other operation will be to thin the seedlings. Pull the early sowings as required. Lift roots for storage with a fork in October. Twist off tops and store in boxes of sand or peat in a frostproof place.

Broccoli

The heading types are really winter Cauliflowers. For methods of raising plants and soil treatment see under Cabbage. By careful selection of varieties they can be had through autumn, winter and spring. In very severe winters the heading types may suffer from frost damage and it is wise to have also some plants of the hardier Sprouting Broccoli.

Brussels Sprouts

This vegetable needs a long growing season and a soil of high fertility. The ground should have been well manured for a previous crop, but not recently dug. A dressing of a general fertiliser should be applied when the plants are growing freely on the main plot. Remove lower leaves as they turn yellow, and gather the Sprouts as they are ready, beginning from the bottom of the stem. (See under Cabbage for methods of raising brassicas from seed.)

Cabbage 'Copenhagen Market'   J. E. Downward

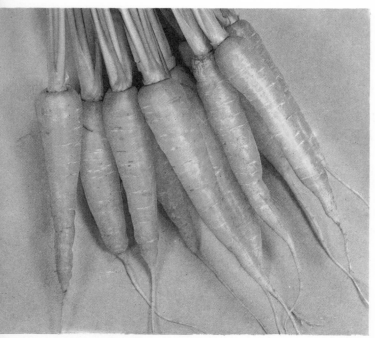

Carrot 'Early Horn'   J. E. Downward

Cabbage

All brassicas (Cabbage, Cauliflower, Kale, Brussels Sprouts, Broccoli) are sown in rows 9 in. apart on a seed bed and subsequently transplanted on to the main plot when plants are about 6 in. high. Thin sowing is essential to avoid drawn plants. A row of plants will take up at least ten times more space in the main plot than in the seed bed. Transplant with a dibber and make plants very firm in the ground. The land on which brassicas are to be grown should have an autumn application of hydrated lime at rate of 8 oz. per sq. yd. Before transplanting, prick into surface of soil sulphate of potash and superphosphate of lime (both kinds at rate of 2 oz. per sq. yd.). When plants are established and growing freely apply a further top dressing of sulphate of ammonia (1 oz. per yd. run).

Carrot

As for all root crops the soil for Carrots must not have been freshly manured. On shallow or stony soils it is best to grow only the stump-rooted varieties

Cauliflower   Fisons Horticulture

Celery

Celery responds well on ground which has been richly prepared. Dig a trench well in advance of planting time and work rotted manure or compost into the bottom. The trench should be 18 in. wide and the soil stacked each side. If the trench is taken out 12 in. deep, some of the soil can be returned after manuring to leave the final depth at 6 in.

After planting, water copiously during dry weather and apply liquid manure at the beginning and end of July. In August remove suckers, tie stems together just below the leaves and commence earthing up. A second and third earthing should take place at three-week intervals, never earthing up higher than the bases of the leaves. Black polythene sheeting can be used instead of earth.

Celery is lifted as required, but in severe winters will need protective material: e.g. bracken or straw. Self blanching varieties, e.g. 'Golden Self-Blanching', need no earthing up.

Cress

This is a popular salad crop that can be produced at any time of the year, but a warm greenhouse is needed during winter. Cress can be sown outside every few days in spring and summer, in good soil with a fine tilth. In the greenhouse, sow thickly in boxes of fine compost. Sow three days before the Mustard with which it is usually associated. The seed need not be covered — merely pressed into the soil.

such as 'Tip Top'. During the growing season apply a general fertiliser along the rows in showery weather.

Pull the early sowings as required when large enough for eating. Lift the maincrop in October with a fork, twist off the tops and store in boxes of peat or sand in a frostproof building.

Cauliflowers

The Cauliflower is less hardy than Broccoli and fills the gap between late spring and autumn crops of the latter. Cauliflowers need very fertile soil, and must never receive a check to growth. The ground should therefore have been deeply dug and well manured. During the growing season dress with 1 oz. nitrate of soda per yd. run at three-week intervals. When curds have formed and are not immediately required their colour and texture are preserved by breaking a leaf or two over them. See under Cabbage for method of raising plants. If raised in the greenhouse Cauliflowers should be pricked out into 3-in. pots to avoid a check at transplanting time.

Brussels Sprouts 'Irish Elegance'   J. E. Downward

Cucumber

All members of the Cucumber family (Gherkins, Melons, Marrows and Pumpkins) have three major common requirements — warmth, moisture and a soil rich in organic matter. In greenhouses and cold frames special beds of compost are made up, 9 in. deep and comprising 2 parts fibrous loam and 1 part rotted manure. Under the bed good drainage is essential.

Shade the greenhouse or frame in sunny weather, and syringe daily to maintain a high humidity. Stretch training wires from end to end of the greenhouse or growing area, 12 in. apart and 12 in. from the glass; then tie strings every 2 ft. at right-angles to wires, to train the leader growths towards the ridge of the house. Tie side shoots to wires and stop at second leaf; stop sub-laterals at first leaf.

Male and female flowers are produced, but males are picked off as they appear, as pollinated females produce bitter Cucumbers with large seeds.

A cold frame 4 ft. by 4 ft. can accommodate one plant which is stopped a week after planting. Four side shoots are retained and one is trained to each corner of the frame, when they too are stopped. Sub-laterals will bear fruits, and these are pinched at one leaf beyond a fruit.

Ridge Cucumbers may be grown outside without protection. They are grown on 9-inch-high ridges of rich, fibrous soil. Stopping is carried out as for frame Cucumbers.

Endive

Endive will grow in most gardens but a fibrous soil which retains moisture ensures quick and steady growth. The leaves are blanched when quite dry by covering with a flower pot, or by gathering together and tying with raffia. Plants for winter supplies should be lifted in the autumn and planted closely together in a cold frame.

Kale

Cultivation and raising is exactly the same as for Cabbage.

Leek

The Leek is a hardy crop that can be taken straight from the garden any time during the winter. The soil should be deeply dug and well manured and a general fertiliser pricked into the soil first before transplanting. During the growing season give a dressing of nitrate of soda at 1 oz. per yd. run.

Planting is done by making a 6-inch-deep hole with the dibber and dropping the plant into it. As the

Lettuce 'Sutton's Improved Unrivalled'

Leek 'Sutton's Improved Musselburgh'   Sutton & Sons

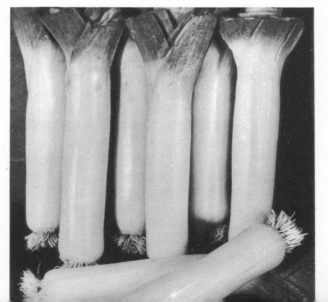

Sutton & Sons

stems broaden they expand and fill the hole. If the weather is dry, water each plant.

Lettuce

Lettuces can be had all the year round with the use of a greenhouse and cold frame. They may be grown in 6-inch-deep boxes of John Innes Potting Compost in the greenhouse, or in the greenhouse border. For outside Lettuces the soil should be well cultivated, fibrous and yet moisture-retentive.

Lettuces transplant well at all seasons except the middle of summer when they tend to bolt, and then it is best merely to thin out the seedlings. Sow little and often is the rule for continuous supplies.

Cabbage Lettuce forms a flat rosette of leaves whilst Cos Lettuces have elongated foliage and often have to be tied with raffia to keep a good shape.

Marrow

The soil where Vegetable Marrows are grown must be well enriched with decaying organic matter. They need good drainage but must never lack water, for which reason they are often grown on low heaps of compost. Bush types are best where space is limited, but with trailing kinds pinch out the growing point at the seventh leaf, and then pinch out the growing points on all side shoots at one leaf beyond a fruit.

For summer use cut Marrows young, and about 9 in. long. The later ones can be allowed to grow to their full size and ripened for storage in a dry, well ventilated but frostproof position.

Mushroom

Mushrooms can be grown outside during the summer months, but for the rest of the year it is necessary to use cellars, sheds, garages or greenhouses. Under cover it is more convenient to place the compost in 6-inch-deep boxes. A ready-for-use compost can be purchased, but if fresh stable manure is used the heap must be turned at least three times until it becomes dark in colour and has lost all smell of ammonia. The compost, when placed in the boxes, should be just moist and not sodden. It will be warm because of fermentation, and when the temperature drops to 75°F. pieces of Mushroom spawn, the size of a Walnut, are inserted at 9-in. intervals and 1 in. deep.

After about a week cover the surface of the compost with a 2-in. layer of moist, fine sandy loam. Apply water through a fine rose, and then only sufficient to keep the casing soil moist, i.e. water must not reach the compost below.

Mushrooms will appear in 6–8 weeks and should be gathered by giving them a twist and a pull.

211

Radish 'French Breakfast'   J. E. Downward

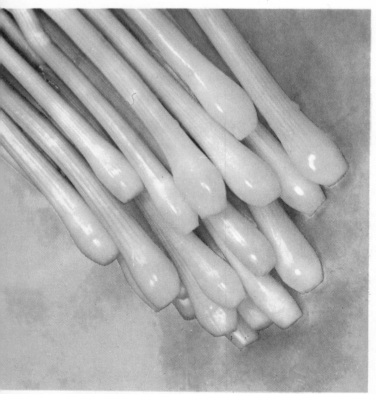

Spring Onion   J. E. Downward

Outdoor beds can be made up early in June. They are usually ridge-shaped, 2 ft. 6 in. wide at the base and 24 in. high. These too must have a 2-in. soil casing, and over all a 6-in. layer of straw to conserve heat and moisture.

Mustard

Grown in exactly the same way as Cress. See p. 209.

Onion

Dig ground deeply in autumn, incorporating liberal amounts of compost. In February give a dressing of 1 oz. of sulphate of potash and 2 oz. of superphosphate per sp. yd., forking into surface soil and creating a good tilth.

Onions may be grown from seed or from sets (small bulbs), the later method giving very good results with far less trouble.

Before sowing in the open or transplanting make sure the soil is firm. Transplant with a trowel, keeping the base of the plant $\frac{1}{2}$ in. below ground, and allowing the roots their full depth.

In August the tops are bent over to hasten the ripening of the bulbs. At the end of the month lift bulbs, and when dry and clean make up into ropes to hang in a dry airy place.

Parsnip

A deep, well worked soil is needed to obtain long roots. If, however, the soil is shallow or stony, holes 2 ft. deep can be made with a crowbar and filled with good, sifted soil. Sow two or three seeds at each station and thin seedlings later, leaving the strongest.

No fresh manure must be used in preparing the soil, but a dressing of a general fertiliser may be applied during the growing season.

Parsnips should be left in the ground in winter and lifted as required. Their flavour improves after frost.

Peas

Like all legumes the Pea thrives best in a deep soil containing plenty of organic matter. No nitrogen manuring is needed, but 2 oz. superphosphate and 1 oz. of sulphate of potash should be applied before sowing. Flat drills 8 in. wide are taken out with a spade or draw hoe so that two or three rows of seeds may be sown to each drill.

Tall varieties need staking, and where space is limited it is better to make repeated sowings of dwarf varieties, when the rows can be closer and support is not needed. From May onwards a mulch of compost will help to preserve moisture. Pick the pods as

Vegetable Marrow 'Long Green Bush'   J. E. Downward

soon as they are ready. During drought it may be necessary to water the ground thoroughly if the pods are not swelling.

Potato

This plant, with 3,000 years of history behind it, is today the most important single vegetable.

Dig the ground and incorporate animal manure or compost in the autumn. Place the tubers in trays to sprout February — March in a light, frostproof position. Reduce number of sprouts to three before planting.

Protect the young growths of early varieties from late frosts by covering them with soil, straw, bracken, etc.

Apply a general fertiliser and hoe between the rows prior to the first earthing up in mid-May. Give a second earthing in early June. Lift tubers of early varieties for immediate use in July, and those of maincrop varieties in September for storing in a dark frostproof place.

Radish

Radishes need to be grown quickly if they are not to taste hot and dry. They therefore lend themselves to catch-cropping between main rows of vegetables. Avoid sowing in summer as plants usually bolt to seed. Thin sowing is the rule.

Rhubarb

Rhubarb needs deeply dug, well manured ground, as the plants remain in position for several years. After planting do not pull any sticks the first year, and only sparingly in the second season. Established Rhubarb can be pulled until July. Flowering shoots must be removed.

To force Rhubarb select a few strong roots from December to February and place them in boxes of moist soil in the dark: e.g. under the greenhouse bench. Hessian or black polythene can be hung downwards from the edge of the bench to exclude light. A temperature of 55°F. is sufficient.

Outside, the Rhubarb may be covered with barrels surrounded by strawy manure. This will give stems for pulling later than the greenhouse crop but before the unprotected plants outside.

Each winter the outdoor plants should receive a top dressing of rotted manure.

Savoy

These are very hardy Cabbages with crinkled leaves. For details of raising plants and cultivation see under Cabbage p. 208.

Cucumber 'Telegraph'   J. E. Downward

Seakale

This plant is native to the western and southern coasts of Britain and grown solely for the blanched stems. To obtain strong roots for forcing the soil should be deeply dug and have liberal quantities of farmyard manure incorporated.

In autumn plants are lifted and roots treated in exactly the same way as greenhouse-forced Rhubarb. The blanched heads are cut when about 6 in. long.

Forcing may also be done in the open by putting boxes or tubs over the plants in succession to obtain a supply of blanched shoots through winter and early spring. Tubs should be surrounded by fresh farmyard manure and leaves to keep up the necessary temperature.

When plants are lifted for forcing make root cuttings (4—6 in. long) from straight side roots. These cuttings are stored in damp sand until spring, when all buds except the two strongest should be removed on each cutting. These cuttings are planted outside in March with their tops covered by 1 in. of soil and spaced 18 in. apart each way.

Shallot

Being another member of the Onion family, the Shallot may be grown on the same piece of ground that has been prepared for Onions. Plant the bulbs by pushing them into the soil to about half their depth.

The clusters of new bulbs are lifted at the end of July and left to dry for a few days. They can then be split into separate bulbs, cleaned and stored in a dry, frostproof but airy place. The smaller bulbs can be saved for planting the following year.

Spinach

The round seeded form is not hardy and is for summer use only (Summer Spinach). Prickly seeded or Winter Spinach is for winter use but may need cloche protection in severe weather. Both kinds need a soil rich in organic matter, especially the Summer Spinach which must never be short of water. During the growing season a top dressing of sulphate of ammonia at 1 oz. per yd. run will encourage quick growth.

Pick leaves regularly during the summer, and in winter pick *largest leaves only* as required.

A third type known as Spinach Beet or Perpetual Spinach is grown in the same way as the other two, and is particularly useful as it will provide leaves from midsummer until the following spring from successional sowings.

Swede

More nutritious than the Turnip, of which it is a close relative, the Swede requires a longer growing season. Roots can be used in August, pulled as required, or stored for winter like Potatoes. Alternatively the crop can be left in the ground, as some people prefer them when they have been subjected to frost.

Potato 'Duke of York'

H. Smith

Tomato

Although Tomatoes are usually grown in greenhouses they may be cultivated in frames, under cloches and on the open plot, always remembering the plants need a growing temperature of 60°F.

In the greenhouse the plants may be grown in the border soil, in pots of good compost, or by the popular ring culture method. In this system the plants are put in large bottomless pots containing John

Turnips 'Golden Nugget'   Copyright Ryder & Sons

Innes No. 3 Potting Compost, placed on a 6-in.-deep bed of ashes or coarse sand and shingle. As the ashes will hold a large quantity of water the plants do not suffer from drying out as they do when in ordinary pots. Liquid feeding is applied to the compost in the pots at ten-day intervals from the time the first truss has set. Plain water is applied *only* to the ash or shingle base.

The plants must be trained on canes, wires or strings and side shoots regularly removed.

For outdoor work the soil must be well drained and contain plenty of organic matter.

Before planting apply 2 oz. sulphate of potash and 4 oz. of bone flour per sq. yd. Liquid feeding may be carried out as for greenhouse plants, if growth is not satisfactory. Outdoor plants should have the growing point removed when four trusses have set, as the weather is unlikely to allow a greater number of fruits to be ripened.

Turnip

The Turnip is a member of the Cabbage family, and in the rotation scheme should be linked with the brassica section.

The earliest crops may be produced in cold frames, and if a hot-bed or soil warming equipment is available, sowings may be made in January and February.

Before sowing in the open garden apply a general fertiliser and prick lightly into the soil, at the same time breaking surface down to a good tilth.

Pull early varieties as required and in autumn lift carefully those required for storage. Twist off tops and store in boxes of sand or soil in a dry frostproof position.

Savoy Cabbage 'Late Ormskirk'   H. Smith

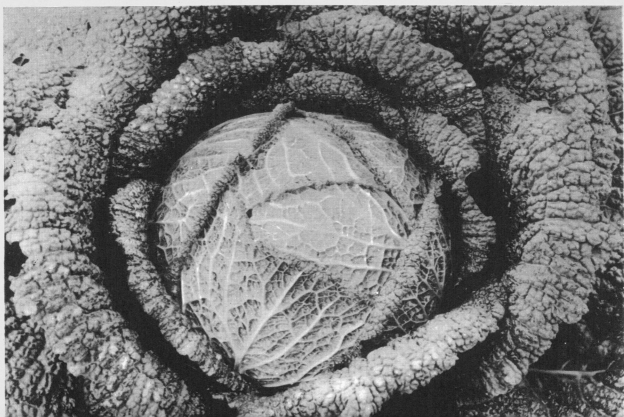

Tomatoes

Fisons Horticulture

The following are recommended varieties and sowing times (all in open, except where marked*)

Beans, Broad. Seville Longpod (Nov.), Green Windsor (Feb.) Broad Windsor (March).

Beans, French. Masterpiece, Canadian Wonder (mid-May, *mid-April 55°F.); Lightning or Early Giant (*early April).

Beans, Haricot. Brown Dutch, Comtesse de Chambord (mid-May).

Beans, Runner. Prizewinner, As Long as Your Arm, Scarlet Emperor (end May, *early May 55°F.).

Beet. Globe: Crimson Globe (April); Long: Perfection, Housewives' Choice (May).

Broccoli. Early: Veitch's Self Protecting; Mid: Winter White; Late: St George (April—May, according to variety, *Feb. 50°F.).

Brussels Sprout. Early: Cambridge No. 1; Late: Cambridge No. 5 (March—April).

Cabbage. Flower of Spring (Aug.), Greyhound (April, *Feb. 50°F.), January King (May).

Carrot. Early: Early Market (April); Maincrop: James' Intermediate (July).

Cauliflower. Early: Snowball (*Feb. 50°F.); Maincrop: All the Year Round (April).

Celery. Early: White Gem; Maincrop: Giant White (*Feb.—March 55°F.).

Cucumber. Greenhouse: Telegraph (*Feb.—March 65°F.); Frame: Conqueror (*April); Ridge: Long Green (*April).

Endive. Green Curled (May—June), Round Leaved Batavian (July—Aug.).

Kale. Hungry Gap (May—June).

Leek. Musselbrugh (April, *Feb. 50°F.).

Lettuce. All the Year Round (March—July), Arctic King (Aug.), Early French Frame (*Oct. 50°F.).

Marrow. Trailing: Long Green; Bush: White Bush (end May, *mid-April).

Onion. Giant Zittau (Aug.), Ailsa Craig (*Feb. 50°F.), Bedfordshire Champion (April); *Spring Onion:* White Lisbon (April).

Parsnip. The Student (March).

Pea. Early: Little Marvel; Maincrop: Gradus (March—May, according to variety); Late: Onward (Nov. under cloches).

Potato. Early: Arran Pilot (plant March); Maincrop: Majestic (plant April).

Radish. French Breakfast (*Dec.—Feb. 50°F.), Scarlet Globe (March—May), Round Black Spanish (Sept.).

Rhubarb. Champagne (plant March), Glaskin's Perpetual (April).

Savoy. Early Drumhead (April), Omega (May).

Sea Kale. Snow White (April).

Shallot. Large Yellow (plant Feb.—March).

Spinach. Summer: Long Standing (March—June, successional sowings); Winter: Prickly (Aug.).

Spinach Beet. Perpetual (April and Aug.).

Swede. Purple Top (early May).

Tomato. Moneymaker — under glass (*Feb.—March 60°F.), Harbinger — outside (*April 60°F.).

Turnip. Early Snowball (*hot bed in frames), Golden Sunrise (April—June), Orange Jelly — for winter storage (mid-July), Green Top White — for Turnip tops (early Sept.).

Purple sprouting Broccoli J. E. Downward

Kale, dwarf curled H. Smith

Kohl-rabi

H. Smith

THE MORE UNCOMMON VEGETABLES

Artichoke

Chinese Artichoke

Plant tubers 4 in. deep in April in a sunny position on well drained friable soil. Allow 9 in. between tubers and 18 in. between rows. When foliage dies down in October tubers are ready for use, but only lift as required and do not expose to light for long periods before using as they soon become discoloured.

Globe Artichoke

This is a herbaceous perennial and plants should be grown 3 ft. apart each way. Plant in April on well manured ground. Propagation is carried out each year to provide one-third of the total number of plants required, so that eventually the three-year-old plants are destroyed at the end of each season. Propagate

by removing rooted suckers in October. Pot up in 6-in. pots and winter in a cold frame, finally planting out in April.

Remove dead and yellowing foliage in autumn and protect plants from winter frosts by covering with straw. The edible portions are the immature flower buds.

Jerusalem Artichoke

Plant tubers Jan. — March 6 in. deep and 2 ft. apart, with 3 ft. between rows. The soil should be well cultivated and manured and not deficient in lime. Earth up plants like Potatoes when 12 in. high and provide stakes, as high winds easily break the tall stems.

Stems can be cut down to 6 in. when leaves are withered, and as plants are hardy they can be left in the ground and tubers lifted as required.

Asparagus

This is a herbaceous perennial, and as the plants

Asparagus Pea　　　　　　　　　　　　　H. Smith

will be in position for many years it is essential to incorporate liberal amounts of well rotted farmyard manure in the soil. Good drainage is important and the beds are often raised about 9 in. above the general level. A bed 3 ft. wide will take two rows of plants 18 in. apart each way.

One-, two- or three-year-old plants may be purchased for planting in April. The one-year-old plants transplant better, but no crop must be cut from them until the third year after planting.

The crowns are planted with 4 in. of soil covering them. Stakes at the ends of the rows with string running between them will prevent the tall foliage being blown about. Keep the bed clear of weeds and cut down and burn foliage when it turns colour, then dress the bed with well rotted animal manure.

Do not cut Asparagus *after mid-June*, so that foliage develops and builds up crowns for the following year.

It is worth while selecting male plants (which have no berries) and destroying the females. The females not only litter the bed with unwanted seedlings but are not as productive or as early yielding as males.

Asparagus Pea

This plant produces winged, rectangular pods which are eaten whole when about 1½ in. long. It is very prolific and attractive with its dark red flowers. Seeds may be sown in drills 2 in. deep in April, the plants being thinned later to 18 in. apart. Allow 3 ft. between rows. Stakes with twine stretched between them on each side of the row will prevent plants sprawling.

Aubergine

Often called the Egg Plant, the Aubergine is, like its relative the Tomato, a tender plant and must be grown in greenhouses, cold frames or under large barn cloches.

Seed is sown February—March for growing on in pots in the greenhouse, but if plants are to go under cloches or in frames, delay sowing until mid-April. Sow thinly in seed pans of John Innes Seed Compost and germinate at 60°F. Prick off seedlings into 3-in. pots and three weeks later pot on into 6-in. pots of John Innes No. 1 Potting Compost. If plants are to be fruited in pots transfer them to 8-in. size in May, using John Innes No. 2 Potting Compost. A week later pinch out growing point to induce bushy habit and insert a bamboo cane to provide support by regular tying. Planting under cloches may be done in early June, allowing 2 ft. between plants. To obtain reasonably sized fruits do not allow more than five to mature on each plant.

Capsicums (Peppers)

The fruit of Sweet Peppers can be picked and eaten whilst still green or may be left to ripen before use. The small hot Peppers or Chillies, used for making Cayenne Pepper, must always be allowed to ripen before picking, and are best grown in a heated greenhouse.

The Sweet Peppers are sown and raised in the greenhouse in exactly the same way as Aubergines and can either be grown on in 7-in. pots in the greenhouse or planted out under large barn cloches or deep frames about mid-May. Allow 18 in. between plants, keep well watered, and syringe twice a day to prevent attacks by red spider. It will be necessary to raise the cloches on elevators as the plants eventually grow to more than 2 ft. As fruits begin to swell, feed plants once a week with a general liquid fertiliser.

Cardoon

The Cardoon is grown for its blanched stems like Celery, and also needs a rich soil and plenty of moisture. Sow seed in March in a heated greenhouse (50°F.) 3 seeds to a 3-in. pot, and thin out seedlings later to one per pot. If no greenhouse is available, outdoor sowings may be made about mid-May when 3 seeds are sown at stations 18 in. apart, each group being thinned later to leave the strongest plant. Plants raised under glass must be hardened off in a cold frame at the end of April.

Like Celery, Cardoons are best planted in trenches 12 in. deep, the bottom spit enriched with well rotted animal manure. Blanching starts in October when the leaves are tied loosely together, wrapped in brown paper or polythene, then earthed up until only the leafy tops are exposed. Blanching takes 6—8 weeks and the Cardoons can be stored, if lifted before frosts, with a good ball of soil round the roots. Keep moist and leave wrappings round stems unless the storage place is completely dark.

Celeriac

This is merely a variety of Celery with a swollen stem base. The plants are raised in the same way as Celery, hardened off and planted out in May 12 in. apart in rows 2 ft. apart. Trenches are unnecessary. Lateral growths are removed, and frequent applications of liquid manure given. The crop is lifted in October, leaves removed and bulbous stems stored in sand or soil in a cool, dry place.

Chicory

The blanched heads of Chicory provide valuable winter salads, whilst the roots may be cooked and eaten like Parsnips.

Seed is sown outside in early June, ½ in. deep in drills 12 in. apart, and the seedlings later thinned to 9 in. in the rows. Remove flower heads.

In November lift as many roots as will fill a 9-in. pot. Cut off tops and pack roots into the pot, surrounded with moist peat. Treat further roots similarly in succession as required through winter. Keep the pots in the dark, at a temperature of 50°F. Blanched leaves which appear in two to three weeks' time are broken off and a second, smaller crop will be produced. After the second cutting the roots are thrown away.

Chinese Cabbage

This is a true brassica but looks rather like a Cos Lettuce. The tender heart can be used raw in salads and the mid-ribs of the leaves treated as Asparagus It is also often used as a cooked vegetable.

The Chinese Cabbage soon bolts in dry weather and sowing is usually delayed until mid-July between other crops which will offer slight shade. It is best to sow two or three seeds every 15 in. or so in a ¾-in. deep drill, eventually thinning seedlings to one at each station. Keep plants moist and use heads as soon as cut.

Corn Salad or Lamb's Lettuce

Successional sowings of this salading may be made from March until August, the last providing crops in early spring. Sow the seed ½ in. deep in drills 6 in. apart and thin seedlings to 6 in. in the rows.

Pick leaves from several plants when harvesting. If selected plants are cut over each time, the older ones soon become coarse and tough.

Couve Tronchuda (Portugal Cabbage)

This plant is also called the Braganza Cabbage and Seakale Cabbage. It is raised and transplanted in the same way as ordinary Cabbages by sowing on a seed bed in April. Extra large plants may be obtained by sowing in heat in February, and, after hardening off, planting out in April, spacing the plants 3 ft. apart each way.

Celery, Giant Red J. E. Downward

Capsicum, Bull Nosed Red   J. E. Downward   Turnip 'Golden Ball'   J. E. Downward

The mid-ribs of the large outer leaves may be cooked like Seakale, whilst in autumn a loose-hearted Cabbage is left at the top of the plant. It is one of the few brassicas resistant to Club Root disease.

Cress (American)

This plant is as much a native of Europe as it is of parts of North America. It looks and tastes like Watercress and needs almost as much water.

The soil must have plenty of organic matter to hold the moisture, but must not be badly drained.

For a summer salading seeds may be sown in April, but as the plants are difficult to establish in a hot summer it is better to sow at end of August and use for winter salads. Sow in very shallow drills ($\frac{1}{4}$ in. deep), 9 in. apart, and later thin the plants to 4 in.

Kohl Rabi

This is another member of the brassicas, but the edible portion is a round swollen stem.

Quick growth is essential for tender stems, so that a very fertile, moisture-retentive soil is necessary. Seed is sown between March and July in drills $\frac{3}{4}$ in. deep and 18 in. apart. The plants are thinned to 6 in. and finally to 12 in. in rows.

Kohl Rabi is perfectly hardy and late sowings can be left outside to be pulled as required during winter.

New Zealand Spinach

This plant is not related to the true Spinach but has a similar flavour and will succeed in hot dry summers which cause ordinary Spinach to bolt.

New Zealand Spinach is not perfectly hardy and seed is sown in March in the greenhouse at a temperature of 50°F. Seedlings are pricked out into 3-in. pots of John Innes No. 1 Potting Compost. In May plants are hardened off in the cold frame and planted out in early June 3 ft. apart each way. Although very resistant to drought a better and more tender crop is obtained by watering thoroughly in dry weather.

221

Sweet Corn 'John Innes'　　　H. Smith

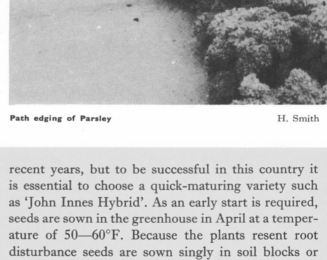

Path edging of Parsley　　　H. Smith

Salsify

Often called the Vegetable Oyster because of the delicate flavour of the roots, Salsify is sown in April in drills 12 in. apart and plants later thinned to 9 in. apart in rows. To obtain good straight roots that are easy to prepare for cooking, make holes 12 in. deep and fill with compost. Sow three seeds at each station (9 in. apart) eventually reducing seedlings to one per station. On light dry soils roots may be lifted as required from October onwards, but it is usually necessary to lift and store in damp sand.

Scorzonera

Scorzonera has a black-skinned root and is grown in exactly the same way as Salsify. Being a perfectly hardy perennial the roots may be left in the ground and lifted as required during autumn and winter.

Sweet Corn

Corn on the Cob has become very popular in recent years, but to be successful in this country it is essential to choose a quick-maturing variety such as 'John Innes Hybrid'. As an early start is required, seeds are sown in the greenhouse in April at a temperature of 50—60°F. Because the plants resent root disturbance seeds are sown singly in soil blocks or paper or peat pots. Plants are hardened off in cold frames during May and are ready for planting out the first week in June.

As male and female flowers are produced and pollination depends on the wind, Sweet Corn should not be planted in rows but in rectangular blocks, spacing plants 18 in. apart each way.

Earth up about 9 in. of the stem when the plants are 3 ft. high to give support against strong winds. Female flowers appear about the end of June and three weeks later the first cobs are ready for harvesting. To decide when to cut a cob, press the thumbnail into one of the grains, when the contents should appear like clotted cream. If watery it is not ready, if firm and solid it is over-ripe.

New Zealand Spinach   Vilmorin-Andrieux

Swiss Chard (Silver Beet or Seakale Beet)

This is a very profitable and useful vegetable since the leaf blades can be cooked as Spinach, the fleshy stems may be used as a substitute for Seakale or Asparagus, and the smallest tender leaves are excellent in salads. If the plant is left in the ground to produce flower stems in the second year, these may be picked when young and used in the same way as the shoots of Sprouting Broccoli.

The ground should be well manured, and seeds are sown in April and again in August to provide pickings from autumn until the following June. Sow 1½ in. deep in drills 18 in. apart, later thinning to 12 in. apart. The thinnings may be used in salads.

Water thoroughly in dry weather and feed with liquid manure. Harvest by breaking stems at bases, but do not completely strip any one plant.

Squashes, Pumpkins and Gourds

These are all closely related to our Vegetable Marrow and are raised and grown in exactly the same way (see p. 211). They are often grown for their decorative as well as edible value because of the great variety of size, shape and colour. There are both summer and winter Squashes; the latter, as well as the Pumpkins, must be allowed to ripen on the plants. Harvest in October and use as needed from a dry, frostproof store. Summer Squashes are eaten when young and tender, like Vegetable Marrow.

Seeds should be sown individually in 3-in. pots in the greenhouse (temperature 60°F.) during April, hardening off plants in a frame in May. Plant out in early June 3 ft. apart each way.

CULINARY HERBS

Generally speaking, the site for a herb garden should be a warm, sheltered border receiving plenty of sunshine. The soil needs to be light and well drained. Heavy manuring is not usually necessary, but those herbs needing a richer soil are noted in the list at the end of the chapter.

Where the chart stipulates propagation by seed it is important to cultivate the soil to a fine tilth before sowing. Division of plants may be carried out in spring or autumn. Where cuttings are mentioned for propagation these will be young shoots, and some form of propagating frame will be needed. For details of taking soft cuttings see p. 238.

Freshly gathered herbs have a finer flavour than when dried, but drying ensures supplies when green leaves are no longer produced outside. The aromatic flavours of herbs are at their best in well developed leaves just before flowering commences. Leaves for drying should therefore be cut at this period, on a fine day and preferably in the morning.

Quick drying preserves aroma and colour. A temperature of 70°F. and good ventilation is ideal. Oven drying is not a good method as the temperature is likely to be too high and to cause evaporation of the essential oils. The herbs may be tied in bunches and hung outside on a sunny day, or in a warm well ventilated kitchen. Alternatively they may be placed on wire-mesh trays so that air circulates below as well as above them. It is important to prevent the drying herbs re-absorbing moisture, as in a steamy kitchen, or outside at night when there are heavy dews.

When dry, the leaves may be stripped from the stems, rubbed through a fine sieve and stored in well stoppered glass bottles. Any trace of moisture will lead to the development of moulds.

223

Easily grown Culinary Herbs and methods of propagating them are as follows:

Angelica. Seed (July). Moist loam. Shady site.

Balm. Division, seed (May). Rich, moist soil.

Basil (Sweet and Bush). Seed (May). Sunny, well drained soil.

Bay. Cuttings (Aug. in frame), layering (Sept.). Sunny, well drained soil.

Borage. Seed (April). Sunny, well drained soil.

Caraway, Seed (Aug.). Light soil.

Chervil. Seed (July). Light soil.

Chives. Seed (April), division. Light but rich soil.

Fennel. Seed (April). Sunny position, light soil.

Garlic. Plant bulbils (cloves) in March. Sunny position, rich, light soil.

Marjoram (Pot). Division, seed (April). *Marjoram (Sweet).* Seed (May). Both sunny, well drained, rich soil.

Mint. Division. Moist rich soil. *Bowle's* var, or Round-leaved Mint less subject to rust.

Parsley. Seed (April and Aug.). Semi-shade. Rich, moist soil.

Sage. Cuttings, division, seed (May). Sunny position, light, well drained soil.

Savory (Summer). Seed (April). *Savory (Winter).* Cuttings, seed (April). Sunny site, light, well drained soil.

Sorrel. Seed (April), division. Damp situation.

Tarragon. Division, cuttings. Light, well drained soil. Sheltered sunny position.

Thyme. Division, cuttings, seed (April). Light, rich soil. Sunny position.

Harvest from the well-stocked garden

Flower Arrangement

The art of arranging flowers for decorative purposes dates back many centuries.

The earliest known use of blossoms dates from 2500 B.C. when flowers were used in Egypt for religious festivals and on the banqueting table. Among the plants known at this period were the Poppy, Anemone, Lupin, Jasmine, Polyanthus, Narcissus, *Iris sibirica*, Delphinium, and Scillas.

In ancient Greece flowers were made into wreaths and garlands, especially to decorate men of distinction. Blossoms and rose petals were also much used during the heyday of the Roman Empire for indoor decoration, and flowers were forced out of season by growing them round the hot-water pipes which supplied the Roman Baths — a forerunner of the modern hothouse.

During the Middle Ages many herbs and flowers were grown by monks and in manor gardens for medicinal and culinary purposes. Petals of sweet-smelling flowers were also strewn among the rushes on the floors of the houses to sweeten the atmosphere, and were often made into posies for guests.

At the beginning of the 15th century flowers appeared in paintings by Italian and Dutch masters, arranged in vases and urns, and their lavish use for decoration in this way soon spread all over Europe. As time passed arrangers paid more attention to the style, texture and colour of their compositions, so that this became known as the 'Bouquet Style.' This type of arrangement continued until the early part of the present century.

In the Orient, however, flower arrangement was

Upright arrangement on plate by Julia Clements

Farmer & Stockbreeder

Face Front Triangular arrangement in urn

well developed in China and Japan by the 6th century. It was used mainly for decoration in Buddhist temples and, in contrast to the Western style, very few flowers were used. Instead, the arrangements were designed with seven lines or branches.

This continued until 1926 when Sofu Teshigahara founded the Sogetsu School of Japanese Floral Art and created the relatively simple modern three-line style of Heaven, Earth and Man.

The three-line style of the Eastern world and the 'Bouquet Style' of the West have become the basis of modern Flower Arrangement.

DESIGNING ARRANGEMENTS – WESTERN STYLE

The basic principles of floral design are:

1. *Proportion*
This means a correct relationship between the size of flowers and container. As a general rule, the tallest stem in an arrangement should be one-and-a-half to twice the height of a tall vase (or the same proportion in relation to width with a low container), with the side flowers about three-quarters of this measurement.

2. *Balance*
This denotes the equal division of plant material on either side of an imaginary central line in a symmetrical arrangement, although in asymmetrical arrangement, the longest stem is naturally off centre. In both, the balance is achieved by placing a focal point, or centre of interest, at the base of the longest stem, or by the use of stands or bases to the containers.

3. *Scale*
This refers to the relationship in size of the plant material and the container, also the suitability (in size) of the finished arrangement to its allotted space.

4. *Contrast*
Contrast is achieved by using materials of varying shapes: e.g. round, irregular or pointed. An arrangement using only one type or size of flower would be very monotonous, but greater interest can be achieved by using stems of different lengths and a mixture of materials.

5. *Transition*
This term refers to the gradual scaling down in size of the plant material from the outside to the centre of an arrangement, i.e. buds and small flowers on the outside, larger flowers in the centre. A successful arrangement must also have height, width, and depth. Depth is achieved by recessing, or putting short-stemmed flowers between the longer ones or placing material at the back of the arrangement.

6. *Colour*
Another point to consider is the controversial subject of 'colour'. The colour scheme plays an important part in the balance, and has a considerable effect on the finished design.

There are three primary colours, yellow, red and blue. Between these are the secondary colours: green (made by mixing blue and yellow), orange (by mixing red and yellow), and violet (by mixing red and blue). All the other colours are a mixture of two or more of these.

The reds and oranges are warm or 'advancing' colours; they have a bold effect, catch the eye and should be used for emphasis. Greens and blues are cool or receding colours, and are used for calm, restful effects.

It is perhaps best not to use more than three colours in any scheme; the best results are obtained by making the main body of the arrangement in one colour, half that quantity of another colour and only small touches of the third colour.

Keep in mind also the type of lighting that will be used. Under artificial light all colours tend to lose their effectiveness, therefore strong and intense colours are better in these instances: e.g. red, yellow, white, orange and pink. Under fluorescent light reds lose their brilliance and appear dull. With natural lighting the most effective colours are pale or pastel shades, blues, greens and all the tints and tones.

EQUIPMENT AND MODERN AIDS

With the increased interest in Floral Art much new equipment has become available, but the basic tools are cheap and easy to obtain.

1. *Wire Netting* — for holding material in place. 1½—2 in. mesh is the best size to use.

2. *Scissors*. Any sharp scissors can be used, but florists' stubb scissors are designed especially for flower work.

3. *Pin Holders*. Flat lead holders fitted with brass pins and obtainable in many shapes varying in size from ½ in. to 6 in. diameter. They are essential to hold leaves, branches, etc., in modern arrangements, and have many other uses.

4. *Well pin holder* — a special type fixed in its own small water-holding container.

5. *Plasticine* — to fix the pin holder to the container. Buy good quality material.

6. *Bostick*. Can be bought in strips and is used in the same way as Plasticine.

7. *Stubb Wires*. Obtainable in various lengths and thicknesses. Useful in first aid for broken stems and in dried Christmas arrangements.

8. *Mosette and Florapak*. Sterile, water retentive materials, which, when dampened and packed into the container, will keep flowers fresh. Very useful in shallow containers or delicate china or glass where metal holders would cause damage.

9. *Oasis*. A new form of water-holding, plastic material. It is cut from the block, soaked in water and then wedged into the container or wired on to a flat disc. It helps in building up height (beyond the dimensions) in a container.

10. *Aluminium Foil*. Used to cover Mosette or Florapak to prevent it drying out. Also useful to line baskets and porous containers.

11. *Glass Balls*. Used in clear vases to hold flowers, in place of wire netting.

12. *Branch Holders*. Consists of a lead base fitted with a screw which can be fixed to drift wood or heavy branches, which are too big to be held with a pin holder or wire netting in the usual way.

Nagiere Upright, using Oak and 'Peace' Roses
Designed by Stella Coe for Mullard Ltd

CONTAINERS AND ACCESSORIES

For pleasing results, containers should be simply designed with little or no decoration. They should be correct in size, colour, shape and texture for the intended purpose and plant material. Vases, urns, goblets, Victorian sugar bowls and dishes, plates and candlesticks can all be used. If the container is too shallow to hold water, supplementary bowls or small dishes are used inside and hidden by leaves, moss, stones etc.

A few basic containers suitable for a beginner are: an urn, sugar bowl, a candlestick, flat dish, trough and two small bowls, one wooden and one pottery.

Accessories

Candle Cup Holders — metal holders made of brass' copper and aluminium in various sizes. They fix into any ordinary candlestick, turning it into a useful flower holder. Each holder has a slot in the base to fit a candle.

Universal holders — small bowl-shaped holders in three sizes which are fitted with a universal screw designed to fix to figurines, dolphins, negresses, shepherdesses, etc. — and available in white, black and gold.

Spring arrangement, Daffodils, Willow and Bark   E. Lyall

Nagiere Slanting style using Lilium speciosum
Designed by Stella Coe for Mullard Ltd

A Christmas arrangement   E. Lyall

MAKING THE ARRANGEMENT

Before beginning an arrangement choose your flowers and think out the details of the style, proportions and colour harmony.

1. Choose your container.
2. Fix your wire-netting or pin holder carefully.
3. Pour in a little water.
4. Place your 'outline' firmly in the container.
5. Fix your centre of interest.
6. Place in the auxiliary material, following the outline.
7. Place leaves or flowers over the rim of the container so that it makes a composite picture.
8. Stand back and look critically at the arrangement, make any adjustments and fill up with water.

Arrangements which display a massed profusion of flowers and foliage are known as MASS arrangements. Those which stress linear outlines, using a dramatic line in their design and a selective amount of material, are known as LINE arrangements. A combination of both of these, is known as a LINE MASS. The main art forms or designs used in flower arrangements are as follows:

Based on Lines

1. *Vertical*. This is usually arranged in a flat container, such as a dish. The highest stem should be one-and-a-half times to twice the width of the container with flat leaves at the base; or the height can be balanced by placing the arrangement on a wide base. This is the best style of arrangement for Iris, Gladioli and stiff-stemmed flowers.

2. *Horizontal*. Width is emphasised to at least twice the width of the container, at the expense of height. Troughs are the best containers. These make good table decorations.

3. *Pyramid*, or Face Front Triangle. Perhaps the most useful design, as it lends itself so well to the popular Mass style of arrangement. It can be used for all types of flowers in bowls, urns, goblets and pedestals. It is symmetrical in outline, the highest stem being one-and-a-half times to twice the height or width of the container, and the side placements three-quarters of this length.

4. *Asymmetrical Triangle*. Here the main stem has been moved off centre — either right or left — so that one side becomes long and the other short. The focal point is then at the base of the longest stem.

5. *Fleur de Lys*. A version of the Pyramid or Face Front Triangle, built up in the same way, but omitting

229

some of the shorter stems between the vertical and horizontal lines, thus emphasising the outline and focal point.

6. *Diagonal.* Good for a jug or tall pottery container, effective with branches of flowering shrubs, which are placed at an angle of 45 deg. upwards and downwards from the horizontal, with a good strong focal point of contrasting flowers or leaves.

7. *Letter L.* This is based on the same dimensions as the asymmetrical triangle, leaving out the shorter side of the triangle and so called because of its shape. Good for Show work.

Based on Curves

1. *Crescent.* This outline is part of a circle. It should be placed in a tilted position, with the upper segment slightly longer than the lower, which forms the base. Centre of interest is below the tip.

2. *Hogarth Curve.* So named after Hogarth's 'line of beauty'. It is an 'S' curve and should be made with soft-flowing, graceful material that can be moulded to the required curves. Looks best in pedestal type container. It can also be used on its side for ordinary table arrangements.

3. *Inverted Crescent.* Most attractive in a pedestal or in candlestick types of container. It is a crescent upside-down and can be arranged as a face front arrangement or all round. Good for dinner tables. Soft-flowing materials are best.

4. *Spiral.* A good basic form which can be used for many types of flowers, mainly for advanced arrangers. It makes a good table or buffet centre when some height is required.

5. *All Round.* This is one of the best known outlines, particularly useful for table decoration. The centre stem should not be too tall (about 9 in. high) and overall measurements should not exceed one-sixth of the table area.

Japanese Arrangements

In order to practise Japanese Flower Arrangement, certain terms have to be mastered, as the aids to arrangement and placement of stems are always described in Japanese. The main terms are:

Ikebana — the art of flower arrangement.
Kenzan — a needle point holder.
Tokonoma — an alcove.
Jushis — added flowers.
Moribana — flowers in a low arrangement.
Nageire — arrangement of flowers in a tall vase.
Shin (Heaven) ⎫
Soe (Man) ⎬ placement in Sogetsu Ryu.
Hikae (Earth) ⎭

230

Sogetsu Ryu School

The main characteristic of Japanese Floral Art is its linear form. Colour and mass have no part in the composition — the emphasis being on outline and spaciousness, rather than mass effects.

Branches and flowers (Jushis) must be carefully chosen and conditioned (the former being pruned), and each stem placed in the exact position for the chosen design.

Branches also have 'right' and 'wrong' sides, the

Ornamental Grasses　　　　　　　Sutton & Sons

Miniature arrangements

right side being the way it faced the sun when growing. This must always be turned towards the arranger. The material used is also placed in relation to its habit of growth: i.e. Water-lilies low down in the design, garden plants taller in the arrangement and branches highest in the design.

The arrangements are also designed to depict the seasons. Flowers play an important part in Spring arrangements, water becomes part of the display in Summer designs, with berries and seed heads in Autumn, and bare branches in Winter.

Example of arrangement lacking outline, shape or focal point Copyright R. & G. Cuthbert

The Placement of Stems

SHIN (Heaven) is always the tallest stem, generally a carefully pruned branch. This is the first placement — fixed to the needle holder or Kenzan. The angle at which it is placed acts as a guide to the rest of the arrangement.

SOE (Man) is the second tallest stem and should be pruned so that it does not touch or intrude on the Shin stem.

HIKAE (Earth) is the shortest stem in the arrangement and is placed low down.

JUSHIS (or the flowers which are used with branches) are never longer than three-quarters of the main (Heaven) stem. They are placed forward and upward in odd numbers (1—3—5—7) according to the type of design, with the stems placed at different angles from the upright. If, for example, the main stem of Shin is 10 deg. from the Upright, Soe should be placed at 45 deg. and Hikae at 75 deg. Different designs are made by interchanging the angles at which these stems are placed.

Two styles used in Sogetsu Ryu are known as Moribana and Nageire.

Moribana are really natural arrangements made in flat dishes and held in place on Kenzans or needle holders.

The main forms of Moribana are:

1. *Risshin-Kei, or Upright*
   Shin 10°   Soe 45°   Hikae 75°

2. *Keishin-Kei, or Windswept*
   Shin 45°   Soe 10°   Hikae 75°

3. *Oyo-Kakei, or One and One* arrangement
   Shin 10°   Hikae 75°
   (2 stems only are used in this style)

4. *Divided Kenzan*

Two pin holders (Kenzans) are used in this to hold the material. Shin at 10 deg. and Soe at 45 deg., both placed on front Kenzan, and Hikae at 75 deg. on Kenzan at back of the container.

Nageire

This style is always arranged in tall vases —with the material held in place by means of forked twigs (instead of pin holders). The same measurements and angles, however, are as used in Moribana.

ACCESSORIES

Kenzan. These are used for all arrangements in low dishes. It is not correct to use Plasticine to fix the Kenzan, for the arrangement should be so balanced that such precautions are not necessary.

Forked Twigs are used to hold branches in Nageire arrangements in tall vases.

231

Plant Propagation

RAISING PLANTS FROM SEED

This is Nature's method of reproducing countless millions of plants and weeds each year.

Species are plants which grow wild, whose seedlings are more or less identical with the parents. No two seedlings are blueprints of each other; there are always slight differences — in height, time of flowering, hairs on the leaves, etc., but virtually indetectable. Only when something sensational occurs, such as a new colour, doubling in the flowers or variegated foliage, does the gardener normally take notice. The new plant is known as a 'sport' or 'muta-

tion' and if it makes a good garden subject it is named and becomes a new variety.

However, if one wishes to propagate the variety, it will not come true from seed, so must be reproduced by other means, such as cuttings, layers and grafts.

Again, when two species are crossed (pollen from one being put on the stigma of the other) the offspring, known as hybrids — will show much variation. Only when the grower has made a deliberate cross, in the hope of raising new plants, would he bother to raise chance forms from seed. Bees, crossing

Planting Strawberries Valerie Finnis

Schizanthus – requires warmth of greenhouse for germination

H. Smith

232

Cinerarias also need greenhouse protection   H. Smith

Germination

Garden seeds are usually treated by one of the following methods:

1. Those which are reasonably hardy are sown directly into the open ground at the appropriate period: e.g. Lettuce, Beans, Lupins.

2. Those which require uniform conditions of light, moisture and warmth for germination, find this under a cloche or in a cold frame: e.g. most hardy perennials, and Celery.

3. Similar to 2 but requiring the greater warmth of a greenhouse: e.g. Schizanthus and Cinerarias.

Germinating seeds require:

1. *Warmth.* Nothing grows in the coldest period of winter and although germination requirements vary a temperature between 55° and 60°F. is appropriate for a wide range of plants. Nothing germinates much below 45°F. and 110°F. destroys life, even with tropical seeds.

2. *Air.* Oxygen is needed very early on in the life of the young plant, so unless the soil is porous and well drained, it may suffocate at birth. Waterlogged soil is fatal to seed germination, except in the case of aquatic plants.

3. *Moisture.* Whilst the seed is kept dry it remains dormant.

4. *Light.* This is not necessary for the actual operation of germination, but vital immediately the shoot comes through.

from Brussels Sprouts to Cabbage Flowers, for example, would ruin the long, patient, selective work of the seedsman, so plants of this family are always well separated when grown for seed purposes.

It is through constant 'roguing', i.e. removing all deviating seedlings, that we can confidently grow so many varieties of vegetables and flowers with practically one hundred per cent of them coming true to name; and although colour purity cannot always be guaranteed we grow certain strains of plants knowing that they will give us good, if not exactly similar flowers or foliage.

Sowing out of Doors

Spring and autumn are obviously the best seasons for sowing, spring being the more important. The soil should be broken up, dug, weathered and reduced to fineness by adequate raking. Digging immediately prior to sowing leaves the surface crumbly and loose, so tread over the ground, moving forward with a shuffling motion, feet together; then rake over to remove footprints.

Except in the ornamental garden, always use a line whilst sowing. Stretch it tautly between stakes at each end of the row and work backwards, keeping one foot on the line and meantime drawing out the drill with a draw hoe. Use only the corner of the hoe for shallow drills. Large seeds, such as Peas and Beans, are often raised in double or treble lines, 2 in. apart. Here the flat blade of the hoe is used and pulled out to a depth of 2 in.

Always sow seed thinly, and cover with fine soil,

Lettuces, Beans etc. are raised from seed sown in open ground
Valerie Finnis

233

either by scuffling it back with the side of the foot, or, in the case of very small seed, by using the head of the rake. Label seeds after sowing, giving the date.

Broadcast Sowing

This is usually practised in the annual border for seeds like Marigolds, Shirley Poppies and Nigella, but may also be used with early crops in frames like Lettuce, Radish and Carrots. Rake soil finely, sow seed very thinly and rake in.

Sowing under Glass

Most ornamental plants are raised by this method, the seed being sown in scrupulously clean pots, pans or boxes. Crocks are placed over the drainage holes of the pots or along the central drainage slit of the boxes. A layer of roughage (leaves, sifted peat, etc.) spread over these prevents fine soil drifting down and fouling the drainage.

The John Innes Horticultural Institute (at Bayfordbury, Herts) has evolved a number of basic seed and potting composts which are designed to suit a very wide range of plants.

John Innes Seed Compost is made up as follows:
2 parts by bulk medium loam
1 part   ,,   leaf or peat
1 part   ,,   coarse sand
To every bushel of the above add:
$1\frac{1}{2}$ oz. superphosphate of lime
$\frac{3}{4}$ oz. ground chalk or limestone.

John Innes Composts can either be made up at home (after partially sterilising the loam) or bought ready made. Fertilisers should not be added until just before the compost is used. When all the ingredients are mixed the compost should be moist but not wet.

Threequarters fill the pot or box with compost, pressing well down at the edges, and levelling the surface. Now sow the seed very thinly (mixing it with equal parts of sand if it is very fine) and cover lightly with silver sand or finely sieved compost. Exceptionally small seeds such as Begonia need no covering at all, although some growers lay a little Sphagnum Moss over the surface, removing this on germination.

After labelling, water the container, using a fine rosed can for the larger seeds, but the immersion method for fine ones. This involves placing the pans, etc., in a bath of water in which the liquid comes just below the level of the pot rims. Here they remain until the soil surface appears moist. Cover the tops later with glass or paper to prevent rapid drying out and stand pots in the frame or on the greenhouse bench.

As soon as the seeds germinate, remove the cover-

Air layering on Mahonia   By courtesy of Home Magazine

Half ripe or heel cuttings of Cupressus

ing, and when large enough prick them out into boxes (approximately 2 in. apart with most varieties), keeping in a close atmosphere for a day or two. Later they may be hardened off in a cold frame for a week or so before being planted in flowering positions outdoors.

Greenhouse plants may be potted straight from the seedling pan into small pots. As growth progres-

Rubber Plants rooted from stem cuttings. They are dipped in hormone powder to accelerate rooting By courtesy of Home Magazine

ses, transfer to larger pots without breaking the soil ball. Turn the plant from the pot by tapping against a bench. It should be nicely rooted but not have so many that they are twisted all round the pot. Crock the new pot as usual, add roughage and a little soil and stand the plant in the centre (after removing its crock). Drop new compost into the space between pot and plant, firming with the fingers or a dibber, not pressing the old soil ball. When finished, the level of the plant should be the same as before.

The compost for potting should still follow the John Innes formula as follows:

John Innes No. 1 Potting Compost
7 parts by loose bulk of medium loam
3   ,,   ,,   ,,   good horticultural peat.
2   ,,   ,,   ,,   coarse sand.

To every bushel of this mixture add:
$1\frac{1}{2}$ oz. hoof and horn $\frac{1}{8}$ in. grist ⎫
$1\frac{1}{2}$ oz. superphosphate   ⎬ Known as
$\frac{3}{4}$ oz. sulphate of potash   ⎬ the John
$\frac{3}{4}$ oz. ground limestone or chalk ⎭ Innes Base

John Innes No. 2 Potting Compost, used for stronger growing plants in later stages of potting, e.g. Chrysanthemums, consists of the same formula with *twice* the amount of John Innes Base. John Innes No. 3 Potting Compost has *three* times the amount.

Acid Plants

Certain greenhouse plants, notably Rhododendrons and Azaleas, Heathers etc., should have lime omitted from the compost. They may also be grown in the new loamless composts, made up of peat, sand and fertilisers, which can be purchased ready mixed.

Difficult Seeds

Some seeds take longer to germinate than others. As a general rule, the more quickly the seed is sown after harvesting the better the results. This is particularly true with Meconopsis, Primulas and many alpines. If these are gathered one day and sown the next, one hundred per cent germination is obtained. When kept several weeks the returns will be halved, whilst a lapse of several months may result in no seedlings at all.

Other plants have exceptionally hard-coated seeds, as the Coconut, and to a lesser degree, Cannas, Horse Chestnuts and Acorns. These have to be softened by natural weathering, and there are various ways of hastening this process.
1. *Soaking.* Fleshy seeds like Peas and Beans germinate more quickly if they are soaked overnight.
2. *Chipping.* Dates, Cannas and similar hard-coated seeds may have some of their hard outer coat chipped

away with a knife or a nail file. Be sure to do this on the opposite side to the eye.

3. *Stratification.* Effective with Holly, Rose, Berberis, Cotoneaster and other berried plants. The seeds, hips, berries, etc., are spread out on boxes of sand as soon as possible after harvesting and placed outside in an open position. Covering the tops with small mesh wire netting prevents birds or mice getting at them. Contrasting weather conditions break down the fleshy part, so that the seeds germinate at once when sown the following spring. Without stratification they take at least another year.

4. *Artificial Frost.* A modification of the preceding method, valuable for many alpines and herbaceous plants. Place seed in a shallow dish of water and leave to swell. Then place the container in the refrigerator for 24 hours, which freezes both water and seeds; remove, thaw out gradually and sow immediately.

5. *Chemical Means.* Various chemicals have been used to accelerate germination, such as formic acid, soda, chlorine and sulphuric acid; also watering the compost with a pale pink solution of permanganate of potash. But for the amateur the safest and surest measures are (*a*) stratification, (*b*) using fresh seed and (*c*) in some instances, soaking.

VEGETATIVE PROPAGATION

Other methods of propagating certain plants come under the collective heading of VEGETATIVE PROPAGATION. This means that pieces of vegetative or living growth are taken from the plant and either induced to root, or made to grow on other plants.

Plants normally reproduced in this way are:
1. Named varieties which do not come true from seed.
2. Plants with special foliage characteristics: e.g. variegations or unusual shapes which might not be transmitted via the seed.
3. Plants with poor rootstocks of their own, liable to die through inherent weaknesses.
4. Plants which make taller, stronger or finer specimens on the rootstocks of other species.
5. Abortive plants which do not produce seed: e.g. double varieties.
6. Plants which rarely seed.

Division

This is the simplest method, but only practical with plants which produce basal shoots and have plenty of fibrous roots. Rhizomatous plants with long snaky rootstocks running horizontally in the ground, such as *Iris germanica* and Solomon's Seal, can also be divided, the rhizomes being cut into sections, each having a fan of leaves or growing shoot as well as a few roots.

Large clumps of herbaceous perennials, e.g. Mich-

Primula helodoxa. Primulas should be sown as soon as possible after harvesting

aelmas Daisies, Phlox, Heleniums and Achilleas, split readily when two digging forks are thrust back to back in the centre of the clump, and the handles levered outwards. Smaller plants can be cut up with a sharp knife. The individual units should always have one or more shoots and some roots.

Spring and autumn are the best seasons to divide plants, although *Iris germanica* is usually split in July, after flowering. Fleshy rooted subjects such as Delphiniums and Lupins are best divided early in the

H. Smith

Meconopsis cambrica. Treat in a similar way to Primulas H. Smith

year. Other plants which are best left until spring are *Aster amellus*, *Scabiosa caucasica*, Pyrethrums, Chrysanthemums and Catananches.

Layering

Layering is one of the oldest and simplest methods of plant propagation — and perhaps the safest. While the young plant is making roots, the parent continues to provide it with nutriment until it can fend for itself. It is a slow method, except for Carnations, but for obtaining several more specimens from a choice shrub, it is infallible.

1. *Layering Border Pinks and Carnations.* In late July and August, select sturdy, strong-jointed growths, removing all leaves except on parts which are to remain above the soil. Spread some gritty or sandy soil around; then, taking each shoot separately, make a cut with a sharp knife just below a joint and half-way through the stem. Turn the knife and run it horizontally through the joint and stem for about half an inch. Push the shoot into the soil with the wound open and pin firmly in place with a layering pin or a hairpin. Keep the soil moist and the layer should root in 6—8 weeks, when the young plant should be separated from its parent and planted in its flowering position (normally in September).

2. *Layering Strawberries.* Take layers only from healthy plants, the first to appear and not secondary or later runners. Four or five from one individual are enough. Peg them down into the open ground, or root them into small pots of sandy soil sunk into the ground near by. With the latter method the plants can be lifted later without damaging roots.

3. *Rooting Shrubs.* Any shrub or tree with branches close to the ground can be layered, young shoots rooting more quickly than old ones. To stimulate rooting, the flow of sap from the parent tree must be restricted in some way, either by:

(*a*) Cutting a tongue, as with Border Carnations. This is only possible with young, soft stems.

(*b*) Cutting a thin layer of bark away or twisting a piece of wire tightly round the stem.

(*c*) Twisting the branch in the hands so that the outer tissues are split.

The wood should be painted with hormone powder or dusted with charcoal and pegged down into gritty soil. Rooting may take from 6 months to 2 years, depending on the plant.

Plants which make long, wand-like shoots, such as Wisteria, can have several layers on the same stem. After the cuts are made the layer is pegged down like the coils of a snake. This is called Serpentine Arching or Layering.

4. *Air Layering.* An alternative method of layering choice shrubs (Camellias, Magnolias, etc.) and trees,

237

also woody house plants such as Ficus. Either remove a slim ring of bark ($\frac{1}{4}$ in. wide) all round the branch, or else make a tongue cut and keep open with a matchstick. Pack the wound with damp Sphagnum Moss, tie in place and slip a polythene sleeve over the branch, securing it firmly at each end with adhesive tape. When roots appear, cut the branch immediately below and pot the young plant.

Cuttings

This is the measure chiefly adopted by nurserymen for soft fruit, herbaceous perennials and shrubs. There are five main methods:

1. *Soft Cuttings*, in which young soft shoots of the current season's growth are used.
2. *Half-Ripe or Heel Cuttings*, taken July—August, mostly from woody plants, with soft pieces of new growth and a heel or sliver of old wood attached.
3. *Ripe or Hardwood Cuttings*. These are pieces of ripe or seasoned wood of the current year's growth, taken in autumn.
4. *Root Cuttings*, in which pieces of root are used.
5. *Leaf Cuttings. Begonia rex* and African Violets are propagated by this method.

The main difference between a cutting and a layer is that the former is severed from the parent plant and has to be kept alive and healthy until such time as it makes its own roots.

Cuttings possess a number of advantages over seed and other methods. The young plants will be of a standard height, make the same type of plant and share the same characteristics of doubling, colour or foliage variation. On the other hand, they will also have the same weaknesses, so that cuttings should only be made from healthy plants.

Soft Cuttings

Usually taken in spring or early summer, soft cuttings can be induced later in the season simply by cutting down old plants. New young shoots appear which can be cut off when they are about 3 in. long and made into soft cuttings. Catmint *(Nepeta faassenii)*, Aubrieta and other rock plants are often propagated in this way in July and August. Again, Chrysanthemum stools kept warm and moist in a greenhouse over the winter will break into growth. The shoots which appear are then used for cuttings.

Never take soft cuttings from spindly, deformed, diseased or over-sappy shoots. Trim selected cuttings, removing some of the lower leaves and then cut the stem straight across *immediately* below a joint (node). Insert the cuttings with a dibber in pans or boxes of very sandy soil and water them in. Crock the containers in the usual way and fill to within $\frac{1}{2}$ in. of the top with compost (two parts each of coarse sand and peat to one of loam).

The rooting material must be free-draining, for

Taking Geranium cuttings   Fisons Horticulture

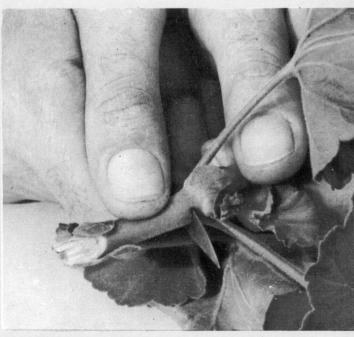

The cutting should be made immediately beneath a joinst
Fisons Horticulture

Cuttings – before and after making   Fisons Horticulture

Inserting the cuttings   Fisons Horticulture

oxygen plays an important part in the operation. It is essential to pot the cuttings in good compost immediately they have rooted, and to keep them in a close humid atmosphere until new roots appear. The necessary close atmosphere can be obtained by keeping them under glass or polythene as in a greenhouse, frame, bell jar, cloche or even beneath jam jars. A temperature of 60–65°F is suitable for most soft cuttings, although 70–80°F may be necessary for tropical plants.

Cuttings may also be rooted very simply on a windowsill. Insert the cuttings in a pot and bend two pieces of wire into an inverted U, pushing the ends into the soil so that they cross at the top and stand about 6 in. above the soil. Slip a polythene bag over the top, fastening it with an elastic band.

Many growers use bottom heat in their propagators. Soil warming and electric propagating units are so convenient and easily managed that the majority of gardeners today consider them an essential part of equipment.

The electronic leaf and mist propagation technique is employed by many growers and, small units are now available for the amateur. The principle involved is an electrically controlled device with a sensitive point or 'leaf' standing amongst the cuttings. When a certain stage of air dryness is reached, the contact is broken and a fine mist-like spray drifts for a few seconds over the cuttings.

Half-Ripe or Heel Cuttings

These are usually found as twiggy side shoots of the current year's growth on the main stems or branches of shrubs and trees. About July they will be between 2 and 4 in. long, just right for cuttings. Pull them downwards from the main stem, taking a 'heel' of the previous year's wood attached to the base. This fragment of older wood should be retained and trimmed, if necessary. In its absence the cutting must be made as for a soft cutting. If the heel is too long, shorten it a little at the top rather than lose it.

Inconveniently large-leaved plants like Hydrangeas should have some of the foliage clipped in half. Many half-ripe cuttings will root in a cold frame without artificial heat, some (like Rosemary, Lavender and Santolina) may even be struck in the open ground, but difficult or more uncommon plants give a higher percentage of 'takes' if given a little bottom heat. Summer-struck cuttings should be placed in north-facing frames.

Hardwood or Ripe Cuttings

These are made from ripened pieces of the current year's wood, usually from late September until early November. Used for Black, Red and White currants, Gooseberries and many shrubs.

Small cuttings between 5 and 10 in. long are best. They are placed directly into the cold frame or open ground and left until spring. Select straight, healthy shoots, cutting just below a joint at the base and just above a joint at the top. This applies to shrubs and Black Currants, and because some buds are buried, underground shoots always appear in succeeding years.

Gooseberries and Red and White Currants, however, fruit on the old wood, so rub out all buds which will go below the soil (usually the bottom two-thirds) when the cutting is made.

The cuttings should be inserted 4 to 6 in. apart in shallow trenches of light sandy soil. Two-thirds must be buried, with one-third only above the surface when the soil is returned.

Root Cuttings

Some plants do not lend themselves easily to stem cuttings. Oriental Poppies, for example, produce basal leaves and flower stems which come straight out of the ground, and yet seed may be an inappropriate method of increase, because the variety for propagation is of hybrid origin.

Certain of these subjects possess bud potentials in the roots which (cut up during autumn or winter) may be used instead of normal cuttings. Herbaceous plants like Poppies, Anchusas and Acanthus can be lifted (partially or entirely), the roots washed and then cut up into thick thongs 2–3 in. long.

For small quantities use deep pots, inserting the cuttings about 1 in. apart in sandy soil and covering them with ½ in. of sand. Place the pots in a cold frame and leave to sprout.

Slender root cuttings like those of Phlox, Catananche and *Primula denticulata* are best placed in boxes. They should be cut into 1- or 2-inch lengths, laid thinly over the sandy soil and then covered with ¼ in. of the same compost.

Echinops, Robinia and Xanthoceras can all be increased from root cuttings, also Seakale in the vegetable garden.

Leaf Cuttings

Leaves form a natural means of increase in many plants. Thus the North American *Tolmeia menziesii*, often called Pick-a-Back Plant, or Youth on Age, has rough, hairy leaves, each of which carries a baby plant towards the end of summer. When detached, these root readily in sandy soil. The fern, *Asplenium bulbiferum*, has lacy leaves with dozens of tiny ferns growing along the fronds. Some species of the greenhouse succulents called Bryophyllums likewise have baby plantlets growing from the notches at the leaf margins. Often these drop off naturally and root in the soil of the pot or bench.

Gloxinias possess root potentials in their foliage and may be propagated by leaf cut

Chrysanthemums are reproduced from cuttings   Bakers of Codsall

H. Smith

Phlox, an herbaceous perennial propagated by division or cuttings
Valerie Finnis

Plants not normally addicted to leaf propagation, but which have certain root potentials in their foliage, include *Begonia Rex* and its varieties, Haberleas, Streptocarpus, Gloxinias, Ramondas, Saintpaulias and Echeverias. These all need the stimulus of bottom heat and the humidity of a frame to make successful young plantlets. The leaves can be inserted upright in a pan of sandy compost, but to stimulate cell activity and rooting make a nick with a knife, at the back of the leaf, where it joins the stalk. The wounded part should lie just under the soil. Begonias should be flat.

Budding

This is a method by which a 'bud' of the desired variety is inserted in the tissues of a host plant. It is normally carried out in July and August when the sap is running freely and the bark parts freely from the wood.

The individual receiving the bud is known as the stock, but both bud and stock must come from similar or closely related species. Thus, it is useless to put Broom on to Apple, although Broom can be budded on Laburnum, for both come from the same family and will readily unite. Similarly, Lilac will take on Privet and Plums on Hawthorn. To check whether sap is circulating freely, cut gently into the outer rind with the point of a knife; if this separates readily from the inner wood all is well.

The choice of stock is important, for on this may depend many factors which ultimately affect the new plant. These may be summarised as follows:
1. Hardiness of the plant.
2. Resistance or susceptibility to pest and disease.
3. Flowering or fruiting qualities.
4. Ultimate size.
5. Ability to grow in normally uncongenial soils. These stocks are recognised by growers, and would-be purchasers can ask for special types to suit individual circumstances. Stocks are occasionally offered by nurserymen for those who wish to experiment with budding or grafting. The main types are:

ROSES
Bud on briars Dog-Rose (*Rosa canina*), *R. rugosa*, *R. laxa*, *R. manetti*.
APPLES
Malling IX ('Jaune de Metz') for Dwarf Trees.
Malling VIII for Semi-dwarf Trees.
Malling I or II for Medium Trees.
Malling XII or XVI for Vigorous Trees.
PEARS
Malling Quince A, B and C.
Pear Stock (for very vigorous trees).

PLUMS
Myrobalan
PEACHES AND NECTARINES
Plum, Brompton Stock.
ORNAMENTAL PLUMS, PEACHES, ETC.
Common Mussel Plum.
CHERRIES
Common Gean or Cherry (*Prunus avium*) Mazzard.

Buds are taken from a branch of the current year's
wood; in Roses normally from the flowering stem
of a full-blown flower. The bud is detached by inserting a sharp knife in the stem about ½ in. below
the bud, drawing it up through the centre of the stem
and the joint, and coming out again about ¼ in. the
other side. This leaves a half-moon-shaped sliver of
wood, with the bud and leaf-stalk attached. The small
pieces of white wood behind the bud must now be
gently removed with the finger and thumb, taking
care not to injure the bud. The leaf — but not the
leaf-stalk — can be removed at the same time.

No time must be lost in inserting this bud into
the stock, but meantime it must be kept moist by
laying it on damp moss or in a dish of water.

The stock is prepared by cutting a T mark into
the bark with a sharp knife (normally near the
ground) but 2–3 ft. up the stem for standard Roses
and trees. Lift the rind on each side of the downward
cut and slip the bud into the opening thus made,
working it down until it sits snugly inside the leg
of the T cut. Gently press the tissue back into place,
cut off any surplus rind and tie securely with damp
raffia. Cover all cut parts in this way, leaving only
the bud exposed. Buds are normally inserted on the
north side of the stock, to prevent sun drying.

All top growth is left on the stock until the bud
'takes' and starts to swell, when the raffia ties should
be severed and any growths *above* the bud removed.
The bud now goes on to make a bush or tree of the
desired variety.

The budding of ornamental Peaches, Plums,
Apples and Pears is carried out in exactly the same
fashion, except that once the bud has taken it is
usual to retain a few inches of the old wood when the
top growth is removed. This is useful for tying in
the young new shoot during its first season.

Grafting

There are many variations of grafting, which, like
budding, involves the insertion of part of one plant
into another, so making the former grow on foreign
roots. The part involved in this case consists of
a piece of the stem with one or more buds, and is
known as the SCION. Success depends on com-
patability between stock and scion and close contact

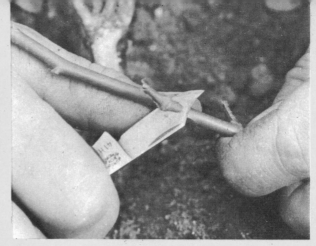

Removing the bud from the flower stem of a Rose
Fisons Horticulture

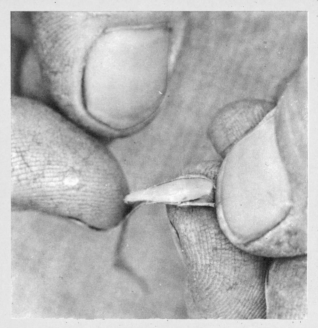

Fisons Horticulture
Removing the wood at the back of the bud

Making a T-shaped cut in the stock and lifting the side flaps
Fisons Horticulture

between the inner barks (cambiums) of both, so that the two fuse together perfectly.

Season

In Britain grafting is usually done between February and June, according to the type of plant and the form of graft to be used. The grafting of Paeonies, Gypsophilas, Rhododendrons or Camellias may, however, take place at various seasons.

Grafting Fruit Trees

The stocks commonly used for grafting fruit trees (see p. 241) are increased by layers and reach the gardener in the form of rooted slips or cuttings, with a single straight stem. These should be planted in rows in the propagating bed.

Scions are normally obtained from winter prunings. Sturdy young shoots of the desired variety are tied in bundles of 20 or 25, and half buried in a shady corner. This keeps the buds plump but retards and prevents them from opening.

Whip and Tongue Grafting

This is the commonest method employed for young trees and takes place in March. First the stock is cut down to within 5 in. of the ground with a pair of secateurs. Now, using a really sharp knife, make a sloping cut, starting about $1\frac{1}{2}$ in. down the trunk and draw the knife upwards so that it comes out in the middle of the stem. Half-way along the cut area make a small downward nick to form a tongue, which will hold the scion whilst this is being tied in place.

To prepare the scion, first remove the unripe top, for it is the firm, middle wood which is required. Measure this against the stock and make a clean slanting stroke on its base of about the same length, cutting a tongue in the centre to correspond with the nick in the stock. The completed scion should have several inches of stem, together with three of four buds above the cut area.

Join the two parts together, linking the tongues, and making the barks on one set of cuts (both if possible) touch, so that food from the stock is taken through to the scion. Tie firmly with moist raffia and cover wounded area with grafting wax.

A variation known as Splice Grafting is sometimes used for plants raised in pots. Thus Roses, Brooms and Clematis may be grown along under glass, both stock and scions of the required variety being made in exactly the same way (but without the notched tongues) and tied closely together.

Double Working

A few plants seem unable to grow with any degree of permanence on certain stocks. The favourite 'Williams Bon Cretien' Pear, for example, will thrive on wild Pear stock, but only lives for a time (before

Slipping the bud in the opening in the stock   Fisons Horticulture

Securing the bud in position with moist raffia. All cut parts must be covered
Fisons Horticulture

snapping suddenly) on Quince. Since the latter stock .gives small compact trees but wild Pear stocks make tall and unmanageable ones, the difficulty must be overcome by double working. Thus a vigorous variety such as 'Beurre Hardy' is first grafted on to Quince and the following season the 'Williams' is grafted on the 'Beurre Hardy'. Pear 'Dr. Jules Guyet' is treated in the same way.

Saddle and Wedge grafting

Herbaceous Paeonies are sometimes grafted on to a strong growing kind such as *P. officinalis*. The eyes or buds are removed from the stock and a wedge cut out thus: The scion is then trimmed to a shape and slipped into the stock. Tying is not normally necessary but the grafts must be kept moist (moss helps in this respect) until the union is complete. This Wedge Graft usually takes place about August and is carried out in a cold frame. By reversing the cutting technique one obtains a Saddle Graft.

Rhododendron varieties are often Saddle Grafted on *R. ponticum*, and Tree Paeonies on *P. moutan* stock.

Framework Grafting

This method can in a matter of two years change a large tree of outmoded, poor type Apples into a heavy-cropping, different variety such as 'Cox' or 'Laxton Superb'. The identity is completely altered by anything from 50 to 500 grafts (according to the size of tree) made between February and June.

Start by preparing the old tree, removing entirely any badly placed branches, e.g. running towards the centre, rubbing, centrally placed or inconveniently positioned. This leaves a framework of well balanced branches, which must be further reduced by cutting out any spur formations and most of the side or lateral growths. No fruit buds of the old variety must remain, but any conveniently placed small lateral branches can be retained for stub grafting.

Four methods are common in framework grafting: 1. *Top or Rind Grafting*. Used only at the *ends* of branches, which must be sawn to remove shoots of the old variety.

Pare the wood carefully with a sharp knife and make a downward cut (starting at the top), about 2 in. long, in the rind of the branch. Now take the handle of a budding knife or a wooden label and lift the lips of the slit thus made to take the scion. Prapare the latter by making a slanting downward cut, about $1\frac{1}{2}$ in. long at the base of a young stem. This should have a bud half-way down at the back of the cut and three or four buds above. Run the tail of the scion out very finely so that it does not leave a raised bulge when placed in the stock, and make a notch, if required, at the top of the cut, so that it fits securely

Hemerocallis sometimes have young plants in their leaf axils

Saddle grafting may be practised with Tree Paeonies

244

H. Smith

on the shoulder of the branch when placed in position. Slip it into the opening on the branch, tie with raffia, and cover with grafting wax.

Incidentally, whilst one top graft may be sufficient for small branches, two or three should be inserted round the tops of large ones or limbs.

2. *Stub Grafting.* Used to change the identity of small existing side branches from ½–1 in. across.

Prepare the scions in the form of a wedge at the basal ends, leaving one side slightly longer than the other. Leave six to eight buds on each.

The side branch to be changed should be cut from above, half-way through its thickness and about ½ in. along in the direction the branch is to take (that is, left or right according to branch placement on the tree). Open the cut by pressing on the end of the branch and slip the scion in place with the longer cut downwards. Release the branch and the scion will be firmly held.

Cut away the old branch as close to the graft as possible and seal round with grafting wax.

3. *Inverted L or Bark Grafting.* Although stub grafts take care of those areas where there are laterals, long stretches of unfurnished wood will inevitably remain on the old branches. To arrange for new laterals at these points it is necessary to insert grafts actually into the bark at such places where a branch or spur seems desirable.

The scion is prepared with a long, sloping cut (about 1½ in.) on one side, followed by a very short cut alongside. Now turn the scion over and make a third cut, shallower than the first but directly opposite. It should have six or eight buds. With a sharp knife make two slits, like an inverted L, in the bark of the branch, lift the edges and slip the scion in place. The angle of the cut will decide the direction in which the new branch will grow. Hold the scion steady with a gimp pin and seal with grafting wax. If space allows, grafts should be made at intervals of about a foot, alternately up every branch.

4. *Oblique Side Grafting.* This is another method of clothing large, bare limbs, particularly useful with thick bark. Scions are prepared with two 1-in. sloping cuts, made so that they meet and form an angle of 30–45° on one side. Shallow oblique cuts are then made round the limb and the scions inserted in such a manner that the cambium layers (green tissues) unite. After sealing, the operation is complete.

The attraction of framework grafting lies in the fact that one is left with a mature tree. Also there is no urgency to complete the grafting within a few days, for the task can be extended over several months (February–June) if the scions can be kept from sprouting.

PROLIFERATION

Under this collective heading are included methods of vegetative reproduction, which produce plantlets on other parts of the plant than the root. Thus the Tree Onion (*Allium sepa var. proliferum*) carries bunches of small onions at the top of 2–2½ ft. stems; these can be detached and planted in the normal way to make new plants.

Plants which adopt such measures of increase are usually shy-flowering or their seed is sterile. Thus *Dentaria bulbifera* often carries plantlets on the abortive flower heads; Hemerocallis and Lupins sometimes have young plants in the axils of the leaves, and many Lilies have bulbils in the leaf axils. Left alone these would eventually fall to the ground and root.

Hedges & Fences

Visitors to Britain are often intrigued by our neat gardens and trim hedges. Indeed, for most of us an enclosing hedge or fence is more than a boundary; it is a symbol of privacy and security.

Walls and hedges may also be used in the garden to separate the flowers from the more utilitarian vegetables and fruit, or as a windbreak; or they may provide harmonious backgrounds for specific features, as, for example, a dark green Yew hedge behind herbaceous borders, or a line of Beech enclosing a Rose garden.

HEDGES

Hedges for boundary use should grow thickly enough to keep out dogs and yet be economical in upkeep, without needing constant clipping. As a light barrier between one part of the garden and another, however, they need be less formidable, so that ornamental plants like Lavender, Roses, Jasmine, and even Heather, can be used in this way.

Privet has the merit of being cheap and easy to grow, and makes a good dense barrier. Unfortunately, it is a soil robber and plants within 2 or 3 ft. of it are usually drawn and starved. It also shelters a number of garden pests and diseases, and needs frequent clipping. The latter task has now been eased by the introduction of a hormone growth-inhibitor called Hedgeset. Spraying after the first cut of the season halts growth for about three months, but the spray must not be allowed to fall on other plants.

For a quick hedge plant bushes in two rows, staggering plants 12 in. apart with 8 in. between rows. All hedges should be cut back hard in their early

Retaining walls, hardboard fencing and trellis Woodmans, Pinner

years to encourage a dense, thick bottom. Height follows afterwards.

Normally Privet is clipped about twice a year, in May and September. Golden Privet makes a more ornamental hedge, but costs five or six times as much as the green.

Beech and Hornbeam are suitable for any soil except the excessively wet, and stand clipping well. Plant in double staggered rows with 8 in. between rows and 15 in. between plants. Do not cut tops of shoots for the first two years, but after that clip normally (preferably in July). Copper and Purple Beech are also obtainable and look particularly well interplanted with green. Hornbeam is more suitable for heavy soils.

Yew is perhaps the best evergreen hedge but rather slow-growing. Establish in October or May, setting plants 18 in. to 2 ft. apart. Clip in May and August whilst young, then once, in August or early September.

Berberis stenophylla makes a dense, evergreen, 'boy-proof' hedge, with prickly, shining foliage. In April it bears golden flowers. It grows quickly and even thrives on heavy clay. Plant 20 to 24 in. apart and prune when flowers fade.

Ornamental Plum is fairly new for hedging purposes, with pink blossom in March and April, followed by bronze, red or green deciduous foliage. Clip mature hedges in early spring, immediately after flowering. Set plants 18 in. apart. Varieties include 'Purple Flash', with purple leaves; 'Pink Paradise', double pink flowers and wine-red leaves; 'Blaze', purple leaves and single pink flowers; 'Crimson Dwarf', white flowers and deep purple leaves; and 'Geenglow', green leaves and white flowers.

For Boundary Hedges try also Hawthorn — very prickly. Plant in two rows, 9 in. apart with 12 in. between plants. Clip July or August; Lawson Cypress, growing up to 15 ft. Plant 18 to 24 in. apart. Clip May or June; *Lonicera nitida*, a low hedge with small evergreen leaves. Plant 12 in. apart. Clip May and September; and Holly, which should be planted 18 in. apart and clipped annually in April or early. September.

For Ornamental Hedges to be used *inside* the garden there are Roses. Use strong-growing kinds like Penzance Briars such as 'Meg Merrilees', crimson; or 'Lady Penzance', copper-yellow; or sturdy varieties like 'Frensham', deep red; or 'Queen Elizabeth,' deep pink. Plant 30 in. apart and simply remove old or useless shoots.

Fuchsias (in warmer areas), Lavender, Rosemary, Tree Heathers (*Erica arborea* or *E. lusitanica*) and

Plastic covered Gro Mesh fencing, useful for keeping plants against a wall
Woodmans, Pinner

Cotoneasters may also be used for hedging. Plant them about 18 in. apart and merely shorten long shoots.

FENCES AND WALLS

A wall provides a perfect background for many fine shrubs or climbers. Dry walls are useful when the garden is on two levels. (See pp. 170 for procedure and suitable plants.)

Fences vary in design and price. The closeboard type may either be set close together vertically or woven in basket fashion. The first lasts many years if regularly creosoted. The woven type is available in finished sections and also lasts years with care. Panels are usually 6 ft. high but come in various other lengths, e.g. 4 ft., 5 ft.

Wattle fences are cheaper and have a more rustic appearance but do not last as long. Galvanised chain-link fencing (some covered with plastic to prevent rust), Chestnut palings and concrete block walls can also be obtained.

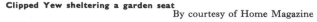

Clipped Yew sheltering a garden seat
By courtesy of Home Magazine

The Greenhouse

Greenhouses are a common feature in many town and country gardens nowadays and provide the opportunity for growing a miscellany of plants, both edible and ornamental.

TYPES AND SIZES

Always go for the best greenhouse you can afford. It will cause less trouble in the long run, for blistering sun, winter rains, fog and internal humidity are punishing to all materials and ruinous to poor ones. If wood is used the timber must be well seasoned, otherwise employ teak or one of the other hardwoods.

The main points to look for are:
1. Quality of the timber, aluminium, etc., used in the main structure.
2. Good horticultural glass.
3. Sufficient ventilation, both along the ridge and sides, with convenient methods of opening same.
4. Gutters should be fitted and run into a tub or tank outside the house. Indoor tanks have been proved a bad source of infection for plant diseases.
5. Solid paths — concrete, stone slabs or bricks. It is not advisable to hard pave the whole floor as humidity is more readily maintained with soil under benches.

TYPES OF HOUSES

The three main types of greenhouse are:
1. *Span-roofed.* There are free-standing houses, with the glass running up both sides to a central ridge. The sides may rest on brick (usually up to 2 ft. 6 in.) or have glass down to floor level. Staging can be erected on one or both sides, with a central path, or along both sides and middle with paths all round the central stage. As light comes from both directions pot plants in particular grow more evenly in this type of house. Erect away from trees or buildings.
2. *Three-quarter Span.* This has one full side running towards the ridge, but the other has glass for only half its length — the rest consisting of brick wall. Good height is available towards the back (useful for tall plants and climbers), or tiered staging can be erected. This kind of house is popular for fruit (Peaches and Vines). It should preferably face south, west or south-west, so as to receive all possible light.
3. *Lean-to Greenhouse.* This type is usually attached to the side of a house or building and should face south, or west or south-west so as to receive plenty of light in winter and spring. Both this type and type 2 may need shading in summer.

HEATING

The quantity of heat required will to a great extent depend upon (*a*) facilities available, and (*b*) the kinds of plants it is intended to grow.

Thus, winter temperatures at night in the various types of houses will roughly conform to the following.

COLD HOUSE .... as temperature outside
COOL HOUSE .... 40–45° F.
TEMPERATE HOUSE ... 48–55° F.
STOVE HOUSE .... 60–65° F.

The main heating methods are:
1. *Water* — from a slow-burning boiler furnace, circulating round 3-or 4-inch pipes, varying in number according to the temperature required.
2. *Electricity.* Various methods including tubular heaters on the principle of the immersion heater.
3. *Gas.* Boiler outside, heating water in pipes inside.

Crewe Greenhouse   Robert Hall, Tonbridge

A small greenhouse   H. Smith

4. *Oil-fuelled boilers.*

5. *Paraffin Heaters.*

The ultimate choice will depend on personal preference, available fuel and comparative installation and maintenance costs.

STAGING

Staging upon which plants can stand may be made of slatted timber, sheets of corrugated asbestos sheeting (which does not rust) or slate. The last two should be covered with an inch of pea-sized shingle or granite chippings, which can be kept wet in summer, thus creating the damp, humid conditions which growing plants so enjoy.

CULTURAL ROUTINE

Methods of propagation, pricking out and potting are dealt with in the various sections devoted to seed and vegetative propagation, but the three main things to watch in the greenhouse are:

1. *Temperatures.* Apply air whenever possible, especially in the cool greenhouse. This applies even in winter, although the vents should always be shut tight in frosty weather.

249

2. *Light*. Plants require plenty of light during dark winter days. Young seedlings must also be kept close to the glass or they will become drawn and weak. Excessive sunlight in summer, however, can damage many plants, so these must be shaded with blinds, newspaper or a colour-wash on the glass.

3. *Watering*. Amounts must be carefully judged. An experienced grower knows that a damp, earthy smell in summer indicates good growing conditions, but a damp, fusty smell usually denotes over-watering; stale air, or diseased plants.

Lifting the pot or tapping the sides (of clay pots) with a tapping mallet (a bamboo cane with a small wooden head) are guides to the plant's requirements. If dry, the pot gives a ringing note; if wet, a dull thud. Heavy pots are wet, light ones are dry. Polythene pots require less watering than clay ones, because they are not porous.

DAMPING DOWN means watering the floor, paths and walls, usually in the early morning and possibly again at midday. This helps to promote an ideally warm humid atmosphere. Syringing with a fine spray is practised in spring and summer when the ventilation is full on, but not in winter, because moisture on the foliage at that time often causes disease or leaf drop.

HYGIENE is vital in all greenhouses. Pots and pans should be scrupulously clean, new loam for potting sterilised, tanks cleaned out periodically and the inside paint and woodwork scrubbed annually with a good insecticide, and occasionally repainted.

The exterior should be painted every three years (or oiled if of hardwood), locks and hinges regularly oiled and the glass cleaned.

THE PLANTS

The types of plants to grow will depend on the room available, temperatures and individual preference, but may include early seedlings, bulbs, doubtfully hardy plants from the garden for over-wintering, ornamental subjects and climbers.

Since most amateurs favour the cool greenhouse, with night temperatures around 45 °F. in winter, plants suitable for this type of structure have been chiefly considered in this chapter.

Climbing Plants

Many greenhouses can be made more interesting with a few climbing plants, though too dense a covering of creepers is undesirable, darkening the house and preventing light from reaching pot plants.

Most climbers do best in a soil bed and to this end the border should, if possible, be dug 2 ft. deep and filled with good soil (3 parts fibrous loam to one each of peat and sand, together with a little rotted manure). Plants should be tied in to keep them shapely and in place

250

Greenhouse with glass to floor level

Modern heat propagation, Humex Propagator

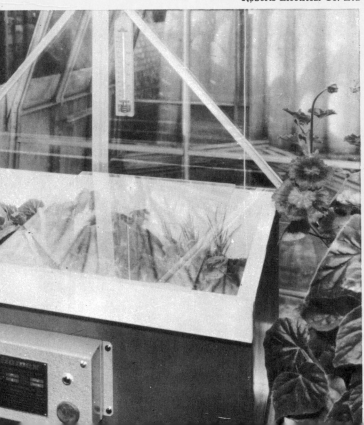

LIST OF GREENHOUSE CLIMBERS

(winter temperatures given in Fahrenheit)

ARISTOLOCHIA Dutchman's Pipe
A. sipho. Curious flowers with twisted tubes and wide corolla. Yellow and purple. 45°. Half-ripe cuttings July—Aug.

BOUGAINVILLEA
B. glabra sanderiana. Brightly coloured bracts, usually deep mauve. Rest in winter, start in Feb. 45°. Half-ripe cuttings in sandy soil.

CESTRUM
C. aurantiacum, evergreen, flowers in dense orange racemes. *C. purpureum,* reddish-purple. Prune hard in spring and summer. Free loamy soil. 45°. Half-ripe cuttings July-Aug.

CLERODENDRON Glory Bower, Bleeding Heart Vine
C. fragrans, heart-shaped leaves, fragrant white flowers. *C. thomsonae,* red and white chequered flowers. Grow over trellis or wire shapes in pots. Dryish soil. 60°. Cuttings.

COBAEA Cup and Saucer Plant
C. scandens. Mauve, bell-shaped flowers, oval leaves. Fairly rich soil. For arches and trellises. Annual, sow seed in spring.

HOYA Wax Flower, Porcelain Flower
H. carnosa. Evergreen, white and red waxen flowers. *H. bella,* purple and white. 40°—45°. Cuttings or layers.

IPOMAEA Syn. Pharbitis
I. rubro-caerulea, Morning Glory. Rich blue Convolvulus-like flowers, gone by evening. Seed. *I. learii,* Blue Dawn Flower. Evergreen, also blue. Cuttings. 45°.

JASMINUM
J. mesnyi. Yellow, tubular blooms, March—April; *J. polyanthum,* Chinese Jasmine, white scented flowers Feb.—March. In pots or planted out, well drained, rich soil. Spray with nicotine. 40°—45°. Cuttings of ripe wood.

LAPAGERIA Chile Bells
L. rosea. Large pink, waxen flowers. *L. rosea var. albiflora,* white flowers, evergreen leaves. Dislikes lime. Peaty acid soil. 45°. Layers or seed.

PASSIFLORA Passion Flower
Showy flowers, red, purple, blue and white. Deciduous are. *P. racemosa, P. x 'John Innes'.* Rapid growers, plenty of water in summer. Prune in spring. 50°. Seed, half-ripe cuttings.

PLUMBAGO Leadwort
P. capensis. Light blue summer flowers; also pink and white forms. Good rich soil. Prune hard in winter. 40°—45°. Cuttings.

RHODOCHITON Purple Bellvine
R. volubile Syn. *R. atrosanguineum.* Dark purple flowers, light purple calyces. Often blooms first year from seed. 50°.

SOLANUM
S. wendlandii, Costa Rican Nightshade. Showy mauve-blue flowers; *S. jasminoides,* Jasmine Nightshade, Potato Vine. White. Vigorous climber, cut back each year. 45°. Cuttings.

STEPHANOTIS Clustered Wax Flower
S. floribunda. Shining leaves, white, waxy, scented flowers. Rich compost. Prune back hard. 55°. Cuttings struck in heat.

STRETOSOLEN Yellow Heliotrope
S. jamesonii. Orange scarlet flowers all summer. Rich compost, well drained. 45°. Cuttings taken in sand under glass.

THUNBERGIA Black-eyed Clockvine
T. alata. Quick growing annual, heart-shaped leaves, masses of round flowers, variously coloured. Sow seed March—April. Syringe freely. Plenty of water in summer. Seed.

GREENHOUSE PLANTS

Name	Colour	Description	Remarks
Abutilon Indian Mallow *A. megapotamicum* 'Golden Fleece' 'Red Ashfold'	Red and gold Good yellow Gold Deep red	Summer flowering. Semi-shrubby with Sycamore-shaped leaves and hanging, bell-like flowers. Usually 2—4 ft.	Compost, equal parts loam, peat leaf-mould with some sand. Water freely. Cuttings in spring and summer.
A. striatum-thompsonii			
Acacia Mimosa *A. dealbata*	Yellow	Eventually small tree, winter flowering.	Rich soil, dislikes lime. Seed, half-ripe cuttings.
Achimenes Cupid's Bower *A. langiflora*	Purple and Mauve	Tubular summer flowers. About 1 ft.	Start tubers in sandy compost from Jan. Dry off after flowering. Division.
Ageratum *A. houstonianum*	Mauve-blue, white or rose	Summer flowering bedding plant. Few inches to 1 ft.	Sow autumn and early spring. Half-hardy annual.
Alonsoa Mask Flower *A. warscewiczii*	Brick red or scarlet	Bushy plant, June-autumn. Masses of flowers.	Sow Sept. Pinch tops for bushy plant.
Azalea Indian Azalea *A. indica*	Shades of pink, red and occasionally white	Winter flowering shrub, often used for house decoration.	Not hardy. Compost of peat and sand. Syringe to prevent leaf drop.
Begonia Tuberous Fibrous *A. semperflorens*	Pink to deep red, yellow, white Pink, red	Tuberous-rooted kinds have showy flowers, fibrous-rooted kinds masses of small flowers. Also many grown for foliage.	Tuberous kinds started in peat moss early in year. Seed or tubers. Fibrous kinds easier. Seed or cuttings.
Beloperone Shrimp Plant *B. guttata*	Pink and white	Summer flowering. Reddish-salmon bracts. 2—3 ft.	Good well drained soil. Summer cuttings.
Boronia *B. elatior* *B. heterophylla*	Rosy-pink Red	Summer flowering, fragrant flowers. Both 4—5 ft.	Loam, sand and peat. Spring cuttings.

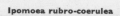

Ipomoea rubro-coerulea

J. E. Downward

Tuberous rooted Begonia

Cyclamen

Passiflora quadrangularis

Name	Colour	Description	Remarks
Browallia Amethyst *B. speciosa major*	Rich blue	Small, flat flowers covering plant Sept.—Oct.	Perennial, usually grown as annual. Seed.
Brunsfelsia Franciscan Nightshade *B. calycinum* Kiss-me-Quick	Purple-blue	Trusses of flowers, shining leaves. Long time in bloom.	Rich soil, humidity. Half-ripe cuttings. Stove.
Calceolaria Slipper Flower *C. x herbeo-hybrids* *C. x frutico-hybrids*	Coloured pouches, often spotted in various shades. Yellow, orange	Spring flowers, at best in May or June. Herbaceous types. Sticky leaves. Shrubby types, summer and autumn blooming.	Sow seed May—June on very fine soil. Final potting March. Cuttings struck in Aug. and Sept.
Callistemon Bottle Brush Plant *C. citrinus splendens*	Scarlet	Australian evergreen trees, flower heads resembling bottle brushes.	Light, sunny dry conditions. Live years in pots. Cuttings.
Campanula Bellflower *C. pyramidalis* *C. isophylla*	Blue or white Blue and white	Tall, stately plants; spikes up to 5 ft. Drooping plants; wide, saucer-shaped flowers.	Biennial. Sow seed May—June. Feed well. Good for hanging baskets. Cuttings.
Canna Indian Shot	Reds, oranges, yellows, many spotted	Fine broad leaves and large, spectacular summer flowers.	Fleshy roots, kept away from frost. Heavy soil and a little lime. Dry off in winter.
Celosia Cockscomb *C. cristata* *C. plumosa*	Mostly red Gold, red and yellow	Summer flowering with large, showy plumes of flowers. 9 in.	Sow seed in April. Use John Innes Compost. Likes humidity.
Celsia Cretan Bearstail *C. arcturus* *C. cretica*	Yellow with mauve anthers	Perennial. Biennial.	Sow seed Feb.—March for late summer blooms of July for spring.
Chrysanthemum Marguerite *C. frutescens*	White	2—3 ft. Yellow variety 'Comtesse de Chambord'.	Sow in Feb. Bed outside in May.

Name	Colour	Description	Remarks
Cineraria (Botanical name *Senecio cruentus*)	All shades of blue, pink and red	Spring plant, masses of Daisy flowers. Dwarf, tall, intermediate types.	Sow at intervals April—Aug. Loamy soil. Grow in cold frames but bring inside to bloom.
Clivia *C. miniata*	Orange-red	Spring flowering, fleshy rooted, strap-like blooms.	Loam, with very little peat. Seed or division. Plenty of water.
Coleus Flame Nettle *C. blumei* Painted Leaf *C. thyrsoideus* Bush Coleus *C. frederici*	Blue flowers Bright blue flowers	Grown chiefly for nettle-shaped, coloured foliage. Winter flowering species with fragrant leaves.	Foliage forms strike readily from cuttings any time; others from cuttings Feb.—March.
Columnea *C. G. B. banksii* *C. gloriosa* *C. glabra*	Scarlet or orange	Trailing plants with greyish-green or reddish small leaves, spectacular tubular flowers.	Two parts loam to one each sand and peat. Needs warmth and humidity. Cuttings.
Cyclamen Sow Bread *C. persicum*	White, pink, red, mauve	Winter and spring flowering. Back-turned flowers.	Sow seed Aug. Rich compost. Keep tubers.
Cytisus Genista *C. canariensis*	Yellow	Spring-flowering, bushy, Pea-shaped flowers.	Loamy soil, peat and sand. Cuttings.
Epacris Australian Heath *E. impressa* Erica Heath esp. *E. hyemalis*	White and pink	Useful for spring work. 3 ft. Bushy plants, brilliant Heather flowers. 1½—2 ft.	Buy as plants, pot on in peat and sand. Cuttings in spring. Ericas similar but hardier.
Erythrina Coral Tree *E. crista-galli*	Deep scarlet	3—5 ft. plant, large Pea-shaped flowers.	Rich loamy soil. Cuttings.
Eucomis Pineapple Flower *E. comosa*	Yellow and green	Summer flowering bulbous plants. Flowers have Pineapple tuft of leaves.	Pot new bulbs in spring and keep moist. Propagated by offsets.
Exacum *E. affine*	Mauve with gold eyes	Grown for powerful scent. Free flowering. 6 in.	Sow Feb.—April in sand and peaty soil.

Callistemon, Australian Bottle Brush Tree

Achimenes

Clerodendron thomsonae

Name	Colour	Description	Remarks
Francoa Bridal Wreath *F. ramosa*	White or pinkish	Summer and autumn flowering. 2—3 ft.	Sow seed June, flowers next summer.
Freesia *F. refracta*	Mauves, whites, yellows, reds, pinks, etc.	Fragrant plants, spring flowering, Newer varieties have double forms.	Pot bulbs Aug.—Sept. or raise from spring sown seed.
Fuchsia Lady's Eardrops *F. fulgens* (innumerable varieties)	Pink, red mostly; also white	Summer and autumn plants with hanging flowers. Can be trained as bedding plants, standards, etc.	Start in Feb. Feed and water well, keeping cool at all times. Soft or half ripe cuttings.
Gerbera Barberton Daisy *G. jamesonii*	Pink, red yellow	Summer flowering, Daisy-like flowers.	Dry, sunny conditions. Sow seed March.
Gloriosa Glory Lily *G. rothschildiana* *G. superba*	Brilliant scarlet and gold	Beautiful plant with tuberous roots and Lily-like flowers. Climber.	Repot tubers in spring in well drained soil. Increase by offsets.
Gloxinia (Botanical name *Sinningia speciosa*)	Red, pink, white, blue, purple, etc.	Summer flowering, velvety leaves, trumpet-shaped flowers. Many hybrids.	Start tubers March in boxes of leafy soil. Keep humid. Seed or division.
Godetia Farewell to Spring *G. amoena*	White, pink, crimson, red	Slender branching plant, satiny flowers.	Easily grown annual. Sow seed Sept.
Haemanthus Blood Lily *H. coccineus* *H. katherinea*	Scarlet Red	Bulbous plants. *H. coccineus* has brush-like flower, *H. katherinea* circular.	Sandy compost. Liquid manure while growing. Offsets.
Hedychium Ginger Lily *H. gardnerianum* *H. coronarium*	Yellow White	Robust plant, fleshy rhizomes, broad leaves, sticky flowers. 4—5 ft.	Good loamy soil. Divide and pot early in year. Dryish in winter.
Heliotrope Cherry Pie (Botanical name *Heliotropium peruvianum*)	Lavender-purple	Fragrant shrub, summer and autumn flowering. Can be trained as standard.	Summer cuttings, potted in Sept. Feed well, repot in spring.

Name	Colour	Description	Remarks
Hippeastrum Amaryllis Lily Varieties of *H. equestre*	Crimson, red and pink shades, white	Winter and spring flowering bulbous plants, trumpet-shaped flowers.	Start in Feb. Sun essential. Loamy soil. Offsets or seed.
Hydrangea *H. macrophylla*	All shades	Summer blooming shrubs, massive flower heads.	Summer-struck cuttings, individually rooted.
Hymenocallis Spider Lily *H. calathina* Lily Basket	White	Spring flowering bulb, tubular flowers, fragrant.	Well drained soil. Dry in winter. Division.
Impatiens Water Fuchsia *I. sultanii* Busy Lizzie and vars. *I. hostii* Snap Weed	Carmine, pink, etc. Scarlet	Good window plants, in flower for weeks. Masses of flat flowers, soft smooth leaves.	Loamy soil plenty of light and water in summer. Grow from cutting or raise from seed.
Isoloma syn. *Kohleria* *I. erianthum*	Bright scarlet	Beautiful plants with tubular flowers, plushy leaves and stems.	Peat, little loam and sand. Shade from bright sun.
Jacobinia *J. coccinea* *J. pohliana*	Flesh pink Pinkish-red	Clusters of tubular flowers Sept.—Oct. Opposite entire leaves.	Good loamy compost. Take young shoots March—April as cuttings.
Kalanchoe *K. blossfeldiana* *K. flammea*	Scarlet	Succulent plants with vivid clusters of blooms. Spring flowering. 1 ft.	Sow seed in March or strike Cuttings. Do not shade.
Lantana *L. camara* varieties	Usually two shades, white-gold, pink-gold, etc.	Small, compact Verbena-like flowers. 'Cloth of Gold' is yellow, 'Chelsoni' red, 'Delicatissima' violet.	Loamy soil and airy, sunny house. Fairly dry in winter. Seed or cuttings.
Nepenthes Pitcher Plant various species	Flowers insignificant	Green, cream and red fly-catching pitchers at ends of leaves.	Grow in slatted baskets. Cuttings, seed.
Nerium Oleander *N. oleander*	Pink also white, cream	Shrubby evergreen with masses of summer flowers.	Grow in large pots. Late summer cuttings.

Fuchsia   H. Smith   **Isoloma erianthum**

Lantanas   **Strelitzia reginae**   Copyright Samuel Dobie & Son

Name	Colour	Description	Ramarks
Pelargonium Geranium	Reds, whites and pinks	Main groups *Zonal*, blooming all year if warm; *Ivy-leaved*, trailing habit; *Scented-leaved* and *Regal or Show*.	Soil on heavy side, not too large pots. All propagated by cuttings, usually late summer.
Pentapterygium Syn. *Agapetes* *P. serpens*	Red, yellow or white with spots	Attractive plan with oval, opposite leaves and lantern-shaped flowers.	Well drained soil. Pots or hanging baskets. Cuttings.
Petunia	Various	Summer flowering, with trumpet-shaped flowers.	Pinch for bushy plants. Seed or cuttings.
Primula Primrose *P. obconica* *P. malacoides* *P. sinensis* syn. *P. stellata* *P. x kewensis*	Mauve Pink to red, mauve and white Yellow	Mostly spring blooming. Sow March—May. Sow June. Sow April—May. Sow March.	Bring in Sept. Bring in Nov. Bring in Sept. Bring in Oct.
Rehmannia *R. angulata*	Rosy-pink	Large flowers, like Foxgloves. Toothed leaves.	Treat as biennial. Sow in May. Heavyish soil.
Saintpaulia African Violet *S. ionantha*	White, pink, red, mauve	Masses of small, flat flowers. Velvety leaves.	Peaty soil. Keep warm. Leaf cuttings or seed.
Schizanthus Butterfly Flower *S. pinnatus* Poor Man's varieties Orchid	All shades	Spring flowering plants, multicoloured Orchid-like flowers.	Sow seed Aug.—Sept. Keep well ventilated and cool.
Solanum Winter Cherry *S. capsicastrum*	White flowers, scarlet berries	Grown for round berries about Christmas. 1—2 ft.	Sow Feb.—March or use cuttings. Loamy soil.
Sparrmania African Hemp *S. africana*	White, with gold anthers	Evergreen shrub, large leaves, summer flowers.	Open soil with some peat. Half-ripe cuttings.

Name	Colour	Description	Remarks
Sprekelia Jacobean Lily *S. formosissima*	Crimson or white	Bulbous plant, with showy Orchid-like flowers.	Cultivate as for Hippeastrum.
Strelitzia Bird of Paradise *S. regina* Flower or Crane Plant	Bright blue and gold	Flowers like head of tropical bird. Up to 5 ft.	Loamy soil. Suckers, started with bottom heat.
Streptocarpus Cape Primrose *S. x hybridus* *S. wendlandii*	Pink white, mauve. Mauve	Like Gloxinias but smaller flowers, long leaves. Showy flowers, one leaf.	Sow seed Jan. or July. Keep moist and shaded. Leaf cuttings.
Torenia *T. fournieri*	Blue with yellow throat	Summer flowering. Pansy-coloured flowers.	Annual. Sow March.
Trachelium Cloud Plant *T. coeruleum*	Mauve or white	June—July. Masses of cobwebby flowers. 2—4 ft.	Sow seed June. Loamy soil.
Tulbaghia *T. violacea*	Purplish-violet	Narrow leaves and umbels of small flowers.	Sandy loam and peat. Offsets or seed.
Vallota *V. speciosa* Scarborough Lily	Bright red	Blooms late summer, trumpet-shaped flowers.	Loamy soil. Keep moist in winter. Offsets.
Zantedeschia Arum Lily *Z. aethiopica* *Z. elliotiana* Calla Lily *Z. rehmanni*	White Golden Rose	Large Arum flowers with golden centre, polished, heart-shaped leaves.	Lift plants and divide Sept. Repot (4 loam, 1 peat, ½ sand and some dried manure.

Hymenocallis, the Spider Lily
Walter Blom & Son

Hibiscus x archeri

In addition the following bulbs and plants are particularly recommended for cool house display. They should be grown in pots. For further details see under the appropriate headings; bulbs, annuals, etc. Agapanthus, Antirrhinum, Bartonia, Calendula, Camellia, Carnations, Chrysanthemum, Clarkia, Crocus, forms of Hyacinths, Iris (bulbous kinds), Lachenalia, Lilium, Mignonette, Narcissus, Nemesia, Nerine, Nicotiana, Roses, Salpiglossis, Salvia, Tulip, Verbena, Zinnia.

Bog & Water Plants

Most of the world's great gardens use water in their settings, for many obvious reasons. It is beautiful in its own right, with an ever-changing surface varying with the moods of the weather. The dripping waterfall or murmuring stream brings music to the garden; the charms of waterside plantings are enhanced by reflections; and, most important of all, water makes it possible for gardeners to grow some of the world's most interesting and beautiful plants.

A large garden is not essential for water plants, but for success three things are vital:
1. Full sunshine. Water plants live but rarely flower in shade.
2. Water which is not too deep. Excessive depth checks flowering.
3. Suitable compost. If this contains too much organic material, cloudy or green water will result.

TYPES OF PONDS

Any receptacle capable of holding water may be looked upon as a potential water garden.

For construction purposes, however, the chief media are:
1. Concrete, suitable for formal or informal shapes, raised or sunken.
2. Prefabricated pools of aluminium, fibreglass and similar materials.
3. Polythene sheeting.

ROCK AND WATER GARDENING

When constructing a rock and water garden it is advisable to start with the pool. Excavated material can then be used for the higher ridges of the rock

Iris pseudacorus var. variegata

Nymphaea chromatella

garden. Formal pools, too, should be built before tackling the lawn or other near-by features.

Choose an open position for the water garden, protected if possible towards the north and east by some form of screen, such as a belt of trees, a hedge, a wall or part of the house. Even a solitary tree or a bank will afford some protection against icy winds in early spring.

Shape and size of the pool is an individual matter, and may largely be dictated by circumstances. A conventional shape with bold, stone-slab sides is desirable for a formal water garden laid out with straight paths and geometrical beds, whereas informality should be the keynote in a rock garden. Here, the pool — or series of pools — should fit in unobtrusively and naturally with the rock surrounds.

Nymphaea marliacea rosea

Tropical Water-lily, N. stellata

The deep central part where fish and Water-lilies live, however, should always be made to conventional shape. This part must be completely watertight, and straight or slightly sloping sides ensure this condition. A marginal trough can be constructed later round the inner portion, if informality is desired. If the outer walls of the trough are left an inch higher than the walls of the central section the water will flood over to the outer extremities, and the pool's final contours will be those of the trough. A shallow surround also makes the pool look much larger, and requires less labour and materials.

The Cement and Concrete Association issue some excellent leaflets on pond construction. Ready-mixed concrete is a boon to the busy gardener and often procurable from a local builder.

The central part should be excavated to a depth of 2 ft. 6 in., and 6 in. of concrete will be needed for a good watertight job. Water-lily roots will require about 6 in. of compost, thus leaving 18 in. of water, ample for most hardy Lilies and deep enough to protect the fish and prevent a complete freeze-up in winter. The main thing is to ensure a minimum thickness of 6 in. for the floor and walls of the deep parts of the pool, and 4 in. for the marginal trough.

New concrete is poisonous to plants and animals due to the presence of free lime. If the pool is kept filled with water for several months most of this will seep out and be rendered harmless. Then the pond can be emptied, rinsed and made ready for planting.

Before planting new pools, however, chemical measures must be adopted to neutralise the harmful effects of the lime alkalis. Commercial syrupy phosphoric acid, applied in sufficient quantities, twice in twenty-four hours, to give an *acid* reaction to litmus paper, is the best antidote to alkalinity. Waterproofing materials can also be bought which seal the pores, and render the concrete harmless as well as watertight.

DRAINAGE

This must be considered while the pond is under construction. Bailing is a labourious method, while siphoning is only possible when there is a lower level near the pool into which the water can run.

There are a number of pumps on the market which either eject the water into a ditch or drain, or, in the case of a rock garden, set off streams or waterfalls and then pump it back so that the same liquid is used over and over again.

Building an outlet during construction is a wise precaution. A length of drainpipe should be cast into the concrete near the base of the pond, leading down to a ditch or sump. A stopcock should be fitted near

A prefabricated pool sunk in position W. & R. Perry

by, enclosed in a small brick or stone chamber, to be operated by a removable long-arm key. The top of the chamber may either be finished with an iron cover, or disguised, with, say, a loose paving stone.

In the absence of a ditch or land drain (to which the pipes can be connected) a drainage sump must be constructed. This need not be far from the pool and will consist of a pit dug *at least 3 ft. deep* and approximately 3 ft. square, and filled practically to the top with clinkers. The drainpipe will run into it, and the pit should then be filled to ground level with soil. Very large pools may require more than one sump.

PREFABRICATED POOLS

These are available in a variety of shapes and materials, including fibreglass. They are light, easily handled, and may be set in place and planted in

Planting pockets for Lilies and other aquatics W. & R. Perry

tageous to line the shell with moist sand) and then spread the polythene sheeting.

Use stout material for the purposes, preferably 1,000 gauge, but not less than 500 gauge, and conceal the edges by burying them under 6 in. of soil or with rocks or paving stones. Fill the pool with water and introduce the Water-lilies and other aquatics in baskets or pots.

Polythene pools will last years if carefully treated, but two important factors should be remembered:
1. Never use sharp tools in their vicinity — a leak cannot be repaired.
2. Always keep them brim-full of water. The sun striking on polythene weakens the fabric, and leaking may result.

PLANTING SEASON

Water-lilies, Aponogetons, Nuphars and other tuberous-rooted aquatics are best moved between the end of March and early June, when growth is just commencing. This is also the best time to move marginal or shallow water aquatics. Underwater plants and floaters may be moved at any time during the spring and summer months, and waterside plants in the spring or early autumn.

Compost

For Water-lilies and tuberous-rooted aquatics use heavy, fibrous loam, stacked until the plant roots and organic material have rotted away. Add to its bulk one sixth of decayed cow-manure or coarse bonemeal, the latter at the rate of half a pint to each 2-gallon bucket of loam.

Avoid leafmould, peat, spent hops, artificial fertilisers or other types of animal manures or compost if you wish the water to remain clear. For marginal aquatics use plain loam.

Waterside plants (above water level) should be provided with a rich vegetable compost. Add peat, leafmould, sand and rotted manure or compost to the original soil to improve moisture and food content.

Planting

Use the compost in a wetter condition than is usual for potting, so that it sticks to the hands. Plant Water-lilies in baskets or in containers with holes in the sides, rather than in completely closed receptacles.

Trim the plants beforehand, removing any unwanted rhizome and the old anchorage roots. These are white, thick and fleshy, whereas young feeding rootlets are slender and covered with black root hairs.

Plant very firmly with the crown of the Lily exposed, or in the case of the *odorata* and *tuberosa* Water-lilies (which have rhizomes like a bearded

A polythene pool, showing material in place and being covered with soil
British Visqueen Ltd

a matter of hours. Some even have punched-out planting holes to take the larger aquatics. The main drawback with many is lack of depth and insufficient provision for the marginal aquatics. 9 in. is a minimum depth, and marginal and Lily pockets *must* have a ledge all round to hold the soil in position.

There is little point in having a pale, painted lining, as algae and debris inevitably turn all pools to a uniformly murky shade. Black is the most practical colour as it is cooler in summer, warmer in winter, and also looks more natural.

In any case, site the pool in an open sunny position and test it carefully with a spirit level before planting.

POLYTHENE POOLS

This is the cheapest method of pool-making and has much to commend it. Simply excavate the area to the required shape and depth (or series of depths), remove any prominent stones or sharply pointed obstacles (in very stony ground it may be advan-

Nymphaea 'Sunrise'

Caltha palustris plena

Cotton Grass

way, with the roots spread out. These need a soil which will not dry out, yet will not become water-logged.

AFTERCARE

1. Keep the pond filled with water all the time, especially in winter.
2. Remove scum on the surface either by flooding it over or by drawing a newspaper across the top of the water.
3. Remove dead leaves and flowers, and never let seedlings develop indiscriminately.
4. Do not over-feed the fish. This may cause water discoloration. Feed always in the same place and only give as much at one time as can be consumed

Iris), with the tops of the rhizomes running horizontally and just showing above the soil. Drop the baskets very carefully into the pond and prop them on bricks so that the Lilies are *only just below* the surface. This is most important. If plunged to their full depth immediately they may rot away before making new roots. The same applies to plants put into soil which is actually spread over the base of the pool. Run in sufficient water afterwards barely to cover the crowns, and only raise the level when new growth becomes apparent. It may take six or eight weeks to fill the pool by this method, but it ensures the safety of the Lilies and usually encourages flowers the first season.

Other aquatics may be planted in similar fashion, except that submerged oxygenators can either be dibbled into pans or boxes, or weighted with strips of lead or stones and dropped into position. Floaters are simply placed on the surface of the water.

Waterside perennials are planted in the normal

in 5 minutes. Cease feeding entirely between December and March.
5. Use Goldfish and Golden Orfe for preference, as they are easily seen and keep close to the surface. Many fish (especially Tench and Carp) remain at the bottom of the pond and constantly stir up the mud.
6. Never let any single type of aquatic get out of hand. Those with underground creeping rootstocks will, if unchecked, take over a pond in a few years. Watch particularly Glyceria, Typha, Water Forget-me-Nots and certain under-water oxygenators.
7. In winter leave a rubber ball or block of wood floating in one corner. When ice forms, pour boiling water over the ball and lift it out. This keeps a hole open for the fish. Breaking the ice with a hammer is liable to injure them. If frost persists, bail out some of the water and throw a sack over the hole, thus protecting fish and plants as with a 'greenhouse light'. Refill the pond directly a thaw sets in.

8. It takes eighteen months or two years for a new pool to settle, so that green water may give trouble in the early days. This is caused by myriads of small plants — called *algae* — which feed on the dissolved mineral salts in the water but need abundant light in order to reproduce. Remedial measures comprise:

(*a*) *Cutting down light*. Normally performed by the floating leaves of Lilies and marginal aquatics. Artificial shading with hurdles, etc., may sometimes be helpful.

(*b*) *Reducing the flow of mineral salts*. Best ensured by using the right compost — free from fibre and organic material.

(*c*) *Providing competition*. Plenty of underwater vegetation is the answer here. Plant Anacharis, Lagarosiphon and *Potamogeton crispus* in good quantities. They can always be thinned out later. There are chemical means of control, but poisons are risky and misuse may easily destroy the ornamental plants and fish. Also the build-up of chemicals affects the water for months. Daphnia (Water Fleas) will clear a pond in forty-eight hours, but the method is not very practical as fish eat them on sight.

9. Fish must be introduced to ornamental waters to keep down mosquitoes. The plants must be established first, however, so as a general rule allow six to eight weeks to elapse between planting and adding the fish.

10. Never let leaves from trees drift into a pond. Laburnum and Walnut, for example, are poisonous, but all leaves are organic and charge the water with salts during their breakdown. Trap them with a roll of wire netting stretched across the pond at the end of September or dredge them out as they fall.

The floating Water Hyacinth

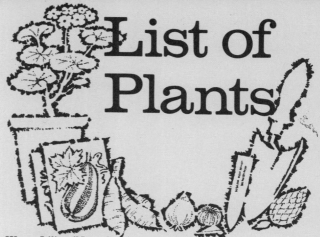

List of Plants

Water Lilies (Nymphaea)

Very widely distributed plants, all countries except New Zealand having their representative species. Much variation in colour (white, flesh pink, rose, crimson, red, yellow, copper, orange, light and dark blue, and mauve) also in size, with flowers varying from 1 to 12 in., and habit — either floating on the water or standing several inches above it. Some bloom by day, others at night, some have plain leaves, others attractively mottled foliage.

The blue varieties are not hardy and have rounded, tuberous rootstocks which dry bulb-like in their native habitats. They must be grown under glass in Britain and stored away from frost in winter. Other species have rhizomatous rootstocks (*Nymphaea odorata* and *N. tuberosa*), or downward pointing, Celery-like rootstocks (e. g. the British species *N. alba*).

When selecting varieties it is important to choose from the group within the depth range of your own pool.

Water Lilies for Deep Water

Depth 2—2½ ft.; surface area 6 feet square.
'Albatross', white; 'Attraction', large garnet-red; 'Colonel Welch', strong grower, yellow, not too free flowering; 'Escarboucle', large, deep dark red; 'Gladstoniana', very large white, golden stamens; 'Marliacea albida', white, fragrant and very free; 'Marliacea rosea', fine shape, rose-pink, paler towards centre; 'Picciola', large, amaranth-crimson; *tuberosa rosea*, N. American, fragrant, soft pink, strong grower.

Water Lilies for Medium Pools

Depth 15—20 in.; surface area 4—6 feet square.
'Brakleyi rosea', very fine rose-pink, fragrant 'Conqueror', red, flecked white. 'Gloriosa', large red, very free; 'Indiana', orange red deepening with age to copper red, spotted foliage; 'James Brydon', one of the best; squat, deep carmine-red flowers sitting flat on the water, extremely free; 'Loose', fragrant white flowers standing above the water; 'Marliacea chromatella', soft Primrose-yellow, fine shape, fragrant, mottled foliage; 'Masaniello' globular, fragrant, deep rose; 'Richardsoni', white, cup-shaped, fragrant, very prolific; 'Rose Nymph', fragrant, deep rich rose; 'Sunrise', the deepest yellow, mottled leaves; 'Virginalis', snow-white; 'Wm. Falconer', deepest' in colour, dark crimson.

Water Lilies for Small Pools, Tubs and Prefabricated Ponds

Depth 9—12 in.; surface area 2 feet square.
Caroliniana, soft rose, fragrant; 'Comanche', rosy-apricot, deepening to copper red; 'Laydekeri fulgens', crimson, 'L. lilacea', soft rose, and 'L. purpurata', crimson spotted white, all very free, with dozens of blooms in a season; 'Paul Hariot', open apricot-yellow changing through orange to pink to orange-red.

Water Lilies for Bowls and Rock Pools

A few inches of water only.
'Pygmaea alba', white, deep green leaves; 'P. helvolva', soft yellow, mottled foliage; 'P. rubis', rosy-red.

Other Water Plants for Deep Water

APONOGETON Water Hawthorn

A. distachyon Tuberous roots, floating, strap-shaped leaves and fragant, forked white flowers with jet-black anthers. In bloom all summer. Suitable for various depths (6 in. to 18. in.) but must have sunshine. *A. krausseanum* is less hardy and has uniformly coloured, creamy flilowers on forked spikes held 4—6 in. above the water. Only suitable for very shallow, warm pools.

NUPHAR Pond Lily

Strong growing, Water-lily-like plants with fine foliage but inferior flowers, strong smelling, usually deep golden. Underwater leaves waved and crimped, surface foliage broadly heart-shaped. Will grow in very deep, shaded or running water. The best kinds are *N. advena* and *N. japonicum var. rubrotinctum.*

NYMPHOIDES Water Fringe

N. peltata is like a small Water-lily with round, floating chocolate-blotched leaves about 2 in. across and three-petalled golden-yellow flowers. Very adaptable, spreads rapidly but easily kept in check.

SHALLOW WATER OR MARGINAL

Unless otherwise stated, all require shallow water, 1—2 in. over the roots and are increased by division.

ACORUS Sweet Flag

A. calamus var. variegata is the best form, with variegated foliage, and flowers, resembling brown cattle horns, situated near the tops of the leaves. Root and leaves very aromatic when bruised, secreting oil used in perfumery. 2—3 ft. July.

ANEMOPSIS

A. californica has an aromatic rootstock, heart-shaped leaves and small Anemone-like white flowers. 12—15 in. Wet ground. July.

BUTOMUS Flowering Rush

B. umbellatus is a British plant with triangular, long, bronze-green leaves and showy umbels of rose-pink flowers. 2 ft. Summer.

CALLA Bog Arum

C. palustris is a scrambling plant very useful for masking the pond edge, as it is equally happy in shallow water or wet mud. Leaves shiny-green, heart-shaped; white flowers like small Arums, followed by red berries. 9 in. June.

CALTHA Kingcup; Marsh Marigold

Invaluable for their early flowers (April). *C. palustris* is a native plant with heart-shaped leaves and large, golden, Buttercup-like flowers. Its variety *plena*, with full double flowers, is perhaps the best; *C. leptosepala* is white. 1 ft.; *C. polypetala* is later (May—June) and taller, with branching stems. 3 ft. This last species increases from runners and has to be kept in check.

DECODON Water Willow

D. verticillatus is a shrubby aquatic with Willow-like leaves and purple, Evening Primrose-like flowers. In autumn the foliage turns scarlet. 3 ft.

DRACOCEPHALUM Dragon's Head

D. palustre has Salvia-like flowers, rose-pink. 12—15 in. July—Aug.

ECHINODORUS

E. ranunculoides A British native with narrow leaves, tapering at each end, and terminal heads of rosy-white flowers. 12 in. May—July.

ERIOPHORUM Cotton Grass

Shallow water plants with showy silky cotton seed heads in summer and autumn. *E. latifolium* and *E. angustifolium* are the best. 10—12 in.

Calla palustris, Bog Arum

GLYCERIA Manna Grass

G. aquatica var. variegata (Syn. *G. spectabilis*) An attractive grass with cream-striped leaves, rosy pink, when young. Inclined to spread. 1½—2 ft.

HOUTTUYNIA

H. cordata is a marginal subject for bog or shallow water with small white flowers, a protruding centre like Rudbeckia and bluish-green, heart-shaped foliage. 18 in. July.

IRIS

Among the truly aquatic Irises *I. laevigata* stands supreme, with handsome foliage and rich blue flowers, the lower petals marked with gold. 2 ft. Plant in 2—4 in. of water. Varieties include *alba*, white; 'Rose Queen', pink; 'Colchesteri', blue and white; and 'Regal', rich royal purple. June—July, occasionally late summer. *I. pseudacorus* is the Yellow Flag, supposedly the original of the French fleur-de-lis, with stately sword-shaped foliage and bright golden blooms. *var. variegata* with gold striped leaves is the better garden plant. 2—3 ft. June—July.

JUNCUS Rush

A large family of mostly weedy plants of little horticultural value. Exceptions are J. *effusus var. aurea-striatus* and *var. spiralis*. The former has smooth round rushy stems, each marked with a longitudinal golden bar, the latter grows spirally, like a corkscrew. 1—2 ft.

MENYANTHES Bog Bean

M. trifoliata is a scrambling plant like *Calla palustris*, with the same uses. The leaves, however, are divided into three, Clover-like, and the flowers — pink and white with fringed petals — grow in clusters. 6—9 in. May—July.

MYOSOTIS

M. palustris, the Water Forget-me-not, with bright blue florets in early summer. Suitable for shallow water or wet mud. The variety 'Mermaid' is the best. 6—8 in. Seed or cuttings.

ORONTIUM Water Club

O. aquaticum, an aroid with large fleshy roots, needing a good depth of soil, has large silvery leaves, heavily coated with wax. The white spadix is attractively studded with small yellow flowers. Suitable for 4—12 in. of water (when the leaves float) or deep mud (when the leaves stand upright). 1—3 ft. July.

PONTEDERIA Pickerel Weed

P. cordata, one of the most popular and dependable marginal aquatics, has smooth heart-shaped leaves and spikes of soft blue flowers. 1½—2 ft. All summer.

RANUNCULUS

R. lingua grandiflora is the Great Spearwort, with very large, Buttercup-like flowers on branching stems, and neat strap-like leaves. Needs to be kept under control. 2—3 ft. Late spring and summer.

SAGITTARIA Arrow-head

A large family characterised by spikes of three-petalled, usually pure-white flowers and handsome arrow-shaped foliage. *S. sagittifolia var. japonica plena* is the only one recommended for the water garden for, unlike most of the species, it never gets out of hand. Flowers very handsome, fully double, like a Brompton Stock. 2 ft. Summer.

SAURURUS Swamp Lily

S. cernuus has bright green, heart-shaped leaves and 4—6 in. spikes of nodding, fragrant, creamy-white flowers; *S. chinensis* is very similar and known as Lizard's Tail due to shape of flower spikes. 12—16 in. Summer.

Aponogeton distachyon, Water Hawthorn

Aponogeton krauseanum   W. & R. Perry

Iris kaempferi growing in Japan

SCIRPUS Bulrush

This is the true Bulrush with fat round rushes, although the common name is often used to refer to the Typha (*below*) *S. lacustris var. zebrirus* is a fine waterside perennial, the rushes horizontally barred in green and white, it is often known as Porcupine Quill or Zebra Rush; *var. albescens* is similar, except that the stripes run longitudinally. 2—4 ft.

THALIA

T. dealbata is a stately aquatic which unfortunately can only be grown outside in warm climates. Alternatively, pot plants may be plunged at the poolside in summer, lifted in September and stood (reasonably dry) in a frostproof house for winter. Leaves glaucous, strongly ribbed on long stems (3—5 ft.), somewhat resembling Canna. Flowers purple on arching stems. Late summer and autumn.

TYPHA Reedmace

Often erroneously called 'Bulrush' on account of the brown, poker-like heads of flowers. Leaves sword-shaped. The majority spread so quickly from seed and underground stolon roots that they soon become a menace in small pools. Avoid planting any but *T. minima*, with diminutive poker heads on 12-in. stems or *T. laxmanni*, with very narrow leaves and 3—4-ft. flower stems.

FLOATING AQUATICS

The chief importance of floating plants is their ability to cast shade and provide sanctuary for the myriads of small creatures which inhabit a natural pond.

Unfortunately, under favourable conditions, the majority spread at an alarming rate (witness the menace of Salvinia in the Kariba Dam), so some sorts — such as Lemna (Duckweed) — must be rigorously excluded. Several mentioned below are not hardy and therefore present no problems in countries which normally experience winter frosts. Instead it is necessary to preserve stock from year to year by over-wintering a few plants in shallow pans of loam and water in a frostproof place.

Azolla, Hydrocharis morsus ranae (Frogbit) and *Stratiotes aloides* (Water Soldier) are all hardy, but disappear in winter, forming winter buds or turions which lie at the bottom of the pool until spring. The spectacular Water Soldier has spiky heads of foliage resembling, and about the size of, a Pineapple top, lying just under the water but coming to the top to flower. The blooms are white and rather small.

Among the tropical kinds *Eichhornia crassipes major* (Water Hyacinth) and *Nymphoides indica* (Water Snowflake) are the most attractive. The former has tough, heart-shaped leaves arranged in a rosette and supported on the water surface by the swollen, spongy, leaf stalks, which resemble sausages more than stems. Flowers are pale blue, with conspicuous peacock-eye

with Holly-like floating leaves upheld by swollen, air-filled footstalks. Seed is only set in warm summers or under glass.

The Water Poppy, *Hydrocleys commersonii*, is a spectacular aquatic, but not hardy, and must be grown under glass in Britain. It produces bright golden, Poppy-like flowers in great profusion, the leaves being fleshy, dark green and round to oval.

SUBMERGED AQUATICS

As already suggested, the chief use of submerged aquatics in an ornamental pool is to maintain water

Day Lilies make good waterside plants

Hydrocleys commersonii, Water Poppy

markings, and borne on showy spikes. Long black roots hang down into the water and form a favourite nursery for fish eggs and fry.

Although Water Hyacinths can be grown outside in summer, they flower better under glass. They are best over-wintered by packing several plants in a bowl of soil with very little water, keeping this in a light but frostproof place until June. Reproduction takes place by means of runners in the same manner as the Strawberry.

The Water Snowflake is a dainty little plant with small round leaves and delightful fringed white flowers. The leaf-stalks support it in the Water. Very suitable for bowl culture.

Trapa natans is an annual, often called the Water Chestnut on account of the edible qualities of its large spiny seeds. These lie at the bottom of the pool all winter and germinate in spring to trailing stems,

clarity. They also — through the process of photosynthesis — take carbon dioxide from the water and replace it with oxygen, a vital operation for the animal life in the pond. The dense leafy masses provide nurseries where fish can lay their eggs and hiding places for the young fry on hatching, as well as sanctuaries for many small water creatures which sooner or later form food for fish.

They should be planted freely, especially in the pond's early years. If growth becomes too prolific, they can easily be thinned. The most important point to watch is that they do not too tightly enmesh the Water-lilies.

The best oxygenators and most attractive species for a small pool are:
Anacharis canadensis, Canadian Pond Weed; *Hottonia palustris*, the Water Violet, with spikes of mauve flowers above the water in June; *Lagarosiphon major*

(Syn. *Elodea crispa*), perhaps the best; all the Milfoils or Myriophyllum species; *Potamogeton crispus*, Frog's Lettuce, and *Ranunculus aquatilis*, the Water Crowfoot, with small white and gold flowers in spring.

WATERSIDE OR BOG PLANTS

These must never have their roots in water or they will rot and die; their needs are a rich, moist soil which never dries out. Their main use in the garden is to link the water with the land, and for best effects plants should be grouped in bold clumps.

The majority favour plenty of sunshine and benefit from occasional top dressings of rotted manure or compost. Most of the plants mentioned are best established in spring and nearly all are propagated by spring division. Many are more fully described in the chapter on Herbaceous Plants.

ACONITUM Monkshood
Helmet-shaped flowers on tall spikes and dark green, much cut leaves. For details of cultivation and kinds see p. 25.

AJUGA Bugle
Ground carpeting plants which help to keep ground moist. See p. 26.

ANAGALLIS Pimpernel
A. tenella Bog Pimpernel. Attractive little plant for damp place with bell-shaped, rosy-pink flowers and small opposite leaves.

Eichhornia crassipes, Water Hyacinth   Wilh. Schacht

It is an annual, which if left alone soon establishes a little colony. 2—4 in. Summer.

ARUNCUS Goat's Beard
A. sylvester (syn. *Spiraea aruncus*). Impressive plant with deeply cut, Spiraea-like foliage and heavy plumes of creamy-white flowers, *var. kneiffii* has more finely cut foliage. May remain years in same situation. 4 ft. June.

ARUNDINARIA Bamboos
The hardy Bamboos are most impressive at the waterside and make good windbreaks. They need free watering during their first season. Other genera, coming under the general heading of Bamboo include Sasa, Pseudosasa, Pleioblastus and Phyllostachys, and may vary in height from 1 to 10 ft. All are evergreen (although the leaves may be cut in a very severe winter) with narrow or broadly grassy foliage. They rarely flower, and if they do usually die afterwards.

ASCLEPIAS Milkweed
A. incarnata has umbels of flesh-pink flowers and grey-green fleshy leaves. Stem contains a milky juice. 3 ft. July—Aug.

ASTILBE False Goat's Beard
Important perennials for pondside planting, which associate particularly well with Hemerocallis, Iris and Primulas. The roots always remain close to the surface so need frequent mulches to retain the moisture. See also p. 29.

ASTRANTIA Masterwort
A. carniolica. Quaint plant with Buttercup-like leaves and round heads of white or pinkish flowers set off by ring of green and white bracts. 1 ft. July—Aug.

BRUNNERA See p. 29.

BUPHTHALMUM Ox Eye
B. speciosum syn. (Telekia speciosa) is a vigorous perennial with large, golden, shaggy-petalled 'Daisy' flowers and big, heart-shaped leaves. Needs careful placing as liable to smother smaller neighbours. 3—4 ft. July—Sept.

CAMASSIA Quamash
One of the few bulbous plants suitable for the bog garden. For details of cultivation see p. 89.

CARDAMINE Lady's Smock
C. pratensis, Cuckoo Flower or Lady's Smock of damp meadows, with slender spikes of lilac flowers. Its double form *flore-pleno* is most attractive subject for water garden. 1 ft. April—May.

CIMICIFUGA Bugbane
Useful for late flowers and suitable for drier parts of bog garden. See also p. 30.

EUPATORIUM Hemp Agrimony
Good bold perennials for rougher parts of the bog garden. See p. 33.

FILIPENDULINA See p. 33.

GUNNERA
Perhaps the largest leaved land plant, with enormous, Rhubarb-like foliage 10 ft. by 7 ft. across on thick spiny stems, growing 8—10 ft. tall. Flowers resemble gigantic bottle brushes and on yard-long stems carry hundreds of greenish-brown flowers. *G. manicata* is most impressive but only suitable for a large garden; needs plenty of water in summer.

Rheum palmatum   H. Smith

Gunnera manicata, largest leaved land plant
By courtesy of Home Magazine

HEMEROCALLIS Day Lily

Indispensable for water garden and happy associate of Astilbes, Iris and Trollius. See p. 34.

HOSTA See p. 35 and 201

INULA See p. 35.

IRIS

Important family for water garden, which should receive full representation.

I. sibirica and *I. delavayi* (see p. 37), are excellent bog plants, also *I. forrestii* with clear yellow flowers on 18-in. stems and grassy leaves in June. *I. kaempferi*, the Clematis Iris, is probably the most exciting of the waterside species, the flowers with their lower petals held flat, looking like gaily coloured parasols in shades of blue, white, pink, red and purple, or blotched and striated in a mixture of colours. Varieties frequently have Japanese names, but mixed sorts are usually very good and cheaper to buy. This is not an easy family to grow as plants require plenty of water in summer but comparative dryness in winter. Growing them in an area which can occasionally be flooded over is one way of meeting the difficulty, or enriching the ground with plenty of rotted manure increases the moisture content in summer so that the roots do not suffer from dryness. The species dislikes lime and is often confused with *I. laevigata* (see p. 267), but easily distinguished by the leaves which have a distinct midrib. June—July. 2 ft.

LOBELIA

L. fulgens and *L. syphilitica* are two excellent bog plants with brightly coloured flowers; the former also has attractive foliage. See p. 38.

Primulas by the streamside   W. & R. Perry

Iris kaempferi, showing diversity of colouring

LYSICHITUM

L. americanum is a large aroid with attractive, deep yellow, Arum-like flowers in early spring (May), often 18 in. in height and appearing before the large, glaucous-green leaves. Not really suitable for a very small garden, thrives happily in shallow water and bog. 2—3 ft.

L. camtschatcense is rarer, with white flowers.

LYSIMACHIA See p. 39.

LYTHRUM See p. 39.

MIMULUS Musk

Useful genus for late summer with very bright Antirrhinum-like flowers. Many can be raised from seed or named sorts propagated by soft cuttings. In exposed parts or cold climates it is advisable to root these in a cold frame towards the end of August or September, leaving under cover all winter and planting out again the following May.

Hybrids from *M. guttatus* are the most useful, especially 'Bee's Dazzler' and 'Whitcroft Scarlet', both vivid red. Hybrids from *M. cupreus*, *tigrinus* and *maculosus* have red, pink, orange and yellow flowers, many with spotted throat. 'Hose in Hose' has a double corolla ring, so that one flower seems to grow inside another. 12—18 in. June—Sept.

MONARDA See p. 40.

PRIMULA Primrose

A large family, the majority appreciating a moist, but not waterlogged soil. They are averse to strong sunshine, and associate most happily with ferns, Bamboos and Meconopsis. An occasional mulch of well rotted manure and leafmould is most beneficial, and seed should be allowed to drop around parent plants to form colonies. Propagation by seed sown *directly* after gathering or by spring division.

The most important types for the bog garden are the candelabras, which bear flowers in a succession of whorls up the stems. They include *P. beesiana*, rosy-carmine; *P. japonica*, white, pink and crimson; *P. helodoxa*, golden yellow, and *P. pulverulenta*, 'Bartley Strain', an excellent race which has produced many fine varieties with soft rose and pink flowers on mealy stems. 2—3 ft. June.

Another good species is *P. rosea*, particularly the improved form 'Micia de Geer', with deep pink flowers on 6—9-in. stems in April. This is the only Primula which will tolerate standing water (for short periods).

P. sikkimensis is the Himalayan Cowslip with 2-ft. stems carrying many nodding, fragrant, pale yellow flowers in July.

RHEUM Rhubarb

The ornamental Rhubarbs give an air of tropical luxuriance to the waterside, although a single specimen will be suficient in most instances. *R. emodi* has bronze-green, glossy leaves with large red veins and heavy plumes of white flowers. June-July. 5—10 ft.; *R. palmatum* has deeply lobed, palmate foliage and deep red flowers in a dense, terminal panicle. Its variety *tanguticum* has more deeply dissected leaves. 5 ft.

RODGERSIA Bronze-leaf

Fine foliage plants with spikes of Astilbe-like flowers, suitable for a moist situation and light shade.

R. aesculifolia has deeply cut, Horse-chestnut-like leaves and flat sprays of fluffy white flowers. June—July. 3ft.; *R. podophylla* has heavily netted, palmately-divided, bronzed leaves and creamy-white flowers. 4 ft. June—July; *R. tabularis* has almost round leaves on a central stalk. 2—3 ft. across. Flowers creamy-white. 3 ft. July—Aug.; *R. pinnata* has showy branched panicles of reddish flowers and pinnately-divided leaves. July. Varieties have white, pink, rose and deep red flowers. 3—4 ft.

Nymphaea 'Conqueror' By courtesy of Home Magazine

Nymphaea 'James Brydon'

SENECIO Ragwort

Bog members of this genus are robust perennials with fine leaves and heads of Daisy-like flowers. They need plenty of moisture in summer. One of the most impressive is *S. pulcher* with long, lobed, leathery, silvery leaves, somewhat stem clasping, and large flower heads, composed of reddish-purple flowers with yellow centres. Autumn. 1—2 ft.

S. clivorum, *S. veitchiana* and *S. wilsoniana*. See Ligularia, with which this family is often linked.

TROLLIUS Globe Flower

Handsome relations of the Buttercup with almost round, ball-like heads of yellow or orange flowers and Buttercup leaves. Suitable for sunny places in wet soil. 'Bee's Orange', orange gold; 'Earliest of All', butter-yellow, and 'Salamander', fiery orange, are good varieties. See also p. 47.

Cacti & Succulents

Cacti and other succulents, being natives of deserts and dry rocky plains, have the ability to withstand long periods of drought. Their outer skin is usually thick and coated with wax or sometimes with very long and shaggy hair which reduces the loss of moisture. In Cacti the foliage is reduced to mere filaments, for the thorns are the leaves whilst the green fleshy parts are really stems. Succulents also absorb moisture quickly when rain falls, storing it in their fleshy stems or foliage, and drawing upon these reservoirs in times of need.

Most succulents inhabit tropical countries, where they are baked up for the greater part of the year and then subjected to torrential rains, interspersed with bright sunshine. It is during this latter period that Cacti make their growth and flower. At other times they are at rest and undergoing a ripening process.

To secure these conditions under cultivation the plants should be started into growth about April with copious waterings, and syringed occasionally from then until June. Towards the end of June gradually reduce the watering and give as little as possible for the rest of the season. Give them plenty of light in winter and adequate ventilation during hot weather.

POTTING

Grow all succulents in small pots with plenty of drainage, repotting occasionally, not necessarily every year. Potting is best carried out during April and May.

The soil should be very open and free draining. The following mixture makes an excellent medium:

7 parts by bulk medium or fibrous loam
3 ,, ,, ,, horticultural peat
2 ,, ,, ,, crushed brick
4 ,, ,, ,, coarse sand
½ part ,, ,, mortar rubble or limestone chippings
4 oz. bonemeal to every bushel of the above mixture.

Pot firmly, up to the old planting mark, gripping the plant by a twist of newspaper round its middle,

Agave   By courtesy of Home Magazine

or alternatively use padded tongs or gloves. Be very careful of the spines, which can be painful, or in some cases poisonous, if they pierce the skin.

CULTIVATION

Always water round the sides of the pot, never over the leaves or into the crown. A little soft soap in water helps to remove dust, and large leaves can be wiped over with damp cotton wool.

When Cacti or Succulents are grown indoors give them all possible light, especially in winter. A windowsill is the best position, but in an unheated room precautions must be taken against frosting at night, and against draughts. Water very little in winter, just enough to keep them from shrivelling.

PROPAGATION

Few plants root so easily from cuttings, many are readily raised from seed, others throw off suckers, whilst a great number may be propagated by leaf, stem, or joint cuttings. Cuttings and suckers must be allowed to dry a little before being inserted in practically dry, very sandy soil. Unless the wound is dry before the cutting is put into the compost, it will probably rot.

Seed should be sown very thinly, in well crocked pans of John Innes Seed Compost and germinated in a frame with bottom heat in a temperature around 70° F. February or March is the best time. Prick off and pot up as soon as possible in very small pots.

CACTI

The majority have curious shapes, sharply pointed thorns, often handsome flowers and sometimes highly coloured berries.

Cacti may all be propagated by cuttings of the branches in a warm frame. Those which do not produce branches may be increased by cutting the apex of the plant, which either causes latent buds to push and grow or suckers to be thrown up. Some kinds are apt to rot at the base and so are frequently grafted on more robust species. Soft wool must be used for binding the grafts, which can be made during the most active growing season.

The seed soon deteriorates and does not readily germinate after two years. 80–95 per cent of a Cactus is water.

The chief troubles are Root Rot — caused by overwatering. Root Aphis — use a nicotine insecticide.

Among the most popular and easily grown Cacti are the following.

APOROCACTUS Rat-tail Cactus

A. flagelliformis. Long, trailing stems covered with soft brown hairs and prickles. Pink or red flowers, late spring. Rich lime-free soil; keep warm in winter. Best grown in basket. Cuttings.

Cacti, showing wide range of shapes   Copyright Ryder & Sons

CEPHALOCEREUS Old Man Cactus

C. senilis. Large, columnar with long white hairs. Sunny window, little water, add extra lime to compost. Slow growing. Minimum winter temperature 50°F. Seed.

CEREUS Torch Thistle; Night Blooming Cactus

Thick branches with ribbed spines, often bluish. Large flowers, open at night. *C. jamacaru,* white flowers, *C. chalybaeus,* red and white flowers. Rather moist soil spring and summer, not entirely dry in winter. Cuttings or seed.

CHAMAECEREUS Peanut Cactus

C. sylvestrii. Branching, pale green shoots with small, white spines, scarlet flowers. Nearly hardy. Cuttings.

Cacti and Succulents, Aloes, Agave, Kalanchoe, Cotyledon and Crassulas   Smallholder and Home Gardener

ECHINOCACTUS Hedgehog Cactus; Barrel Cactus

E. grusonii, ball-shaped, flattened at top, strong golden spines. Easy but slow growing, rich soil. Minimum winter temperature 50° F. Seed.

ECHINOPSIS Sea Urchin Cactus

E. eyriesii, prickly, ridged growth. Pink or white flowers. Easy to grow, likes sun. Cuttings or seed.

EPIPHYLLUM Orchid Cactus

Beautiful flowering varieties with flat stems and upright growth, few or no thorns. Flowers open at night. Rich soil, liquid feeding when in full growth. Moderate sun, careful watering when in flower. Minimum temperature 50° F. Cuttings.

MAMMILLARIA Pincushion Cactus

Dwarf kinds, covered with warts, many small flowers. Stand cold if dry, semi-shade in summer, like lime. Seed and cuttings.

OPUNTIA Prickly Pear

Some have prickly pads or ears, others warted. Flowers red, orange or yellow. Fruits edible. Full sun, keep dry in winter. Seed or cuttings.

ZYGOCACTUS Christmas Cactus; Lobster Cactus

Z. truncatus, flat lobster claw-like shoots. No spines, trailing growth. Cultivate as for Epiphyllum. Good basket plant. Cuttings.

SUCCULENTS

These plants have fleshy stems and leaves which store water. Occasionally they have prickles, but unlike Cactus this is a rarity rather than the rule.

When grown they should be kept on the dry side, especially in winter, or they will easily rot. A top dressing of granite chippings or brick rubble over the soil surface is beneficial.

There are hundreds of species and varieties, but the following are some of the commonest and most easily grown.

AEONIUM House-leek Tree

A. arboreum. Upright woody growth like miniature tree, with leaves and yellow flowers. Protect from brightest sunshine. *A. tabulaeforme*, overlapping leaves in flat rosette. Propagated from leaf rosettes or cuttings.

AGAVE Century Plant

A. americana, well known 'Cactus' with broad leaves and vicious spines. Flowers on upright spikes, but only after many years. Fairly hardy, full sun, store away from frost. Slow-growing but can make enormous specimens.

ALOE

A. filifera, white threads covering plant. Full sun; *A. variegata*, Partridge Aloe, triangular dense leaves, striped white. Light position; *A. aristata*, makes rosette with narrow leaves edged and covered with white teeth. Flowers often showy, red, orange or yellow. Seed, offsets or leaf cuttings.

BRYOPHYLLUM

B. daigremontianum, long triangular leaves and yellow or pink

Echinopsis   Worsfield Gardens

Flower on Astrophytum graft   Worsfield Gardens

Rancho 'Santa Fé'   Worsfield Gardens

Echinocereus   Worsfield Gardens

Echinocactus   Worsfield Gardens

flowers. Baby plants round leaf edges; *B. tubiflorum*, long thin leaves like spikes with small plants at ends. Need winter light and warmth. Propagates from plantlets on leaves.

CRASSULA

C. arborescens, Jade Plant, like small tree with fleshy, spoon-shaped leaves; *C. lucens*, Scarlet Paint Brush, is similar, with red-edged leaves; *C. rupestris*, Necklace Vine, has foliage arranged like beads on thread. All need good light, occasional feeding with liquid manure. Good pot plants.

ECHEVERIA Hen and Chickens

Many kinds. Leaves grow in rosettes, often glaucous, flowers coral or orange-red. Water when dry, avoiding leaves. Stem or leaf cuttings.

EUPHORBIA Medusa's Head

E. caput-medusae. Cactus-like plant with sinuous branches like snaky hair. Others are branched and knobbly. All exude milky juice and bleed when cut. Plenty of light and heat. Stem cuttings.

GASTERIA Ox-tongue

Long, warted and often spotted leaves, long-lasting scarlet flowers. Very little water, no feeding. Seed, offsets or leaf cuttings.

HAWARTHIA Cushion Aloe

Squat plants with rosettes of pudgy leaves, small flowers, white or greenish. Moderate watering in winter. Seed or offsets.

KLEINIA Candle Plant

K. articulata, jointed, fleshy stems and lobed leaves. Keep very dry in summer and never overwater. Cuttings and runners.

LITHOPS Living Stones; Pebble Plants

Fleshy plants, variously coloured, resembling pebbles. Very sandy soil, no water in winter and little at other times. Yellow or white flowers. Seed or division or cuttings.

ROCHEA Crassula

R. coccinea, stems up to 2 ft., triangular, leaves arranged cross-wise. Showy red flowers. Light, cool conditions in winter. Seed or cuttings.

Epiphyllum 'Innocence'   Worsfield Gardens

Opuntia, Prickly Pear Cactus   Worsfield Gardens

Flowers for Cutting

It is a great satisfaction to grow your own flowers for cutting, and yet have enough over to keep the garden bright with colour. But few people can grow all their indoor floral requirements. The solution is probably to grow what you can, particularly background or unusual material, treating the flowers carefully when cut.

General Treatment of Cut Flowers

1. Gather the blooms in the coolest part of the day when they are fresh — usually early morning or evening — and put them in water immediately.

2. Leave in deep water for several hours before arranging.

3. Reduce the foliage, especially on woody plants and never keep leaves under water.

4. Crush or slit ends of stems of woody plants.

5. Keep flowers away from sunshine, hot air, draughts, gas and other fumes.

6. Use hot water to revive tired flowers.

7. Take flowers out of a hot room at night.

8. Change water and cut stems frequently with long-lasting flowers like Helianthus 'The Monarch' and Chrysanthemums. Mixed flower arrangements need topping up daily.

9. Syringe blooms occasionally with soft water at room temperature, using a very fine spray.

INDIVIDUAL FLOWERS

1. *Violets*. Immerse the whole bunch in cool water, shake and arrange. This more than doubles the lifespan.

Anaphalis triplinervis

2. *Astilbe*. Immerse in water, remove a few leaves and dip the ends of the stems in dilute (10 per cent) hydrochloric acid or glacial acetic acid. The latter acts as a styptic.

3. *Apple Blossom*. Cut in bud, crush stems and stand overnight in deep water.

4. *Daffodils, Brodiaeas, Alstroemerias*. Place in not more than half an inch of water. One drop of T.C.P. discourages bacteria.

5. *Camellias and Magnolias*. Salt water dropped into the blooms prevents petal browning.

6. *Lupins*. Turn stems upside-down and fill with tepid water. Plug with cotton wool or place a finger over the cut end and invert into vase of water. This prevents petal drop and extends the life of the blooms.

7. *Delphiniums*. As with Lupins.

8. *Hydrangeas*. Cut stems should be charred with a taper or painted with glacial acetic acid. Remove some foliage and immerse stem and flower head occasionally in cold water.

9. *Rhododendrons and Azaleas*. Remove some foliage and dip cut end in dilute alcohol or hydrochloric acid.

10. *Tulips*. Wrap in newspaper and stand up to the flower heads in cold water all night. This keeps the stems straight.

11. *Forsythia*. Cut branches early in tight bud stage.

12. *Wisteria*. Spray continuously and soak ends in strong, alcohol for some hours. Alternatively, try burning the ends.

13. *Iris*. Place stems first in hot water and then in cold.

14. *Chrysanthemums*. Strip off most of the leaves, jog stems up and down in a jug of hot water to remove green sap, crush ends and arrange. Add one or two drops of *oil* of peppermint (not the essence) to the water.

15. *Asters*. Add half a teaspoonful of sugar to each pint of water to raise flower heads. Soak in cold water overnight.

16. *Beet, Cabbage and any large leaves*. Lie flat in shallow water overnight, but do not submerge.

17. *Sweet Peas*. Burn tips of the stems and stand in a cool draught-free place.

18. *Lilac*. Remove all leaves, hammer stems and place in water. Use foliage separately.

19. *Carnations*. Slit the ends of the stems and keep away from gas. Carnations live longest in deep water.

20. *Roses*. Remove underwater thorns. Gather in bud, protect blooms with paper or cloth an boil ends of stems for a few seconds.

21. *Water-lilies*. Take out of container at night, shake and lie by side of bowl.

22. *Philadelphus and Lime Blossom*. Pick in bud, remove leaves.

23. *Macleaya*. Pick the older sprays which last longest.

24. *Fennel*. Flower and foliage — as Macleaya.

25. *Stocks and Wallflowers*. Remove some of the leaves: scrape and split ends of stems.

26. *Poppies, Geums, Eschscholtzias*. Gather in bud, dip ends for a few seconds in boiling water, then in cold.

27. *Hollyhocks*. Steep ends of stems in boiling water for a few seconds (protecting flowers and foliage from steam).

28. *Anemones*, which will not open. Cut the ends of the stems and stand in a basin of hot water. Cover the whole with a polythene bag or tin and leave for an hour.

29. *Mimosa*. Cut the ends, remove leaves, stand first in boiling water then in cool. Keep in a cool room. Drawing the flowers through steam will make them fluffy for a short while, as will the glycerine method. See p. 280.

30. *Bluebells and Daffodils*. A drop or two of a non-oily disinfectant, like permanganate of potash, T.C.P. or Milton, in ½ pint of water keeps the water fresh. A penny in the water also helps, the copper acting as a mild germicide.

Helichrysums

Buying flowers

Remember that most of the 'Daisy' family last well when cut. Coreopsis, Gaillardia, Erigerons, Cornflowers and Chrysanthemums are all good buys provided they are fresh. Never take flowers which look flabby or discoloured at the cut end. The leaves should be fresh and green; if yellow they have been picked for some time.

Stamens often give an indication of age. Pollen of Lilies and allied genera should be light gold not dark or dry-looking. With Carnations press blooms gently. On release the petals should spring back to their original position. If not the flowers have been too long in a refrigerator chamber.

Avoid bulbous subjects such as Narcissus if these have a papery transparent look. If the stems have split and curled back and become brown they are not fresh. Similarly, Rose petals should be as crisp as a Lettuce. Limpness should be avoided in all flowers.

The inner petals of Marigolds, Chrysanthemums

and Dahlias should still be tightly folded on purchase. Spiked flowers, e.g. Gladioli, Larkspurs and Chincherinchees, should have the lower flowers open, the rest in bud.

The age of Orchids is more difficult to detect. Old flowers look lustreless or wear a strange pockmark on the petals. Look for blooms with a smooth, glistening appearance.

Drying Flowers

Flower and foliage material for drying should be gathered when the blooms are nearly full and before the seed pods open.

Strip foliage from stems and hang them upsidedown in small bunches in a dark, airy, dry place. Helichrysums, Statice (Limonium), Anaphalis, Larkspurs and others should be treated in this way.

Seed pods of Cape Gooseberry *(Physalis franchetti)* are ornamental as grown, or the scarlet outer covering can be cut up with scissors and turned back like petals round the red inner berry.

Berries in seed pods, such as *Iris foetidissima*, tend to shrivel when brought indoors. They can be kept plump by painting over with colourless nail varnish or shellac. This is also useful with Gourds, Rose Hips and other fruits.

The ornamental part of Honesty (Lunaria) is the silvery inner wall of the seed pods. To expose this, remove the outer coverings and seeds by rubbing between finger and thumb. Other interesting seed pods are found in Poppy, Mullein, Larch, Acorns and Fir and Pine cones.

Very many grasses are attractive, particularly Quaking Grass (Briza); Wheat, Barley, Timothy (which dries green) and Millet (dark brown). They can be given extra colour by standing them for a night (before drying) in water containing a little soluble dye, such as red or green ink. Pampas should be gathered before it is fully out, and broken up for small arrangements.

Hydrangea flowers should be left on bushes until the desired colour is attained, then dried off in vases containing a very little water.

Many ingredients for dried flower arrangements and bouquets can be bought from florists; together with dead branches, Fungi, Acorns, Thistle heads and seed pods, and a little evergreen, they make most attractive arrangements.

Preserving Leaves

The main methods are as follows:
The Glycerine Method. This gives the most natural and satisfactory results. The twigs should be gathered

Annual Chrysanthemums   Copyright Ryder & Sons

Larkspurs can be used fresh or dried   Copyright Fidlers of Reading

whilst the sap is still rising: i.e. in the case of Beech or Hawthorn, when the leaves are green.

Wipe off dust, trim away any blemished foliage. Now slice up or crush the ends and stand the branches upright in a solution of one part glycerine to two parts warm water. Leave in a cool place for 2 or 3 weeks, topping up with *water* if necessary. The leaves will gradually change colour and assume a polished appearance, when they may be arranged — with or without water — in vases. Beech, Laurel, Eucalyptus, Hawthorn, Sweet Chestnut, Eleagnus and Oak can all be preserved with glycerine. Small leaves like Ivy and Mahonia should be immersed in the solution and left until they change colour.

Oiling. Evergreens can be preserved for a time with oil. Wash the foliage, using tepid water and a little cotton wool. When dry, smear with a trace of olive oil or petroleum jelly on the upper and under surfaces. This blocks the *stoma* or pores through which they transpire moisture, and is a quick method with Laurels, Ivy and Holly for Christmas.

Pressing Method. Leaves, single flowers, Fern fronds and grasses may be preserved by pressing. Spread the plant material thinly over several thicknesses of newspaper or blotting paper, cover with newspaper and apply a heavy weight. This is the best method for decorating table mats, screens or pictures.

Skeletonising Leaves. Skeletonised leaves last indefinitely when properly prepared. Strongly veined foliage like *Magnolia grandiflora*, Camellia, Iris and Galax give the best effects, but Poplar, Bergenia and Laurel may also be tried.

Soak the leaves for a week or more in a strong solution of caustic soda, or boil for half an hour in same solution (half a teaspoonful of soda to a pint of water). Next rinse in clear water and pat lightly dry with a soft cloth. Place a pad of blotting paper over the foliage and beat lightly with some object like a clothes brush. This should leave a network of veins, but you may have to repeat the process.

It is also possible to stain them with colour washes or dilute ink mixtures.

GROWING FOR FLOWER ARRANGEMENT

Perennials

Erigeron, perennial Scabious, Alstroemeria, Gaillardia, Michaelmas Daisies, Coreopsis, Iris, Astilbe, Helianthus 'The Monarch', Liatris and Violas.

Annuals and Biennials

Marigolds, Larkspurs, annual Chrysanthemums, Clarkia, Antirrhinums, Asters (Callistephus), Centaureas (Sweet Sultan and Cornflowers), Nigella (Love-in-a-Mist), Stocks, Zinnias, Rudbeckias, annual Scabious, Matricaria, Wallflowers and Foxgloves.

Everlastings and Plants for drying

Catananche coerulea, Gomphrena, Lunaria, Helichrysum, Helipterum, Limonium (Statice), Molucella, *Achillea eupatorium*, Acanthus, Larkspurs, Bullrushes and Physalis.

Ornamental Grasses

Agrostis (Bent Grass, *Avena sterilis* (Animated Oats), *Briza maxima* (Large Totter Grass), *Coix lachryma-jobi* (Job's Tears), Eragrostis (Love Grass), *Hordeum jubatum* (Squirrel-tail Grass), *Lagurus ovatus* (Hare's Tail Grass), *Phalaris arundinacea picta* (Gardener's Garters) and various forms of variegated Maize (*Zea japonica vars*) and Pampas Grass (Cortaderia species).

Bulbous Plants for Cutting

Snowdrops, Tulips, Narcissi (not necessarily new but saved from previous year's display beds), Lilies, Gladioli, Chincherinchee, Brodiaeas, Lily of the Valley, Agapanthus, Anemone, Freesias, Ranunculus.

Silver-Leaved or Coloured Foliage Plants

Senecio greyi, Artemisia (many species), Cornus, Rosemary, Lavender, Dianthus, Golden Privet.

Bedding or Tender Plants.

Dahlias, Carnations, Gerbera, Orchids, Penstemons.

Annual Asters come in a wide variety of shades
Copyright Samuel Dobie & Son

Wall shrubs & Climbers

Many beautiful shrubs which normally require glass protection can be grown in the open on walls; and climbing plants can also be used for draping fences and walls, covering old tree stumps and festooning arches and pergolas. They provide a pleasant green background to the flower beds and offer in addition their own fine fruits and autumnal tints.

Before planting shrubs against a wall, clear a space 1½–2 ft. wide and as much deep. Work in some decayed manure or peat when the soil is naturally light, but if very heavy add a fair proportion of coarse sand as well. A handful of bonemeal can also be added to the top layer.

Set the plants carefully about 1 ft. in front of the wall, spreading out the roots of deciduous types but leaving the soil ball intact in the case of evergreens. Water may be necessary at times during the first season, and a mulch of straw spread over the near-by soil helps to conserve moisture.

Some climbers, like the Ivy, support themselves by means of aerial roots; others, such as Passion Flowers and Vines, have curling tendrils which catch on anything in their upward climb, and plants like the Honeysuckle twine themselves round any convenient support and then spread themselves all over their host.

Some plants need tying periodically into place. One method is to pass a strip of cloth round the shoot and then nail it to the wall; a more satisfactory method is to string the wall horizontally with stout, plastic-covered, straining wires. These should be about 8 in. apart and secured by hooked or eyelet-holed metal pins.

A lattice work of narrow laths painted green or stained with Cuprinol may be rigged up for low-growing shrubs; alternatively, plastic-covered wire trellis can be fastened to the fence or wall, or even used free-standing. (See p. 52).

A few Pea-sticks strapped to the trunk will help annual climbers like Hop or *Cobaea scandens* to scramble up an old tree. For moderately tall climbers like Clematis and some of the garden Roses, poles or tripods of Larch or Spruce (left with short stumps of their side branches) can be very useful. Before insertion in the ground, stand parts for burying for 24 hours in creosote.

SHRUBS AND CLIMBERS FOR SUNNY WALLS

These most favoured spots in the garden should be reserved for the tenderest or most beautiful plants. Species especially suitable for town conditions are marked with a T. S.C. denotes Soft cuttings; S., seed; H.R.C., half-ripe cuttings; L., Layers; Div., division; R.C., root-cuttings; H.C., hard-wood cuttings; D., Deciduous; E., Evergreen.

ABUTILON
Two hardy species are suitable for wall culture. *A. vitifolium* which has Maple-shaped downy leaves and lilac-blue Hollyhock-like flowers in June and July, 6–12 ft.; D., and *A. megapotamicum* E., very slender, with small leaves and conspicuous handing scarlet and gold, bell-like flowers, June—October, 3 ft. Little or no pruning. S. or S.C.

ACTINIDIA
A. kolomikta is chiefly valuable for its foliage; some are

Magnolia denudata　　　　　　　　J. E. Downward

Camellia japonica, 'C.M. Wilson'　　Copyright Wood & Ingram

variegated with white and pink at the terminal part, others patterned. The flowers are small but white and fragrant. D. 6—10 ft. Prune to keep in bounds and occasionally take out old wood. H.R.C. July.

AKEBIA D.

A. lobata has leaves divided like Clover, in threes, and small purple flowers, followed by large grey edible fruits, 3—5 in. long. Good for training over small tree or summerhouse. No pruning. S.L. or H.R.C. July.

CAMPSIS D.

T. Trumpet Creeper. Also known as Tecoma. *C. chinensis grandiflora* and *C. radicans* are two hardy and vigorous climbers, with Ash-like leaves and sprays of funnel-shaped rich orange flowers. Good for covering sunny wall or pergola, or for masking an old tree. Leave alone when young, but later the side shoots can be cut back in November (like Vines) almost to the old stem. August—September R.C. Suckers and L.

CEANOTHUS T.

All the Ceanothus are best suited to a south wall, though in town they will also do well on walls facing east and west. Most varieties have flowers of some shade of blue. They can be grown in any well drained soil and are deciduous or evergreen, with small neat toothed flowers. The flowers are borne in clusters. H.R.C. in pure sand in Aug. or Sept. under glass. *C. dentatus* blooms in May and June with rounded clusters of bright blue flowers. Cut back strong side shoots to within 1 or 2 ins. of main branches when flowers fade. *C. hybridus*. This group contains a number of good garden varieties of mixed origin. 'Henri Desfosse' is deciduous with deep indigo flowers; 'Gloire de Versailles', bright blue and fragrant, also deciduous; 'Autumnal Blue', evergreen, soft blue, and 'Perle Rose', crushed strawberry-pink, deciduous. These all flower between July and October and should be pruned Feb.—March by removing any weak wood and shortenig back strong shoots to 6 or 12 ins. from old wood.

CLEMATIS T. Mostry D.

These do surprisingly well, even in towns, provided one remembers the maxim 'Clematis like cool feet and a hot head'. If shade is unavailable, rest a stone slab on the ground near by until the plant becomes established. S.L. or H.R.C. in July, also grafting on *C. vitalba* or *C. viticella*. *C. armandii* is only hardy against a wall. It has leathery three-pointed leaves which are evergreen, and clusters of small white flowers in April. Prune to shape.
C. x jackmanni. This is the well known, large-flowered purple variety blooming between July and Sept. Many varieties including 'Crimson King', bright red; 'Gipsy Queen', rich dark purple; 'Comtesse de Bouchard', soft pink; 'Mme Edouard André', the best red; and 'Victoria', purple-mauve. Cut old growths in Feb. to within a foot or two from the ground.
C. macropetala blooms in spring and has drooping, violet-blue, double flowers. Not as robust as most, but will reach 5 ft. on wall.
C. montana is very vigorous and hardy and has white flowers something like a wood Anemone. There is a pink-flowered form called 'Elizabeth' also scented; *var. rubens* has pinkish blooms and bronzy foliage. Normally flowers May—June. No regular pruning beyond occasional thinning. *Vedrariensis* is another *C. montana* variety with pale pink, sweetly scented flowers. May—June. Var. 'Highdown', is an improved form of it, with 2½ in. blooms. No pruning, will grow on north walls.
C. patens, with white or bluish flowers, has given rise to a number of good garden varieties, such as 'Nellie Moser', pink with deep carmine red bars up the centre of each sepal. 'The President', dark violet with pale blue bars; 'Barbara Dibley', deep Pansy-

violet; 'Mrs. George Jackman', satiny-white with cream bars and 'Edouard Desfosse', violet-mauve with deep violet bars. These bloom between May and July. Shorten back occasionally after flowers fade.

C. spooneri, not as rampant as *C. montana* but with larger flowers. Suitable for a north wall. *Var. rosea* is a good pink form with 'winged' sepals.

C. tangutica. The best yellow species. Aug.—Oct. 10 ft.

C. viticella. Hybrids include 'Ernest Markham', petunia-red; 'Minuet', cream and purple; *kermesina*, crimson. July—Oct. 8 ft.

COBAEA SCANDENS T.

An annual which must be started from seed under glass. Self-clinging, with large Canterbury Bell-like flowers, greenish-white, darkening to purple. Late summer.

GARRYA T.

G. elliptica. The Silk Tassel Bush. A beautiful evergreen with roundish or oval leaves, shiny green above and woolly grey beneath. Male and female catkins borne on separate plants. They hang in bunches from Nov. until Feb. in suede-green pennants. Always buy male plants, and propagate in Aug. from cuttings. Little pruning, but shelter plants from cold winds. Suitable for a west, south or east position. H.R.C. under glass in Aug.

HYDRANGEAS T.

All kinds flower better when given wall protection. They are easy to grow and readily kept in bounds. See also p. 69.

JASMINES T.

A large genus of climbers, some more tender than others, but all easily cultivated in ordinary loam or peaty soil. Propagated by suckers or Aug. struck cuttings. Especially useful is the winter flowering *Jasminum nudiflorum T.* which has yellow, tubular blooms on leafless green shoots. It usually flowers from Christmas until Feb. or March, the leaves appearing about the time the blossoms fade. Prune when this occurs, cutting back shoots which have just bloomed nearly to old wood; strong new growths will appear during summer.

J. officinalis T. does well in an east or west position as well as south, and grows quickly with dark green leaves and fragrant white blooms appearing off and on all summer.

J. x stephanense has pink and *J. floridum* yellow flowers during summer. Both need south wall protection.

MAGNOLIA

M. grandiflora T. A fine evergreen for a large wall expanse, as it is extremely vigorous. Leaves large and glossy, with enormous flowers, 8—10 in., globular, fragrant, creamy-white. July—Sept. In very mild climates makes a tall pyramidal tree but on walls can be kept to required height. Propagation difficult, but layering may be tried.

OLEARIA E. Daisy Bush

Evergreen, sun-loving shrubs with small daisy flowers; all of Australian origin. Need light, well drained soil. H.R.C. in warmth.

O. gunniana. Tasmanian Daisy Bush. One of the most popular with narrow, grey, toothed leaves and branching clusters of white, orange-centred Daisy flowers. Also forms with blue, lavender and pink flowers. May. 3 to 5 ft.

O. haastii T. This is the hardiest and may also be grown away from the wall. It has small dark leaves and masses of small, white, fragrant flowers. July—Aug. 5—8 ft.

Wistaria   Copyright Wood & Ingram

Clematis 'Madame Edouard André'   Fisk's Clematis Nurseries

Ceanothus must have wall or fence protection

Clematis spooneri rosea

O. illicifolia also has fragrant white flowers, in June. Leathery leaves, 2—4 ins., with spines like Holly. 6—10 ft.

OSMANTHUS

O. delavayi. Evergreen shrub with small leaves and fragrant tubular white flowers in April. Sun. Makes a small bush (about 6 ft.) with glossy, pointed, Holly-like leaves. H.R.C. in bottom heat in July. Prune to shape end April.

PASSIFLORA D. T.

P. coerulea T. Passion Flower. Favourite climber for a sunny wall, with grey-green, Vine-shaped leaves and very handsome flat flowers. Seed or cuttings.

PHYGELIUS

P. capensis T. Cape Figwort. Evergreen with spikes of rosy-scarlet, tubular flowers arranged candelabra-fashion on four-sided stems. 3—5 ft. Smooth oval leaves. Light but rich soil; propagated from seed or cuttings Aug. See also p. 42.

PIPTANTHUS See p. 71

PUNICA D. Pomegranate

P. granatum flore pleno. Small shrub with double fiery scarlet flowers which have a fleshy red calyx and crumpled petals. Smooth oval leaves. No specific pruning but needs full sun, well drained, rather light soil and shelter from cold winds. C. or L. June—Sept. 3—12 ft.

ROSES T. D.

Practically all climbing roses are suitable for town as well as country gardens, with the large, single flowered, sulphur-yellow 'Mermaid' as first choice. This blooms from July through to autumn. Will even grow on north wall. There are also climbing roses with pink, red, white and yellow flowers in both single and double types. See also p. 104.

SOLANUM D.

S. crispum Potato Tree. Only suitable for sheltered areas where it grows up to 14 ft. with large clusters of bluish-purple Potato-like flowers. Very showy climber, blooming June—Aug. Prune to shape, in spring. R.C.,C.

STACHYURUS

S. praecox (syn. *chinensis*). Winter-flowering deciduous shrub with beautiful sprays of waxy, yellowish flowers. An east, west or south wall gives sufficient protection. Soil well drained. Leaves oblong, smooth and green. H.R.C. with bottom heat. No regular pruning but occasional shortening back and removal of old stems. Feb.—March. 6—8 ft.

VITIS T. D. Vine

Useful group of plants for quick coverage on old buildings, walls and pergolas, easy to grow, many handsomely coloured in autumn. Require no regular pruning unless they get out of hand, when they may be thinned or new growths shortened back to 1 in. in Nov. Propagated by cuttings or layers.
V. coignetiae is the Glory Vine with large heart-shaped, 3—5 in

Lonicera periclymenum belgica, Honeysuckle   H. Smith

Cotoneasters are useful berrying shrubs in autumn   J. E. Downward

lobed leaves, green above and rusty beneath, changing to crimson and orange in autumn; very vigorous; *V. henryana* green leaves, picked out along veins with silver and pink; *V. vinifera* is the hardy Grape Vine, with varieties having red-purple leaves as in *purpurea*, and much cut leaves, in *apiifolia*. *V. quinquefolia* is the well known Virginia Creeper, a self-clinging climber, turning brilliant red in autumn.

WISTARIA D. T.

Beautiful climbing shrub with Ash-shaped leaves and pendulous sprays of mauve, purple or white Sweet Pea-type flowers. Full sun and good soil, otherwise will not flower. Wistarias make a great deal of growth in a season but must be watched lest snake-like shoots get under slates or tiles. Cut back fairly hard, but leave flowering buds which are usually arranged in clusters, on spurs at the branch bases. Shorten young shoots in winter to within three or four buds of old wood. This results in finer trusses of flowers. Where there is space leave unpruned. Propagated by layers.
W. floribunda has long drooping sprays (5 to 10 ins) of slightly fragrant, violet-blue flowers in May and June.
Var. alba is white and var. *macrobotrys* pale mauve with tremendously long trusses, sometimes 3 ft. or more.
W. sinensis has rich mauve blossoms and there is a white-flowered and also a double variety.
W. venusta is the best white, the flower sprays fairly short (4 to 6 in.), but exceptionally richly scented.

SHADY WALLS

CAMELLIAS T. E.

These do well in towns, possibly because the glossy leathery leaves throw off dust. Varieties of *C. japonica* are particularly suitable with white, pink, red or striped flowers, either single or double. Foliage is beautiful too, lasting weeks when cut. Avoid lime. A woodland type soil of coarse sand mixed with moist peat or leafmould, makes excellent mulch. Apply annually. Air layers. C. under glass.

COTONEASTERS T.

Certain Cotoneasters such as *C. horizontalis* and *C. microphylla* cling naturally to walls, with a fishbone arrangement of branches. The small leaves are evergreen. *C. horizontalis* has small pinkish flowers and *C. microphylla* white, both succeeded by scarlet berries which persist in winter. S. or C.

FUCHSIA T.

Most Fuchsias are not hardy and so have to be put in the greenhouse in winter. Those listed are hardy enough against a south wall, particularly in milder areas. Well drained loamy soil. Increase by soft cuttings struck in warmth. Cover crowns in Oct. with 4—6 in. of weathered ashes or soil and leaves and let this remain until spring. *F. magellanica* has small, scarlet and purple flowers; *var. variegata* has variegated foliage and *riccartonii* bears sealing-wax red and purple flowers June—Oct. All these are 4—8 ft.

HEDERA T. E.

Most Ivies do well in towns and succeed in shaded situations. They are not particular as to soil and are self-clinging. They bear

Vitis coignetiae, Glory Vine

J. E. Downward

hard and repeated clippings without ill effects and will even creep over the ground and so disguise manholes or old tree stumps. There are many varieties, with large and small leaves, and also showy variegated forms. C.

HYDRANGEA T.

Two Hydrangeas are genuine climbers which cling naturally to tree trunks like Ivy. They make good wall coverings provided the mortar is not fresh. C. *H. petiolaris* is deciduous with long stalked leaves up to 4 in. long, pointed and sharply toothed. Flowers are white and open in June in flat clusters 6—10 in. across. *H. integerrima* is evergreen, and the flower heads are smaller (1 in.).

LONICERA T. Honeysuckle

Most Honeysuckles like some protection from hot sun, so are best on shady walls where soil can be kept moist in summer. In more exposed positions they can be afforded more sunshine. H.R.C. Aug. in gentle heat or H.C. in Oct. The evergreen *Lonicera japonica* has creamy-yellow, pink-tinged flowers in the leaf axils of the young growing shoots. They bloom all summer and autumn and are very fragrant, especially at night. A variegated form, *aurea reticulata* is useful for cutting, with rounded yellow and green leaves on long trailing stems. Thin growths and remove old and weak shoots in spring or after flowering. H.R.C. in gentle heat July or H.C. outdoors in Oct. *L. periclymenum* is our native Honeysuckle or Woodbine. It loses its leaves in winter but has more showy flowers than *L. japonica*. They appear between June and Aug., the individual blossoms carried in rounded whorls on short stems. These are beautifully fragrant and creamy-white flushed with red. *L. tragophylla* is scentless but has bright golden yellow flowers in June. The scarlet Trumpet Honeysuckle *L. x brownii* has showy orange-scarlet blooms, likewise without fragrance. Both these kinds are deciduous and lose their leaves in winter.

POLYGONUM T.

P. baldschuanicum. Silver Lace Vine. Extremely vigorous climber for sun or shade, which will cover an unsightly fence or building in a season. Deciduous, with smooth heart-shaped leaves and lace-like sprays of creamy flowers. Plant for a specific purpose or quick screening. Aug.—Oct. H. C.

PYRACANTHA T.

Firethorns grow freely even on a north wall, although they berry better when given some sun. They are easy to raise, succeeding even in heavy clays and have a neat evergreen habit. If left alone, berries hang until Feb. or March. *P. coccinea* has coral-red fruits, *var. lalandei* orange and *P. rogersiana* yellow. The flowers in all cases are white and spectacular in May and June. When grown as trees Pyrecanthas are often left unpruned, but against a wall they should be kept in shape by shortening back longest growths in April. S. or H.R.C.

SCHIZOPHRAGMA

S. hydrangeoides Japanese Hydrangea Vine. Self-clinging climber, which loses its leaves in winter and has showy clusters of white Hydrangea-like flowers. The leaves are long stalked, something like Ivy. They are very vigorous and grow well over old buildings or up tree trunks. July. Propagated by layers. *S. integrifolia* has larger leaves.

Jasminium nudiflorum

J. E. Downward

Winter Flowers

'I doe hold it, in the Royall Ordering of Gardens, there ought to be Gardens, for all the Moneths of the Yeare; In which, severally, Things of Beautie, may be then in season.'

Francis Bacon, the Elizabethan writer, expressed these sentiments nearly 400 years ago, when the opportunities to indulge them were far from easy. Even today, it takes thought and planning to produce an attractive garden in winter. Yet at no other season are flowers more welcome.

Select a sheltered spot or else hedge round an area so that it is protected from cold winds. A hedge such as Beech, Yew or *Berberis stenophylla* is ideal. In a large exposed garden a shelter belt of trees of *Chamaecyparis (cupressus) lawsoniana* or *Cryptomeria japonica var. elegans* may be used on the windward side, with a Yew hedge or hardy evergreens such as Bamboos in front, to provide protection whilst the hedge is developing.

The greatest winter treasure in my garden is *Viburnum bodnantense*, which usually produces its first pinky blossoms whilst trees are in leaf in October and continues in character until they return in April. At Christmas, the dark, naked branches are festooned with bunches of fragrant flowers. It needs well drained soil, but requires no pruning beyond an occasional thinning and grows 6 to 10 ft. high. *V. fragrans* is also grown here but is not as attractive. *V. tinus* is evergreen with less conspicuous flowers. All these may be increased from layers.

Witch Hazels *(Hamamelis)* make good winter standbys. There are a number of kinds, all making small, spreading shrubs with gold, yellow or reddish flowers on the naked wood.

Carefully chosen Winter Heathers provide a succession of bloom from November until April. Try 'King George V' (Nov.–Feb.); 'Springwood White' and 'Springwood Pink' (Jan.–March) and *atrorubra*, a deep red kind (March–April). These are tolerant of most soils and grow about a foot high.

A comparative newcomer to gardens is *Abeliophyllum distichum*, a small bush with white, tubular

The bright winter berries of Pyracantha lalandii
Copyright Wood & Ingram

Iris unguicularis

flowers which are very fragrant and last when cut.

Mimosa (*Acacia dealbata*) can be grown and flowered outdoors in the milder parts of this country, though most gardeners prefer an unheated glasshouse, where it thrives with little trouble.

Another winter gem is the yellow Jasmine (*J. nudiflorum*) which blooms from Christmas until March. The green catkined Garrya has unusual charm, with its swinging green flower tassels from November onwards, whilst the Winter Sweet (*Chimonanthus praecox fragrans*) is a most fragrant garden plant.

Two winter-flowering trees should be included in every winter garden, one evergreen the other deciduous. The first is the Strawberry Tree, *Arbutus unedo*, which has dark green, glossy leaves and clusters of pinkish-white flowers which develop into edible

Rhododendron 'Winter Cheer'

round fruits, about the size of a Strawberry. *Prunus subhirtella rosea* makes a small tree, the black branches studded with rosy-white blossoms during mild winter periods. Underplant it with the early lavender-blue *Crocus sieberi* or sky-blue *Iris histroides*.

Algerian Irises are indispensable for those with a south or west facing wall. I prefer the old name *I. stylosa* to the more correct *I. unguicularis*, as it draws attention ot the style (or stalk) of the stigma which is connected to the seed pod, and is 9 to 12 in. long. Tuck the plants close to a warm wall in well drained, rather poor soil. Gather in bud, pulling them from the ground. Arranged with a little dark foliage such as Juniper or Cupressus, and a few sprigs of winter Jasmine or Viburnum they make an ideal table display.

In the shady areas of the garden *Helleborus corsicus*, *orientalis* and *lividus* bloom for weeks on end. *H. orientalis* is also known as the Lenten Rose, with flowers in green, cream, pink, rose and deep red.

For the Christmas Rose, *H. niger*, an east or west facing position under trees is ideal. The round, white blossoms are often marred by the weather or slugs, so place a sheet of glass on bricks or a belljar over the buds in November with a little slug bait nearby.

When room permits, some of the winter flowering Rhododendrons such as 'Christmas Cheer,' *nobleanum* and its varieties *venustum* and *album; rivieri* and the crimson *barbatum* are invaluable.

A number of Camellias flower early in the year and the small golden-flowered *Cornus mas* makes a fluffy mist in February or March. It forms a shrub 8 to 10 ft. high, with a round, twiggy head.

Early-flowering bulbs can brighten up the garden too. The Crocus Tulip shows its red blossoms with the Snowdrops in February, following closely on the yellow *Iris danfordiae*. Dwarf Narcissi such as *cyclameneus* and *asturiensis* are admirable in a rock garden pocket, also many Crocus species and the Narcissus hybrid known as 'February Gold'.

Shrubs which hold their berries — Cotoneasters, Skimmias, Pyracanthas and the like also bring colour to the winter garden, as do the beautiful barks of many trees and shrubs. *Acer pennsylvanicum*, the Snake Barked Maple, has green and white stripes down its straight stems; Silver Birch is grey and silver and many Cherries have a polished mahogany finish which often flakes to reveal lighter patches. The new white shoots of *Rubus leucodermis* and *Cornus sanguinea*, with red shoots, both make a cheerful display.

There are many more — fragrant Daphnes, Mahonias and winter Honeysuckles — all serving to prove that the garden is never 'dead' but always has something to show.

Pests & Diseases

Pests and diseases have existed ever since gardening began and many are the methods employed through the ages to combat them — from powdered dried roots to arsenic mixed with honey.

Peter Collinson, the British botanist, in 1746 suggested spraying nectarine trees with water in which tobacco leaves had been soaked, surely the original nicotine insecticide!

Garden hybrids are the chief victims of pests in the flower garden — and in all cases good cultivation, propagation only from disease-free stock, burning rubbish, and prompt recognition and treatment in the early stages of attack are the main measures of control.

PESTS AND DISEASES COMMON TO MANY PLANTS

Ants. Loosen soil round plants, especially alpines; also move Aphides about, causing fresh outbreaks. Sprinkle round nests with proprietary Antkillers like NIPPON. Dust with DERRIS.

Aphis. Suck sap from foliage and young stems, producing curling and distortion. Spray or dust with B.H.C. or MALATHION or NICOTINE at first signs. Repeat 10 days later.

Capsid Bug. Particularly troublesome on Chrysanthemums and Dahlias, often breeding on Groundsel and Dock. Treat as for Aphis.

Caterpillar. Larvae of many moths chew margins or bite out holes of leaves. Hand pick and destroy, or spray / dust with a DERRIS, trichlorphon or B.H.C. preparation.

Chlorosis. Yellow leaves, especially of shrubs or trees. Leaf veins show dark green. Usually associated with chalk soils. Water soil with sulphate of iron (1 oz. per gallon) or spray foliage with a SEQUESTRENE IRON preparation.

Damping Off (Seedlings). Fungus attacking stems of many seedling plants. Good cultivation. General hygiene. Under glass water seedlings with CHESHUNT COMPOUND.

Die-Back. Attacks Roses and other shrubs, fruit bushes and trees. Young shoots die back from tips. Burn infected wood. Apply sulphate of potash to soil (2 oz. per sq. yd.).

Downy Mildew. White or grey downy growth on undersides of leaves, due to fungus attack. Onions may be severely checked. Dust with DISPERSIBLE SULPHUR. Avoid wet, badly drained soils. Crop rotation.

Earwig. Feed on foliage and developing flower buds at night, hiding in canes, hollow stems or refuse by day. Trap in canes of flower pots containing straw. Spray or dust with Lindane.

Eelworm. Stunted growth, wilting leaves often turning black. Microscopic pests invading roots and stems. Burn infected plants, particularly Phlox and Chrysanthemum.

Frog-hopper (Cuckoo Spit). Larvae surrounded by white foam while feeding on growing points and side shoots of numerous

Cherry Fruit Moth, adult   A Shell photograph

290

Gooseberry Sawfly: defoliated and normal foliage

A Shell photograph

Common Green Capsid: effect of attacks on Pears

A Shell photograph

Gooseberry Sawfly: eggs on underside of leaf   A Shell photograph

herbaceous plants and Roses. Spray with water to remove foam, then with B. H. C.

Goat and Leopard Moth, Attacks trees and larger shrubs. Large caterpillars feed on pith of trunk or branches, sometimes killing latter. Block entrance hole by inserting crystals of PARADI-CHLOROBENZENE and plug with clay.

Leaf Miner. Larvae of grubs feed between upper and lower surfaces of leaves. White serpentine marks on foliage. Hand pick affected leaves, or spray with MALATHION or B.H.C.

Mildew. Several species of fungus attacking wide range of host plants. Spray with COPPER FUNGICIDE or KARATHENE.

Millipede. Soil pest, with round black body. Feeds on decaying matter and may attack plant roots. Fork soil frequently and dust with B.H.C. Burn nearby rubbish where pests hibernate.

Red Spider. Sucks plant sap, giving leaves a silver or whitish appearance. Foliage may drop prematurely. Spray proprietary material containing PARATHION or KELTHANE. Spray frequently under glass or maintain cooler atmosphere.

Root Rot (Honey Fungus). Trees or shrubs die suddenly in full leaf. Honey-coloured toadstools sometimes evident in nearby soil. Burn infected plants; dig out and burn old tree-stumps, probable source of fungus.

Scale Insects. Cling to stems and bark and suck sap. Attack many plants under glass, also fruit trees, Rhododendrons, Camellias, Orchids, Ferns, etc. Outdoors, spray in Jan. with TAR OIL WASH. Remove with knife if only few involved under glass, or spray with NICOTINE.

Silver Leaf. Attacks Prunus species and closely related shrubs and trees. Affected leaves have metallic appearance. Branches then die. No effective cure, but cut out and burn infected wood. Paint wounds and pruning cuts with white lead paint or MEDO. Avoid winter pruning.

Slugs and Snails. Feed on stems at or just below soil level. Trap with poison bait containing METALDEHYDE.

Thrips. Discolour and distort foliage and blooms, especially Gladioli, Carnations and Chrysanthemums. B.H.C. or MALATHION sprays or smokes.

White Fly. Most troublesome under glass. Tiny white flies over fruits and foliage. Fumigate with TETRACHLORETHANE or a LINDANE SMOKE. Outdoors, spray with NICOTINE and PETROLEUM EMULSION WASH or MALATHION, twice, 14 days apart.

BRASSICA CROPS

Cabbage Aphis. Distorted foliage, often sticky with honeydew. Spray or dust with DERRIS, MALATHION or B.H.C.

Cabbage Root Fly. Leaves of young plants become blue and cease growth. Legless maggots tunnel into roots and stem. Dust planting hole with 4 per cent CALOMEL DUST when transplanting.

Cabbage White Fly. Plants often sticky with honeydew. Remove badly affected lower leaves. Use NICOTINE or DERRIS.

Caterpillars of Cabbage White Butterfly. Holes in leaves and at edges. Remove by hand and destroy. Dust or spray with a Lindane preparation.

Club Root of Brassicas. Swellings on roots just below soil level, becoming soft and slimy when plants decay. Also attacks Turnip, Mustard and Wallflowers. Similar to Cabbage Root Fly but distinguished by solid swellings when cut across and strong smell. Practise crop rotation. Maintain good lime content in soil. Dip roots in CALOMEL PASTE before planting out.

Cutworm (Surface Caterpillar). Stems of young plants severed at soil level. Dust soil with B.H.C.

Flea Beetle. Foliage of seedlings riddled with small holes. Dust plants with a FLEA BEETLE DUST.

Turnip Gall Weevil. Swelling at base of stem contains grub. Good cultivation reduces effects. Dust with Lindane soon after transplanting.

LEGUME CROPS

Bean Aphis (Black Fly). Clusters at growing point and on

developing pods severely check and cripple plant. Nip out tops as soon as discovered. Dust or spray with B.H.C. or MALATHION.

Pea and Bean Beetle. Eats holes in Pea and Bean seeds in storage, reducing germinating power. If seed is to be stored dry for later use, dust or spray with Lindane immediately after flowering.

Pea Fusarium Root Rot. Fungus causes premature discoloration in Pea and Bean plants, foliage and stems yellowing while pods developing. Adequate crop rotation is best safeguard.

Pea and Bean Weevil. Seedling damage. Adults eat leaf margins, giving notched appearance to leaves of seedlings. Clean cultivation. Provide good tilth for plant growth. Spray or dust with Lindane or DERRIS at first sings of damage.

Pea Moth Caterpillar. Hatch from eggs laid near flowers and enter developing pod, feeding on young Peas. Crop rotation. Clean cultivation. Spray with Lindane 7—10 days after beginning of flowering.

Pea Thrip. Skin of pods mottled and silvery in appearance. Spray as for Pea Moth.

ROOT CROPS

Beet Eelworm. Stunted plants, wilted and dying foliage. Excessive number of lateral roots producing 'whiskered' appearance. Crop rotation. Do not grow Beet on infested land for 4—5 years. Keep infected soil off tools, shoes, etc.

Canker (Parsnip). Brown or black cracks and corky areas at top of root; common in wet autumn. Avoid too much nitrogen. Maintain good lime content.

Carrot Fly. Grubs burrow into roots. Foliage turns bronze or red and often wilts. Avoid early sowings. Crop rotation. Dust rows with B.H.C.

Dry Rot (Potato). Occurs in storage of 'seed' Potatoes. Tubers shrivel and may show white pustules on sunken areas. Sort tubers in store and before planting. Burn infected ones.

Leek Moth Caterpillar. Tunnel into leaves, causing yellowing and wilting. Spray or dust with Lindane when planting out.

Mangel Beetle Fly. Pale blotches on leaves of young plants. Grubs tunnel into leaf tissue, causing blisters. Good cultivation Top-dress with fertiliser. Burn affected leaves.

Onion Fly Larvae. Small grubs burrow into bulbs; leaves and stemps yellow and wilt. Crop rotation. Dust seedling rows with B.H.C.

Potato Root Eelworm. Plants weak and stunted. Foliage dull, sometimes yellow and withered. Poor root system and few tubers. Small brown cysts visible attached to roots. Rest heavily infested land for 5—8 years. Crop rotation. Use only certified seed Potatoes. Keep infected soil off tools, shoes, etc.

Scab (Potato). Scab patches and raised areas on skin of Potato tubers. Peeling usually reveals sound flesh below. Dressing of compost or organic manures in planting trenches will reduce trouble. Avoid too much lime.

Wireworm. Larvae of Click Beetle. Feed on roots of many plants. General treatment of soil with B.H.C. and WIREWORM DUST before sowing or planting.

OTHER CROPS

Asparagus Beetle. Damage to buds and shoots. Eggs laid and grubs later feed on foliage. Remove nearby rubbish where beetles hibernate. Spray with Lindane or use DERRIS if within 14 days of cutting.

Blight (Potato and Tomato). Brown patches on leaves contain fungus spores, which later infect tubers and fruits by rain splash. Spray foliage with COLLOIDAL COPPER around end June and repeat fortnightly in humid seasons.

Blossom-end Rot (Tomato). Blossom end of fruit rot, becoming black or brown. Mulch around plants with peat. Top-dress with sulphate of potash.

Woolly Aphids on Apple   Fisons Horticulture

Caterpillars on Cabbage   Fisons Horticulture

Black Spot on Roses   Fisons Horticulture

Greenfly on Roses   Fisons Horticulture

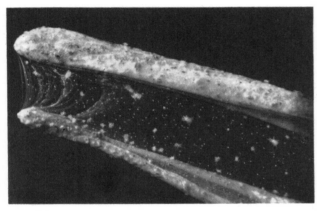

Red Spider   Fisons Horticulture

Codling Moth   Fisons Horticulture

Aphids   Fisons Horticulture

Buck-eye Rot (Tomato under glass). Red-brown spots on fruit, with dark brown rings. Reduce watering. Increase ventilation. Remove infected fruits.

Celery Fly. Larvae hatch and burrow into leaves, causing brown blisters. May check plant growth. Dust with B.H.C. when first seen, and occasionally with soot after planting.

Celery Leaf Spot. Brown spotting of leaves and stems. Seed-borne disease which can spread rapidly. Spray with a COLLOI-DAL COPPER spray, or dust with BORDEAUX MIXTURE. Obtain seed from reliable source.

Grey Mould (Botrytis). Attacks Lettuce, Tomato and many crops under glass. Grey patches on stems or leaves, eventually causing decay. Good cultivation. Under glass, ventilate well and avoid excess moisture or too close planting. Dust with proprietary dust, e.g. BOTRYLEX.

Leaf Mould (Tomato under glass). Yellow spots on upper surface of leaves in early summer. Grey or purple patch on under surface. Leaves shrivel. Good ventilation reduces spread of fungus. Spray plants with COLLOIDAL COPPER preparation. Grow disease-resistant variety.

Lettuce Root Aphis. Colonies on roots form white wool-like clusters. Clean cultivation. Crop rotation. Spray soil with MALATHION.

Mosaic Virus. Attacks Potato, Tomato, Cucumber, Lettuce, etc. Leaves appear with light mottled yellow and green areas, among normal green colour. Growth may be stunted. Spread largely by Aphis, so control this pest.

FRUITS AND NUTS

American Gooseberry Mildew. White fungus patches on tips of shoots, spreading to leaves and maturing fruits. Tip the leading shoots when winter pruning. Spray in May with 1 lb. Washing Soda, ¼ lb. Soft Soap to 5 galls. water.

Aphides (Black Fly, Green Fly, etc.) Many species, some of which attack only one crop plant. All cause distortion and curling of leaves. Spray or dust with MALATHION, B.H.C., DERRIS, NICOTINE. Destroy nearby weeds. Do *not* use B.H.C., preparations on Blackcurrants or other soft fruits near harvesting time.

Apple Capsid Bug. Rough corky patches on mature fruit. Spray with D.N.C. PETROLEUM WASH during dormant season or B.H.C. at green cluster stage of flower buds.

Apple Codling Moth. Larva enters fruit in June or July, through bird or insect damage. Spray with DERRIS mid-June and again early July.

Apple Mildew. White powdery fungus on tips of young growths in summer. Spray with KARATHENE when first seen and repeat 2—3 weeks later. Cut out badly infected shoots.

Apple Sawfly. Larva enters young fruit and feeds, often causing it to drop while small. Spray with B.H.C. or NICOTINE within 7 days of petal fall.

Apple and Pear Scab. Brown or black areas on leaves. Black areas on fruits, which often become cracked. Spray with LIME SULPHUR or CAPTAN at appropriate stage of bud development. (See fruit tree spray programme.)

Bacterial Canker (Stone Fruits). Cracks in bark of trunk, causing excessive gumming. Bacteria enter through wounds or broken branches. Also causes shot-hole effect in leaves. Protect pruning cuts with paint or pruning compound. Spray with BOR-DEAUX MIXTURE 3 weeks after petal fall and again after leaf fall in autumn.

Blackcurrant Big Bud Mite. Swollen appearance of buds in winter, Mites transmit Reversion Virus disease. Also attacks Red Currants. Spray with LIME SULPHUR at 'Grape-stage' of flower bunches. Remove and burn affected buds in winter.

Blackcurrant Midge. Larvae feed on leaves of young growth tips, causing curling, twisting and blackening. Spray young shoot tips with B.H.C. at 'Grape-stage' of flower bunches.

Blackcurrant Reversion Virus. Leaves reduced in size and 'oak-leaf' in outline. Fruit much reduced in quality. Treat against

293

Big Bud Mite, carrier of the virus. Burn badly affected plants.

Brown Rot (Apple, Pear, Plum). Grey or brown pustules on fruits on tree or in store. Remove and burn. No effective cure. Remove 'mummied' fruit left on tree in winter.

Cane Spot (Raspberry, Loganberry, Blackberry). Small purple spots on young canes in May or June, later forming small pits and cankers. Spray side growths when ½ in. long in March with COLLOIDAL COPPER. Burn badly infected canes.

Cherry Fruit Moth. Larva enters trusses of blossom buds and feeds on petals and stamens, later attacking young fruits. Spray with TAR OIL WASH in Dec., also with DERRIS at bud-burst stage.

Die Back (Gooseberry shoots, etc.). Wilting or dying of branches. Spreads from decaying vegetation. Cut out and burn infected wood.

Fruit Tree Red Spider Mite (Apple, Peach, etc.). Leaves become dull green and later bronze. Spray during summer with MALA-THION or CHLOROBENZIDE.

Gooseberry Sawfly. Larvae feed on leaves, rapidly defoliating bush in severe attack. Can also occur on White and Red Currants. Spray bushes with B.H.C. or DERRIS when damage first seen.

Nut Weevil. Adults lay eggs in young nuts in May and June. Larvae hatch and feed in developing nutlet, leaving escape hole. Spray or dust bushes with B.H.C. in late May. Cultivate around bushes in winter.

Peach Leaf Curl. Leaves distorted and swollen with red blisters. Shoots and flowers may be affected. Spray with COLLOIDAL COPPER wash at bud burst in Feb.

Pear and Cherry Sawfly. Black, slug-like larvae feed on upper leaf surfaces, leaving veins intact. Spray attacked foliage with DERRIS or B.H.C.

Raspberry Beetle Sawfly. Larvae tunnel into developing fruits of Raspberry, Loganberry and Blackberry. Spray with DERRIS or B.H.C. after blooming.

Raspberry Mosaic Virus. Mottled leaves, stunted cane growth. Prevent Aphis attack. Remove badly infected wood.

Silver Leaf of Plum. Fungus infects wood, entering through wounds. Leaves have silvered appearance. Avoid pruning in autumn or winter. Burn dead wood before mid-July. Burn badly infected trees.

Mealy Plum Aphid   A Shell photograph

Strawberry Mildew. Curled leaf margins. Fruit also often affected. Spray with KARATHENE but not near picking time.

Strawberry Seed Beetle. Eats seeds of developing fruits, causing discoloration and shrivelling. Cultivate around plants; apply ALDRIN DUST before strawing.

Strawberry Rhynchites. Larvae feed on stems of leaves and blossom trusses, causing them to wither and die. Spray or dust with Lindane when first flower truss is formed.

Strawberry Tarsonemid Mite. Feeds on leaves, which become pale and brittle. Hot water treatment of runners in autumn (7 minutes at 115°F.) before planting.

Vine Weevil. Adults bite holes in foliage of Vine, Peach, Cyclamen, Ferns, etc. Spray or dust with Lindane but if edible crops, not within 2 weeks of harvesting.

Woolly Aphis (Apple). Colonies enclosed in dense white woolly masses on stems. Small outbreaks can be treated by hand, with methylated spirits, or spray with MALATHION any time after petal fall.

LAWNS

Earthworms. Some species throw up casts on surface during autumn and winter. MOWRAH MEAL applied to surface at 6—8 oz. per sq. yd. and well watered in, or DERRIS POWDER (1% ROTENONE) at 10 oz. per sq. yd,. watered in.

Fairy Rings. Ring of toadstools forming on grass. Spike area and apply sulphate of iron (¼ oz. in 1 gall. water per sq. yd.).

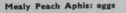

Mealy Peach Aphis: eggs   A Shell photograph

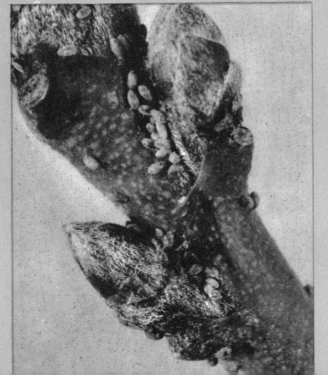

Fusarium. Reddish-brown patches which join and spread, killing grass. MERCURY fungicide spray.

Leatherjackets. Grubs feed on grass, causing it to die in patches. Bad in dry weather. Dust with B. H. C.

Moss. Kills out grass. Usually a sign of an acid or poor soil. LAWN SAND, 4 oz. per sq. yd. in mid-March. Rake out when it goes black. Feed lawn.

ORNAMENTAL PLANTS

Black Spot of Roses. Irregular black spots on leaves. Burn infected leaves. Mulch with grass cuttings or compost. Spray with CAPTAN several times at 14 day intervals.

Hollyhock Rust. Rust pustules on foliage. Burn badly affected plants. Cut to ground level in autumn and burn growth. Spray in spring with a COPPER fungicide.

Leaf Spot. Attack many plants. White or brown spots on foliage. COPPER fungicide or BORDEAUX MIXTURE.

Narcissus Fly. Fat grub burrows in bulbs. Leaves weak and twisted. Burn affected bulbs and change site.

Sweet Pea Streak. Deformed growth, leaves and stems brown streaked. No cure. Change site. Avoid excessive use if nitrogenous manures. Add potash to soil.

Tulip Fire. Stunted plants, withering and grey patches on leaves. Burn affected bulbs, spray others with TULISAN.

Verticillium Wilt (Asters etc.). Foliage withers and branches die. Burn affected plants.

Viruses (many plants). Various symptoms: e.g. dwarfing, leaf streaks, blindness, flecked flowers. No cure. Transmitted by Aphides, which should be kept under control.

HOUSE PLANTS

Root-Rot. Plants rot at soil level. Usually due to overwatering.

Shot-hole. Small holes in leaves. Shoots often die from tips. Avoid water on foliage in winter. Provide better drainage.

American Gladiolus Thrip: damage to flowers   A Shell photograph

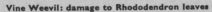

Vine Weevil: damage to Rhododendron leaves   A Shell photograph

WEED DESTRUCTION

Read the directions carefully and follow them explicitly. Be careful of 'drift' which may destroy neighbouring plants. Wash all receptacles out thoroughly after use.

Some sprays are poisonous, others inflammable; keep away from children and pets. Wear gloves during application.

To kill all vegetation: Arsenical weedkillers (very poisonous); Sodium chlorate (inflammable) Dalapon; Monuron; Simazin.

Selective weedkillers: Broad-leaved weeds (as on a lawn): 2:4 — D and M.C.P.A. Brushwood Killers: 2:4:5 — T. Weeds among bulbs: Penachlorophenal (applied a week or more before shoots come through soil). Pre-emergence Sprays: made after sowing but before crop germinates. Oil Herbicides.

index

PROPORTIONS FOR POOL MAKING

1 part by bulk cement
2 parts by bulk sand
3 parts by bulk aggregate (shingle, stones etc.
grading between $\frac{3}{4}$ and $\frac{3}{16}$ in.)
Sufficient water to make a stiff mix.

1 cubic yard of concrete will
cover 54 sq. ft. to a depth of 6 in.
1 cubic yard of concrete will
cover 81 sq. ft. to a depth of 4 in.
3 yards of concrete requires 21 cwt. cement
$1\frac{7}{8}$ yds. sand
$1\frac{7}{8}$ yds. aggregate

TO CALCULATE
THE GALLON CAPACITY OF A POND

Multiply the length in feet by breadth by depth
(inside measurements)
Multiply the result by $6\frac{1}{4}$

TO REMOVE TREE STUMPS

Drill holes with an auger 2 in. deep and
3-4 inches apart all over stump

Recently felled Trees Half fill holes with Sodium
Chlorate, top up with water and plug with clay.

Old Stumps Fill with saltpetre and plug.
After 6 months remove plugs and fire
the stumps.